THE DESERT

THE DESERT

Lands of Lost Borders

Michael Welland

REAKTION BOOKS

For Fotinoula

Published by Reaktion Books Ltd
33 Great Sutton Street
London EC1V 0DX, UK

www.reaktionbooks.co.uk

First published 2015
Copyright © Michael Welland 2015

Printed and bound in China by 1010 Printing International Ltd

A catalogue record for this book is available from the British Library
ISBN 978 1 78023 360 4

**Aboriginal and Torres Strait Islander people should
be aware that this book contains the words and images
of people who have since passed away. Care and
discretion should therefore be exercised.**

Contents

Preface

OUR GROUP HAD camped in the heart of Egypt's Western Desert, close to the Libyan border. In fact, we might have actually been *in* Libya, for, with the exception of the rare, unexpected, sand-blasted and lonely marker post, the border is lost. I am not by nature an instinctively gregarious individual and, relishing an opportunity for solitude, I wandered off to climb one of the desiccated and rocky hills that ringed the camp. The desert offers solitude in a way unequalled by any other setting on earth – with the exception of the polar regions, which are, after all, deserts themselves. It takes a while to escape the sounds of one's companions in the still desert air, but I found a quiet place above a cliff where not only the silence but the view of the landscape was overwhelming.

In the crystal light of the desert day, I viewed the landscape through the eyes of a geologist. Details of the multicoloured rock layers in the flanks of flat-topped tablelands and pyramid-shaped hills held stories of times when this now hyper-arid land was covered by seas; changes in the texture and folds of the intervening dune fields told of the wind-blown journeys of the sand, funnelled through gaps in the hills, filling the topography, spontaneously forming inexorably moving dunes. Boulders and rubble on the slopes were witness to the source of the sand, the slow but never-ending erosion of the staunch, but ultimately futile, resistance of the cliffs.

It's a problem that geologists have – an inherent inability to deflect attention from the contents of a scene, whether it's the setting of a movie, a road cut or a glorious panorama that should be experienced simply for itself. But at night all this inevitably changes and in the desert night dramatically so. After dinner, I retraced my steps in the dark to my lookout. But 'dark' is not the word. Although it was only a half-moon, I had no need of my head torch and it seemed as if, even without the half-moon, the light from the stars would have been enough.

Night in the desert is unique. It reveals and reminds us what the rest of the universe really looks like from our humble planet. The Milky Way dazzles. But here I was in the Saharan night, overlooking the same geological landscape that I had enjoyed earlier, but now set out before me in the light of the moon and the galaxies, its colours subdued but still luminous. It was a different place, solitude amplified, silence enveloping, geology irrelevant. The experience of the desert is, essentially, a solitary one, and isolation in the desert night requires taking a measure of oneself. It is no wonder that the great religions, not to mention mystics, ascetics and fanatics, have more often than not emerged from and returned to the desert.

A century ago, Mary Hunter Austin was a prolific and eloquent writer on the deserts of the American southwest and an early enthusiast for the peoples and environments of the 'Great American Desert'. In 1909 she published *Lost Borders*, in the first chapter of which she wrote:

> Out there, where the borders of conscience break down . . .
> almost anything might happen; does happen, in fact, though
> I shall have trouble making you believe it. Out there, where
> the boundary of soul and sense is as faint as a trail in a sand-
> storm, I have seen things happen that I did not believe myself.

Out there, in the utter silence of that Saharan night, I sat for I don't know how long and understood intimately what she meant. It suddenly occurred to me that nothing would surprise me there and, despite my non-religious nature, I very clearly and specifically felt that, should God or the Devil – or both – sit down beside me, then this would not be at all strange or shocking. It was, I suppose, the response that Paul Bowles, writing half a century after Austin but echoing her words, termed the 'baptism of solitude' that the desert provides.

The deserts of the American southwest have provoked a large body of literature and art, to which Mary Austin was one of the first, and rightly celebrated, contributors. Fifty years after her, these lands produced one of the first vociferous environmentalists (some would say 'eco-terrorists'), Edward Abbey. In his most well-known work, *Desert Solitaire*, Abbey writes:

But the desert is a vast world, an oceanic world, as deep in its way and complex and various as the sea. Language makes a mighty loose net with which to go fishing for simple facts, when facts are infinite . . . Since you cannot get the desert into a book any more than a fisherman can haul up the sea with his nets, I have tried to create a world of words in which the desert figures more as a medium than as material . . . evocation has been the goal.

I am no Edward Abbey, but this resonates. I am, after all, a geologist, and this book will contain plenty of material on the desert as a fundamental player in the workings of our planet. But my interest in the desert extends far beyond the science, and it is my hope that this book will also provide an evocation, a celebration, a consideration of our responses to the desert, the idea of the desert. And not only ours, the outsiders', but those of our billion companions for whom the arid lands are home.

There is a Tuareg saying, 'There are lands full of water for the well-being of the body, and lands full of sand for the well-being of the soul.' The desert is a place of contrasts, of extremes, a place of staggering beauty and unimaginable violence, a place where the margins between success and failure, between life and death are slim, a place of timelessness and ephemerality, a place of good and evil. The desert is a place, in reality and in our minds, of tension, of conflict between civilization and the wilderness. Arid lands have always been – and continue to be – a challenge, both to those who would 'conquer' them and those who would make a living within them. Historically, culturally and politically, the desert has played a leading role in, and not simply provided the stage or the backdrop for, dramas of nations, species and individuals.

The scope of the topic is as vast as its subject. Since I explore it in terrains beyond my own professional expertise, this book can be only a sampler, not an exhaustive treatment. I find myself frustrated by some of my own omissions: for example, the deserts of the polar regions and those beyond our own planet; the constructive role of fire in arid lands and their biodiversity; the impact of desert tourism; and numerous artists, writers and epic journeys. Just as what we don't know about the desert far exceeds what we do know, what is left out far exceeds what is included and what is included is driven by personal fascination. No, you cannot get the desert into a book, but perhaps the following pages will begin to cast what Paul Bowles called the 'spell of the vast, luminous, silent country'.

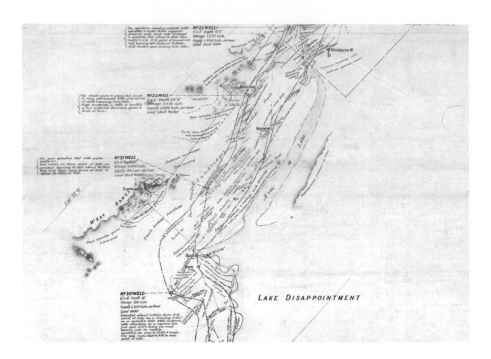

LAKE DISAPPOINTMENT

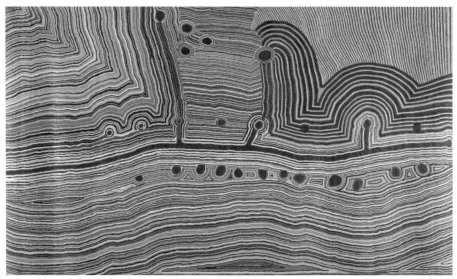

1, 2 Two contrasting perceptions of Australia's Great Sandy Desert:
Alfred Canning's map and *Martumili Ngurra*, 2009, Martumili Artists.

ONE

Wet and Dry, Hot and Cold

IN MAY 1906 a survey team of eight men, twenty-three camels and two horses left the Australian outback mining town of Day Dawn in the borderlands of the Little Sandy Desert. A century later, and a thousand kilometres northeast of the now long-abandoned town, six artists gathered in the Great Sandy Desert to begin a huge collaborative work.

The endeavours of both groups would result in an image of the same area of desert terrain, but the two images are utterly different, fundamentally irreconcilable as depictions of the same subject and representative of two profoundly contrasting views of the desert.

The survey team was headed by Alfred Wernham Canning, the group of women artists by Kumpaya Girgiba. The goals of the two groups were as different as their views of the desert: Canning would carve a path through the desert to allow stock to be herded from the northern pastures of the Kimberleys nearly 2,000 kilometres to the markets of the southwestern goldfields. For Kumpaya Girgiba and her fellow Aboriginal Martu artists, the need was to tell the stories of their country and the journeys of their ancestors, and to provide instruction in caring for the land and its traditions. The results were both maps, but maps in the broadest sense. Look at these two maps, each covering the same 200 kilometres north–south, and look for the common features, for they are there (illus. 1, 2).

Above is a section of Canning's *Plan of Wiluna-Kimberley Stock Route Exploration*, below is *Martumili Ngurra* ('This is all Martu's home'). Canning's map is one of bare necessity: the route itself, annotated locations of the wells he planned and sank, and details of the topography in the immediate vicinity of the route. On either side, away from the stock route, there is essentially nothing, the map is empty, blank space.

David Carnegie, prospector and explorer, had passed through this 'vast, howling wilderness' ten years earlier and described the 'heartbreaking country, monotonous, lifeless, without interest, without excitement'. Canning saw the desert the same way.

Below is the *Martumili Ngurra* painting, in reality more than three by five metres in size. It is a map in a very different sense from Canning's, but the dark lines are the tracks, the circular motifs along them are the wells and other water sources, and every line, every colour, has meaning. There the similarities end, for the focus of the painting is not on the route but the details of the land and its stories: the blank desert spaces of Canning's map are filled with exuberant colour, covered in intricate designs and motifs. This is a map in the sense that it depicts places – importantly, like Canning, the locations of water – but it is much more. It is a seamless image of the real and the spiritual, for each place has a deeper meaning than simply the cartographical. It is a view through the mind's eye of a people for whom the land is everything, for whom the desert is home, for whom the desert is the spiritual foundation as well as the supermarket, the pharmacy and the hardware store.

In 2006 the Western Australian arts initiative FORM began an ambitious project that would document the intercultural history and stories of the Canning Stock Route from the viewpoint of the people whose lands it crossed and whose families were intimately affected by it. This project was titled Ngurra Kuju Walyja (One Country, One People) and it assembled a vast multimedia treasury of narrative and art, including 140 new paintings, of which *Martumili Ngurra* is one. The collection was acquired by the National Museum of Australia and toured the country as a groundbreaking exhibition. Among the diversity of the stories told runs a constant thread: as noted in the exhibition materials, the Aboriginal depictions of the land appear to be 'a complete inversion of Canning's map', and tell an old story 'in which the incursions of twentieth-century history, however radically disruptive they may have been to the material conditions of people's lives, remain merely as scratches on the surface'.

There is a long, often brutal and sordid, narrative that links Canning, his stock route and the saga of the desert's indigenous peoples; we shall return to it later. But these two images are a compelling illustration of the theme of this book: 'The desert' plays a powerful and staggeringly diverse role in the human imagination and it means many different things, in reality and in the mind.

The very word 'desert' carries a wide range of meanings, formal and otherwise. It means nothing to the indigenous inhabitants of the Australian centre or, indeed, to any of the more than 1 billion people across the world for whom arid lands are home. It is a word coined by outsiders and, in its origins, carried no specific correlation with aridity but simply with wilderness, an absence.

'Desert' was originally synonymous with 'wilderness' – uninhabited, uncultivated places, regardless of vegetation or ecology. In Shakespeare's *As You Like It*, Orlando describes the forest as 'this desert inaccessible'. In the nineteenth century Thomas Medwin, cousin and biographer of Percy Bysshe Shelley and friend of Lord Byron (who referred to 'The leafless desert of the mind' in 'The Giaour', 1813), wrote of the distinctly non-arid Welsh moors, 'A more uninteresting desert cannot be conceived.' Today, nestled in the verdant gorges of the Herault, and officially one of 'Les Plus Beaux Villages de France', is Saint-Guilhem-le-Désert.

For centuries the European concept of the desert was formed by its role in the Bible and, despite the arid reality of the Holy Land, paintings of desert temptations and exile (notably those of Saint Anthony and Saint Jerome) depicted relatively verdant settings – plenty of rocks, yes, but trees, rivers and 'civilization' within what seems to be but a short walk.

Yet accurate descriptions of the biblical desert reality were available. In the late fifteenth century, at roughly the same time that the thirteen-year-old Michelangelo completed his first painting – a surprisingly serene Saint Anthony beset by devils while floating above an idyllic river landscape, complete with sailing vessel – a German Dominican friar was enduring the hardships of the real desert. Felix Fabri made two pilgrimages to the Holy Land, first in 1480 and then in 1483, and wrote accounts of both. The description of his second journey, originally written in Latin, is remarkably detailed, carefully documenting his travails in crossing the 'horrible desert tracts' and mixing vivid descriptions of the landscapes and environment with biblical references. *The Book of the Wanderings of Felix Fabri* provided Europeans with their first significant source of accurate information on the desert.

In a fascinating section titled 'A description of the wilderness, the solitary place or desert, setting forth its length, breadth, and barrenness, in the course of which description the four ways wherein the word is used are explained', Fabri sets out the various meanings:

First, a place is called a wilderness or desert when folk might dwell therein, but do not . . .

The second way in which a place may be called a wilderness is solely because men do not dwell there, albeit there be gardens, fields, meadows, pastures, orchards, and the like . . .

Thirdly, by a wilderness is meant a place in the woods or fields, either covered with bushes or bare, where men do not dwell, but where lions, bears, deer, wolves, and other beasts run wild . . .

Fourthly, and most properly, that part of the world is called the wilderness wherein nothing grows for man or beast to eat, neither trees nor herbs, and wherein neither men, beasts, nor birds can live, both because of the want of water and because of the intolerable heat of the sun, the barrenness of the ground, and, in short, because of the lack of all things appertaining to the support of life. Such a wilderness is that which reaches from Gazara to Mount Sinai; not, indeed, everywhere, but in the greater part thereof. No such wilderness is to be found in Germany, France, or Italy, albeit desert places, according to the first, second, or third meaning of the word, may be found there.

He goes on to set out twenty characteristics of the desert, beginning with:

Firstly, this country is called the desert because it seems to be, so to speak, deserted by God, by the heavens, and by the world. It is deserted by God, because it is empty and void, as though God had used it to improve or adorn the rest of the universe.

Fabri continues to catalogue the features of 'this country . . . called the lonesome place . . . this country . . . called the solitary place', a waterless salt land, pathless, where no man dwells and no man passes through, a land of serpents, scorpions, dragons, fauns and satyrs, a place of devils and temptation but, nevertheless, a place also of meditation, devotion and contemplation, 'a place where great merit is acquired'.

We shall revisit Fabri's accounts of the landscapes of the desert, of sandstorms and foul water, of extremes of temperature, of endless gravel plains, but it is his image of the desert as 'empty and void' that endures

– it is precisely Albert Canning's view of the land beyond his stock route. If there is a terrain that is psychologically and physically linked with blank, empty areas of a map, it is the desert.

In AD 75 Plutarch described how

> geographers . . . crowd on to the outer edges of their maps the parts of the earth which elude their knowledge, with explanatory notes that 'What lies beyond is sandy desert without water and full of wild beasts', or 'blind marsh', or 'Scythian cold', or 'frozen sea' . . .

To begin the North African campaign in the Second World War, the Allies had maps on which areas of thousands of square kilometres were essentially blank, relieved only by the occasional dashed line marking the 'approximate route of camels'. While cities grew around the benign coasts of Australia, the interior was referred to as 'the ghastly blank'. Maps of the world's deserts bore a close resemblance to the 'Ocean-Chart' produced, to the crew's delight, by the Bellman in Lewis Carroll's *The Hunting of the Snark* (1874–6): 'A perfect and absolute blank!' Yet it has been exactly those empty areas on the map that have stimulated exploration, science and discovery.

In the North African campaign, a key strategic advantage was provided by a small, highly mobile group who, indulging in 'some piracy on the high desert', would appear out of the 'impassable' sands to harry Axis facilities and troops before rapidly disappearing whence they came. Erwin Rommel, the Second World War German Field Marshal known as 'the Desert Fox', later confessed that the Long Range Desert Group (LRDG) caused him more damage than any unit of comparable size, and the LRDG was the inspiration of a man seduced by the blank areas on the map. In 1927 Ralph Bagnold, then a young British Army officer, had driven modified Ford Model T cars hundreds of miles across 'the great lifeless desert that rolls like a sheet of blank paper westward across North Africa from the western banks of the Nile'. At the oasis of Siwa (home of the oracle visited by Alexander the Great), Bagnold took an evening stroll to 'the very edge of the real unexplored':

> For beyond Siwa to the south and southwest lay the Great Sand Sea, where the map of Egypt faded away into a blankness

stippled vaguely to indicate sand, and ended with the final stimulating remark, 'limit of sand dunes unknown'.

Thus was the tide of war in North Africa influenced, for Bagnold's fascination with the desert – and its scientific as well as cartographic blankness – led him not only to extensive further exploration, but to a pioneering scientific study of how the desert works. When war broke out, no one other than the Bedouin knew the Western Desert as well as Bagnold: he had, after all, filled in many of the blanks on the map. It was this knowledge, together with his engineering and logistical skills, that led to the success of the LRDG.

Blank spaces on a map are intensely seductive and the urge to penetrate them, to find out what is there, to describe, name, map and exploit them, has driven the human imagination and the exploration of our planet for millennia. The lure of the unknown, and the possibilities of the exotic, of treasures, lost cities, fabulous beasts and primitive tribes, have been powerful stimulants to intrepid men and women, real and fictional. For Joseph Conrad's Marlow, the blank spaces on the map had been a childhood obsession, and ultimately it was 'the biggest, the most blank, so to speak' that led him into the heart of darkness. At the time of Marlow's childhood, Africa offered vast areas of blankness. Marlow's hankering was for the rivers and jungles, for others it would be the deserts. By the time Marlow's boyhood dreams became a reality, the Congo 'had ceased to be a blank space of delightful mystery', for the pace of map-making, of exploration – and colonial exploitation – during the nineteenth century was rapid.

The blank spaces were perceived as wilderness, 'desert' in the original sense of the word, whether covered by rainforest or sand. But as they were filled in by explorers and cartographers, it became clear that they were not uninhabited and that their ecologies were complex and diverse. The jungle proved to be indeed 'teeming' and the desert was far from 'monotonous' or 'barren'. And with these discoveries came confrontation, for when it was found that a blank space was inhabited, then exploration became a 'mission', the mission was one of 'civilizing', and civilization was, of course, defined as European and Christian. 'The desert' came to be defined through Western eyes and Western thinking, its character associated with adjectives evoking the challenge it threw down to intruders: 'merciless', 'pitiless', 'unforgiving'. It seems that 'the desert' came to occupy a space in the Western imagination far broader and more threatening than simple geography. 'The desert' carries with it today a resonance of the blank spaces as a threat and a symbol of something that, if it cannot be avoided, has to be crossed, a barrier that we must conquer to find somewhere better. We have transferred its threatening character from the natural wilderness to our own social settings: we suffer not only from urban deserts, but food deserts and medical deserts. And there are, as Robert Frost described, like Byron, the awful deserts of the mind, the psychological and spiritual empty spaces that for Robert Frost have the ability 'to scare myself with my own desert places'.

And yet, in the same way that the desert has become symbolic of threat in the Western mind, it has also become associated with a strong sense of romance – the lure, the seduction, the beauty of empty spaces and different cultures. It is a place of extremes both physical and psychological. The spectrum and emotional strength of the outsiders' response to what is, in simple terms, just a landscape, is startling. But the inhabitants of arid lands would hardly recognize these responses: the desert has so many different meanings for so many different people. And therein lies our first problem. If we are to embark on a contemplation of the desert, what exactly do we mean by that term?

Lost borders

Dominic Louis Serventy was one of Australia's leading ornithologists of the twentieth century, and in editing a volume on the biology of desert birds in 1971 he wrote that 'A desert occurs wherever it is said to occur. A definition by acclamation!' He was expressing a frustration with what was, at the time, a lack of scientific consensus on the apparently simple task of defining a desert. In the intervening decades much thought has gone into this issue, but little has emerged by way of consensus and what we have is a bewildering array of definitions.

This is hardly surprising, given that the diversity of deserts is matched by the range of interests in them. How you choose to define a desert depends very much on why you wish to do so in the first place. Geologists, geographers, archaeologists, historians, anthropologists, hydrologists, agronomists, biologists, botanists, climatologists, politicians, economists and industrialists – not to mention artists, tourists, photographers and writers – all have their own particular interest in the desert. And, more often than not, their interest lies specifically in their desert, not that different desert on the other side of the world. What we end up with is a variety of definitions, each one of which best suits the priorities of the end-user.

The most basic stage of the process has always been to give the area of interest a name, which can then be put on a map, thereby locating it. If the view is that the area is a desert, then the word 'desert' is appended to the name. These names may or may not bear any relation to the names given to the area by the people who live there. The word *'sahraa* in Arabic more or less means 'desert' and so, when we mark the 'Sahara Desert' on a map, we are naming the desert 'desert'. On a map of China and Mongolia, 'Gobi Desert' means 'gravel plains desert'. But never mind – we now have a place on the map. But what to do next? Our desert must begin and end somewhere, its extent must be delineated on the map, ideally by a boundary of some sort, a line. It is here that we encounter the next problem: nature does not deal in lines and boundaries. Should we decide to start in the most desolate, arid, barren part of our desert, the *désert absolu* of Victorian Saharan travellers, and walk out until we encounter terrain that we would instinctively describe as 'not-desert', we will be hard-pressed to put any kind of line on the map. Does the desert end when the first struggling blades of grass appear, or when clumps of grass – or perhaps some shrubs – dot the landscape? This approach simply doesn't work. Our journey takes us, in general, across less and less arid landscapes, each merging imperceptibly into the next.

Analysing our observations, we understand that what we have encountered are changing levels of aridity, reflected in the changing vegetation. Aridity, the lack of water, is what all deserts have in common – although some deserts are more arid than others, and areas of any one desert are more arid than others. This, then, offers the possibility that we can somehow measure that variation in aridity and delineate it on the map, using it to show where the desert begins and ends. This seemingly logical approach does indeed form the basis for many desert definition schemes, and for the inevitable terminology of subdivisions, but it is applied in many different ways.

It is obvious that aridity reflects a deficiency of water, and so the simplest approach would be to decide on the maximum average annual rainfall for an area to be considered a desert – the common figure is 250 millimetres. But there are vast swathes of the Australian outback that are called desert (a definition anyone travelling in those parts would strongly agree with) that receive 400 millimetres of rainfall on average. In the nineteenth century most of the western United States was referred to as the 'Great American Desert', and large areas do receive less than 250 millimetres of rain a year, but would we really refer to central Washington State as a 'desert'? Large areas of the world's oceans receive less than 250 millimetres – but this merely emphasizes the assumption that a desert is on land. The largest desert by this simple definition is Antarctica – the entire continent typically receives less than 50 millimetres of precipitation each year, so indeed, it is extremely arid, but we do not normally think of it as a desert.

Average annual precipitation is an immediate and evocative measure of a desert and dramatically illustrates extremes, but it suffers from the problems of all averages. Arica, in Chile's northern Atacama Desert, has an *average* rainfall of 0.6 millimetres per year, a figure calculated on the basis of three rains in seventeen years. Arica is probably the driest city on earth, on average, but it was struck by devastating floods in 2012. The region of the Great Sand Sea over which Ralph Bagnold gazed (and ultimately explored) is one of the driest parts of the Sahara, but an expedition in 1874 was stranded by two days of continuous downpours. In 2012, the filming of the latest post-apocalyptic *Mad Max* movie, which explicitly required a desiccated and barren desert setting, had to be moved from Australia to Namibia because after a prolonged drought, the rains had come and the outback was in exuberant bloom. Averages can be misleading in many ways. The image of rain in the desert, when it comes, is one of a deluge, but, in spite of the genuine dramas of flash floods, they are not common events. It doesn't rain often in the desert, but when it does, how much does it rain? Taking measurements of rainfall and the number of rainy days over decades in arid lands (both of which can vary by orders of magnitude) reveals that the average rainfall per rainy day across North Africa is essentially the same as London. It's just that there are, of course, far more rainy days every year in London than in Algeria. The *way* in which water is delivered to the desert is critical to our understanding of how arid processes work, and many of our long-held assumptions are in need of re-examination. It has always been appreciated that historical measurements of, for example, rainfall, over long periods of time show dramatic extremes. However, there has also been the assumption that even the extremes fall within a statistical distribution that is fixed and valid and forms a reliable basis for addressing environmental issues. But in today's context of climate science 'mega-data' and a more sophisticated statistical approach, it is now apparent that this assumption of 'stationarity' is not only simplistic and misleading, but potentially dangerous when applied to environmental management.

Rainfall is not the only way that moisture arrives in the desert. The great cold ocean currents that well up along the southwestern coasts of South America and Africa not only help create the Atacama and Namib Deserts, but bestow them with life-giving water through condensation and fog. Data from the Atacama reveal that up to 2 litres of water can be provided by this means over every square metre of the ground, even more than 10 kilometres inland. The importance of these desert fogs is reflected in their being given specific names: the *garua* of Peru, the *camanchaca* of Chile, the *nieselregen* of Namibia, the *Mal-mokkie* of Namaqualand. The *nieselregen* provides coastal Namibia with seven times the moisture of the (rare) 'normal' rains, and entire and extraordinary ecosystems in these deserts depend on fogs and dew for sustenance. *Tweeblaarkanniedood* is an Afrikaans word meaning 'two leaves, cannot (or will not) die', and describes the unique and bizarre plant, *Welwitschia mirabilis* (illus. 3). 'Unique' is an entirely correct adjective – it is the single species of a single family and is literally alone on the tree of life. It seems to have combined the characteristics of widely different families of plants and is seen as a survivor, a 'living fossil'. It has only two leathery leaves, but they are huge, growing up to 9 metres long and 2 metres wide, the whole thing spreading out over the ground and only achieving a typical height of less than a metre. The appearance of multiple leaves is a result of their being shredded by the wind and the blowing sand.

There are male and female plants and they can live for perhaps 2,000 years – the weird and wonderful ('mirabilis') characteristics of this plant seem endless. Austrian botanist Friedrich Welwitsch, who discovered it in 1859, felt that he 'could do nothing but kneel down and gaze at it, half in fear lest a touch should prove it a figment of the imagination'. *Welwitschia* can have extremely long roots to seek out any available subsurface moisture, but its primary source of nourishment is the fog and dew generated by the coastal currents. Go very far inland in the Namib, away from the sustenance of the coast, and *Welwitschia* cannot survive. But where it does, it provides moisture, nutrients and shelter for desert mammals and insects. The delightfully rainbow-coloured gecko *Pachydactylus rangei* boasts a number of clever adaptations to

3 Welwitschia mirabilis.

this harsh environment, including the habit of licking dew from its own eyeballs. The flattened body of Peringuey's adder not only assists with its sidewinding motion but also collects condensation. And among the insects is a remarkable beetle, *Stenocara gracilipes*. A wonder of nano-engineering, its wings have a structure of water-attracting (hydrophilic) and water-repelling (hydrophobic) micro-patterned surfaces that conspire to collect and channel the moisture from the morning dew and fog. So clever is this beetle's technology that it is being replicated in many different water-harvesting research and development projects for application in arid lands around the world.

In the Atacama Desert, the role of *Welwitschia* is played by cacti whose surfaces collect water from the *camanchaca*, the windblown coastal fog, and on which grow lichens, with a structure cleverly adapted for moisture collection. The entire desert ecosystem depends on this.

The critical role of fog and dew in certain desert environments illustrates the many problems with simply using rainfall as a measure of aridity. It is also clear that there are plenty of what we would instinctively call desert areas that receive as much rain as those that we emphatically would not. There must be other pieces to the puzzle, other components of the equation. The obvious missing piece is temperature.

After all, in addition to being dry, we think of deserts as typically being hot.

'Typically' because, while heat is intuitively a necessary characteristic of the desert, not all deserts are searingly hot, and certainly not all of the time. Various locations compete for the title of 'the hottest place on earth' and they are all in the desert. For many years, El Azizia in Libya claimed the prize, having registered a temperature of 58°C in 1922. However, a recent re-evaluation has suggested measurement inconsistencies, and the record has been awarded to Furnace Creek in Death Valley, where the temperature of 56.7°C was recorded in July 1913. The difference is hardly significant: these temperatures are intolerably hot. And they are merely the official *air* temperatures – the ground temperatures can easily exceed them. Satellite measurements of ground temperatures have measured values of over 70°C in Iran's Lut Desert and 69°C in the outback of Queensland. Sand temperatures of over 83°C have been reported from the hills bordering the Red Sea.

However, the desert is a place of extremes, and high temperatures are but one end of the spectrum. The temperature *range* in parts of the Gobi Desert is +50°C to –40°C and it is so dry that the snow doesn't melt, it simply evaporates. Mongolian herders dread the arrival of the *dzud*, a devastatingly severe and prolonged winter of low temperatures, snow and wind. The *dzud* of 2009–10 lasted from December to March and, with an average temperature of –18°C, in some areas only a third of the livestock survived. Under normal circumstances in the Saharan winter months, a sleeping bag is a necessary piece of equipment. The nights are cold and it can snow, even at low elevations.

So, like precipitation, temperature in itself does not a desert measure. But combine these two factors and progress towards definitions can be made. If an area is arid, it is a consequence of the inability of any water that may arrive to last. Not only is the ground dry, and the rain soaks rapidly into the parched ground, but the rate of evaporation is high. The land simply has the ability to return the water to the atmosphere – its capacity to evaporate far exceeds any precipitation. The rate of evaporation is something we can measure, simply by putting a bucket of water out in the desert and seeing how long the water takes to disappear. The actual meteorological instruments are only slightly more sophisticated than this (illus. 4).

Wind will increase evaporation rates, and so wind speed measurements are also taken. A continuous record over the course of a year,

4 A pan evaporator at the Giles Meteorological Station in Western Australia.

combined with a sufficient distribution of weather stations like Giles, allows a map to be made of average annual pan evaporation rates across the entire continent. Compare this map with one of average annual rainfall (illus. 5), and the aridity of Australia's red centre becomes dramatically clear. Areas of the outback that receive 400 millimetres of rain per year (as we noted, much more than the simple desert definition of 250 millimetres), have a pan evaporation rate of 3,600 millimetres per year. In other words, the land has the capacity to rid itself of nearly ten times as much water as actually falls on it: aridity rules.

This then is the basis for delineating the arid areas of our planet: their capacity to return water to the atmosphere far exceeds the capacity

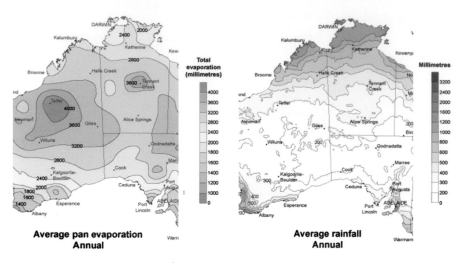

5 Australia: evaporation versus precipitation.

of the atmosphere to provide water and there is a net moisture deficiency. However, it becomes more complex. The capacity of the land to remove water is not simply measured by the drying out of a bucket. Rather than just evaporation, we need to measure total evapotranspiration. Vast areas of the desert are not completely bare rock and sand, but support cleverly adapted vegetation: the flora of the outback of Australia is stunning. All plants transpire, breathing in their own way, losing water from their leaves, and even in the desert this contributes to the ability of the land to lose water. Despite the common adaptations of desert plants to minimize transpiration, it is still an important process. So what we need to measure is this total of potential evaporation and transpiration – what the land could get rid of if enough water were available – and compare it to actual precipitation. This will then allow us to quantify aridity, produce an index of aridity and thereby a comforting measure of the desert, something we can, at least in theory, all agree on.

The aridity index, AI, is the ratio of precipitation (P) to potential evapotranspiration (PET): AI = P/PET. It appears simple but, naturally, it is not. There are two major problems: data availability and nature. Even to take the inadequate measure of pan evaporation as a surrogate for PET, these instruments are hardly scattered widely and consistently around the arid regions of the world. And direct measurements of transpiration are even more difficult and more rare. Furthermore, nature is complex: the rate of evaporation from a surface of wet sand is not the same as from a bucket, solar radiation and atmospheric turbulence are key but quantitatively elusive factors, the biophysics of plants varies with species and time of year, and so on and so on. Dedicated scientists have wrestled with these problems for decades without finding a satisfactory solution, developing complex formulae, empirical and otherwise, whose performance is always at best an approximation of reality.

Charles Warren Thornthwaite was an American geographer who in 1948 published a paper titled 'An Approach Toward a Rational Classification of Climate'. A major part of this heroic endeavour was devoted to grappling with the thorny issue of potential evapotranspiration, and resulted in this equation:

$$\text{PET} = 16 \left(\frac{L}{12}\right) \left(\frac{N}{30}\right) \left(\frac{10T_a}{I}\right)^\alpha$$

In the same year, Howard Penman, a British meteorologist, published his own formula that attempted to reflect more details of the energy components of surface and atmospheric physics, and this was subsequently combined with other analyses of vegetation effects to yield the Penman-Monteith equation:

$$\lambda ET = \frac{\Delta(R_n - G) + \rho_a \, c_p \, \frac{(e_s - e_a)}{r_a}}{\Delta + \gamma \left(1 + \frac{r_s}{r_a}\right)}$$

That I have not attempted to explain the basis for these formulae, nor the meanings of their components, is a reflection of their inevitable sterility and spiritual removal from our topic, not to mention the fact that they do not work very well (and certainly not globally). However, equations such as these are important, because arid lands must be defined in order for the United Nations and other interested parties to have some common framework and language with which to evaluate and collaborate. As we will examine in the final chapter, identifying, understanding and making any attempt to manage our planet's arid lands depends fundamentally on such collaboration.

The search for a scheme of terminology and of, in today's jargon, 'metrics' of what we mean by the desert can be bewildering and complex. It seems that the definitions are endlessly variable and often contradictory, depending on the needs and agendas of the end user. For a global viewpoint, and one that at least respects an attempt at consensus, the United Nations is arguably the best source. But even to begin such an investigation is to become rapidly entangled in a jungle (or desert) of acronyms, and differing UN programmes have differing goals, representing, in their own ways, differing end users. For example, the purpose of the United Nations Decade for Deserts and the Fight Against Desertification (UNDDD) is declared as follows:

> With more lands around the world facing increasing deterioration and degradation, the United Nations General Assembly declared the United Nations Decade for Deserts and the Fight Against Desertification, which runs from January 2010 to December 2020 to promote action that will protect the drylands. The Decade is an opportunity to make critical changes to secure the long-term ability of drylands to provide value for humanity's well being.

This 'Decade for Deserts' employs the term 'drylands', which, it declares explicitly (and somewhat confusingly), 'generally excludes deserts'. However, in 2011 the United Nations Environmental Management Group published a valuable and wide-ranging report (from eighteen contributing agencies) titled 'Global Drylands: A UN System-wide Response'. In this report, 'drylands' explicitly include deserts, and are defined in the following extract:

> Drylands are land areas with one overriding characteristic: they receive relatively low overall amounts of precipitation in the form of rainfall or snow. Although conceptually easy to grasp, drylands are difficult to define precisely. This report uses a broad definition in which drylands are land areas with an aridity index of less than 0.65. The aridity index is a measure of the ratio between average annual precipitation and total annual potential evapotranspiration. Drylands can be further sub-divided (see Table 1) into: hyper-arid deserts (<0.05 index of aridity), arid (0.05–0.20 index of aridity), semi-arid (0.20–0.50 index of aridity), and dry sub-humid (0.50–0.65 index of aridity).

For the purposes of drawing to a close our complex journey through attempts to measure the immeasurable, a simplified version of the table referred to will be taken as the source for our definitions:

DRYLAND SUB-HABITAT	ARIDITY INDEX	SHARE OF GLOBAL AREA (%)	SHARE OF GLOBAL POPULATION (%)	PROPORTION CULTIVATED (%)
Hyper-arid	<0.05	6.6	1.7	0.6
Arid	0.05–0.20	10.6	4.1	7
Semi-arid	0.20–0.50	15.2	14.4	35
Sub-humid	0.50–0.65	8.7	15.3	47
Total		41.3	35.5	25

For the aridity index, the UN has conventionally returned to the (relative) simplicity of Thornthwaite's formula. Note that all the aridity indices are substantially less than one, signifying varying degrees of net water deficiency, and the inclusion of the 'sub-humid' category in drylands reflects the impossibility of actually defining where (and when) aridity ends. Through the rest of this book our wanderings will take us through hyper-arid, arid and semi-arid lands, with the occasional foray into the sub-humid. But even excluding the latter, we will be travelling through lands that represent almost one-third of our planet's land area and contain one-fifth of its population – almost 1.5 billion people.

The UN translates these categories into a global map (illus. 6). This is arguably as good a conventional map of the world's arid lands as we can make. The scale can, of course, be increased and specific areas shown in more and more detail – until the data runs out.

As a delineation of aridity based essentially on climate, this approach is not alone. In terms of classifying and mapping the world's climatic zones, the scheme first presented by the German climatologist and botanist Wladimir Köppen and his student Rudolph Geiger in 1928 remains, even after a multitude of refinements, one of the leading schemes in use today. The Köppen-Geiger Climate Classification is based on temperature and precipitation, moderated by the timing

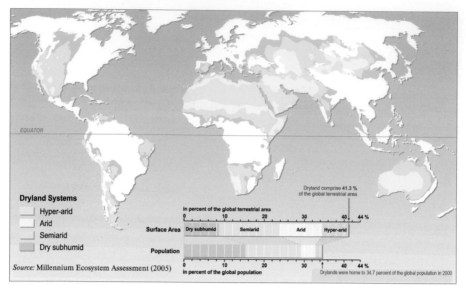

6 Drylands of the world as defined by the UN.

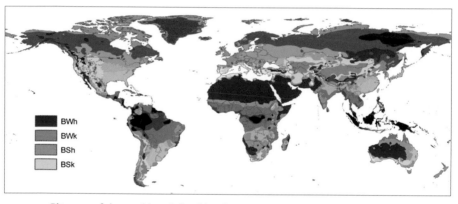

7 Climates of the world as defined by the Köppen-Geiger Climate Classification.

of the dominant precipitation during the year and, given Köppen's botanical background, coloured by considerations of vegetation. The arid zones (or the drylands) within this classification appear in two main categories, steppes (BS) and deserts (BW), each further subdivided into hot (H) and cold (K) (illus. 7).

The UN drylands map and the Köppen-Geiger map demonstrate strong similarities with respect to where the arid lands are, but there are also some clear differences in the details. However, they share one important feature: none of the lines separating the different zones mean anything at all on the ground. The boundaries have no real meaning whatsoever. To return to our earlier mind experiment of walking out of the hyper-arid desert core and observing the changes in aridity, we see no changes, no boundaries that in any way resemble the lines on these maps. Nature has no time for lines or boundaries but works with lost borders.

A conventional map, of which these are examples, is, by definition, a distortion. The reality of a three-dimensional world is depicted on a flat two-dimensional surface, we impose human conventions, reality is abstracted and uncertainty is rarely admitted. And there are still blank spaces, simply because the data used to make the map are not universally distributed and because we must severely scale down reality. But today we have a completely different means of observing, describing, measuring, mapping – and imagining – our planet, one that provides a far more objective image of reality: remote sensing, the extraordinary technology of satellites.

Desert heat is notorious, desert light is inspirational: the desert is perhaps the environment in which we are most aware of the engine of solar radiation. Much of the incoming energy from our sun is absorbed by the atmosphere or reflected by clouds. Of the remainder much is absorbed in one way or another and harnessed to drive the complexity of the organic and inorganic processes of our planet. Much is also reflected back into space by vegetation and the land and ocean surface, not just as visible light, but across the entire energy spectrum from the hot wavelengths of the infrared to the cool of the ultraviolet. Every rock, every grain of sand and every leaf reflects its own characteristic radiation signature, a unique part of the spectrum, and this is what our satellite sensors, our eyes in the sky, can capture with remarkable and ever-increasing precision.

The proportion of incoming radiation that any surface reflects is referred to as its albedo. Fresh snow and clouds have, unsurprisingly, a high albedo, but dry sand and the desert in general are the next most reflective surfaces on earth, returning typically 40 per cent of the energy they receive, compared to less than 15 per cent for forests and 15 to 25 per cent for croplands. As we shall see, the high albedo of the desert is in itself an important factor in influencing its climate, for this energy input into the atmosphere creates feedback effects that, in turn, moderate conditions on the ground. For our satellites, given the combination of the amount of reflected energy and its spectral signatures, arid lands provide a feast of data. For the last decade or so there have been large

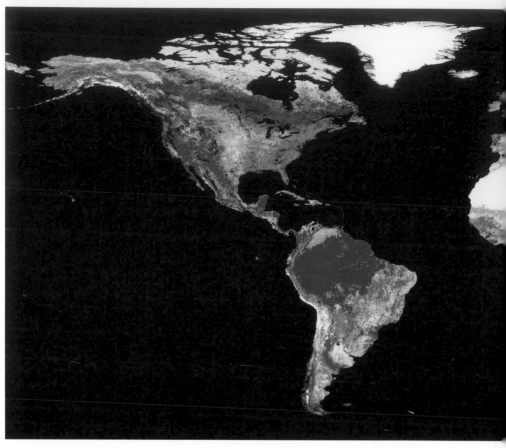

8 Land cover types of the world; our entire planet shown in all its glorious detail.

numbers of satellites circling the earth carrying instruments dedicated to collecting the details of the spectrum radiated from every part of the earth's surface and translating those data into maps that measure changes in space and in time. It is because of this technology that our understanding of our planet's changing environments becomes less imperfect on a daily basis.

Thanks to NASA, the European Space Agency (ESA) and the Internet, many of the results of these earth monitors are available to all. Not only do they powerfully illustrate the problems with defining the desert, but they provide satisfying imagery around which to settle on the viewpoint of this book. But first, how do they work and what do they tell us?

In March 2002 ESA launched Envisat, a satellite with ten different instruments on board, the entire package weighing in at a massive 8 tonnes. Envisat took up a polar orbit, allowing its sensors to monitor

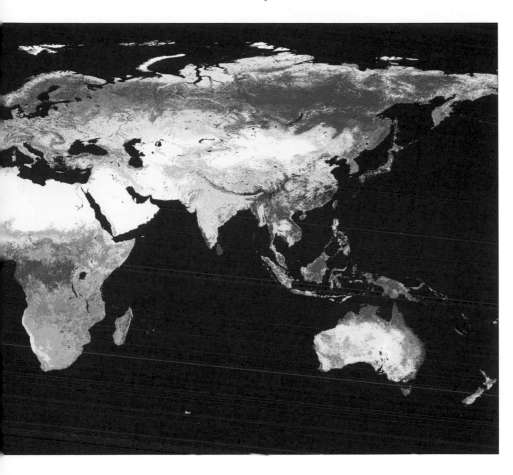

essentially the entire surface of the earth on a routine basis. For ten years the instruments sent back vast volumes of data, enough that, even after communication with the satellite was mysteriously lost, processing and reprocessing of the data continues today. The key instrument on board that is of interest to us here was the Medium Resolution Imaging Spectrometer (MERIS). As its name implies, MERIS gazed at individual areas of the earth's surface and measured the radiation spectrum they emitted. But it divided the spectrum up into fifteen different segments (bands) so as to be able to read the different signatures of the different materials from which that radiation was coming. Incredibly, the dimensions of each patch of the surface over which these measurements were made were less than 300 by 300 metres: it could monitor the radiation from London's Olympic Stadium. The blank spaces on the map had all but disappeared.

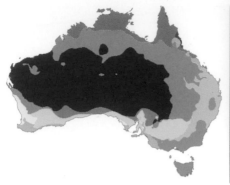

9 Australia, as mapped by the Köppen-Geiger Climate Classification
and from remote sensing analysis of land cover types.

So what, then, to do with these data which are, after all, just
numbers, measures of the amount of energy over different bands of
the spectrum? For scientific research purposes, the data are fundamental,
but for our purpose we need a map, an image. The way in which a
satellite-derived image is created is very much the same as the way in
which a photo is produced from the data that a digital camera collects.
The data are calibrated, registered to the character of their origin (in
the case of a pixel of a digital photo, the colour of the object covered by
that pixel) and then coded, assigned a colour for display from a palette
that properly reflects the range of data values. The result is a map image
– not, in itself, a photograph of the earth's surface (that is the domain
of spy satellites), but a representation of the varying characteristics of
neighbouring patches of the surface. In the case of the MERIS data, they
have been calibrated to the signatures of different kinds of land cover
and displayed, using the UN land cover classification, as a stunning
image, 'GlobCover' (illus. 8).

The different colours depict the 22 primary categories of land
cover (there are further levels of detail), the deserts and drylands of
illus. 6 and 7 being subdivided into such categories as 'closed to open
shrubland', 'closed to open grassland', 'sparse (<15 per cent) vegetation' and, finally, 'bare areas'; they appear in predictable (but artificial)
shades of brown, orange and beige. Finally, instead of lines and boundaries, we can see a meaningful depiction of what we know to be the
subtleties and variations of the real landscape. The difficulty we had
in defining the desert's edge is resolved – there is none. The reality is
a changing patchwork of grasses, shrubs and trees, captured by the
satellite data far more accurately and comprehensively than sterile

lines on a map. We can see this illustrated dramatically (illus. 9): on the left, the Köppen climate map of Australia, on the right the GlobCover image, filled with the real subtleties and variations of the natural environment.

And the spectacular resolution of the data (the Olympic Stadium) allows zooming in to details of small areas of the earth's surface – where, then, do we draw a line that represents the boundary of the Sahara in this land cover image (illus. 10)?

The value and revelations of these kinds of data go much further. This image, for example, is but a snapshot in time, displaying the changes in ground cover conditions only geographically. But the satellite data are collected continuously and therefore have the extraordinary power to show these changes over time, to reveal the shifting patterns of the desert borders. The close relative of MERIS that is run by NASA is called MODIS (Moderate Resolution Imaging Spectroradiometer) and is carried on two satellites, again in polar orbits but hurtling along in opposite directions. This provides complete coverage of the earth every one or two days, and the data are collected over 36 bands of the radiation spectrum. The scope and the detail are breathtaking.

In the U.S. the National Oceanographic and Atmospheric Administration (NOAA) generates readily available images from the MODIS data that visualize vegetation changes over the year across the entire globe. This is done using the differences between the radiated

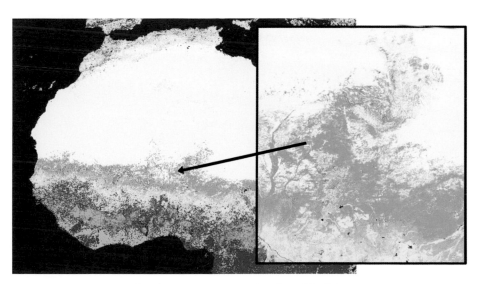

10 Land cover variation on the edge of the Sahara.

11, 12 Vegetation changes on the edge of the Sahara over the course of 6 months.

spectrum of healthy, chlorophyll-rich plants and poorer, struggling shrubs and grasses, mapping the changes week by week throughout the year. The measure is called the Normalized Difference Vegetation Index (NDVI), a powerful tool in understanding changing arid lands. Two such images are shown here, of the Sahara and its southern borderlands, in which increasingly deep shades of green indicate, literally, increasing greenness of plant cover (illus. 11, 12). Conversely, shades of orange and red are areas of struggling vegetation or none at all. Below are the conditions in March 2012, at the top, September of the same year.

Like the daily tides of the ocean, the yearly tides of greenness and barrenness roll across the borders of the desert, the landscapes constantly changing. It is not surprising that these southern borderlands are called the Sahel – the Arabic for 'shore' or 'coast'. They are the ever-changing 'shore' of the desert.

The writing of Mary Austin, the radical, eloquent and meticulous observer of the desert of the American southwest, was quoted in the preface. Those words came from the second of her two most well-known works, *Lost Borders*. In the first, *The Land of Little Rain*, her opening words are as follows:

> East away from the Sierras, south from Panamint and Amargosa, east and south many an uncounted mile, is the Country of Lost Borders.
>
> Ute, Paiute, Mojave, and Shoshone inhabit its frontiers, and as far into the heart of it as a man dare go. Not the law, but the land sets the limit. Desert is the name it wears upon the maps, but the Indian's is the better word. Desert is a loose term to indicate land that supports no man; whether the land can be bitted and broken to that purpose is not proven. Void of life it never is, however dry the air and villainous the soil.

Mary Austin's view of the desert is a compelling literary and cultural one compared to that of NDVI's scientific and technical view. But both images are powerful, and they converge. In *Lost Borders* Austin comments that 'Here you have the significance of the Indian name for that country – Lost Borders. And you can always trust Indian names to express to you the largest truth about any district in the shortest phrases.'

It is this truth that provides us with far more evocative imagery than any conventional definition of the desert, and it is in this spirit that we shall proceed. The hyper-arid desert core has its own fascination and character, but it is also as we approach its dynamic lost borders that we find a wealth of history, a richness of culture – and a multitude of challenges. And it is appropriate that we look for this inspiration in the voices of insiders, people for whom the desert and its lost borders are home, whose culture and way of life originates, in the words of *The Rubaiyat of Omar Khayyam*, 'along the strip of Herbage strown/ That just divides the desert from the sown'.

TWO

Big and Small,
Fast and Slow

'STILL, WE HAVE TO START SOMEWHERE, and a desert is one of those entities, like virginity and sans serif typeface, of which the definition must begin with negatives.' These words of the science and nature writer David Quammen are from *Desert Sanitaire* (1983) and echo the challenges of definition addressed in the first chapter. The title itself is an echo of Edward Abbey's *Desert Solitaire*, encountered in the Preface, and the overwhelming negative that Quammen refers to is water – never mind all the other associations of barrenness and emptiness. However, Abbey himself makes a provocative, and more positive observation:

> Water, water, water . . . There is no shortage of water in the desert but exactly the right amount, a perfect ratio of water to rock, water to sand, insuring that wide, free, open, generous spacing among plants and animals, homes and towns and cities, which makes the arid West so different from any other part of the nation. There is no lack of water here unless you try to establish a city where no city should be.

Look closely and even the most hyper-arid desert is far from empty, and its lost borders are rich. The narrative of this book, then, is to celebrate what is there rather than what is not, taking a viewpoint from the heart, the indisputably arid core, of the 'absolute' desert and venturing out into the lands of lost borders where aridity may still rule but its grip is more tenuous.

Every desert is different. Australia is the most arid continent but contains essentially no areas that can be described as hyper-arid in the sense of the central Sahara or the Atacama, but few would disagree that the 'red centre' is a desert. Similarly, the northern Kalahari typically receives the same amount of rain each year as the drier parts of England, but it easily soaks away and, regardless, the land is capable of evaporating three times the amount of moisture that falls on it: the Kalahari is a desert. The Gobi of Mongolia is a cold desert, the Rub' al Khali, the Empty Quarter of the Arabian Peninsula, an indisputably hot one. The Rub' al Khali contains the greatest continuous expanse of sand dunes on earth, but dunes play only a minor role in the landscapes of the Mojave Desert. Add in the factor of time, the fluctuations of temperature, rainfall, vegetation and climate, and the diversity of the places we call 'the desert' becomes vast. But therein lies the fascination and a dramatic character that all deserts display: scale. 'The desert' comes with adjectives: vast, endless, boundless, interminable, infinite, timeless. The sense of scale is both physically real and psychologically powerful, at the same time compelling and intimidating, seductive and terrifying. This sense of scale is perhaps so immediate, so overwhelming, because the desert reveals all – there is no challenge of not seeing the forest for the trees. And what the desert reveals are the extremes of scale, from the micro to the planetary, the instant to the aeon. A single sand grain provides a measure of something almost invisibly small, the number of sand grains in the Sahara an approximation of infinity. Deserts operate on a vast range of scales, and to understand them we need to think across more than ten orders of magnitude of time and space – from a rock coating a few millionths of a millimetre thick to the 650,000 square kilometres of the Rub' al Khali and from a few minutes of a flash flood to tens of millions of years. It should come as no surprise that so many of the desert's mysteries are, enticingly, not yet revealed.

Look at any of the views of the world shown in illus. 6, 7 or 8, and it is clear that arid lands play a prominent role across the face of the globe, occupying roughly one-third of the total land area. It is, however, misleading to think of these lands as being relatively sterile and static, mere bit-players in the dynamics of our planet. Indeed, this was the conventional wisdom for many years, but, like so much conventional wisdom, it could hardly be more wrong. In recent decades, many of the great steps in science have been taken by innovative experts in diverse fields making the brave decision to talk to one another, to explore the lost borders between different disciplines. This has been particularly true of the planetary sciences, where taking a more holistic and cross-disciplinary view has led to what is now referred to as 'earth system science'. Systems theory has flourished in a wide variety of fields from cybernetics to biology, sociology and engineering, its power being derived from the identification and analysis of relationships and interactions, feedbacks and interfaces, the analyses only made possible by the increasing capabilities of computer modelling and the ever-easier access to more and more data. Earth system science puts geologists, geophysicists, geomorphologists, oceanographers, atmospheric scientists, climatologists, biologists and botanists of every stripe together in the same real or virtual room and asks the apparently simple question, 'how does the earth work?' The answers are, of course, not simple at all, but the complexities in themselves are revealing. The land, the atmosphere, the oceans and the biosphere are all participating in a real-time multiplayer game in which the action takes place on every conceivable scale. The deserts reveal themselves as anything but passive spectators; they play a major role in the way the earth (and other planets) work, influencing, dampening and amplifying the dynamics of the system. Cold air sweeping down from the Hoggar and Tibesti mountains of the Sahara may cause low pressure systems that move westwards out of the desert and spawn Atlantic hurricanes. However, the star player, the big gun, is dust, a desert export that has such a profound effect on climate, life and human history that we will examine its role in detail in later chapters. But first, what exactly goes on in the desert, what processes are at work in desert landscapes and desert life?

Why, indeed, do deserts exist? Although the extent of arid lands varies through time, their lost borders surging back and forth over years, decades and geological eons, they are not the end products of some 'desertification' process, but rather an inevitable and enduring result of planetary-scale processes, the games of the earth system. Evidence from the Namib suggests that it has been a desert for perhaps 80 million years; the Atacama and the Australian deserts have existed for tens of millions of years, and it is difficult to identify any period of our planet's history when deserts have not existed somewhere. It is clear that we are looking at something much more fundamental than simply prolonged droughts, but it also becomes clear that widespread and prolonged aridity can occur for different reasons, different dynamics of the earth system and conspiracies of topography, climate and oceans.

However diverse the deserts of the world may be, they all suffer from thirst, a net moisture deficit. On relatively local levels and over time, our atmosphere is a series of moving maelstroms, but on a global scale there is a broad structure governed by heating and cooling and the rotation of the earth. The familiar east–west bands of the trade winds, the Horse Latitudes, the Westerlies, remain essentially in place throughout the year, shifting a little north and south, conspiring with the oceans to create different environments and climates. Illus. 13 shows this broad atmospheric structure as the air masses both rise and descend and migrate around the earth; the process of particular interest here is the circulation of warm air up and away from the equator in two rolling loops, the Hadley cells. The warm air rises from the equator and moves north and south to the tropics where it descends, the higher pressure causing it to warm and dry out – creating deserts. The air then circulates back towards the equator as the trade winds. The Sahara and the Arabian deserts are the most dramatic examples of these low latitude hot deserts, but in the southern hemisphere the same effect contributes to the aridity of southern Africa. These sub-tropical high-pressure belts are quite stable, maintaining aridity throughout the year. However, they are not continuous around the globe, for local perturbations such as the monsoons of Asia disrupt the system.

But, as usual, things are not simple: the aridity of Namibia or the Atacama, for example, does not originate primarily from atmospheric circulation patterns. For these coastal deserts, the atmosphere and the ocean conspire, bringing deep, cold ocean currents that rise to the surface along the coasts, reducing evaporation from the ocean surface, chilling the air and locking in what moisture there is. It is from the resulting ephemeral cold coastal fogs that the beetles and geckos harvest their moisture, but otherwise the air is as dry as a bone. The 'Skeleton Coast' is so-called not because of bones in the desert but from the countless shipwrecks caused by the fogs. The conspiracy story of the Namib Desert does not even end there: the winds from the east have blown so far across the continent that they have given up their moisture long before they reach the west coast.

All the southern oceans swirl anti-clockwise, the great ocean gyres turning and turning, bringing cold waters to the west coasts of the continents. The climates of Africa, South America and Australia all fall under their influence. In the case of Australia, the coastal aridity is amplified into the interior. As the rain systems fail to make it across the continent of southern Africa, so do their Australian equivalents become exhausted long before they reach the red centre. The outback is a desert

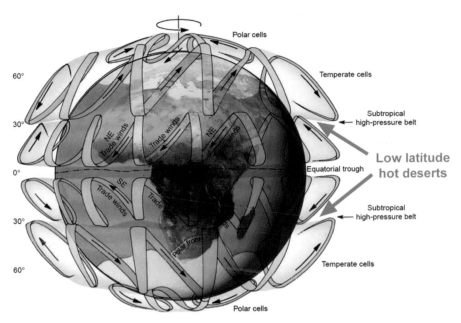

13 The atmospheric structure and the setting of the low-latitude hot deserts.

of simply too much continentality. In the case of the Atacama, the desiccating effect of the cold coastal gyre is amplified by the role of the Andes. The easterly rain-bearing winds encounter this great topographic mass and rise, dropping all the water they have, and by the time they reach the western side of the mountains they are dry: the Atacama is also in part a rain-shadow desert. The 'Great American Desert' lies in the rain-shadows of the Rockies and the Sierras, but the greatest realm of topographically induced aridity is the Gobi. The deserts of China and Mongolia lie in the wide shadow of the greatest mountain range on the planet, *plus* the Tibetan Plateau and, as we have recently come to realize, the younger mountain ranges that prevent moisture from the north reaching this vast area of aridity.

These conspiracies result in a number of great dryland zones stretching across the continents. Starting on the northwest coast of Africa, you could walk almost to Beijing without ever leaving one; three-quarters of Australia is desert. The 'Great American Desert' stretches from Mexico into Canada. South America may only host less than 10 per cent of the arid area of the world, but the Atacama and the Patagonian deserts cover a great swathe of the continent. And – while they will not be a focus of this book – let us not forget the frozen polar deserts, the dry valleys of Antarctica and the sandy arid wastes of Iceland. The very names of the earth's deserts conjure up the allure, the diversity, and the mysteries of these lands: the Lut, the Tanami, the Kyzylkum, the Tengger, the Dzungarian, the Ordos, the Armagosa, the Strezlecki, the Taklimakan, the Thar, the Mu Us, the Forty Mile, the Lop, the Great Sandy, the Rub' al Khali, the Umm as Samim, the An Nafud, the Sechura. All different, each with its own character, some covered in sand, others largely rock, some settled on the most venerable and stable parts of the earth's crust, others close to the constant conflicts between tectonic plates, routinely shattered by earthquakes. For centuries into these inhospitable lands have gone explorers, merchants, soldiers, prospectors – and, eventually, geologists. James Hutton, sometimes called 'the father of modern geology', first revealed, in the late eighteenth century, to a militantly doubting audience the depths of geological time and the ways in which the earth's surface is testament to constant change. This is, he argued, 'a subject in which we find an extensive field for investigation, and for pleasant satisfaction'. He continued:

> The hideous mountains and precipitous rocks, which are so apt to inspire horror and discontentment in minds which look at sensible objects only for immediate pleasure, afford matter of the most instructive speculation to the philosopher, who studies the wisdom of nature through the medium of things. As, on the one hand, the summit of the mountain may be supposed the point of absolute sterility, so, on the other, the sandy desert, moved by nothing but the parching winds of continents distant from the sources of abundant rains, finishes the scale of natural fertility, which thus diminishes in the two opposite extremes of hot and dry, of cold and wet; thus is provided an indefinite variety of soils and climates for that diversity of living organised bodies with which the world is provided for the use of man.

However, despite Hutton's encouragement and the pace of exploration, during the following century surprisingly little progress was made in the science of the desert. Geology made great strides during that period, but science was rarely a primary object of an expedition. The earth's character could be observed in greater comfort closer to home, and perhaps the perception was that the 'sterility' and 'barrenness' of the desert meant that it held little of scientific interest. Charles Montagu

Doughty was the somewhat eccentric son of an English clergyman who, more by accident than design, travelled for two years around the Arabian deserts. He was a self-made poet first, a geologist second, and always an openly aggressive Christian. The fact that he survived these journeys has been described as miraculous, particularly given that he travelled with a pilgrim caravan to Mecca, a visit to which would incur the death penalty for non-Muslims if they were discovered.

Doughty took several years to write his *Travels in Arabia Deserta*, eventually published in 1888. This was a monumental work (the abridged edition, published in two volumes in 1908, amounted to a thousand or so pages), and it was written in an idiosyncratic and inaccessible style, based, apparently, on that of the King James Bible. It was only with the support of T. E. Lawrence and later Wilfred Thesiger that it became a classic work of desert travel and it contains some of the most detailed descriptions of desert landscapes that had been written since Felix Fabri. Doughty wrote, for example, that they 'passed soon from the sandy highlands to a most sterile waste of rising grounds and hollows, a rocky floor, and shingle of ironstone. This is that extreme barrenness of the desert which lies about Teyma, without blade or bush.' And, 'We rode upon a plain of sand. Nigh before us appeared that great craggy blackness the Harra, and thereupon certain swarty hills and crests, *el·Hélly*: I perceived them to be crater-hills of volcanoes!' But, reflecting undoubtedly his own deprivation and suffering, Doughty spends much of his time describing the desert with bleak and uncompromising adjectives: 'uncouth', 'inhuman', 'sorry', 'dreadful', 'hostile'. It seems that Doughty had little love for this 'wilderness of burning and rusty horror of unformed matter' and he concludes with a very brief appendix that declares: 'The geology of the peninsula of the Arabs is truly of the Arabian simplicity.' He was misguided on all counts.

In 1900 a pioneering work was published: *Das Gesetz der Wüstenbildung in Gegenwart und Vorzeit* (The Law of Desertification in the Present and the Past). The author was Johannes Walther, a German geologist who had spent years travelling the world's deserts, observing, recording and questioning – it was the first comprehensive attempt to understand desert processes. The Royal Geographical Society review of the book declared that

The work of Prof. Johannes Walther during the last fifteen years has placed him amongst the first authorities on the desert lands of the globe, for he has not only brought an almost unrivalled critical knowledge of travel literature to bear on the subject, but has himself made three considerable journeys in various parts of the world . . . In dealing with the effects of erosive action in deserts, Prof. Walther rightly insists on the futility of attempting comparison with more familiar regions of abundant moisture. The desert is, as he says, the land of geographical paradox, rain-clouds which distribute no moisture, springs without streams, rivers with no mouths, lakes with no outlet, dry valleys, dry deltas, waterless regions below sea-level, intense watering without weathered rock surfaces, and decay of rocks from within outwards; obviously a land where the most skilled interpreter of the topography of moister regions must go warily.

Over a century later, Peter Wild, in his introduction to *The New Desert Reader*, offers his own definition of the desert: 'a place where habits learned in humid areas are bound to fail'. A definition, it would seem, as true of science as sociology. Unfortunately, Walther's work remained untranslated for too long; the first English version only appeared in 1997, published by the University of Miami in their 'Geological Milestones' series. It is now just that, a milestone. It has been barely referred to in subsequent works on the geology and processes of arid lands, and at the time of its original publication 'provoked astonishment and protest'. Walther gathered evidence for the existence of deserts throughout the earth's history, but conventional wisdom held that this 'seemed to exceed the bounds of probability to speak of "fossil deserts"'. Walther was tragically ahead of his time: while he was wrong on a number of things, this was groundbreaking, scene-setting work, but it was controversial and he was not writing in English.

It would not be for decades after Walther that real progress was made on understanding how deserts work. The belief that the desert was sculpted essentially by the wind alone and that desert processes are unique was not seriously questioned until later in the twentieth century. Even the way in which sand is transported by the wind was only revealed in the 1930s through the pioneering and meticulous work of Ralph Bagnold in his enduring classic, *The Physics of Blown Sand and Desert Dunes*. Collaboration on desert research was long inhibited by nationalism and empires, French geologists working in the western realms of the Sahara, British in the eastern. For those 'western' countries that actually contained a desert, it was on their own arid lands that the focus was placed. In addition to the challenges of access and data availability, there were those of scale. For much of the last century, desert studies remained essentially descriptive. Bagnold conducted beautiful quantitative analyses of moving sand in his laboratory wind tunnel, but these could not be scaled up to create a dune. He eventually would move on to study sand and water because further progress on the role of the wind was impossible in the absence of reliable and long-term data. Even today with the extraordinary power of computer modelling, to fully capture the workings of a system whose engine is global and within which a single grain of sand is a player remains beyond our grasp. But despite challenges and controversies, fashionable and unfashionable ideas and theories, we can take, as James Hutton urged, a 'pleasant satisfaction' in the status of our understanding of how the desert works.

Paved, varnished and encrusted

The tyres on a Ford Model T were only 9 centimetres wide. They left distinctive tracks, tracks that can still be seen in the Western Desert of Egypt today, nearly 100 years after these classic cars were adapted for desert use. The tracks of General Patton's tanks can still be seen in the Mojave seventy years after he held his wartime exercises. The paths of ancient camel caravans are marked not only by skeletons but by beaten paths across the desert floor. Not, of course, in the shifting sands, but in the vast landscapes of the flat gravel plains, the reg or serir of the Sahara, the gobi of China and Mongolia, the gibber plains of Australia. Far more of the desert is covered by rock and gravel plains than by sand. On close inspection the surface is often a mosaic of tightly spaced pebbles, frequently coated in a dark, lustrous, metallic veneer, causing the desert to glint in the sun, Doughty's 'shingle of ironstone'. These are the desert pavements and the veneer is desert varnish, both dramatic testaments to scale in the desert. Antoine de Saint-Exupéry, intrepid French aviator and author of *Le Petit Prince*, crash-landed in the Sahara on more than one occasion. In his memoir *Wind, Sand and Stars*, he writes of walking away after one such event across sand 'covered with a single layer of shining black pebbles . . . It is as if we are walking on scales of metal, and all the domes around us shine like armour. We have fallen into a metallic world. We are locked in an iron landscape.' An iron landscape of varnished desert pavement.

Such mosaic surfaces are characteristic of all deserts, and are some of the oldest landforms on our planet (illus. 14, 15). 'Saint-Ex' and his navigator were walking on a pavement unchanged for thousands of years. Pavement landscapes of the Negev Desert have likely remained the way they are today for 2 million years and an age of more than 100,000 years is the rule rather than the exception. A desert pavement takes tens of thousands of years to form and only a few seconds to destroy. It is formed, typically, of but a single layer of pebbles with only sand and dust beneath, so removing those pebbles reveals this pale substrate. Removal allowed the construction and the enduring visibility of the Nazca Lines, those vast and enigmatic geoglyphs of the Peruvian desert. And drive a Model T or a modern four-wheel-drive vehicle across the pavement and the scars will remain for an immeasurable length of time (illus. 16). The destruction of the desert surface by the wars in Iraq and Kuwait has exposed the fine-grained soil beneath, which is now revealed to the wind, creating huge dust storms.

A Model T cost around $300 and, with care, could travel five times as far as a camel in a day. In the First World War the British bought 19,000 Model Ts and many of them were used in the Western Desert by the Light Car Patrols to keep watch on the invisible desert borders. They were the stars of the initial motorized exploration of the desert pioneered by Ralph Bagnold and others in the 1920s, only giving way eventually to the Model A with its improved 23-centimetre tyres. This period was the beginning of the enduring competition between the car and the camel as the preferred means of desert transport. It was the car that enabled Ralph Bagnold and his Long Range Desert Group to contribute to turning the tide of the Second World War in North Africa, but Wilfred Thesiger, writing of his epic post-war travels in the Arabian desert, commented that

> I would not myself have wished to cross the Empty Quarter in a car. Luckily this was not possible when I did my journeys, for to have done the journey on a camel when I could have done it in a car would have turned the venture into a stunt.

Egyptian travellers themselves had differing approaches in the 1920s. Ahmed Mohamed Hassanein (Hassanein Bey) made his epic journeys by camel, whereas Prince Kamal el-Din chose not the Fords but rather Citroën half-tracks, whose distinctive legacy remains imprinted on the

14, 15 Desert pavements, Egypt (top), Australia (bottom).
Each view is approximately 1 metre across.

16 Tracks, old and new.

Egyptian desert today. These 'autochenilles' (caterpillar vehicles) were for a while a prominent feature of André Citroën's global marketing campaign, despite having a maximum speed of fifteen miles per hour and consuming huge quantities of water. From December 1922 to January 1923, they made a well-publicized crossing of the Sahara from Touggourt in Algeria to Timbuktu in Mali, a twenty-day journey that typically took six months by camel. The second expedition (from October 1924 to June 1925) was much more ambitious: over the course of the so-called 'Croisière Noire' (Black Cruise) the whole continent of Africa was traversed. This was followed in the 1930s by the 'Croisière Jaune' (Yellow Cruise) from Beirut to Peking across the deserts of Asia.

The Croisière Jaune followed, in part, the tracks of Roy Chapman Andrews, an American palaeontologist who led a series of expeditions to the Gobi from 1922 to 1930, in the course of which he revealed the fossil treasures of the desert – including dinosaur eggs. Andrews, who is sometimes cited as the inspiration for Indiana Jones, had begun his career sweeping the floors of the taxidermy department of the American Museum of Natural History in New York and by 1934 he was its director. For desert travel, he had a poor opinion of the French half-tracks, preferring Dodges bought straight from the factory; these performed well and were sold at a profit to local Mongolian merchants. Nevertheless, he wrote later that, while they were the trail-breakers of motor transportation, 'Instead of pride at the thought, I reflected sadly that we were violating the sanctity of the desert and destroying the mystery of Mongolia.'

We will return to a contemplation of the camel and its merits – or otherwise – as a mode of desert transportation, but at least the camel caravans followed the same well-worn paths, whereas the four-wheel-drive enthusiast relishes the uninhibited ability to cross the flat expanses of desert pavement, leaving behind a persistent network of scars, a tangible violation. But why is the desert pavement so ancient, why is it typically but a single layer of pebbles – how did it form?

There is an obvious explanation, and one that, like the pavement itself, endured for many years. It seems clear that the pebbles are simply all that remain, a so-called 'lag deposit', after the wind has blown away the sand and dust that accumulates between them. This was the process, originally described at length by Johannes Walther, that came to be known as deflation. This scouring and excavation by the wind does indeed operate in the desert and undoubtedly contributes to maintaining the pavement free of sand and dust. Among Ralph Bagnold's many experiments, he demonstrated how flying sand grains bounce off pebbles and rocks and continue their journey until 'splashing' into a dune and losing their energy. In this way he explained the strange pebble-strewn 'streets' between the dunes, advantageous avenues for desert travel, swept clear of sand while the dunes on either side accumulate. But why the single layer of pebbles, why, so often, are there no pebbles in the sand and dust below the surface? Desert pavement still presents its mysteries, but current thinking suggests that, rather than being evidence of erosion, it is actually an accumulating deposit. The occasional rains will wash sand and dust down below the surface through cracks formed by desiccation, and not only are the pebbles too big to follow, but through wetting and drying, swelling and contracting, heating and cooling, any pebbles below the surface are actually heaved upwards. The pebbles and gravel ride to the surface, leaving only the finer-grained materials beneath. This process is clearly a slow one – but then we know that desert pavements are immensely old.

A close look at the surface of the desert offers many revelations, but for Michel Vieuchange such a scrutiny was involuntary. The 26-year-old Frenchman had served briefly with his country's colonial forces in Morocco, but otherwise had no specific interest in the desert. Except for one obsession: to reach Smara, which was, in 1930, the largest town in the rebellious Moroccan province of Western Sahara. The origins of this obsession are entirely mysterious, but it caused a certain derangement of Vieuchange's mind. Speaking no Arabic or Berber, and having no idea how to actually travel to Smara or, indeed, where exactly it was, he nevertheless, with the help of his brother, set out on 10 September. Travelling for much of the time disguised as a Berber woman, he suffered immensely in his physical health, his security and his state of mind. For long periods he was crammed unceremoniously and in extreme discomfort into a wicker hamper that jolted along with the movement of a camel or a donkey and from this viewpoint, or from beneath the shrouds of his female disguise, his perspective was limited. He therefore wrote in considerable detail about the small-scale features of the desert floor, whose

> surface was covered with myriads of black or tawny pebbles, which bestrew it evenly . . . but without a single heap. It is as though they had been sown broadcast: a covering the same

thickness throughout, which gives the earth its colour. In places
a yellow earth shows where the seeding is not so close . . . like
a crocodile skin, or scales, which cracked under the feet of
the camels.

Vieuchange was successful in reaching Smara, '*ville de nos illusions*',
but on his return to Agadir died, apparently of dysentery, in his brother's
arms. His journals, published (together with photographs) as *Smara:
The Forbidden City*, make startling reading, not least for his detailed
descriptions of the desert floor.

As Saint-Exupéry described, that desert floor is often shining, like
'scales of metal' in 'a metallic world'. T. E. Lawrence wrote of how
his 'eyes ached with the glare of light striking up at a sharp angle from
the silver sand, and from the shining pebbles'. The desert gleams,
glitters with a metallic lustre as if the rocks and pebbles had been
coated with a glinting black varnish. And, in a way, they have – by
nature's meticulous and mysterious brushwork (illus. 17). There are
many different varieties of desert rock coatings, but 'desert varnish' is
the most common and the most perplexing. Break one of these pebbles
open and the coating is revealed to be remarkably thin and the rock
inside fresh and unpainted, a feature that allowed our ancestors to make
the rock art of the world's deserts by removing that surface. Look at the
varnish under a microscope and it is typically less than 200 micrometres
thick – this page is approximately 100 micrometres. It is also micro-
scopically laminated, as if successive coats of alternating dark and light
varnish had been applied. Analyse these layers and they turn out to be
a complex mix of inorganic and organic components. The metallic
lustre does indeed originate from a high concentration of iron oxides,
but helped by substantial amounts of manganese and clay minerals,
the dust particles that blow in the desert winds. But there is also life: up
to 100 million bacteria per gram of varnish have been identified, together
with pollen and a smorgasbord of organic molecules.

This kind of rock varnish is not unique to the desert. Alexander
von Humboldt described a 'brownish black crust' coating rocks along
the Orinoco river in the heart of the South American rainforest. In
his *Personal Narrative of Travels to the Equinoctial Regions of America
During the Years 1799–1804* he sets out a considered evaluation of the
possible origin of these crusts, noting their extreme thinness and the fact
that the underlying rock composition bore little relation to that of the

crust. Noting also the richness of iron and manganese, he concluded that the crusts formed from a process of chemical solution, that those elements are a concentrated residue from the original rock and that 'cementation seems to explain why the crusts augment so little in thickness'. Charles Darwin described similar rock coatings in Brazil, and for the deserts Johannes Walther noted that they 'must be regarded as a true desert appearance'. In 1905 Alfred Lucas, the Chief Chemist of the Cairo Survey Department, published a thorough evaluation titled 'The Blackened Rocks of the Nile Cataracts and of the Egyptian Deserts'. Lucas concluded that the 'peculiar black polished film' had 'formed from inside the rock' but that the process by which this happened remained a mystery of chemistry.

This idea that the varnish formed from some kind of chemical 'sweating' of the rock remained the accepted view for decades, but the evidence was against it. The composition of the varnish was totally different from the rock on which it formed – the concentration of manganese, for example, far exceeded that of the varnished rock – and was essentially the same on pebbles of different rock types. Once the amount of organic material was identified, in particular the living bacteria, it was clear that some other process was going on. There was a school of thought that the coating was analogous to siliceous hot-spring deposits, but while these trap bacteria, the microbes are not part of the process. Furthermore, siliceous coatings form in the desert alongside, but entirely separate from, varnished pebbles (illus. 18).

17 Varnished rocks.

18 Iridescent siliceous rock coatings.

Fascinatingly the origin of this 'true desert appearance' continues to be something of a mystery. There remains the view that its formation is entirely inorganic, but in current thinking the bacteria have a key role to play, possibly in collaboration with the chemically active microscopic clay and dust particles. The micro-lamination results from bacterial activity extracting and concentrating iron and manganese from the dust, the atmosphere and the occasional rains, slowly – extremely slowly – building layer by layer. *Extremely* slowly: radioactive decay of elements in the varnish allows the age to be estimated, revealing that it grows at a rate of 1–40 micrometres per 1,000 years. It could take several thousand years for the thickness of this page to develop.

But exactly how the varnish develops remains unclear. If all the bacteria identified within it were active builders, then it would build much faster than it seems to. At the same time, there are some examples that do show faster growth. Lead smelters were operating in the vicinity of Socorro, New Mexico, from the 1870s to the 1930s, and their emissions, including lead, can be found incorporated into varnish coatings of the surrounding desert. Knowing the period over which the anthropogenic lead was available allows accurate estimates of varnish growth rates: they can be up to 600 micrometres per 1,000 years, still not exactly rapid, but significantly faster than other measurements.

19, 20 Wind-sculpted, sand-blasted formations of the Western Desert of Egypt.

Does this mean that, for older varnish layers, we are not measuring an accumulation rate, but rather a history of alternating growth and abrasion, by sand-blasting perhaps? The story has yet to be told, but however fast desert varnish forms it retains a microscopic record of changing conditions over thousands of years and is a key witness to the history of the desert.

In his uncertain conclusions on the origin of desert varnish, Alfred Lucas observed that it is 'abundantly clear that a comparatively large amount of purely chemical disintegration of rocks occurs in the Egyptian desert, and that probably this chemical disintegration of rocks in dry and tropical climates is considerably greater than is usually supposed'. How prescient he was. It is easy to think of chemical attacks on rocks in the torrid heat and humidity of the rainforests, while in the desiccated and sterile environments of the desert the forces of chemistry lie essentially dormant. But we now understand that this is far from the way things work – the pace of activity in the desert, the rates of weathering (rock disintegration) and erosion (removal of the weathered materials), may be slower than in more humid climes, but the processes are little different.

The desert lays bare its surfaces and its often bizarre landforms (illus. 19, 20), but nevertheless there has been a longstanding debate over how, and how fast, they are formed, the roles of wind versus water, and the formation of desert soils. We hardly even think of the desert as having soil, accustomed as we are in much of the west to the dark, aromatic, fertile, earthworm-infested materials of our gardens and fields. But to a soil aficionado, anything that is 'a complex mixture of weathered minerals, organic and inorganic compounds, living organisms, air and water' is soil, and the desert will not be denied. In 2013 the European Commission, together with the African Union and the UN Food and Agriculture Organization, published the first soil atlas of Africa, an extraordinary and comprehensive report, complete with detailed maps. The legend for the maps is made up of over 140 categories and subcategories of soil types; the map of the northern part of the continent is shown in illus. 21 – the arid lands display far less than that total diversity, but, once again, they are more complex than might be imagined.

The Sahara and its borderlands contain a dozen or so different types of soil, dominated, unsurprisingly, by arenosols, easily eroded, sandy, with little ability to hold water or nutrients, and leptosols, a shallow covering of hard rock and gravel. These are thin soils and can hardly be

21 Soil types of North Africa.

described as fertile, but along the paths of ephemeral or ancient rivers, fluvisols develop: thicker, slightly more nutrient-rich soils, ideal for the valley-filling oases of palm trees and other produce. Over large areas, there are calcisols, the calcium carbonate – the limestone – component precipitating out of the occasional rains and floods, and often cementing the soil into rock. Plinthosols (from the Latin for 'brick') are what used to be called laterites, the startlingly bright red soils rich in clay minerals and iron oxides, and form typically in the more semi-arid borders of the desert. Unique to the desert are gypsisols and solonchaks, soils rich in salt. And not just sodium chloride, but often calcium sulphate, gypsum, formed commonly in the beds of old, long-evaporated lakes, or where water seeping upwards from below the surface has evaporated and deposited its dissolved mineral cargo. It is the gypsum in the soil that creates the spectacular and beautiful 'desert rose' crystals, excavated from the sand and sold along the sides of the desert tourist routes (illus. 22).

While the soil terminology is overwhelming, the message is clear: there is a diversity of soil types in the desert, but, not surprisingly, they are thin and mean, poor in nutrients and challenging for life.

Except for windblown sand, dust and other materials, desert soils are intimately related to the geology of the rocks beneath their thin covering and it is the disintegration, the weathering of those rocks, that contributes the inorganic components. It was long thought that the only means whereby rocks in an arid environment suffered disintegration

22 Desert roses, ~30 cm across.

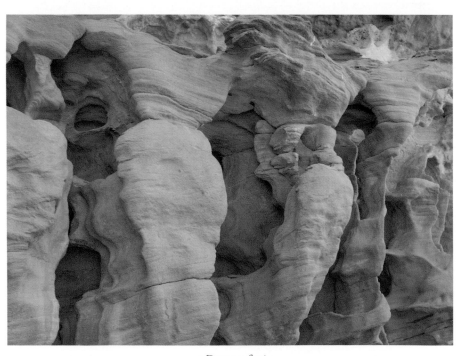

23 Desert tafoni.

was through alternate heating and cooling, expansion and contraction breaking them apart. But Alfred Lucas was right: we now understand that chemical weathering, in collaboration with biological activity, is no less important than in other environments. The gypsisols and the solonchaks hold the clue: salt. In addition to sodium chloride and gypsum, the desert hosts an exotic collection of mineral salts, rejoicing in their chemical complexity under names such as darapskite, glauberite and bloedite. Each member of this saline tribe behaves differently, but they conspire to assault exposed rocks and to clog up the soil. The rate of evaporation in the desert means that salts are more concentrated there than in any other environment, whether the evaporation is of water from the rains or from underground. Once formed, the salts can then be picked up by the wind and blown as dust to land far away from their origins to commence the local battle with the rocks. But how does salt fight this battle?

Even in the smallest micro-fractures in a rock, minuscule amounts of water will contain dissolved salts; lower the temperature a little and the salts will crystallize, creating a real force on the sides of the fracture. Alternate higher and lower temperatures and the repeated solution and crystallization will physically force the fracture apart and break up the rock through the process known, for obvious reasons, as 'salt-jacking' (growing lichens can have the same effect). But it doesn't end there. Some salts, such as gypsum, actually change their crystal form when they take up water into their molecular structure – gypsum is the mineral with water molecules within it, anhydrite is its 'dry' equivalent. The transition from anhydrite to gypsum is marked by a dramatic volume increase: the mineral expands by 63 per cent, creating a pressure equivalent to that inside a bottle of champagne or three times the typical pressure in a car tyre. Reverse the process and the shrinkage is 39 per cent; endless cycles of expansion and contraction cause havoc with solid rock, grain by grain. Salt weathering is by far the dominant process of disintegration in the desert and is responsible for many of the bizarre rock sculptures, including 'tafoni' (illus. 23). This kind of wholesale corrosion of solid rock can take place at a rate that seems surprisingly rapid for a dry climate, and we are only now coming to appreciate the conservation challenge it presents for archaeological sites. At Petra and the magnificent Roman amphitheatre of El Jem in Tunisia there are spectacular examples of tafoni.

The barrenness of desert soils, the compacted surface of the pavements and the salinity may make the environment challenging for life, but life in the desert is obstinate. Nowhere is this more apparent than in desert crusts. So-called 'duricrusts' cover large areas of every desert floor and may be constructed entirely from inorganic minerals – gypsum, silica and limestone form extensive crusts (the last often called caliche). These develop extremely slowly but over vast areas, through combinations of the actions of the atmospheric chemistry, weathering, groundwater and rainfall (even falling raindrops can compact the surface into a crust). Once again, the details are poorly understood, but it is the microbiotic crusts that present the greatest wonders and the greatest mysteries. Without looking carefully, you would miss them, for they are thin and fragile, but of enormous importance to the desert ecosystem. Built by photosynthesizing algae (cyanobacteria), lichens (the symbiosis of algae and fungi), mosses and other organisms with dust and sand as their construction materials, these microbiotic crusts make efficient use of every molecule of water available, together with nutrients blown by the wind. With highly complex internal structures, these communities survive long periods of drought and they commonly form the angular muddy plates with the distinctive curled-up edges that, until it rains, cover the desert floor (illus. 24). The wetting and drying of the crust results in cracks that trap dust and allow moisture infiltration into the soil when it does rain, trapping further dust and nutrients.

Microbial desert life is truly extraordinary, and we are only scratching the surface, so to speak, of what is there. Analysis of the biological components of soils from three different areas of the American southwest has revealed vastly different genetic signatures and biomolecular systems. Given that natural bacteria contribute the majority of new compounds for pharmaceutical development, the diversity of the DNA already identified by a team of researchers from The Rockefeller University, New York, suggests that these environmental bacteria 'have the potential to encode a large additional treasure trove of new medicines'.

Thin, fragile and mysterious they may be, but microbiotic desert crusts are the most stunning illustration of scale. They form a surface seal that collects rainwater and nourishes vegetation; they fix nitrogen from the atmosphere and increase soil fertility; they probably, on a global scale, act as a methane sink, reducing the release of that greenhouse gas into the atmosphere; and they participate in the global carbon cycle, contributing to the surprising ability of the desert to soak up significant amounts of carbon dioxide. Unassuming and microscopic, they play a crucial role in the way our planet works. We have yet to appreciate the

24 Desiccated microbial and clay crusts, Australia. Roughly 2 metres across.

true value of the diversity of desert soils and crusts, but there is one nation whose economy was built on them.

Greek fire in the desert

In *Desert Memories*, Ariel Dorfman, the Chilean-American novelist, journalist and human rights campaigner, wrote that the 'desert entered the modern destiny of Chile with nitrate' and that 'every major, ground-breaking figure of 20th-century Chilean politics' emerged from the Norte Grande, the Atacama's northernmost region – including Salvador Allende. Sodium nitrate, 'Greek fire' to the old Chinese, Arabian and European alchemists, saltpetre, the basic ingredient of fertilizers and explosives, encrusts vast areas of the Norte Grande and for more than fifty years generated more than half of Chile's revenues: it was big business.

Sodium nitrate is almost twice as soluble in water as sodium chloride and will vanish in the slightest amount of moisture. But in the hyper-arid Atacama there is virtually no water and the world's largest deposits of the crystalline material have formed there. Other small deposits are known from Death Valley and elsewhere, but the Chilean nitrates cover thousands of square kilometres of the desert with a mineral crust up to several metres in thickness. The 'salitre' deposits were first mined in the sixteenth century, the salts produced by a long process of excavation, grinding and leaching: lixiviation. The industrial revolution created a huge increase in demand and a series of improvements to the processing method followed. In the 1870s Santiago Humberstone (a British chemical engineer working in Chile) adapted the Shanks process for refining caustic soda to significantly improve yields and purity, but the process remained labour-intensive. By the twentieth century, the Guggenheim empire controlled much of the Chilean economy through nitrates and copper, and it was from their copper mines that a step change in nitrate processing methods was borrowed. The Guggenheim method allowed processing of very low-grade nitrate deposits (the nitrate was originally mixed with a variety of other materials – salts, clay and limestone). But by then the writing was already on the wall for the industrial wealth of the earlier decades.

The nitrate boom was intimately linked to war: the national boundaries between Chile, Peru and Bolivia transected the precious deposits and as a result the War of the Pacific between these countries raged from 1879 to 1883. Chile occupied Lima, annexed large areas of Peru and cut Bolivia off from the sea. The so-called 'Treaty of Peace and Friendship' was eventually signed in 1904 giving Chile control over the entire Atacama Desert and permanently removing Bolivia's access to the Pacific. However, it was the First World War and its demand for explosives that would spell the end of the boom. Germany was blockaded and consequently had little access to nitrate. But German ingenuity resulted in the invention of the Haber-Bosch process which simply takes nitrogen and hydrogen from the air, creates ammonia and thus opens the door to the manufacture of explosives. The result for Chile was the 'nitrate crisis', and the industry had collapsed by the 1930s, with dire consequences for the economy.

But during its heyday the Chilean nitrate business created tycoons and gave birth to social movements that would change the nation. John Thomas North, the 'Nitrate King', was a self-made entrepreneur and multimillionaire by today's standards. Originally sent from England to sell machinery for the industry, he went on to manage operations, buy his own nitrate works, build essentially a monopoly on water supplies and railways, involve himself in dubious stock flotations and securities trading, and die of 'apoplexy' in 1896. An entire social structure grew up

25, 26 Nitrate workings in the 1860s.

around the nitrate towns (illus. 25, 26), the *salitreras*, and the workers fathered the first democratic socialist movements that would, through good times and bad times, continue to shape the nation. The remote locations of the towns made them ideal locations for General Pinochet's concentration camps and they will forever be linked – as Ariel Dorfman so compellingly relates – to the *desaparecidos*, the thousands who 'disappeared' under his dictatorship.

Only one fully functioning mining town remains, Maria Elena, originally started by the Guggenheims in 1926 and bizarrely laid out on the design of the British flag. Maria Elena was devastated by the 2007 Tocopilla earthquake but, together with the UNESCO World Heritage Site of the ruins of the salitreras of Humberstone and Santa Laura, remains testimony to an extraordinary story of national destiny. Today what used to be by-products of nitrate production sustain the business – iodine, lithium and borax. As for how this crust formed, it is again something of a mystery and certainly the subject of considerable debate.

It was originally thought to be formed from seaweed, the decay of marine algae or other ancient plant materials, guano, gases from magma, or the evaporation of ancient seas (a theory that Darwin espoused during his travels on the Beagle in 1835). It has also been suggested that the Atacama fogs were responsible or that, as in other desert crusts and varnish, bacteria play a role. The arguments continue, but careful analysis of different isotopes in the deposits, and calibration with those of atmospheric gases, strongly suggests a unique mechanism. The extreme aridity, combined with photochemical reactions in the atmosphere, results in nitrogen oxides in the air being converted to nitrate and deposited directly as a surficial crust (perhaps moderated by microbial activities). However, this is another excruciatingly slow desert process: the crusts that made a nation themselves grow at a rate equivalent to scattering a few grains of sand on every square metre of ground each year.

Arica, the most northern town in Chile, was originally in Peru, was occupied by Bolivia, and has served as a strategic port for the region's mineral exports since the days of the Spanish occupation. It enjoys what can be described as a 'mild desert climate' with relatively moderate year-round temperatures, earning its reputation as the 'city of eternal spring'. Rain falls only rarely and sparsely, but the city is at the mercy, sometimes catastrophically, of events far to the east across the desert.

Floods

At approximately nine o'clock in the morning of 21 October 1904, Isabelle Eberhardt drowned in the Sahara. She was 27 years old.

Eberhardt was one of those quixotic, unconventional, unfathomable characters whose lives were consumed by the desert. She saw the desert as a mirror of her own unrelenting melancholy – an opportunity for self-exploration – and her writing echoes this obsession. With his own parallel fascination with the 'baptism of solitude', it is not surprising that Paul Bowles translated and introduced *The Oblivion Seekers*, a selection of Eberhardt's essays; when she was not yet twenty she wrote, 'Solitude is *absolute*.' Her life was enigmatic and bizarre: she routinely dressed as an Arab man, she was driven by extremes of experience and introspection, she was a habitual drug-user (and quite probably an alcoholic) and fervently promiscuous. She also, through her writing and her reputation, revolutionized perceptions of colonialism and the desert. The tragic manner of her death was as bizarre as her life – to drown in the desert seems paradoxical, absurd, but it is a fate that is not uncommon.

In 2008 flash floods killed dozens of people in the Algerian oasis of Ghardaïa, a few hundred kilometres east of Aïn Séfra, where Isabelle Eberhardt died. Mud and adobe buildings simply dissolve in the down-pours. On the edge of the Atacama, Arica vies for the honour of the longest dry period on record: no rain fell there from October 1903 to January 1918, more than fourteen years. But Arica lies at the mouths of two of the rivers that actually cross the Atacama, rivers that rise in the Andes and flow to the Pacific. While 'flow' for much of the year is something of an exaggeration, nevertheless stretches of the river valleys above Arica provide irrigation and are verdant, fruit-producing oases. But in February 2012 there was too much water. Torrential deluges in the mountains sent flood waters roaring down the valleys, destroying farms, bridges and homes, burying highways and the railway in mud, and dislodging hundreds of landmines remaining from the 1970s when tensions between Chile and Peru were high.

Typically, the weather that October morning in Aïn Séfra in 1904 was reported as calm, with no rain and no storms in the immediate vicinity. Without warning, a wall of water hurtled down the dry wadi bed, carrying with it trees, buildings, boulders and people. But that is the nature of flash floods in the desert: they are often unexpected. And they are, at any one location, extremely rare – Aïn Séfra may well have seen no rain for decades. Understanding how flash floods work presents an obvious challenge – waiting around for a flood in a dry desert valley is hardly a plan for a successful research grant proposal.

But there have been some successful, if serendipitous, observations and measurements, as well as a few experiments, and results of these are of vital importance, not only to human health and safety but to our understanding of how deserts work. Despite the temptation to view floods in the desert as analogous to the tree falling in the forest, it is clear that flowing water plays a key role in the formation of desert landscapes.

27 A dry river valley in the Gilf Kebir in Egypt's Western Desert.

The view in this image (illus. 27) is westwards from the plateau of the Gilf Kebir on the borders of Egypt and Libya, looking out over the Sahara stretching endlessly and hazily into the distance. It is a dry desert valley, a wadi, but it is also clearly a river valley. Scatter some trees, some grass and meadows and a couple of hamlets over this landscape and it would not be difficult to see it as a mountain river valley in a more temperate setting. Today it is hyper-arid, and any sudden storm over the plateau would send flash floods down those river channels. It is also an old landscape that tells different stories of times past and we shall return to this valley in chapter Seven.

This landscape is a testament to millions of years of change – there were times when it *was* relatively green, with trees and grass, if not hamlets. It is a palimpsest, earlier testaments partly scraped off but still legible. For too long, science, together with the rest of society, regarded the desert as essentially a closed environment, characterized by unique processes dominated by the wind. The role of water was seen purely as a human element, the availability of water at oases or waterholes determining the way of life of desert societies. It is only in recent years that the far more prominent role of water in shaping the desert, past and present, has been recognized. A more holistic approach has been adopted, viewing arid landscapes and the processes that sculpt them as simply end-members in the spectrum of the surface environments of the earth. The view above *is* of a river valley, albeit one that lies dormant for long periods of time, and, when it is active, it is different, but not *that* different, from any river valley in the Alps.

Like many rivers in arid lands, the one that occasionally flows here is certainly – extremely – ephemeral. It is also endogenous and endorheic. Or, to put it simply, today it begins and ends in the desert: any flash flood water runs out into the distant sands and dissipates, dying in the aridity. The flood that killed Isabelle Eberhardt did not travel far beyond Aïn Séfra, but it did change the landscape. It is the sheer power of water in the desert that, even allowing for its rarity, makes it such a potent sculptor.

Weather systems over the desert can be complex and violent, particularly over mountainous areas where great masses of warmer and cooler air engage in combat over the course of the day. An atmospheric convection cell in the desert is typically small and local, as opposed to a full storm front, but can let loose torrential rain over a limited area. The runoff, the amount of water that the ground fails to absorb, instead flowing over the surface, can be immense. This would seem odd, since surely the desiccated land would act as a sponge for the rain? But there are several factors at work here. First, the sheer volume and rate of rainfall is simply too much for the ground to handle. Second, over the bare rock of the mountain wadis there is no vegetation to stem the flow and give it time to soak in. And third, the sand and gravel surfaces of the desert are commonly armoured with various impermeable soil crusts and pavements. These factors make the behaviours of storm waters very different from those of temperate vegetated landscapes. The runoff from a desert storm, funnelled through narrow mountain gullies and canyons, can be catastrophic.

While detailed measurements of a flash flood are difficult and rare, there are plenty of eyewitness accounts, particularly from areas frequented by hiking tourists. In 1997 eleven visitors to the popular but notorious Antelope 'Slot' Canyon in Arizona were drowned; but there are miraculous escape stories too. Havasu Canyon, a tributary of the Colorado River, is also prone to such events, and hikers in the spectacularly beautiful canyon are often caught by surprise, describing no rain in the vicinity but a sudden wall of water surging down the river bed. In 2008 a particularly devastating flood hit the canyon, requiring helicopter evacuations and destroying much of the Havasupai tribe's tourist infrastructure. Impressively documented via videos on the web, the flooding was dramatic, terrifying and landscape-changing. The creek changed its course, two superb waterfalls were abandoned and two new ones created.

The common description of a 'wall' of water can at times be a slight exaggeration, but 'walls' of water 1.5 metres high have been reliably reported. This flood bore (a travelling wave as seen in some tidal rivers, for example the Severn in the UK), in the few cases where real measurements have been made, is typically 10–50 centimetres in height and moves at perhaps a metre per second. The volume of water behind the bore, however, and the rate at which it rises, can be dramatic, the depth increasing rapidly and the velocity of the flow reaching several metres per second – the online videos are gripping evidence of this. Even if the 'wall' is only modest, its unexpected arrival and the surge of the flood behind it, together with its cargo of huge tumbling rocks and tree-trunks, can easily be fatal. There may often be further surges, as the floods from tributary valleys join the main flow, and the torrent can be short-lived or, more often, continue for hours. Peak volumes of water flow can be staggering, equivalent to the contents of more than a thousand full bathtubs passing every second.

This kind of event represents immense power, power to destroy homes and bridges, and power to carve away at the landscape, redistributing monumental volumes of mud, sand, gravel and boulders. The valley in illus. 27 is filled with the chaos resulting from this sediment transport capacity.

A river's cargo, its load, comes in three categories: soluble minerals dissolved in the water, fine particles suspended by the turbulent flow, and gravel, pebbles and boulders rolled and hurled along the bed of the river by the force of the flow and by mutual impacts. This is the case for all rivers, temperate, tropical or arid, but it is the arid and semi-arid rivers that trump all others in their capacity to shift sediment. The observed record for suspended load, 68 per cent concentration by weight – a sort of soup – is held by the Rio Puerco in New Mexico. The Rio Puerco is ephemeral – there are long periods of time in the summer when it doesn't flow at all. But then in a flash flood the thousand bath-tubs per second will hurtle by, and when that happens, the river's cargo is over 2 million tonnes of sediment in a day.

Given this power, it is no surprise that floods in desert rivers change the entire landscape, moving vast quantities of sediment from one place to another. The hills and valleys are scoured, and when the flood abates the cargo is dumped. Where estimates have been made, up to 2,000 tonnes of sediment can be deposited over every square kilometre of the landscape each year. Or none, as the case may be.

The scouring and erosion sculpts and lowers the surface of the earth. Over thousands of square kilometres of the semi-arid catchment area of the Rio Puerco, the land surface is being lowered at an average rate of 10 centimetres every 1,000 years. This may not seem like much, but it is highly effective when it continues for thousands and thousands of years. And the evidence can also be visible on a human time scale: channels metres deep that simply did not exist in photographs from less than a hundred years earlier. So it comes as no surprise that the desert landscape in illus. 27 has been carved by water over the course of time.

The flood that killed Isabelle Eberhardt was devastating; she had just left the hospital that morning, recovering from malaria (and probably syphilis), and was found entombed in debris in the small house that she had been renting by the wadi. The flood was described by Richard Kohn, a German Legionnaire who had known her:

A bubbling, yellow torrent was rushing down the valley of the river bed, between the town and the camp, sweeping along with it a mass of rubbish, trees and bushes. I saw the water swallowing up the place where I had just been. Between the town and the barracks was a river of rapids and whirlpools, swirling along and swelling as it went . . . Suddenly there was a noise

like thunder; I saw half the bridge collapsing into the waters
. . . Now we were all crowded together, watching agonized as
the flood swallowed the town.

Good descriptions of flash floods are rare and the testimony often
tragic, but just occasionally there has been an expert witness. The French
geographer Fernand Joly was working some distance to the west, close
to the Moroccan border, 45 years after the catastrophe at Aïn Séfra.
Among his observations, translated from the French by Julie Woodward,
was the following:

> The rain resumed more violently that night, as heavy down-
> pours, between 7 p.m. and midnight. All of the washes began
> to flow and sheets of flow covered the fans. In the bed of the
> oued, puddles appeared about 9 p.m., due to both rain water
> and the emergence of ground water flow . . . Towards midnight,
> at the same time that the lateral sheet flooding ceased, a wall
> of water 1 m to 1.5 m high, fed by the gullies from the slopes
> and the channels draining the alluvial fan and traveling at a
> speed of 1 to 2 metres per second, appeared in the 15 m wide
> channel. The flood waters began to drop almost immediately
> after this . . .

He goes on to describe the progress of the flood crest for more than 100
kilometres downstream.

Upstream from where Joly was working is the desert town of
Merzouga. Today it is a tourist destination, next to the Erg Chebbi,
Morocco's only major dunes that offer the opportunity for camel treks
and the inevitable assault of 4x4s and quad bikes, as well as sand
baths for rheumatic Moroccans in the fierce summer heat. Merzouga
and neighbouring villages are separated from the dunes by a broad
and flat wadi, an apparently ideal place to construct the hotels required
to accommodate the increasing numbers of dune seekers. Collective
memory is short, and construction proceeded unabated and unregulated
with no recollection of flowing water in the wadis – indeed, they were
probably not even recognized as river beds. But the area is as exposed
to flash flooding from the Atlas Mountains as are the wadis described
by Joly; such an event had not occurred for more than 50 years but, one
night in May 2006 after heavy rains, disaster struck.

28 A ruined hotel in Merzouga, 7 years after the flood.

The flood must have been colossal in order to have had the power to cause the damage it did over flat wadi beds 1 kilometre across. All around the edge of the dunes, the waters surged, breaking through any barriers of sand and overwhelming houses and hotels. A number of people were drowned and over a thousand displaced. When I visited seven years later, rebuilding – in the same locations, but with more brick and concrete than adobe – was still continuing, even with the deserted ruins as stark reminders and oracles (illus. 28).

Landscapes

Crustaceans: a group of creatures more commonly associated with a seafood platter than the desert, but they are there. In the arid lands of North Africa, the Negev Desert and elsewhere lives *Hemilepistus reaumuri*, the desert woodlouse. Not only is *H. reaumuri* monogamous and family-oriented, it is a 'geomorphologic engineer species' – it changes the desert landscape. The family groups share systems of extensive burrows and the population levels are such that huge volumes of soil are routinely turned over, ingested and excreted, 'bioturbated'. The result is a more easily eroded surface, but also one in which the salt content does not build up in the way it would if undisturbed, and one on which vegetation can more easily establish itself. The land would look different if these small creatures were not at work. Such is the way desert landscapes work, atmosphere, climate, water, wind and life interacting on every scale. 'Landscape ecology' has become an interdisciplinary science in its own right, examining the dynamics of patterns and processes, mega, macro and micro over days, seasons and centuries. The landscape is a mosaic patchwork of microclimates, chemistries and ecosystems between which matter, water and energy are constantly flowing.

29 A salt lake east of Uluru in Australia.

H. reaumuri is not the only crustacean to inhabit the desert patchwork landscape. Among the dunes of Libya's Ubari sand sea are the Dawada Lakes, formed because the water table actually reaches the surface, and so-named because they have long been home to people known as the *daw-wada,* the worm-eaters. The harvest is not in fact worms, but *Artemia salina,* brine shrimp. They are dried, crushed and made into cakes, sometimes mixed with dates, which are reputed to have aphrodisiac qualities. The brine shrimp are crustaceans, but more closely related to *Triops,* the three-eyed 'tadpole shrimp', than the shrimp on a dinner-plate. Brine shrimp and tadpole shrimp are found in extremely saline desert lakes from the Sahara to the Australian outback, the Kalahari to Death Valley – even the lakes that only appear every few years. All of these crustaceans have highly efficient and rapid life cycles to take advantage of the availability of water and they lay eggs that are capable of lying dormant for years, or even decades, when their lakes dry up. Rains in Death Valley in 1955 hatched a teeming population of shrimp after at least 25 years of drought.

Lakes, however ephemeral, form significant expanses of the desert landscape, even, like the Dawada Lakes, making an unlikely appearance among the sand dunes. When water is present it is generally extremely saline, and when it evaporates it leaves behind dazzling white vistas of salt, often painted with subtle hues of algal growth (illus. 29).

Salt lakes – playas, chotts in Tunisia, kavir in Iran, salars and salinas in South America – form as the final resting place of waters from ephemeral desert rivers and in topographically low areas where the land surface intersects the water table, often as a result of deflation, the erosion and lowering of the surface by the wind. The Chott el Djerid in Tunisia represents a combination of these factors, and the water levels fluctuate dramatically with seasonal floods from the Atlas Mountains and with variations in the level of the local water table.

Dawn over the chott is a dramatic sight (illus. 30), but these lakes are dangerous places, 'a hell of mud and mire from the time of the first winter rains', as Isabelle Eberhardt wrote in *Prisoner of Dunes.* She recounts how a tribesman described the tragic death of his brother: 'The great chott drank him.' A close observer of the desert environment and a poetic writer, Eberhardt describes the

> treacherous expanses where a thin, apparently dry crust hides
> unfathomed pits of mud . . . And beneath the motionless crystal

30 The Chott el Djerid, Tunisia.

of the salty waters there are countless archipelagos of clays and
multicoloured rocks, in perpendicular and stratified ledges . . .
a labyrinth of deep canals, islets, pitfalls, of deposits of salt and
saltpetre . . . a leprous region where all the earth's secret chemistries are on display in the bright sun . . . An inchoate sadness
hangs over this lonely region 'from which God has withheld
his blessing', a vestige, perhaps, of some forgotten Dead Sea,
with nothing to boast of but bitter salt, sterile clay, saltpetre
and iodine.

Poetic, yes, but also accurate: 'the earth's secret chemistries' are indeed
on display, and the complexity of what is happening in these waters
and deposits as the lake waters rise and fall is extraordinary. The suite
of minerals slowly left behind, the 'evaporites', is far more diverse than
that in seawater, and includes, in addition to sodium choride (halite)
and gypsum, such exotics as natron and trona, mirabilite and sylvite,
epsomite and hexahydrite. Eberhardt's physical description of crusts and
stratified ledges is also accurate: the surface of salt lakes is commonly
broken into polygonal patterns of desiccation cracks and heaved into
crystalline ridges reminiscent of Arctic ice. The chemistry and topography of playas is in constant flux, a complicated game of hydrology,
chemistry and physics.

And, like the nitrates of Chile, these salt deposits are of immense
value. For centuries, Saharan commerce was underpinned by the salt

trade, and natron, a hydrous form of sodium carbonate, was excavated for use as an antiseptic, as an ingredient in early soap, in Egyptian mummification, and as a flux in glassmaking and ceramics. Today, the riches of salt lakes lie in lithium for manufacturing batteries and in a multitude of high-tech applications. The Salar de Uyuni in Bolivia is the largest salt flat in the world, covering more than 11,000 square kilometres, and has been referred to as 'the Saudi of lithium'. The u.s. Geological Survey estimates that approximately 9 million tonnes of lithium – more than a quarter of all the world's known resources – are available in brines beneath the surface of the Salar de Uyuni alone, never mind the other Bolivian salt lakes. However, the environmental and health implications of exploiting these resources remain to be seen.

Salt 'flats' are indeed, where they are not heaved into Eberhardt's 'stratified ledges', the most level surfaces on earth. The Salar de Uyuni is so even and level over such a large area that it is used to calibrate the altimeters on satellites. Rogers Dry Lake at Edwards Air Force base in California has been used for space shuttle landings, with the playa at White Sands in New Mexico as a back-up. Land speed record attempts have routinely been made across the white expanse of Utah's Bonneville Salt Flats, and the current outright record, the first supersonic speed of 1,228 km/h, was set in 1997 across the 'alkali flats' of the Black Rock Desert in Nevada (also home of the Burning Man festival). Car commercials often exploit the opportunity for speed and the image of freedom and escape. But dry desert lake beds, reflecting their remoteness, inhospitableness and perceived uselessness, like the desert in general, have also been used for less admirable endeavours: nuclear tests. Yucca Flat and Frenchman Flat are old salt lake basins pockmarked with the consequences of underground nuclear tests at the so-called Nevada National Security Site and the enormous Lop Nur salt lake in the Gobi Desert has long been the location for a range of China's nuclear activities.

For millennia desert lakes have been vital to human communities as sources of water, nutrition and minerals. Lakeside dwellers became used to adapting their lifestyles to changing water levels and shorelines that were forever coming and going. Isabelle Eberhardt was again right in talking about the chotts as vestiges 'of some forgotten Dead Sea' for many of them are exactly that. The Australian dry lake in illus. 29 is but an isolated remnant of the once much greater Lake Amadeus, Black Rock playa was formerly part of the great Lake Lahontan, and Lake Chad, which once was one of the biggest lakes in the world, spreading

31 Satellite view of alluvial fans along the northern margin of the
Chott el Djerid. East–west scale 10 km.

into Niger, Cameroon, Nigeria and Chad, is now but a shadow of its
former self. Depending as it does on rains and the endorheic flows of
a handful of rivers, the natural fluctuations in the lake's size are substantial, but water withdrawals, damming of those rivers and drought
have reduced the size of the lake by 95 per cent in the last 50 years. A
mere 5,000 years ago the lake covered an area greater than the Caspian
Sea does today; so-called 'Lake Megachad' filled essentially the entire

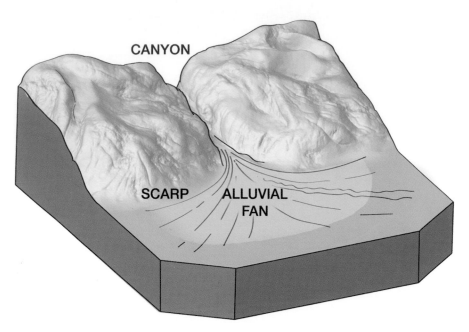

CANYON

SCARP   ALLUVIAL
FAN

32 The construction of an alluvial fan at the outlet of a canyon.

33 Gobi alluvial fans, Mongolia. East–west scale 100 km.

area of the lowpoint called the Bodélé Depression. What is left behind is dust – clay particles, salt and the remains of the microscopic lake life. This region now constitutes the greatest source of windblown dust on the planet.

Great salt flats, endless gravel pavements, barren rock: these, in most areas more than sand, are the components of the desert landscape. And then, as the sun rises over the Chott el Djerid, you will see another. If you were to look northwards from the bizarre white, pink and treacherous landscape of the lake you would see – in addition to many of the filming locations for the Star Wars planet Tatooine – a range of parched and canyoned hills flanked at their base by what appears to be an apron of rocks, sand and gravel, transected by stream channels and their tributaries (illus. 31).

These are the great piles of debris washed down those canyons by the sporadic rains and flash floods and, reflecting their shape and origin, they are known as alluvial fans (alluvial from the Latin for 'washed against'). A single fan-shaped pile of rubble will accumulate at the mouth of an individual canyon where the slope and the water flow decrease, causing the plentiful cargo of rock and gravel to be unceremoniously dumped (illus. 32).

The fan builds upwards and outwards as the sediment is transported down a network of ever-shifting gullies. Eventually, this fan merges and coalesces with those from the neighbouring canyons, and the hills will develop the apron of debris known from the American deserts as a bajada. The break in slope at the foot of the canyons is often caused by a mountain-front fault that lowers the valley floor, and the biggest alluvial fans are formed in deserts that are tectonically active: the western u.s., the Atacama, the Gobi. Alluvial fans are not unique to arid environments, but it is there that they are at their most magnificent. They are some of the great constructions of the desert and they can be truly gigantic: examples from the Gobi shown in the satellite view of illus. 33 are 100 kilometres across. These features are key to supplying water to the string of oases at their feet, clearly visible green against the browns and greys.

Alluvial fans cover vast areas of the deserts of North and South America and the Gobi, regions where the earth's crust is constantly on the move and where topographic relief is consequently dramatic and renewed. In contrast, the icons of the desert, the endless seas of sand, contribute relatively little to tectonically active landscapes: less

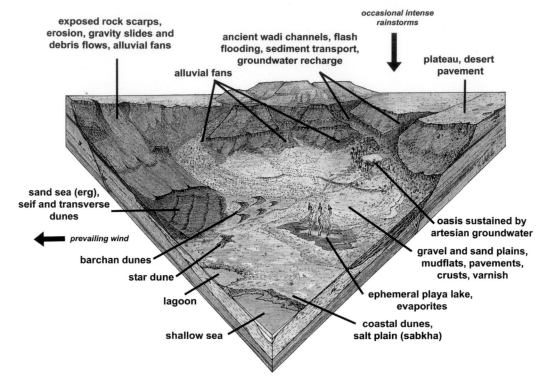

34 The diversity and relationships of desert environments.

than 1 per cent in the southwestern U.S. However, close to one-third of the old and stable regions of North Africa and Arabia and much of Australia's red centre are covered in sand (we shall consider sand seas and dunes in due course).

The landscapes of the desert operate on a range of scales that cover multiple orders of magnitude, from the nano to the global. The processes that form and sculpt them occur in a matter of seconds or over millions of years and to gaze on the desert is to see our planet's history laid bare before our eyes – which is probably why so many geologists love the desert. The desert displays a diversity of landforms and processes equalling any environment on earth, a complexity of interactions and feedbacks that we are still only beginning to understand. An attempt to describe this diversity in its entirety is far beyond the scope of this book, but this diagram, substantially simplified, from a Geological Society of London publication on desert engineering, provides a view of this diversity (illus. 34).

Near and far

Many of these desert features, including some of those resulting from active hydrology, are not unique to our planet. Desert pavements, dunes and sand seas, alluvial fans, salt deposits – and possibly varnish – are characteristic of the Martian landscape. Indeed, considerable progress in understanding our deserts was stimulated by the first missions to Mars, and the links between the study of extraterrestrial arid lands and our own continue to be strong and productive. The desert on earth provides the closest analogue for the environment on Mars and therefore provides not only the training ground for future human missions but also the place to test instrumentation, not least that which is dedicated to the ever-fascinating search for extraterrestrial life.

The desert is full of surprises. We have seen that we do not have to travel to Mars to find new and extraordinary microbial activity in biotic crusts and varnish, but the story does not end there. If life does exist on Mars, it is likely to be microbial and those microbes will certainly be *extremophiles*, forms of life that thrive in extreme environments. On an almost daily basis, the boundaries within which we find life on our planet are being pushed back, with the discovery of microbes that relish high temperatures and pressures at great depths in the oceans and the crust, life that needs no sunlight or oxygen, cares little about radiation, metabolisms that operate to an entirely different and alien set of chemical rules. The desert is proving to be a veritable jungle of exotic life, examples of what has provocatively been referred to as the 'shadow biosphere' that challenges our conceptions and definitions of life. For the moment we can only base our assumptions and instrumentation on the fundamental ingredients of life as we know it, and even searches on that basis are showing extraordinary results.

Researchers from Spain, Germany and Chile have developed an instrument, designed for Mars, termed the 'Signs Of Life Detector' (SOLID) that cleverly uses antibodies specialized in finding, and attaching themselves to, sugars, proteins, DNA and other ingredients of life as we know it. To test this, they went to the seemingly lifeless parts of the Atacama Desert in the old nitrate province, drilled a hole a few metres below the surface of a long-dried-out salt lake, and put SOLID to work. What they found was extraordinary, a veritable 'microbial oasis'. In invisibly small fractures in the salt crystals are not only living bacteria but *archaea*, the third and ancient domain of life that was only discovered in the 1970s. Archaea have no cell nucleus, operate on a unique biochemical system, and their DNA is as different from other microbes as ours is: they are master extremophiles. Salt is *hygroscopic*, absorbing even the slightest amount of water and so microscopic films of water in the crystal fractures are sufficient for the oasis to thrive. Similar communities have been found in bubbles of water ('fluid inclusions') trapped inside modern and ancient salt crystals in Death Valley and neighbouring Saline Valley in California. Many of the microbes are alive and others can be resuscitated, which raises the question: how old are they? It seems likely that they are at least tens of thousands of years old, and quite possibly much, much older. It has even been claimed (very controversially) that the oldest living organisms are bacteria trapped in salt crystals *250 million years ago*. Regardless, growing evidence demonstrates that extreme microscopic life forms thrive in the hyper-arid desert, and this, in turn, serves to inform our search for their possible extraterrestrial analogues and to question our very understanding of life itself.

Life: the desert, even if its rate of bio-productivity is low, is as bio-diverse as any environment on earth. The role of life in the desert system and its landscapes is not – cannot be – portrayed in illus. 34, nor have we considered ourselves. Humans play a vital role in arid lands, one that can be both constructive and destructive, and the desert in turn plays with us.

Playing with scale

Spend time in the desert and it changes your perspective, modifies your view of the world, requires a scale adjustment. In *Baptism of Solitude*, Paul Bowles observes that

> the physical contours of the landscape vary as much here as anywhere else. There are plains, hills, valleys, gorges, rolling lands, rocky peaks and volcanic craters, all without vegetation or even soil. Yet, probably the only parts that are monoton-ous to the eye are regions like the Tanezrouft, south of Reggane, a stretch of about five hundred miles of absolutely flat, gravel-strewn terrain, without the slightest sign of life, or the smallest undulation in the land, nothing to vary the implacable line of the horizon on all sides. After being here

for a while, even a rock awakens an emotion in the traveler: he feels like crying, 'Land!'

Countless desert travellers comment on the way the desert plays havoc with a sense of scale, distant hills taking far more – or less – time to reach than initial judgement suggested, small rocks appearing as boulders, mirages causing distant country to appear in the sky. Part of this distortion of perception is a result of the absence of vegetation and our inability to use the normal yardsticks of trees to judge distance, and part is simply because vision is the only working sense in the silent and odour-free environment. Human vision is, even at the best of times, an approximation of genuine information with much interpolation and guesswork by our brains; in the desert is the reliance on that guesswork increased and the fallibility of our neuro-processing emphasized? 'Then', as Bowles describes, 'there is the sky, compared to which all other skies seem faint-hearted efforts. Solid and luminous, it is always the focal point of the landscape.' Or, as Willa Cather wrote, describing the desert of the American southwest, 'Elsewhere the sky is the roof of the world; but here the earth was the floor of the sky.' The sky, the horizon, a particular pebble, an individual grain of sand are the objects of human perception, and the mind moves constantly, and often bewilderingly, between them.

And then there is *time.* Just as the desert itself is in many ways timeless and sculpted by physical and biological processes that operate over vast lengths of time, so does the human perception of time become distorted. Even Carl Jung was not immune to this. He recounted how 'The deeper we penetrated into the Sahara, the more time slowed down for me; it even threatened to move backward.' Unless you have an urgent destination, a waterhole, for example, time in the desert becomes largely irrelevant, a strange sensation and one difficult for the outsider mind to come to grips with. Which brings us back to the automobile and the camel. Paul Bowles again: 'Of course, the proper way to travel in the Sahara is by camel, particularly if you are a good walker, since after about two hours of the camel's motion you are glad to get down and walk for four' – a truth that I can personally vouch for. But the pace of the camel, the silence of its footsteps, seem correct and allow exercise of the visual senses in a way that hurtling around in a four-wheel drive certainly does not. If you should have the experience of spending a few days crossing the desert on the back of a camel, take off your watch: it is a surprisingly disconcerting sensation to begin with, but becomes refreshing, even liberating.

People for whom the desert is home have little need for a watch, and treat time in a very different way from an outsider. The human response to scale in the desert is utterly different for an insider.

THREE

Insiders and Outsiders, Civilization and Savagery

THE CHARGES WERE READ OUT in Perth, January 1908:

1. Forcing natives to accompany the party.
2. Taking forcible possession of natives' valuables.
3. Chaining by the neck natives who had done nothing to deserve being deprived of their liberty when horse guard would have been sufficient.
4. Chaining natives to trees with too short a chain.
5. Chaining to camels when travelling.
6. Chaining natives to water casks by using handcuffs attached to the ankle.
7. Chaining a native to another by using a handcuff fastened through a hole in the nose, and unnecessarily depriving natives of their water supply by deepening and squaring water holes, rendering it impossible for old men and piccaninnies to reach the water, and causing the water to be polluted by animals falling in.
8. Hunting native women on foot and on horseback, sometimes with rifles, for immoral purposes.
9. Using threats and giving bribes to native men to induce them to direct their women to have connection with members of the party.

This book began with the departure of Alfred Canning in 1906 to survey a 2,000-kilometre stock route from the Kimberleys to the markets of Australia's gold fields. Canning returned from what had been described as the 'howling wilderness' the following year, successful for one reason only: he forcibly coerced the Aboriginal inhabitants to reveal sources of water that he and his men were incapable of locating. There had

THE DESERT

been personal conflicts among the members of his team, in part based on the behaviour of individuals, and one, Edward Blake, felt strongly that Canning failed to adequately control his men. On his return, Blake brought the charges listed above for the attention of the Royal Commission that had been called to 'Enquire into the Treatment of Natives by the Canning Exploration Party'. The route crossed landscapes of which the many different local peoples were the custodians. For them, the scattered waterholes and springs were sacred places, located at intersections of Dreaming stories, inhabited by Ancestors; they were also critical to their way of life and their own survival. To induce them to reveal these places, Canning caught them, chained them, and fed them salt.

Only one Aboriginal witness was called to give evidence. 'Harry' was described in the local press as being 'very ill at ease' – hardly surprising. The *Perth Daily News* reported opaquely and without explanation that 'He announced that he could "Wongi all the Same White Fellah"'. This was an apparent misinterpretation, for the noun 'Wongi' is used by Aboriginal peoples from parts of Western Australia to describe themselves, and Harry would seem to have been simply trying to express racial unity. Harry admitted being chained but went on to describe Canning as a 'good fellah boss' and denied that any of the other members of the party were 'sulky'. The charges of immorality and rape were dismissed and the methods of coercion deemed necessary – they were, after all, only the same as those used by previous explorers. The Commission's final summary declared: 'Your Commissioners feel that in his natural endeavours to provide against disaster he would consider the wise precautions of preceding explorers, and by so doing, not only ensure the safety of his party but an expeditious performance of the work entrusted to him.' Canning then returned to complete 52 wells along the route, but the stories of his treatment of Aboriginal peoples became embedded in local history and lore. Among the many compelling stories told by participants in the Ngurra Kuju Walyja (One Country, One People) project on the stock route were the words of Billy Patch, a native of Wiluna at the southern end of the route: 'They been getting all the black people. They tie him up. No water, just the salt water. They let him go and they follow him 'til they find that rock hole. They make a well there. That's how they been find him all the way up there through Canning Stock Route.' Or listen to Clifford Brooks:

You're trespassing on other people's Country, other people's land. You know that word you say, 'trespassing'? You can't trespass on other people's property. You're breaking the law. Because we've got our own law and where the boundary ends, it's the songlines you follow. That's what the old people showed us. The old people keep it in their head. 'This songline. Ah, that's where my boundary finishes.' And that person in that group where they're having a ceremony, 'Oh, his boundary now, he can sing that area, that's his Country.'

Conflicts, tensions and frontiers

The term '*terra nullius*' originates from Roman law to describe 'nobody's land' but has become emotionally and controversially linked to the history of Australia. It was not officially used until the twentieth century, but its principle was applied in 1835 by Richard Bourke, the Governor of New South Wales, who declared that any assertions of land ownership based on treaties with Aboriginal peoples were invalid and that the land belonged only to the British Crown. In 1889 the Privy Council confirmed that 'from the onset' the colony 'consisted of a tract of territory practically unoccupied, without settled inhabitants or settled law'. Australia was officially empty. It was only in 1992 that the High Court ruled that the continent's indigenous peoples had prior title and rights to land from before the colonial occupation, but by then the cultural destruction had been accomplished.

The desert, whether in Australia, the United States, the Middle East or the Sahara, exemplified the image and the concept of *terra nullius*. The inhabitants of arid lands were, through necessity and choice, nomadic and if they were always on the move how could the idea of land owner-ship and borders possibly be of importance to them? And yet the words of Clifford Brooks, quoted above, make it clear how wrong this is. T. E. Lawrence commented in *Seven Pillars of Wisdom* that 'Men have looked upon the desert as barren land, the free holding of whoever chose; but in fact each hill and valley in it had a man who was its acknow-ledged owner and would quickly assert the right of his family or clan to it, against aggression.' As Australia's desert became the country's frontier, the total inability of the colonists to comprehend the nature of nomadic communities became the source of ever-increasing tension and conflict. As settlers attempted to push back that frontier and to exploit the land

– and, like Canning, its people – their assumption was that, since those people were nomads, they could simply move out of the way. And Australia was not alone: every desert was a frontier, socially and politically, for one nation or another, and 'pioneers' encountering 'natives' routinely resulted in a clash of cultures, an overt conflict between 'civilization' and 'savagery'. Well into the twentieth century, the French still referred to natives of their North African colonies who had received the benefit of a 'proper' education as *évolués*, evolved. Historically the gap in comprehension between the desert outsiders and its insiders was profound and, sadly, remains so in many ways today.

The history and motivations of frontier exploration and exploitation depend very much on whether the desert was a far-flung part of a country's empire or an integral presence in its own backyard. 'Conquering the wilderness' may have been a common, if unfortunately phrased, endeavour, but for the imperial powers of France, Italy, Spain, Germany and Britain the story of their relationships with arid lands is very different from that of the U.S. and, having been in large part self-governing for the critical years of its development, Australia. In the U.S., the beginning of the nineteenth century saw one of the greatest land deals in history, the Louisiana Purchase. For around three cents an acre, President Thomas Jefferson acquired from France all or part of what are now fifteen states east of the Rocky Mountains, regions he described as 'vast and trackless deserts'. By the time the rest of the territory was consolidated in 1853 following the annexation of Texas and the Mexican–American War and the Gadsden Purchase, the desert had taken its place as a key part of the nation's identity, as its frontier and as its 'manifest destiny'. For Australia, the nation's 'dead heart' or, as a Melbourne newspaper termed it, the 'hideous blank', embedded itself in the national psyche as an embarrassment to be conquered, developed and settled with the idea of '*terra nullius*' always in mind. For the U.S., the frontier was western, for Australia interior, the 'civilized' peoples of the east and the coasts pitted against the wilderness and its 'savages'.

For France, the Sahara represented simply an impediment to commerce, exploitation and resource development, plus an exotic land in which its Orientalists and exiles could find comfort. The stories of the deserts of eastern Asia were different again, never having been part of any Western empire but rather the guardians of Chinese civilization against foreign intrusion and barbaric incursion. But China's western frontiers had their own inconvenient inhabitants, and confrontation between outsiders and insiders there was no different from any other desert frontier.

The stories of the interactions between insiders and outsiders and their contrasting views of the world are fascinating and diverse; in this and the following chapter I can highlight only a selection. Throughout, however, there is a trap. Just as mythologies and fictions arose from these histories, so did romance. While it is vitally important to counter the racial prejudice that typically shaped the views of the outsiders, and drove, among a depressing litany of examples, the behaviour of Canning and his men, it is equally important not to excessively romanticize the nomad. As we will see, the art and writing of the desert have contributed much to an understanding of the desert way of life, to a celebration of the distinctive qualities of desert societies, but they have also led to romantic notions that the insiders themselves would hardly agree with. There is a balance that must be sought, an objectivity based not only on fact and science, but on the testimony of the insiders. This is not easy, but let's begin at the beginning.

World views

'Since most of it, however, is not cultivated and is a desert (either because covered by unproductive sand or because of climatic or regional aridity) or else is infested by many harmful species of animal, Africa is huge but not populous.' So wrote Pomponius Mela around AD 44 in *The Description of the World*, the earliest surviving geographical work in Latin. We know little or nothing about the man himself, but his writing was part of an ongoing tradition of geographical fact and fantasy. The shores of the Mediterranean world were well known, but beyond them knowledge dissolved rapidly into myth. He went on to describe the tribes along the Nile and the North African coast, inland from which 'a region, uninhabitable in its entire length, covers a broad and vacant expanse'. This was what had long been known as the Libyan Desert, a term for the eastern Sahara still used today. Mela continues:

> At that point we hear of the Garamantes as the first people to the east; after them, the Augilae and the Trogodytae, and, furthest to the west, the Atlantes. In the interior – if one wants to believe it – at this point the scarcely human and rather

brutish Goat-Pans, Blemyes, Gamphasantes, and Satyrs possess, rather than inhabit, the land. They roam freely everywhere, with no houses and no fixed abodes.

There is at least one fact here: the Garamantes were real, a people warranting being called a 'civilization', whose technology and culture dominated a large part of the eastern Sahara for over a thousand years and who put up a spirited resistance to the Roman invaders. We shall meet these extraordinary people again, but Mela was using as a reference, together with his mention of the 'Trogodytae' (or 'Troglodytae') and essentially all the tribal names, the descriptions of Herodotus five centuries earlier.

In his *Histories*, Herodotus had provided a comprehensive mix of fact and fiction that would be referred to for hundreds of years:

> This region is inhabited by a nation called the Garamantians, a very powerful people, who cover the salt with mould, and then sow their crops . . . In the Garamantian country are found the oxen which, as they graze, walk backwards. This they do because their horns curve outwards in front of their heads, so that it is not possible for them when grazing to move forwards, since in that case their horns would become fixed in the ground. Only herein do they differ from other oxen, and further in the thickness and hardness of their hides. The Garamantians have four-horse chariots, in which they chase the Troglodyte Ethiopians, who of all the nations whereof any account has reached our ears are by far the swiftest of foot. The Troglodytes feed on serpents, lizards, and other similar reptiles. Their language is unlike that of any other people; it sounds like the screeching of bats.

Herodotus and later Greek and Roman historians were well aware of the nomadic nature of the inhabitants of the interior of North Africa, and the diversity of landscapes and agriculture, but Mela was correct in questioning the veracity of some accounts. Herodotus again:

> For the eastern region of Libya, which the nomads inhabit, is low-lying and sandy as far as the Triton river; but the land west of this, where the farmers live, is exceedingly mountainous

and wooded and full of wild beasts. In that country are the huge
snakes and the lions, and the elephants and bears and asps,
the horned asses, the Dog-Headed (Kynokephaloi) and the
Headless (Akephaloi) men that have their eyes in their chests,
as the Libyans say, and the wild men and women, besides many
other creatures not fabulous.

The headless men with their eyes in their chests were the Blemyes
of Mela or the Blemmyes of Pliny's *Natural History*, a work which relied
on Mela as a key source. None of these geographies come with surviving maps. There are versions of Pomponius Mela's 'map', but they are
creations from much later, turning his descriptions into graphics, and the
descriptions of these historians are often the narrative equivalent of
the fantastic images that would be deployed to fill in the blank spaces
on subsequent cartographic efforts. Mela's work never became popular
in the way that Ptolemy's *Geographia* would a century later, a work that
certainly contained maps, although, again, we have no original versions.
Redrawn and reconstructed in the fifteenth century, Ptolemy's influential map shows North Africa as impressively blank, with the exception
of the Nile and an effort to depict the course of the River Niger – which
would remain enigmatic for 1,700 years. But, like his predecessors,

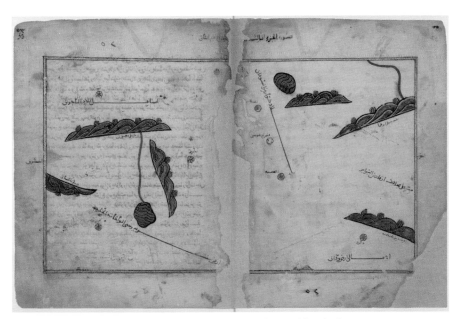

35 Part of the Libyan Desert as depicted by al-Idrisi.

Ptolemy based his geographical description on the names of the inhabitants, real or mythical: 'and below the Samamuci are the Damensi and then the Nygbeni, below whom are the Nycpi; then below the Cinyphi and the Elaeones is Macae Syrtitae and the Libyan desert.' Ptolemy's geography was based on a key innovation that was fundamentally cartographical: latitude. Beginning with Aristotle, the earth had long been roughly divided into zones of different climates. For Aristotle there were five: frigid and temperate in the northern and southern hemispheres and torrid between the tropics – the torrid zone was deemed uninhabitable. A century after Aristotle, the great geographer Eratosthenes, also a poet, described these zones in *Hermes*:

> Five encircling zones were girt around it: two of them darker than greyish-blue enamel, another one sand and red, as if from fire . . . Two others there were, standing opposite one another, between the heat and showers of ice; both were temperate regions, growing with grain, the fruit of Eleusinian Demeter; in them dwelt men antipodean to each other.

The world for Aristotle, Eratosthenes and Ptolemy was not only spherical, but divided by lines of latitude into zones, the *klimata* or climes. And the zone on either side of the equator, torrid and uninhabitable, was the desert. Ptolemy developed the zonal system to include seven, all of them essentially in the northern hemisphere, their boundaries calculated by the length of the longest day – equivalent to latitude. With inevitably less accuracy he laid out a system of longitude, thereby establishing the global grid system that evolved into what we use today. The basis for a cartographic world view was established and there were descriptive geographies, but the two coming together in a rigorous way – at least in a way that survives today – would have to wait for a thousand years. A world map that for all its distortions is startlingly recognizable as such would originate not from European geographers, whose obsession was maritime, but from the sophisticated world of medieval Islamic science.

In 1101 Norman forces took over Sicily from the Arabs under whom it had prospered for more than 250 years. However, the Norman king Roger II was an enlightened and intellectually cross-cultural ruler, determined to improve on the primitive maps and geographies available at the time. He established an academy at his court in Palermo and in 1138 invited the prominent Arab geographer Muhammad al-Idrisi to lead the project. The works of twelve scholars were evaluated and compiled; ten of them were Muslim, a reflection of the land-based knowledge derived from commerce and administration throughout the Islamic world as opposed to the maritime focus of the Europeans. Records of the postal service administrations provided information from far-flung parts. Sicily was also well placed to receive merchants and travellers, and Roger and al-Idrisi carefully identified and interviewed anyone who could fill in the blanks. The work took fifteen years, culminating in the production of a map, the *Tabula Rogeriana*, compiled and engraved on a silver disk over 2 metres in diameter and reportedly weighing 140 kilograms. The only surviving copy of Ptolemy's *Geography* had been preserved in its Arabic translation and al-Idrisi's world was based on the seven climes which, together with Ptolemy's system of longitude, provided the basis for the accompanying detailed text and individual maps. The book was titled *Nuzhat al-mushtaq fi ikhtiraq al-afaq* (The Delight of One Who Wishes to Traverse the Regions of the World) or, more simply, *al-Kitab al-Rujari* (Roger's Book). An example of the 70 maps included in the volume is shown in illus. 35: it depicts perhaps a thousand kilometres east–west of the Libyan Desert and, according to the conventions of the day, north is towards the bottom of the image. Mountains are shown with different designs, together with rivers and bodies of water; inhabited places, most likely oases, are marked with golden rosettes, together with key distances and directions.

This was, however, the Dark Ages, the crusades were raging, and in 1160 local Sicilian warlords rebelled, sacking, looting and burning the palace: it seems that the silver disk and the Latin version of al-Idrisi's works were destroyed. Amid the slaughter, al-Idrisi had fled, taking with him the Arabic version. It would be some time before it was fully appreciated in Europe and it would not be until the nineteenth century that *Roger's Book* was translated into French. In the 1920s a German geographer, Konrad Miller, assembled (and edited) all 70 maps into one image, a view of the world stunningly similar to our own (illus. 36).

Roger's Book contains, perhaps not surprisingly given the scope of the Islamic world (the Arabs were, after all, more or less insiders), detailed descriptions of oases, desert inhabitants, their culture, art, beliefs, commerce and way of life. Itineraries are listed in terms of duration of travel

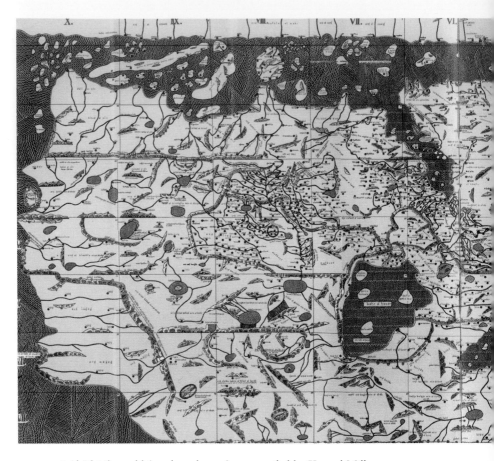

36 Al-Idrisi's world (south at the top) as compiled by Konrad Miller.

for a caravan and availability of water sources; the typical daily routine of a camel caravan is described in detail. Interestingly, the 1830s French translation by Jaubert notes the distinction between the words *sahara* and *madjāba*, the first being the general term for desert – sand, gravel plains, pavements and rocks – and the second specifically referring to '*solitude aride*', expanses of dunes with no water for up to fourteen days of travel. As for the people, 'One finds in the plains diverse tribes of nomads, who cross the country in all directions to search for pasture for their herds . . . They have no fixed home, passing the time in travelling without ever leaving their territory, without being in contact with other peoples, without trusting their neighbours.' The nomads, he reports, look after only themselves; the inhabitants of neighbouring villages, even of the same tribe, steal children in the night and sell them into slavery. 'These people are in general very corrupt and polygamous.'

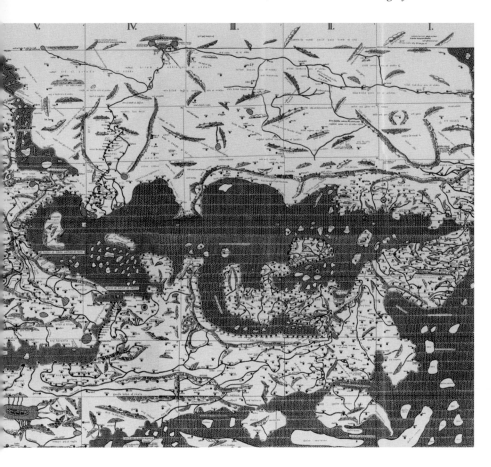

The romantic view of the nomad was not for al-Idrisi – but nor were any fantasies.

The accounts and the maps were revolutionary in terms of accuracy and scope, and remained unparalleled for several centuries. A work that properly mapped and documented the world, recognized the source of the Nile, described Lake Chad and the Niger River (together, probably, with Timbuktu) and discussed changing climates where the evidence showed that the land had been more fertile in the past, emerged from the Islamic world at a time when European armies were ransacking the Levant.

Unfortunately, to the east the Islamic world was also under pressure. By the thirteenth century Genghis Khan and the Mongol nomad hordes were pressing westward against the frontiers of the Muslim caliphates. In 1258 Baghdad was sacked and, although there would be a period of compromise in which the invaders embraced Islam, the fourteenth century saw Tamerlane sweep across central Asia and the Middle East, bringing slaughter and devastation in his wake – much of the cultural and scientific heritage of the Islamic empire was destroyed. Knowledge of medieval Asia was sparse, except among a handful of intrepid travellers spurred by a European desire to use the Silk Road for trade with China and religious conversion. The most celebrated among these were the Polo brothers Niccolò and Maffeo who, on their second epic journey to the lands of Kublai Khan, took along Niccolò's son, Marco – but there had been others. Papal diplomacy had included a plan to take advantage of Mongolian aggression by converting them to Christianity and enlisting their help in the crusades, and a number of monks had been dispatched eastward.

A Flemish Franciscan friar, William of Rubrick (Willem van Ruysbroeck), decided to undertake his own mission and set out in 1253 for a journey that would last three years and provide the most detailed account of the Mongols available at the time. 'Nowhere have they fixed dwelling-places, nor do they know where their next will be', he wrote, describing their felt yurts, ornamentation, travelling methods, clothing, food and drink, including the preparation of their favourite drink, cosmos, or fermented mare's milk. Therein was a problem for William's missionary aspirations, for Slavic Christians had let it be known that drinking cosmos was forbidden and one of his candidates 'said he could not possibly venture to receive baptism, for then he could not drink cosmos. For the Christians of these parts say that no true Christian should drink, but that without this drink it were impossible to live in these deserts. From this opinion I could not possibly turn him.' On his return journey, he describes 'the barriers of Alexander, shutting out the wild tribes, that is the desert nomads, so that they could not get in on the cultivated lands and the towns'. These would likely have been the Caucasian barriers built by the Persians, rather than Alexander, to keep the insiders out, insiders including monsters and the biblical and koranic apocalyptic figures of Gog and Magog. Al-Idrisi referred to 'Yajooj' and 'Majooj' and had located them roughly in Mongolia; they would feature on maps for centuries.

The return of the Polos in 1295, and the imprisoned Marco's dictation of his account of their 24 years of travels, created a further revolution in map-making. In 1375 a Catalan Jewish illustrator and chartmaker, Cresques Abraham, working in Majorca, was commissioned

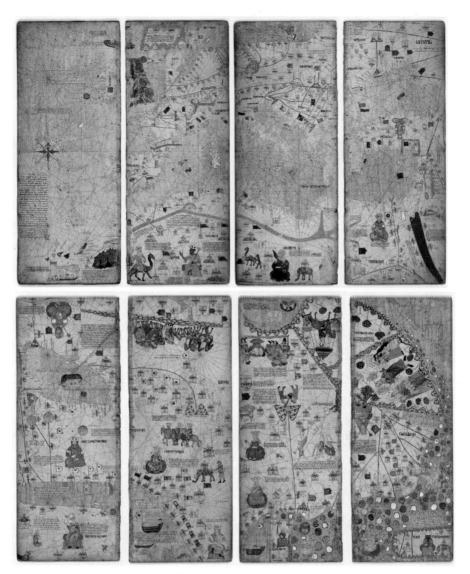

37 The complete Catalan Atlas, the panels shown west to east
from top left to bottom right.

by Peter of Aragon to fulfil the request of Charles v of France for an
'image of the world and of the regions which are on the earth and of
the various kinds of peoples which inhabit it'. The result was the so-
called Catalan Atlas, an extraordinary work of popular and Christian
mythology, fact and imagery. The complete map, originally measuring
nearly 4 metres in width, transferred to a series of wooden boards, is now
preserved in the Bibliothèque Nationale in Paris (illus. 37).

The results of ever-increasing maritime exploration and trade are clear: the coasts and their harbours, together with navigational data, are shown in remarkable detail. But it is the Atlas's glorious images and annotations that fill the land areas that are truly fascinating. The facts and fantasies of Marco Polo's accounts are clearly incorporated into the details of Asia. A Silk Road caravan crossing the Taklamakan Desert appears, inverted (shown normally in illus. 38), with one of the travellers shown apparently falling asleep, quite possibly a direct reference to Polo's warning:

> It is asserted as a well-known fact that this desert is the abode of many evil spirits, which amuse travellers to their destruction with most extraordinary illusions. If, during the day-time, any persons remain behind on the road, either when overtaken by sleep or detained by their natural occasions, until the caravan has passed a hill and is no longer in sight, they unexpectedly hear themselves called to by their names, and in a tone of voice to which they are accustomed. Supposing the call to proceed from their companions, they are led away by it from the direct road, and not knowing in what direction to advance, are left to perish.

Towns named and described by Polo are represented but so are bizarre images of religious mythology. Alexander is shown and described as being assisted by Satan to imprison Gog and Magog, who represent Central Asian tribes of cannibals. Moving westward, the Three Kings are shown, Jerusalem is placed as convention required, approximately in the middle of the map, and the Queen of Sheba sits, contemplating a golden orb, in the middle of the Arabian peninsula, not far from Mecca and Medina. The Red Sea is red, with a bridge-like structure at its northern end to mark where Moses crossed.

The Sahara is only slightly more accurate than al-Idrisi's depiction, but the figures used to fill in the blank spaces are of interest. A veiled Tuareg rides a camel near a group of tents and, close to Timbuktu (Tenbuch), sits, in all his glory, King 'Musse Melly'. This is Mansa Musa, the fabulously wealthy head of the great Malian empire of the fourteenth century. The annotation informs us that he is 'the richest and most distinguished ruler of this whole region, on account of the great quantity of gold that is found in his land'. To the east are the Kings of Organa and Nubia, the latter 'always at war and under arms against the Nubian Christians, who are under the rule of the Emperor of Ethiopia and belong to the realm of Prester John'. The mythical Christian patriarch would appear himself in later Catalan maps, seated in Ethiopia, overseeing Paradise – although this could also be located in central Asia or Mongolia.

Marco Polo's descriptions, real and imaginary, of the Asian deserts would remain the primary source for centuries, with his accounts not only of desert spirits and 'the excessive troubles and dangers that must unavoidably be encountered in the passage of this desert', but the oases, 'plentifully supplied with every kind of provision . . . particularly celebrated for producing the best melons in the world'. The city of Kamul (modern-day Hami, in the borderlands of the Gobi and still renowned for its melons) came in, perhaps not surprisingly, for special attention:

> This district lies in the intermediate space between two deserts; that is to say, the great desert already described, and another of smaller extent, being only about three days' journey across. The inhabitants are worshippers of idols, and have their peculiar language. They subsist on the fruits of the earth, which they possess in abundance, and are enabled to supply the wants of travellers. The men are addicted to pleasure, and attend to little else than playing upon instruments, singing, dancing, reading, writing, according to the practice of the country, and the pursuit, in short, of every kind of amusement. When strangers arrive, and desire to have lodging and accommodation at their houses, it affords them the highest gratification. They give positive orders to their wives, daughters, sisters, and other female relations, to indulge their guests in every wish, whilst they themselves leave their homes, and retire into the city, and the stranger lives in the house with the females as if they were his own wives, and they send whatever necessaries may be wanted; but for which, it is to be understood, they expect payment . . .

Maps of the world's deserts would evolve but little over the years, with the Sahara still being described as 'Desertum Barbariae' and the southern Arabian peninsula by the Roman term 'Arabia Felix' in the eighteenth century. It would not be until the age of empires in the

38 A Silk Road caravan from the Catalan Atlas.

nineteenth century that our knowledge would finally be set on firm – if subjective and often somewhat prejudiced – ground.

'Something hidden. Go and find it . . .'

If the Catalan Atlas was the *National Geographic* of the fourteenth century, then the *Rihla*, the travelogue, of Ibn Battuta was its *Baedeker*. Islamic scholarship had long been the source of much of the world's knowledge, and Battuta followed in the illustrious footsteps of al-Bakri, the eleventh-century geographer, al-Idrisi and others. His travels and his account of them in the *Rihla* – more properly *A Gift to Those Who Contemplate the Wonders of Cities and the Marvels of Travelling* – were spectacular, easily outshining Marco Polo's in their scope. Islam required making the hajj, but the Prophet Muhammad also encouraged the seeking of knowledge 'even as far as China', and it was with these goals in mind that the 21-year-old set out from his home in Morocco in 1325 for travels that would last 30 years, covering 120,000 kilometres and the equivalent of 44 countries in today's world. During the course of his wanderings he made the hajj multiple times, but his main motivation seems to have been study, increasing his own knowledge and simply travelling for the enjoyment of it. He did not see keeping a record of his travels as necessary and we are fortunate that the Sultan of Fez saw differently and required Battuta to dictate his recollections, an oral account and memoir that would become a document of close to a thousand pages in its English translation.

Over the ensuing centuries scholars have argued not only about the truth of some of Battuta's descriptions but also about whether the *Rihla* originated solely from him. Even his contemporary, the great Arab historian and philosopher Ibn Khaldun, cast doubt on the veracity of the account, but there was a strong element of disbelief in the foreign and the exotic and a degree of intellectual prejudice. While some of Battuta's stories may well be fictional, his first-hand accounts more often than not have a ring of truth and contain vast amounts of information on peoples, culture and commerce. Here, for example, he visits Dhofar on the arid Yemen coast, close to the border with Oman:

> Thoroughbred horses are exported from here to India, the passage taking a month with a favouring wind. Dhafari is a month's journey from Aden across the desert, and is situated in a desolate locality without villages or dependencies. Its market is one of the dirtiest in the world and the most pestered by flies because of the quantity of fruit and fish sold there. Most of the fish are of the kind called sardines, which are extremely fat in that country. A curious fact is that these sardines are the sole food of their beasts and flocks, a thing which I have seen nowhere else. Most of the sellers are female slaves, who wear black garments. The inhabitants cultivate millet and irrigate it from very deep wells, the water from which is raised in a large bucket drawn up by a number of ropes attached to the waists of slaves. Their principal food is rice imported from India.

Battuta was travelling in a world that knew no borders in the modern sense and, although surviving the Black Death, many desert crossings and perilous sea voyages, he virtually never seems threatened by the people and tribes he encounters. He shows a remarkable objectivity and egalitarianism, complaining largely about the food. He is certainly critical of customs that do not fit with his view of Islam, but makes few judgements. For example, he is taken aback by the equality of women in the Mauritanian oasis town of Walata, the terminus of an important trans-Saharan trade route, but simply reports:

> Their women are of surpassing beauty, and are shown more respect than the men. The state of affairs amongst these people is indeed extraordinary. Their men show no signs of jealousy

whatever; no one claims descent from his father, but on the contrary from his mother's brother. A person's heirs are his sister's sons, not his own sons. This is a thing which I have seen nowhere in the world except among the Indians of Malabar. But those are heathens; these people are Muslims, punctilious in observing the hours of prayer, studying books of law, and memorizing the Koran. Yet their women show no bashfulness before men and do not veil themselves, though they are assiduous in attending the prayers.

He shows no prejudice, no judgements of the civilized versus the barbaric or the primitive, and viewed skin colour as a result of climate, nothing more. This passage describing the character of the people of Mali is from an English translation made in the 1920s:

> The negroes possess some admirable qualities. They are seldom unjust, and have a greater abhorrence of injustice than any other people. Their sultan shows no mercy to anyone who is guilty of the least act of it. There is complete security in their country. Neither traveller nor inhabitant in it has anything to fear from robbers or men of violence. They do not confiscate the property of any white man who dies in their country, even if it be uncounted wealth. On the contrary, they give it into the charge of some trustworthy person among the whites, until the rightful heir takes possession of it. They are careful to observe the hours of prayer, and assiduous in attending them in congregations, and in bringing up their children to them.

The *Rihla* of Ibn Battuta would be a source for travellers and scholars for centuries (and his name lives on with the Ibn Battuta Mall, 'the world's largest themed shopping mall' in Dubai). Sir Richard Burton, another passionate traveller, quotes Battuta and reportedly read the *Rihla* in the original Arabic. Indeed, if the two men could meet, it would be a fascinating encounter, both authors of very personal accounts, who immersed themselves in the cultures that they encountered, who had both made the hajj. However, they would undoubtedly differ in their spiritual views of the world. Burton, however exotic, manic, controversial and enigmatic, was as much a man of his age as Battuta was of his, but Burton's age was one of empires and the assumed superiority of Western civilization. Since Columbus, Europe's attention had been drawn westward, but the loss of the American colonies and the growth of those of Africa and Asia had shifted the focus back. Motivations for exploration were dominated by aspirations for military and commercial power – yes, the lure of travel for knowledge and 'discovery' was still there, but the benign days of Ibn Battuta were long gone.

The quotation at the start of this section, 'Something hidden. Go and find it . . .', is from Rudyard Kipling's poem 'The Explorer', written as the nineteenth century was drawing to a close. In this fine example of characteristically jingoistic and imperialistic narratives, Kipling describes the divinely inspired explorer who, alone, goes in search of 'Something lost behind the ranges', suffering hallucinations in his desert crossing, 'But at last the country altered – White Man's country past disputing.' His 'discovery' of some kind of promised land would be forgotten by those who followed in his footsteps to take advantage of his efforts:

> Well I know who'll take the credit – all the clever chaps
>   that followed –
> Came, a dozen men together – never knew my desert fears;
> Tracked me by the camps I'd quitted, used the water-holes
>   I'd hollowed.
> They'll go back and do the talking. They'll be called
>   the Pioneers!

Kipling had begun the poem with:

> 'There's no sense in going further – it's the edge of cultivation,'
> So they said, and I believed it . . .

until the narrator was inspired to 'go beyond the ranges'. He ends with:

> Yes, your 'Never-never country' – yes, your 'edge of cultivation'
> And 'no sense in going further' – till I crossed the range to see.

The phrase 'Never-never country' was not his – it had been in use since the middle of the nineteenth century in Australia to refer to the arid and desolate lands beyond the 'edge of cultivation'. Kipling had briefly visited Australia and may have come across the term then, but he stayed firmly in the cities and did not himself venture into the never-never. But the phrase, and the heroism of the poem's character in single-handedly opening up *terra nullius*, perfectly sums up the history of exploration and exploitation of Australia's 'hideous blank'. And, as already described, Australia's history is one of the most dramatic testaments to the contrasting perspectives and seemingly inevitable conflicts between insiders and outsiders.

For centuries the southern continent, Terra Australis Incognita (originally referred to by the ancient Greeks as being required to balance the northern continents), had been nothing but conjecture to Western cartographers and sailors, and would remain so, with the exception of brief landfalls by Dutch, Portuguese and British ships, until James Cook's arrival in 1770. Cook landed at Botany Bay and then sailed northward, charting the coast and, following his secret instructions from George III, claimed nearly 4 million square kilometres as a British Possession and named it New South Wales. Cook's instruction to take possession of the land 'with the consent of the natives' proved frustrating. Natives generally ran away, he had no idea what they were saying when they approached him, and he could see no signs of an organization whose consent he could seek. Sir Joseph Banks, the wealthy botanist accompanying Cook (and for whose efforts the Bay was named), had a poor view of the indigenous inhabitants, describing them as 'the most uncivilized savages perhaps in the world' and 'wandering like Arabs from place to place'. Cook, however, took a more enlightened view, describing how 'the natives of New Holland . . . may appear to some to be the most wretched people upon Earth, but in reality they are far more happier than we Europeans.' In actuality, neither had any means by which to assess Aboriginal society and culture.

When the First Fleet arrived eight years later to establish a colony at Botany Bay, it again came with specific instructions: 'To endeavour by every possible means to open an intercourse with the natives, and to conciliate their affections, enjoining all our subjects to live in amity and kindness with them.' But this endeavour would not begin auspiciously when a group of armed inhabitants greeted them from the shore shouting *'warra, warra!'* – 'go away!' The First Fleet did indeed go away, deeming Botany Bay unsuitable for settlement, but only to sail north to Port Jackson to establish the first colony. Cultural conflict and the introduction of alien diseases were inevitable, and it was probably not helpful that many of the colonists were convicts. It has been estimated that the Aboriginal population of Australia, of which perhaps 10 per cent lived in the arid interior, was greater than 500,000. Most people were described as healthy, with a life expectancy not much different from that of Europeans at the time. By 1920 the population would be approximately 60,000, and 50 years later the desert would be essentially empty.

As far as the new possessors of the continent were concerned, the interior was indeed empty but was assumed to hold great promise. After all, a continent with an unproductive interior would be unique and most certainly contrary to the perfection of the divine plan. The problem, to begin with, was topographic – the aptly named Great Dividing Range is essentially the youngest part of Australia and therefore its most substantial chain of mountains. After the billions of years during which the core of Australia was subjected to the wear and tear of geological time, the east coast suffered the turmoil of a nearby plate boundary and, like the Andes, a great mountain range was heaved up. Even when the colonists arrived a few hundred million years later, it remained substantial, a barrier to exploring the interior. But something needed to be done beyond the ranges: the agricultural resources of the coastal strip were inadequate and the climate challenging. In 1813 the first expedition to succeed in crossing the mountains – closely monitored by the local inhabitants – gazed westward across rolling grass plains, creating great optimism for future development and stimulating the exploration of the inland river system on the western side of the mountains. That river system, today referred to as the Murray–Darling Basin, is the foundation of the country's key agricultural region, but it passes through the semi-arid borderlands of the desert and its water supply is fickle. The rivers were first thoroughly explored in the 1820s and '30s by Captain Charles Napier Sturt, who would then turn his attention to the great interior.

The conviction that the centre of Australia could not possibly be barren had led to the great conjecture of an inland sea. In the 1820s Thomas Maslen, retired from working with the East India Company, sat at home in Yorkshire (his 'Siberian wilds') and wrote a 500-page work titled *The Friend of Australia; or, A plan for Exploring the Interior and for Carrying on a Survey of the Whole Continent of Australia*. Maslen found it outrageous that 'there is still one great blank in the map of the world, staring Britain in the face with a look of askance and reproach' and felt that his experience of the geography and logistics of India equipped him to write in detail a plan for an expedition into the interior of Australia that would be proved to be lush and fertile:

One of the reasons for condemning the interior as an arid
desert, are the fierce hot winds felt occasionally on those coasts;
but, that scorching winds do not always proceed from sandy
deserts, is pretty severely recognised at Sydney sometimes, when
those kinds of winds have been known to be heated by extensive conflagrations of the back country, which, having been
explored in all directions, is well known to be beautiful and
luxuriant in woods and forests, fine natural parks, and fertile
valleys and meadows: why may we not suppose that similar
extensive conflagrations in the woods, far out of sight of the
coast, during the dry season, would produce similar effects
on the thermometer off the north and northwest coasts, instead
of condemning the interior to rank with the burning deserts of
Africa and Arabia.

His planning was, if nothing else, thorough, recommending among
the endless lists of supplies, equipment and provisions, lightweight
chainmail armour in case of attack by natives – 'We have hitherto heard
of no wilder beast than the aborigines in Australia' – and boats, elephants
and (presciently) camels, on which he included a lengthy history and
guidelines for management. The book was published in London in
1830 and included an extraordinary map that, recognizing Sturt's establishment of the northern part of the Murray–Darling River system,
hallucinated a vast interior system of rivers draining into the 'Delta of
Australia' (illus. 39).

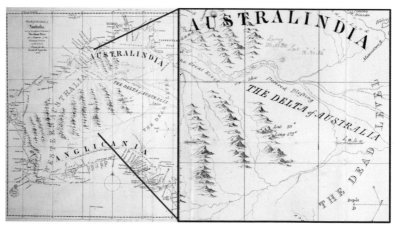

39 Details of Maslen's imaginative map of Australia showing
'The Great River or the Desired Blessing'.

Perhaps following Maslen's vision, when Sturt set off northward from Adelaide in 1844 among the party's equipment was a whaleboat. The expedition set the scene for the series of epic and heroic failures that would continue to characterize exploration of the Australian deserts and embed themselves in the national memory. One of the most enduring and romanticized sagas is that of the eccentric Prussian explorer and naturalist Ludwig Leichhardt. His story, and disappearance in 1848 together with four European companions, horses, mules and 50 bullocks, have been superbly fictionalized by Patrick White in *Voss*, in which he declares: 'The map? I will first make it.' However, as Thomas Keneally comments in his introduction, 'Voss's exploration of Australia is designed to educate him in suffering rather than to give him the euphoria of discovery.'

The 'dead heart' would root itself in the national consciousness as the enemy, exploration a form of conflict. As Sturt wrote:

> Let any man lay the map of Australia before him, and regard
> the blank upon its surface, and then let me ask him if it would
> not be an honourable achievement to be the first to place foot
> in its centre.

Although after considerable hardship they reached a point only 240 kilometres from the centre of Australia, they turned back in desperation, Sturt himself blind and paralysed with scurvy (it would only be native berries that gave him some relief).

> Men of undoubted perseverance and energy in vain had tried
> to work their way to that distant and shrouded spot. A veil
> hung over Central Australia that could neither be pierced or
> raised. Girt round about by deserts, it almost appeared as if
> Nature had intentionally closed it upon civilized man, that
> she might have one domain on the earth's wide field over which
> the savage might roam in freedom.

'I have the melancholy satisfaction of discovering the worst country in the world!' declared Sturt, crossing vast stony gibber plains and endless sand dunes:

> We were then in a perfect desert, from the scrub we got on
> barren sandy flats, bounded at first by sandy ridges at some

little distance from each other, but the formation soon changed, and the sand ridges succeeded each other like waves of the sea. We had no sooner descended one than we were ascending another, and the excessive heat of so confined a place oppressed us greatly.

He was a few million years too late for an inland sea – he described the limestones and the fossils that had formed in it – and could find 'no hope of any inland fertile country'. He did, however, note the ores that would later be developed into the great Broken Hill mining district, and his 'Stony Desert' would be named after him. His encounters with Aboriginal peoples were essentially benign – they largely avoided him and he had no means of communicating with them:

If I except the tribe upon Cooper's Creek, on which they are numerous, the natives are but thinly scattered over the interior, as far as our range extended. The few families wandering over those gloomy regions may scarcely exceed one hundred souls. They are a feeble and diminutive race when compared to the river tribes, but they have evidently sprung from the same parent stock, and local circumstances may satisfactorily and clearly account for physical differences of appearance . . . The personal appearance of the men of this tribe . . . was exceedingly prepossessing – they were well made and tall, and notwithstanding that my long-legged friend was an ugly fellow, were generally good looking. Their children in like manner were in good condition and appeared to be larger than I had remarked elsewhere, but with the women no improvement was to be seen. Thin, half-starved and emaciated they were still made to bear the burden of the work, and while the men were lounging about their fires, and were laughing and talking, the women were ceaselessly hammering and pounding to prepare that meat, of which, from their appearance, so small a proportion fell to their share. As regards the treatment of their women, however, I think I have observed that they are subjected to harsher treatment when they are members of a large tribe than when fewer are congregated together. Both parents are very fond of and indulgent to their children, and there is no surer way of gaining the assistance of the father, or of making a favourable impression on a tribe than by noticing the children . . . As regards their food, it varies with the season. That which they appeared to me to use in the greatest abundance were seeds of various kinds, as of grasses of several sorts, of the mesembryanthemum, of the acacia and of the box-tree; of roots and herbs, of caterpillars and moths, of lizards and snakes, but of these there are very few. Besides these they sometimes take the emu and kangaroo, but they are never so plentiful as to constitute a principal article of food . . . With respect to their religious impressions, if I may so call them, I believe they have none. The only impression they have is of an evil spirit, but however melancholy the fact, it is no less true that the aborigines of Australia have no idea of a superintending Providence.

'You call it desert – we used to live there'

Sturt's summary of the characteristics of the indigenous peoples he encountered could have been written at any time during the remainder of the nineteenth century and, as we have seen from the Canning expedition, well into the twentieth. It was a meeting of two alien civilizations, neither of which had any basis on which to comprehend the other. *You Call it Desert – We Used to Live There* is the title of a book by Pat Lowe and Jimmy Pike, who was born in the Great Sandy Desert of Western Australia, the 'howling wilderness' traversed by Canning. That title provocatively and perfectly captures the conflicting views of the insiders and outsiders. Lowe spent three years living on the edge of the desert with Jimmy and travelling over the landscapes and places he had known as a child, and their collaborative accounts are compelling. She has written:

> The Great Sandy Desert was my frontier. But one person's frontier is another person's home. At the same time that I was experiencing the newness of the desert, a country without settlement or, nowadays, human habitation of any kind for hundreds of square miles, I was learning how differently the country appeared to the people who grew up there . . . At first, the desert appeared to me beautiful but undifferentiated. I saw regular, long red sandhills and swales clad in spinifex, wattle and small trees. Only as I picked up some of the vocabulary of the

Walmajarri people did I begin to distinguish one area from another, and start to perceive pattern instead of randomness.

The vocabulary, as we shall see, tells a story.

The deserts of the Australian red centre are unique. Before I first saw the Great Sandy, my experience had been in the Sahara, Namibia, the Oman, the American southwest. The Great Sandy was unlike any desert I had seen: seemingly infinitely long, red dunes snaking off to the horizon, vast varieties of vegetation, sudden riots of colour (illus. 40).

Australia is quite possibly the most dramatic example of divergent evolution resulting from isolation. The break-up of the ancient super-continent of Gondwana was a prolonged affair, and Australia separating from Antarctica around 80 million years ago was the last major schism. Since then life on the continent has gone its own way and the often bizarre flora and fauna for which Australia is famous developed and adapted to changing times. Nowhere is this more true than in the deserts. The hideous blank was, in reality, anything but, teeming with life, just not life as the outsiders understood it. Homo sapiens first arrived in Australia around 50,000 years ago, at a time when sea level was low and the land area of the continent was a couple of million square kilometres bigger than today. There may occasionally have been land bridges with New Guinea, or the journey may have been made by accidental castaways on small craft or floating logs driven by wind and currents. The distinctive genetics of the indigenous inhabitants demonstrates their original links with Southeast Asia and their isolation since arrival. If the first Australians did arrive by sea, it would have been a one-way journey – their new home lacked the proper materials to build craft with long-term buoyancy and the prevailing winds were against them. The earliest archaeological sites, from perhaps 45,000 years ago, are in the interior rather than on the coasts: climate was arid but fluctuating, there were more extensive lakes than today, and there was big game. The game was literally big, a megafauna typical of the ice ages around the world, but this one was distinctively Antipodean: flightless birds, kangaroos, wombats, snakes and lizards, all of them giant, and most of them about to become extinct. There were probably a variety of reasons for their demise, but again, like elsewhere in the world, the arrival of man was likely no coincidence.

Coping with the disappearance of most big game was probably the only real adaptation that the original Australians had to make.

They were superbly adapted to fluctuating climate, episodes of extreme aridity, seasonal variations in the flora and the complex nature of the land that was their home. The Aboriginal peoples of Australia remained essentially isolated for tens of thousands of years until the arrival of the Western outsiders and had developed a way of life and a culture perfectly suited to their environment. Their social structure was complex, with groupings on every scale, from regional linguistic 'tribes' to fluid bands of extended families, each with its own 'range', more often than not centred around a source of water. They were, in the words of Josephine Flood in her comprehensive account of *The Original Australians*, 'classic nomads', managing the productivity of each patch of land, hunting, gathering – and burning. We have only now come to understand how effective the organized process of 'fire stick' farming is in stimulating and preserving the biodiversity and ecology of the outback. The indigenous society was classless and unstratified, with a cooperative economy, not one which could provide the kind of formal consent that James Cook was seeking: there was no one with whom to make a treaty. But Aboriginal society was far from unsophisticated. Behavioural codes were strong and careful kinship laws, among other guidance, set out the rules of who might marry whom. This was no paradise, but while flies and parasites that plague the outback today have always been there, descriptions from first contacts do not suggest major health problems. The low population density and the nomadic lifestyle reduced the risk of outbreaks of infectious disease and the women ran an extensive pharmacy of barks, roots, leaves and minerals. But this would not last. The arrival and dispersal of the colonists brought diseases that would spare no corner of the continent, however remote. Smallpox, influenza, tuberculosis, typhoid, diphtheria, measles, scarlet fever, venereal disease – and, eventually, AIDS – would be the cause of perhaps 90 per cent of the decimation of the indigenous population.

The structure of Aboriginal society was very much based around language. The Canning Stock Route alone crossed around fifteen different language groups, and there are hundreds of distinct languages and dialects across the continent (more than a hundred have disappeared since records were kept). Josephine Flood comments that the original Australians were possibly the most multilingual people in the world simply because of the need to communicate with neighbours along the hundreds of 'dialect chains' that stretch across the country, some for thousands of kilometres. And with each one containing up to

40 The Great Sandy Desert.

10,000 words (similar to spoken English), these languages are not 'primitive': the vocabulary is rich and the grammar complex (to educate children and keep them healthy, one language has four genders, masculine, feminine, neuter and edible). But this was a purely oral society, with knowledge passed down through stories and song. There was no need for a written tradition and it would only be at the beginning of the twentieth century that the voices of these peoples began to be properly heard – thanks to the work of an extraordinary pair of men.

The first truly scientific expedition to Australia's interior took place in 1894, organized by William Austin Horn, a highly successful entrepreneur who had made a fortune from mining and ranching. Among the scientists was Walter Baldwin Spencer, Chair of Biology at the University of Melbourne, in the team as the biologist and photographer. But Spencer's primary interest was in the newly developing field of anthropology and ethnography, and when he met up with Francis James Gillen, the station master at the Alice Springs post and telegraph, a pioneering collaboration in understanding the Aboriginal peoples began. Gillen was a thoughtful amateur ethnologist but also an inveterate speculator in mining stocks, and the resulting losses would require him to periodically sell his collections of indigenous artefacts to museums. There was much work to be done: the two recount that when they visited Ayers Rock (Uluru), their native guides constantly talked and pointed out features of the landscape important to them 'which they naturally thought would be of interest to us – as, without doubt, would have been the case, if we could have understood what they were saying'. Over the following years they were to rectify this, travelling thousands of kilometres through the outback, using Gillen's knowledge to gain confidence and trust from peoples for whom white men, *kartiya*, were aliens, witnessing and documenting ceremonies and customs, photographing and recording the languages – on wax cylinders in the middle of the desert.

The Native Tribes of Central Australia (1899) would be the first of a series of the publications from their fieldwork and would have worldwide influence on the science of anthropology. In many ways their views were enlightened. But Spencer and Gillen were still men of their times, failing to fully understand the Aboriginal peoples' relationship with their land: 'Like all savage tribes the Urabunna people appear to feel the need of accounting for every prominent natural feature in their country and they therefore have recourse to the invention of myth.' As subsequent work, stimulated by that of those two men, would clearly show, they had this the wrong way round. For Aboriginal peoples, the myths came first, became recorded in the landscape and the naming of places is an inevitable outcome – the land and the stories are inseparable.

Place names tell stories, and this is nowhere more true than in the Australian deserts. David Carnegie, travelling through the Great Sandy Desert a few years before Canning (treating the inhabitants in the same way), wrote: 'In this cheerless and waterless region we marched from August 22nd until September 17th seeing no lakes, nor creeks, nor mountains; no hills even prominent enough to deserve a name, excepting on three occasions.' Compare this with the words of Yami Lester, an elder from the borders of the Simpson Desert, talking in 2011 on the ABC National Radio series, 'The Australian Landscape: A Cultural History':

> You know, a lot of people say it's just a desert, but it's certain type of area to us. The apu area, which is rock or mountain, a hill, we call that apu area. And you find different kind of thing like ilis growing, and that kupata, round there, and these rock holes and euros, yeah, wallabies. Then away from the rock we call puti, which is thick timber land. And puti, which is karukaru, that's where the kangaroos live in the watercourse way, because more grass grows there, more sweeter grass and that's where the kangaroo likes hanging round, that's where you find honey ants and the goannas, they call them sand goannas but we say milpali.

Or the words of Pat Lowe: 'I challenge anyone who comes to the desert for the first time to distinguish between a jilji and a jitpari, a kurrkuminti and a larralarra: terms describing sandhill formations for which English has no words.'

Look on the topographic maps of the Australian interior and the place names tell the story of heroic failure and suffering: there is a Misery Mount, Creek, Gully, Rock, Bluff, Sandhill, Plateau and a Miserable Creek. There are mounts Desolation, Solitude, Hopeless, Deception and Carnage – but one Success Hill and Reward Lake can be found. Names of benefactors and family are common. Find on the maps the indigenous names (or their anglicized versions) and the story is utterly different. For Aboriginal peoples, almost everything in the landscape has a name, because they themselves are part of the

landscape and the living land is their culture. The Canning Stock Route Project is titled Ngurra Kuju Walyja. *Ngurra* can be translated as 'country' and 'home' in the languages of the Western Desert (and is the title of the painting in illus. 2). To say that land, home, country are at the heart of Aboriginal society is an understatement and no English words are adequate to capture the tradition and beliefs of the oldest living culture in the world. 'Dreamtime' and 'the Dreaming' are terms that originate from Spencer and Gillen's work, translated from the central desert Arrernte word *alcheringa*, 'eternal' or 'law'. In the Western Desert, the Dreaming is *jukurrpa*. Everything for the Aboriginal peoples derives from the Dreaming. In the Dreaming, the Ancestral Beings, the spirits, after emerging from the land, the sky and the sea, travelled across the land singing it into life along the songlines, creating everything in it and on it. They were shape-shifting beings, interacting with humans, creating the world in every detail, and finally settling into the land. Josephine Flood quotes Aboriginal explanations about the meaning of the Dreaming:

> It's all linked up with people, land, religion. It's just like one big circle . . . The law is embedded in the stories . . . The Dreaming means our identity as a people . . . These Dreaming creatures were connected to special places and special roads or tracks or paths . . . The great creatures changed themselves into sites where their spirits stay . . . All the land is full of signs.

41 The Olgas.

Place names can be purely and pragmatically descriptive: Sturt's Stony Desert is Marda-purru purru in the local language, *marda* meaning 'stone', *purru*, 'full of', and *purru-purru*, 'very full of'. West of Lake Eyre is a spring, a major Dreaming site for the songs of the Native Cat ancestor; a crooked box tree grew there, which gave the site its name, Pitha-kalti-kalti. The tree was cut down by European settlers to make fence posts (much to the distress of the local Arabana people), and now appears on the maps as Coward's Spring, but the spring is still known as Pitha-kalti-kalti. Some features are named using parts of the human body. For example, any kind of hill is viewed as a head and the correct name for the spectacular hills of the Olgas, west of Uluru (illus. 41), is, for the indigenous peoples (illus. 42), Kata-Tjuta, 'many heads'.

By far the most dominant names are those associated with the journeys and activities of the ancestral spirits, and sources of water, hardly surprisingly, figure prominently in these. In one of her contributions to *Aboriginal Place Names*, Louise Hercus describes the naming of the landscapes of the Arabana people and relates the tale of Muku the Green Ant and the waterholes associated with his Dreaming story:

> Muku the Green Ant in his gigantic ancestral version killed and ate only lizards and was happy like that. Kalthu the Bull Ant, who was even more ferocious in his ancestral shape, killed dingoes, usually two at a time but got Muku to gut them and cook them for him. Their main camp on the lower Macumba was by a waterhole named Minti-thakarna 'pegging together

42 A group of Aboriginal Australians near the Olgas,
photographed in 1926 by Dr Herbert Basedow.

the cleaned out abdomen of an animal ready for cooking'. They
ranged as far up the Macumba as Mudlamirka Madla-mirrka
'dog scratching' waterhole, which is marked on maps. In the
end Muku got tired of having to do the gutting and cooking
day after day. They had a fight and it ended with Muku the
Green Ant cutting the Bull Ant nearly in half – that's why
he looks almost cut in half today. This happened at a waterhole called Kudna-purrunha 'full of guts', i.e. 'guts left in',
the place where Muku decided to stop doing all the gutting
and cooking.

It would inevitably be water that was at the heart of conflict in
the desert. Explorers and settlers had no understanding of the natural
signs of birds and vegetation that signalled the presence of water and
would use the local inhabitants, whose knowledge and preservation of
waterholes, springs and 'soaks' was fundamental to their way of life,
to guide them, voluntarily or otherwise. The wells on the Canning
Stock Route were all sunk or developed from Aboriginal water sources,
every one of them not only vital for survival but sacred. The wells
were, and remain, numbered from south to north, some of them
today just holes in the ground or jumbles of rusted metal and iron,
some restored, for example Well 43, complete with the windlass to
which horses, camels or bullocks were hitched to draw the water,

shown in illus. 43. Many retained their original names. But from the start, they were cased and covered, more often than not making them difficult or impossible for the local inhabitants to use.

Usage was one thing, spiritual destruction was another: one of the greatest of the ancestral beings, and one deeply associated with rain and water supplies, is the Rainbow Serpent. As the Canning Stock Route Project records:

> At Kulyayi, which became Well 42, history and the Jukurrpa collided. During the excavation of the well, either by Canning's original party or by one of the reconditioning teams, the great rainbow serpent Kulyayi was killed.
>
> '[Kartiya] were looking for water . . . They dug down and found that snake . . . They killed him and ate him just like ordinary meat.' (Milkujung Jewess James, 2007) 'People felt empty when he was gone . . . They moved away. Animals moved away. People, animals, they're connected. When they took that snake out, they made that place out of balance.' (Lloyd Kwilla, 2009)

And:

> The story of Jarntu. Many Jukurrpa stories relate to sacred sites. One such site is Jarntu or Well 35 along the Canning Stock Route. Jarntu is a place so sacred that its true name (Kinyu) should only be used by people with close ties to the ancestral being that gives it its common name – Jarntu. Jarntu is the ancestral mother dingo whose puppies inhabit the surrounding rockholes and soak waters, which are linked by a network of underground tunnels. Jarntu has healing powers, but she is also a fierce protector of her home and people. Aboriginal people enter the site ritually and with great respect, sweeping the ground with branches, announcing strangers and leaving food for Jarntu. Jarntu returns this generosity by ensuring successful hunting for her Countrymen and by protecting them from danger. Like many sites in this country Jarntu is simultaneously an ancestral being, a story and a place. 'Jarntu is like a guide dog for the old people, a protector. It's the belly button of the Country. Right in the middle. The Canning

43 A restored Canning Stock Route well.

Stock Route cut the body in half. Jarntu is like the veins of the body.' (Morika Biljabu, 2008)

In the traditional terms of religious belief, Aboriginal peoples are totemist and animist. All natural objects possess a spirit and there is a deep relationship between individuals and animals, plants and landforms. An Aboriginal person sees the land in a way that a geologist can sympathize with: every feature has a story to tell. But these were stories that the colonial *kartiya* could not read and their own beliefs denied that the original Australians had any religion – or even culture – at all.

It was not only religion that shaped the outsiders' view of the indigenous peoples of the Australian (or any other) desert. Charles Darwin published *On the Origin of Species* in 1859 and *The Descent of Man* in 1871. The encounters with Aboriginal peoples in the second half of the nineteenth century and well into the twentieth took place in the aftermath of these works and the vigorous misinterpretation of Darwin's theories that led to the eugenics movement. Darwin had visited Australia in 1836 during the voyage of the *Beagle*, travelling sufficiently to encounter floras and faunas that would astonish him and inform his thinking. He also encountered Aboriginal peoples and described them in *The Descent of Man*. He commented on dwindling food resources, alcohol and disease but, apparently failing to recognize the effects of displacement from their nomadic territories, suggested some 'mysterious agency' to explain that 'wherever the European has trod, death seems to pursue the aboriginal'. While he disagreed with the conventional representation of Aboriginal peoples as 'utterly degraded beings' and admired for some of their skills, he would write about 'savages' the world over, including the Australian Aboriginals:

> Extinction follows chiefly from the competition of tribe with tribe, and race with race. Various checks are always in action, serving to keep down the numbers of each savage tribe, such as periodical famines, nomadic habits and the consequent deaths of infants, prolonged suckling, wars, accidents, sickness, licentiousness, the stealing of women, infanticide, and especially lessened fertility . . . When civilised nations come into contact with barbarians the struggle is short, except where a deadly climate gives its aid to the native race. Of the causes which lead to the victory of civilised nations, some are plain and simple, others complex and obscure. We can see that the cultivation of the land will be fatal in many ways to savages, for they cannot, or will not, change their habits. New diseases and vices have in some cases proved highly destructive; and it appears that a new disease often causes much death, until those who are most susceptible to its destructive influence are gradually weeded out.
>
> The cases which I have here given all relate to aborigines, who have been subjected to new conditions as the result of the immigration of civilised men. But sterility and ill-health would probably follow, if savages were compelled by any cause, such as the inroad of a conquering tribe, to desert their homes and to change their habits. It is an interesting circumstance that the chief check to wild animals becoming domesticated, which implies the power of their breeding freely when first captured, and one chief check to wild men, when brought into contact with civilisation, surviving to form a civilised race, is the same, namely, sterility from changed conditions of life . . .

> At some future period, not very distant as measured by centuries, the civilised races of man will almost certainly exterminate, and replace, the savage races throughout the world.

If this was the atmosphere under which all 'savage races' were judged, then the combined influence of religion and science would indeed be toxic. In 1876 Ernest Giles made the third of his five epic, and essentially successful (barring a few deaths), expeditions, across the Western Desert of Australia. His diary for July of that year tells of how

> an old black man and two lads made their appearance. This old party was remarkably shy; the elder boy seemed a little frightened, and didn't relish being touched by a white man, but the youngest was quite at his ease, and came up to me with the audacity and insouciance of early youth, and pulled me about. When I patted him, he grinned like any other monkey. None of them were handsome; the old man was so monkey-like – he would have charmed the heart of Professor Darwin. I thought I had found the missing link, and I had thoughts of preserving him in methylated spirits, only I had not a bottle large enough.

Unfortunately, the work of Darwin's colleague and rival (and arguably the more thoughtful biologist), Alfred Russel Wallace, would be largely ignored, for Wallace had a far more nuanced view of the 'civilized' versus the 'primitive'. Rather than the conventional view of an ordained linear progression from savage through semi-civilized to fully civilized (in other words, Western and Christian), he saw every group of humans as displaying various combinations of all three. In his classic work *The Malay Archipelago*, which, published in 1869 and dedicated to Darwin, first defined the 'Wallace line' separating the biogeography of Asia and Australasia, he concluded with a chapter on 'The Races of Man in the Malay Archipelago'. He might have surprised some of his readers with the following conclusion:

> Before bidding my reader farewell, I wish to make a few observations on a subject of yet higher interest and deeper importance, which the contemplation of savage life has suggested, and on

which I believe that the civilized can learn something from the savage man. Compared with our wondrous progress in physical science and its practical applications, our system of government, of administering justice, of national education, and our whole social and moral organization, remains in a state of barbarism. We should now clearly recognise the fact, that the wealth and knowledge and culture of the few do not constitute civilization, and do not of themselves advance us towards the 'perfect social state'.

Compared to most of his contemporaries, Wallace had an enlightened and radical outsider view of the insiders.

Pushing back the lost borders

The time when Alfred Canning was chaining the local inhabitants, destroying their songlines and attacking their ancestral beings was a transitional one for Australia. There was still a great sense of national gloom at the prospects for finding any value in the interior, but there was also a substantial effort on the part of the authorities to convince settlers to make their way there. Depending on the weather in any given year, the desert would be more or less productive and its borders were transient – it was imperative in the interests of nation building and the economy to push them back and bring civilization to the outback. These were also the borders of *kartiya* Australia, and racial integrity was at stake.

In 1901 Australia became an independent nation. The six colonies of Queensland, New South Wales, Victoria, Tasmania, South Australia and Western Australia joined to form the Commonwealth of Australia and the first federal elections were held. Littleton Ernest Groom was a fervent nationalist and was elected to the new parliament and soon became Minister of Home Affairs and then External Affairs. He was a strong advocate of science and development and advocated the formation of a Bureau of Agriculture, inspired by the U.S. Department of Agriculture that President Lincoln had created in 1862. It would be through his bureau that Groom believed 'much of the land which is now despised will ultimately become very productive'. During the early years of the twentieth century it would be mining that largely drove the outback economy, but sheep and cattle ranching would continue to push back the desert frontiers. Geology had provided a huge stimulus: the Great Artesian Basin had been discovered and would provide water to vast areas of arid lands in the eastern half of the country where little had been available before. The same series of events that created the mountains of the Great Dividing Range caused thick layers of sand and gravel to be shed westward through erosion into the interior seas and lakes of the largely submerged continent. Those porous and permeable rocks would be buried and charged with water from rains over the Great Dividing Range, which, trapped under pressure, would flow to the surface if pierced by a well – artesian flow. This vast underground water reserve (the largest artesian basin in the world) underlies a fifth of the continent; it was first drilled in 1878, and by 1915 more than 1,500 artesian bores were in operation. It was, of course, this aquifer, when it leaked to the surface naturally, that provided many of the reliable springs known and used by Aboriginal people.

Pastoralism and the establishment of cattle stations relied heavily on Aboriginal labour, drawing the people away from their desert homelands into the relative comfort of life on the stations – and they became highly skilled stockmen, outnumbering the whites by five or six to one. Although rarely acknowledged, many of the hands who drove the herds down the Canning Stock Route were, ironically, locals. The burgeoning cattle business was led by Sidney Kidman, a self-made entrepreneur who, by the time of the First World War, was a millionaire running a series of connected cattle stations across the outback covering an area greater than England; he became a national hero and today Kidman Holdings remains one of the largest landowners in the world.

In 1872 the Overland Telegraph had been completed between Adelaide and Darwin (crossing the arid interior and removing essentially all usable timber en route for the poles). By 1917 the east and west were linked by the transcontinental railroad that included the longest straight stretch of track in the world, 478 kilometres across the desolate Victoria Desert and the Nullabor Plain. Water for the locomotives was a challenge – well water was often brackish and unsuitable, and supplies (often half the total load) had to be carried on the trains. A strategically important staging post for the railroad was Ooldea, on the edge of the Nullabor Plain. It was blessed with a reliable water supply, a soak, a significant sandy area within which excavation almost anywhere would find water, albeit of variable quality. As such it was a place of fundamental importance to Aboriginal peoples from a large surrounding region: it was a location for ceremonies and meetings, a vital refuge in times of drought, and, inevitably, of considerable spiritual significance. It had provided a base camp for exploration of the area, and initial wells were sunk by aspiring sheep ranchers. The railroad ran 6 kilometres south of the soak, which was 'acquired' in 1917 after wells close to the tracks had proved too brackish and attempts at purification using a condensing plant had simply resulted in all the black oaks in the area being felled for firewood to run the plant. The soak depended on water pooling in the sands above an impermeable clay layer: the wells drilled by the railroad would provide, for a while, the 45,000 litres per day that the locomotives required, but would destroy the clay layer and the soak by the early 1920s.

Water, the railroad, the telegraph and the spread of pastoralism irrevocably pushed back the country's arid frontiers, and the national mood began to swing from gloom to optimism unsupported by evidence. In 1918 Edwin James Brady, a poet and journalist, would publish his most successful and highly popular work, *Australia Unlimited*. Brady's purpose was to catalogue the country's industries and argue enthusiastically for the potential for expansion. He had been working on the book for years, along the way interviewing Alfred Canning, who 'had a grey-blue eye, the long distance eye one might call it, which seems typical of these explorers and back-bushmen'. He described what he called 'The "Desert" Myth':

> Very early in the country's history there grew up a stereo-typed conception of the interior as a dry and waterless desert, composed for the most part of shifting sands, scorched by everlasting suns and swept by constant hot winds. Book after book has been written perpetuating this fallacy, which has become so firmly rooted in people's minds that it will probably be another two or three generations before it is finally consigned to the limbo of ancient fallacies. It is doubtful if there are a hundred square miles of true desert within the whole area of the Australian Continent, and it is now an established fact that millions of acres, once regarded as useless for agricultural purposes, are among the most fertile and productive lands in the world.

He maintained that rain was common and droughts only local, that the soils of the desert were fertile, only requiring irrigation and proper treatment and that 'Instead of a "Dead Heart of Australia" there exists in reality a Red Heart, destined one day to pulsate with life.' The book was a tremendous success, fuelling optimism for the future. In the 1920s an estimate was made that the future population of Australia would be between 100 and 200 million; it stands today at around 22 million.

In his vision for Australia, Brady echoed the general view of the time, seeing no place for Aboriginal peoples in the country's glorious future:

> But the hour was approaching when the Hunter would be called upon to make room for the Artificer; when, despite a probable common ancestry, the Man of Iron, by virtue of his superior knowledge and attainments, was to dispossess the Man of Stone.
>
> The neolithic races of Australia, since the elaboration of the theory of Evolution, have become of peculiar interest. During later years scientists of various nationalities have collected valuable information concerning our aboriginals, now only to be met with in an absolutely primitive state in certain parts of Northern and Central Australia.

Brady was right: 'The Man of Stone' would indeed be system-atically and brutally dispossessed over the following decades, dispossessed of land and therefore dispossessed of everything. The Aboriginal peoples had few champions. The missions, for example, were not there to protect; besides, the indigenous inhabitants had spurned the 'gift' of Christian civilization. Droughts would exacerbate the problem, forcing more and more out of the bush and into cattle stations and settlements where they became the people in-between, unable to continue their old life, their culture destroyed, and unable to fit into white society. Welfare dependency, alcoholism, petrol-sniffing and disease would wreak havoc. Government policy, such as it was, shifted between segregation, integra-tion, protection and, disastrously, assimilation. Seemingly well-meaning equal-pay legislation in the 1960s would only make the problem worse: the cattle station employers had been providing family support as well as wages and could no longer afford to do so. Despite the efforts of the anthropologists, there remained – and remains today – a vast cross-cultural chasm of lack of understanding.

And the desert was needed for other things. The Cold War required missiles and atomic weapons, missiles and atomic weapons required testing, and for the UK military where better to test than in the 'empty' Australian desert? The plans for a testing range began immediately after the Second World War, and Len Beadell, then an army surveyor, was commissioned to locate and survey appropriate sites. Beadell was an extraordinary character, a man of the outback who came to be known as 'the last true Australian explorer', with an understated and infectious sense of humour (in addition to his books, audio and video recordings are available). The area of interest was the vast swathe of the deserts of South and Western Australia, and Beadell's initial task was to locate the site for the first weapon testing and survey the ground for the necessary support facilities. He decided on a clay pan that would be named Emu Field, and Woomera (named after an Aboriginal spear-thrower), as the main base. Beadell surveyed and built the roads, and in 1953 two atomic tests took place. This was celebrated as the new destiny

44 A Weapons Research Authority team and Pintupi men
in the Southern Central Reserve, 1950.

for the Australian desert. The *Sydney Sunday Herald* pronounced that 'the very poverty of these areas in surface resources made them valuable in the atomic field, either as a storehouse of uranium riches or as the kind of waste land where experiments can be most safely conducted.' The Australian writer Ivan Southall described the area as an 'open-air laboratory . . . one of the greatest stretches of uninhabited wasteland on earth, created by God specifically for rockets'. But uninhabited it was not (illus. 44).

Emu Field was, however, deemed too remote, and a more convenient site was constructed at Maralinga (home of Yami Lester, quoted earlier, who became blind following the 'black mist' from tests held there). Seven nuclear tests and hundreds of relatively minor experiments would be conducted at Maralinga. But a rocket testing range was also needed between Woomera and the west coast and Beadell set off, alone, into the desert to survey the 'centre line' for firing and prepare to build the necessary roads. His efforts were heroic: more than 6,500 kilometres of roads constructed over an area of 2.5 million square kilometres. Beadell built his 'highways' as straight as possible in order to keep Australia looking 'tidy', and this network remains the backbone of desert access today. As Beadell himself remarked, 'I didn't know it at the time, but this Centre Line would govern the future of Central and Western Australia forever.' He was a national hero, a remarkably modest and entertaining character despite his skills and accomplishments, but he was still a man of his times: giving a talk in 1991 he was still describing the desert as an area 'that hadn't been touched by anybody since the world began'.

The Woomera facility would be the end of desert residency for Aboriginal peoples. At its height, the facility itself covered 270,000 square kilometres – invasive enough in itself, but the rocket-firing range required a wide corridor spanning the entire western half of the continent. It was understood that people lived beneath it, and the possibility of accidents and atmospheric burn-out debris meant that they had to be moved. Small teams of 'Native Patrol Officers' were dispatched to find as many people as they could, round them up and escort them out of harm's way into the towns, missions and 'native settlements'. The problem was that, even in the 1960s, no one really knew anything about how many people lived in the western deserts and who they were – there had been little or no contact since the time of Alfred Canning. In 1964 a group of twenty Martu women and children were tracked for several months and over hundreds of kilometres across the Stock Route country. This incredible story is told in *Cleared Out: First Contact in the Western Desert* by Sue Davenport, Peter Johnson and Yuwali, published in 2005. In 1964 Yuwali was a girl of seventeen and up until then had had no contact with white men whatsoever. Hers is a unique oral account of being chased by the 'devilmen' in the 'rocks that move' (four-wheel-drive vehicles). The saga would only end when the patrol officers used two local Martu men to find the group and persuade them to come to the nearby mission where many of their fellow people had long been resident.

Today 70 per cent of Aboriginal peoples live in towns and cities and, despite a history of legislation on land rights, the establishment of a sequence of different 'reserves' and Indigenous Protected Areas, an indigenous Australian dies twenty years earlier, is fifteen times more likely to be in jail and ten times more likely to be murdered than an Australian white. At the time of writing, the Australian government is declaring the importance of removing racial discrimination clauses from the constitution and the plan to hold a referendum to approve recognizing the original Australians in the country's founding document. Many Aboriginal people remain refugees in their own lands. The tension of civilization versus the savage has simply been renamed as an urban–bush divide, and the empty desert is, arguably, more of a desert than it was 200 years ago.

FOUR

Outsiders and Insiders, New World and Old

THE MID-NINETEENTH CENTURY was a halcyon time for camels to see the world. Within a few years of each other two pronouncements had been made, by influential men on opposite sides of the Atlantic, that would stimulate the involuntary emigration of large numbers of camels from their homelands. Vexed by the frustrations of exploring the mysterious interior of Australia, a founding member of and then-president of the Royal Geographical Society, Sir Roderick Impey Murchison (one of the finest geologists of his time), addressed the society in 1844, the same year Charles Sturt set off for the desert with eleven horses:

> Others again say, with our member, Mr. Gowen, that a thorough exploration of the interior of Australia will never be effected until we import thither camels from our eastern possessions, and thus at once get rid of the vast difficulties attending the want of water.

A few years later, the u.s. Secretary of War, Jefferson Davis (soon to become provisional President of the Confederate States of America), wrote to the President that

> For . . . military purposes, for expresses, and for reconnoissances [sic] . . . the dromedary would supply a want now seriously felt in our service; and for transportation with troops rapidly moving across the country, the camel . . . would remove an obstacle which now serves greatly to diminish the value and efficiency of our troops on the western frontier.

The idea was not new. An enthusiastic and informed lobby had been working hard on it for some time and in 1856 Congress allotted $30,000 for the purchase of camels and the establishment of a u.s. Army Camel Corps. George Perkins Marsh, a u.s. Senator, saw even wider benefits in terms of pacifying the troublesome indigenous inhabitants of the arid west:

> The habits of the Indians much resemble those of the nomadic Arabs, and the introduction of the camel among them would modify their modes of life as much as the use of the horse has done. For a time, to be sure, possession of this animal would perhaps only increase their powers of mischief, but it might in the long run provide the means of raising Indians to a state of semi-civilized life. Products of the camel (wool, skin and flesh) would prove of inestimable value to Indian tribes, which otherwise are fated to perish alongside the buffalo.

Two New World countries with a similar wilderness challenge, but their stories would be radically different. The first camel, named Harry, had actually arrived in Australia from the Canary Islands in 1840. Harry accompanied John Horrocks on an 1846 expedition, but was reportedly bad-tempered and prone to biting people. Among the desert salt lakes of South Australia, Horrocks was in the process of preparing his gun to shoot an attractive bird when Harry lurched, the gun discharged and Horrocks was mortally wounded. On Horrocks's wishes, Harry was destroyed, but not before biting an Aboriginal stockman's head. The first major excursion of camels from today's Afghanistan and Pakistan to Australia took place following, as in the u.s., serious lobbying of the authorities, who in 1859 commissioned the purchase for a grand budget of £302. The initial project was to use camels to support what would turn into perhaps the most iconic of heroic failures in Australian exploration, the Burke and Wills expedition. One Wednesday in June 1860, 24 camels and a number of cameleers ('sepoys') arrived in Melbourne from Karachi. Robert O'Hara Burke took sixteen north, together with four camel-handlers, Samla, Dost Mohamet, Esau Khan and Baluch Khan (illus. 45, 46).

Burke established the expedition base at Cooper Creek, on the edge of Sturt's Stony Desert, and then, unwisely, set out for the north coast with Wills, John King and Charley Gray, six camels and one horse.

Unwisely, because they departed in December in the height of summer. They made it to the edge of the Gulf of Carpentaria, thus completing the first south–north crossing of the continent, but on the return, Gray died and progress was hampered by monsoon rains. They arrived back at Cooper Creek only nine hours after their support group had left; two camels, Rajah and Landa, survived the return journey to the Cooper, but one had to be shot after getting bogged down and the other died – as did Burke and Wills.

Despite the instinctive European preference for the horse (and the mutual antagonism between the two species), camels had proved themselves superior at desert travel and capable of carrying substantial amounts of supplies. From 1870 to 1900 alone, more than 2,000 cameleers and 15,000 camels came to Australia. Their role in exploration was vital. In 1873 camels and three Afghans were in William

45 Burke's cameleers, 'Belooche' (Baluch Khan) and Esau Khan.
46 The expedition departs.

47 Afghan camel drivers at Beltana, 1897.

Gosse's party that first saw, named (after the Chief Secretary of South Australia, Sir Henry Ayers) and climbed Ayers Rock, Uluru. But, far more importantly, their major contribution was to build Australia. Every major infrastructure project, every development of the mining and agricultural economy, was made possible only by camels and the cameleers. They transported everything needed to build the overland telegraph and then the mail and supplies to service the towns that grew up along it. The first piano in central Australia arrived on the back of a camel. Camels made the construction of the Canning Stock Route feasible. They built and supplied the railways: the rail link between Port Augusta and Alice Springs became known as the Afghan Express, later the Ghan – an informal recognition of the contribution of the thousands of 'Afghan' cameleers who made Australia what it is today (illus. 47).

There is a great irony here, because there was considerable bureaucratic and racial prejudice against the Muslim workers of the 'Ghan towns', whose relationships with Aboriginal peoples were far warmer than with the whites. And there is a further irony in that the camels and their handlers were building their own redundancy: by the 1920s the infrastructure of roads and railroads was such that camels and their handlers were no longer needed.

Many returned home, but a substantial community remained, some of the cameleers maintaining camel businesses, others carving out new roles for themselves. In 'Australia's Muslim Cameleer Heritage', Philip Jones recounts how

> In the Adelaide summer of 1952 a young Bosnian Muslim and his friends, newly arrived immigrants, pushed open the high gate of the Adelaide mosque, tucked away in the city's run-down southwest corner. As Shefik Talanavic entered the mosque courtyard he was confronted by an extraordinary sight. Sitting and lying on benches, shaded from the strong sunshine by vines and fruit trees, were six or seven ancient, turbaned men. The youngest was 87 years old. Most were in their nineties; the oldest was 117 years old. These were the last of Australia's Muslim cameleers, who had plied the inland routes before the era of motor vehicles began. Several had subscribed money during the late 1880s for the construction of the mosque which now, crumbling and decayed, provided their last refuge.

Large numbers of camels were released into the outback where, naturally, they have thrived. Today, it is estimated that there are more than a million feral camels roaming the red centre, and they are a highly controversial problem. The *National Feral Camel Action Plan*, published in 2010, describes the environmental, social and economic impacts of these herds and calls for a 'rapid reduction' in the population, with a 'vision' of the 'Comprehensive, coordinated and humane management of feral camels and their impacts that maintains and promotes the biodiversity, agricultural assets and social values of our rangelands for all Australians'. Millions of dollars have been set aside for a culling programme, and, since the 1925 Camel Destruction Act that declared wild camels to be vermin, shooting them has been a national pastime. But humane it is not – today they are shot from helicopters and left to die, rot and be scavenged. This is extremely controversial, anti-culling groups pointing out that, although there may be a million camels in the Australian outback, there are 100 million sheep and tens of millions of cattle. But, more importantly, why are these animals not seen as a resource? Camel milk is lower in lactose than cow's milk, is rich in vitamins B and C and has ten times more iron; it is high in insulin, contains effective antibodies and is the focus of medical and nutritional research.

In the U.S., camel milk sells for $25 or more per litre and the market is growing rapidly. The global market for the milk is huge (it already nourishes millions of inhabitants of arid lands), as is that for camel meat. In a world facing a protein shortage, why leave thousands of tonnes to rot in the desert? And, in parts of the Middle East, a fine racing camel can sell for more than a million U.S. dollars.

When the Aboriginal peoples of Western Australia first saw camel tracks in the sands of the western desert, they had an explanation: these are 'little fellah bums', the tracks of small spirit-beings who make their way across the sands on their backsides. When the semi-nomadic people of the Sonoran Desert, the O'odham, first saw camel tracks, their interpretation was more pragmatic and less spiritual: they did not know what it was, but it would be almost certainly edible.

Manifest destiny

Between 1845 and 1853 the United States, as a result of the annexation of Texas, the Mexican–American War and the Gadsden Purchase, had added to its territory an area of more than 2.5 million square kilometres, more than four times the land area of France. Most of it was arid, little of it was mapped and it was populated by largely un-known peoples. It was, at the same time, an opportunity and a challenge, but a challenge manifestly underpinned by a divine plan. The term 'manifest destiny' was first coined by the journalist John O'Sullivan in the *New York Democratic Review* in 1845, but he had already written in strong and emotional support for nation-building and westward expansion. In an 1839 piece, 'The Great Nation of Futurity', he declared that

> We are the nation of human progress, and who will, what can, set limits to our onward march? . . . The far-reaching, the boundless future will be the era of American greatness. In its magnificent domain of space and time, the nation of many nations is destined to manifest to mankind the excellence of divine principles; to establish on earth the noblest temple ever dedicated to the worship of the Most High – the Sacred and the True . . . Who, then, can doubt that our country is destined to be the great nation of futurity?

With tragic irony, he also rejoiced in the fact that 'Our annals describe no scenes of horrid carnage, where men were led on by hundreds of thousands to slay one another.' Sixteen years later the country 'destined for better deeds' would be torn apart in the slaughter of civil war.

To some extent, the nineteenth-century New World histories of Australia and the U.S. parallel each other – vast, virtually unknown interior desert territories inhabited by troublesome natives, all in need of conquest and exploitation. But the U.S. addressed the issue with far greater urgency and efficiency. Four years before William Gosse and his party first saw Uluru, and 60 years before the Ghan Railway was completed, the first railroad linking the U.S. east and west coasts was constructed, and within twelve years there would be a second, the southern route crossing the deserts of the southwest. The iron horse outpaced the iron camel, and the animal that built Australia was but a footnote to manifest destiny. The idea proposed by Jefferson Davis to solve the desert transportation and logistics crisis met with a mixed reception, but enthusiastic lobbying resulted in Congress allocating $30,000 in 1855 for the purchase of 'fine animals'. A navy supply vessel was dispatched to the Mediterranean, but the procurement was made difficult by the need for camels in the Crimean War. Nevertheless, after a rapid learning curve in terms of identifying inferior and diseased beasts, a shipment of 33 camels and three cameleers left Turkey in 1856 for the voyage back to the U.S.. Accounting for births and deaths en route, 34 camels disembarked at Indianola, Texas, giving children rides around the town as well as fighting among themselves and suffering the scorn of townspeople and cowboys (illus. 48).

Major Henry Wayne, who had travelled with the procurement expedition, was in charge of the camels and went some way to dispelling the scorn by putting on a show: a single camel demonstrated its capabilities by carrying 550 kilograms of hay, more than four times the maximum load for a mule. Meanwhile, an additional 41 camels had arrived, and it was time to put them to use. Major Wayne held the strong view that time should be taken to train and breed the camels, developing a large herd for commercial as well as military purposes. But, supported by the disdain of the equestrian lobby, the military view prevailed: Wayne was reassigned and a former Superintendent of Indian Affairs in California, Lieutenant Edward Fitzgerald Beale, was assigned to take charge of the camels. Meanwhile, France, a country familiar with the value of the beasts, awarded Wayne the gold medal of the newly formed Société Impériale Zoologique d'Acclimatation for introducing camels to the United States.

Beale set out westward with 25 camels and Syrian 'camel-whisperers', tasked with surveying a road from Fort Defiance, in New Mexico, to Fort Yuma on the Colorado River border of Arizona and California. Crossing the deserts of Arizona, and eventually reaching California, the camels performed superbly. Beale, a long-time enthusiast for their skills, reported that 'My admiration for the camels increases daily with my experience of them. The harder the test they are put to the more fully they seem to justify all that can be said of them.' To the surprise and embarrassment of the equestrians, camels even proved superior to horses in crossing rivers and would eat virtually anything, including thorny desert shrubs that horses and mules would not touch. Threatening Apache groups are reputed to have fled at the sight of Beale on Seid, a particularly imposing beast. Camels not only intimidated mules and horses, but also outshone them by transporting water for them across the dreaded Jornada del Muerto, a completely waterless stretch of the New Mexican desert. Furthermore, they never required shoeing. Californians were impressed with their potential, and 45 bactrian camels were imported from Mongolia and Siberia. However, the heyday of the camel in the Wild West was short. In 1861 the Civil War broke out, and although connecting with California and its gold fields was a high priority for the Confederacy, ironically its leader, Jefferson Davis, seized the camels but never made real use of them. The existence of the fledgling u.s. Camel

48 The landing of camels at Indianola, 1856.

Corps was brief and unsatisfactory. After the war, the camels were auctioned off to mining and freight companies and many ended up in circuses. But most were turned loose or escaped to become feral, apparently with some success because members of the United States–Mexico boundary commission reported seeing a herd of wild camels in southern Arizona in 1901. They failed, however, to reach the critical mass that their cousins in Australia did, and the last sighting of a wild camel came from the far south of California in 1941. It was probably eaten by the O'odham.

Camels may not have been part of the developing U.S. economy, but they entered its folklore. A largely forgettable film of 1954, *Southwest Passage*, tells the story of Beale's expedition, starring what would seem to be an inappropriate number of Bactrian camels. Legend has it that the 'Red Ghost', a camel carrying a skeleton on its back, is occasionally sighted galloping across the desert. The skeleton may well be that of Hi Jolly. Hadji Ali, previously Filippou Teodora or Felipe Teatro before his hajj to Mecca, was probably of Greek-Syrian (or possibly Bedouin) parentage and one of the cameleers to arrive in Indianola. It is likely that he had learned his camel-handling skills during a stint in the French Foreign Legion. Through the unfamiliarity of the Americans with Muslims and Arab names, he became Hi Jolly (or sometimes 'Greek George') and accompanied his charges on the Beale expedition. Once the military camel experiment was ended, he was an army scout and packer during the war with the Apaches, established camel freight routes, became a saddle maker and worked at odd jobs with some of his camels around the west. He called himself Philip Tedro, married a Sonoran woman and had two children, but eventually left her to return to a nomadic life. He moved to the small and remote mining town of Quartzsite, Arizona (which today prides itself as 'The Rock Capital of the World', despite misspelling its namesake rock), where he was well-liked and developed a reputation as a storyteller. In spite of his belief that he had become an American citizen and earned an army pension, when he became ill all help was refused. He would round up any feral camels he could find and, when he died in a sandstorm on a desert road in 1902, it is said that his arms were around the neck of a long-lost camel. In 1955 the Arizona Highway Department put up a memorial to Hi Jolly in Quartzsite (illus. 49) which reads, 'Over thirty years a faithful aid to the U.S. Government' – and today is the town's main tourist attraction.

Hadji Ali may have been an early Arab emigrant to the U.S. but he was hardly the first. The American west had been well known to the Spanish since Columbus had stimulated westward exploration and colonization in the sixteenth century. Hernán Cortéz conquered Mexico and the Aztec empire in 1521, and his invasion route to Mexico City would become the first part of El Camino Real de Tierra Adentro, The Royal Road to the Interior that eventually was extended northward to New Mexico and linked up with the Santa Fe Trail. The impetus for its early extension was silver, discovered in the Zacatecas Mountains of central Mexico in such huge amounts that smelters and mints were built in Mexico City to handle the ore. In 1598 the colonizing expedition of Juan de Oñate reached what is today's El Paso after crossing the Chihuahuan Desert and the Jornada del Muerto, a journey of 2,400 kilometres from Zacatecas. El Camino Real was complete and would become the backbone for three centuries of Spanish colonies in Mexico and western North America. Along this route came settlers, supplies and missionaries. The Spanish priests were zealous converters, making their focus the indigenous inhabitants of the Pueblos of New Mexico where they would build hundreds of missions. While these missionaries were anxious to save souls, they also had to adopt a certain pragmatism in order to survive in the New World. The long hand of the Inquisition had spread to Mexico by the time that colonizing expeditions were establishing outposts in today's New Mexico and Arizona, but its control was weak. The sixteenth century saw a diaspora from the Old to the New World that included Arabs from what had, until the end of the fifteenth century, been the civilized world of Moorish Spain. Fleeing the Inquisition and Ottoman conscription, they sought refuge in the wilderness and deserts of Spain's North American colonies.

As the ethnobotanist Gary Nabhan describes from a very personal perspective in *Arab/American: Landscape, Culture, and Cuisine in Two Great Deserts*, these refugees left their mark on the language and culture of the American southwest, which survives today – Hadji Ali may well have encountered much that was familiar. A further diaspora from Syria and Lebanon in the early twentieth century augmented this legacy. In what Nabhan calls 'culinary transportation', manuals of agriculture and recipes arrived with the refugees, together with seeds and spices and water management methods that originated in North Africa. Kebabs in one form or another are global fare, but so are *kibbeh*, fried croquettes of bulghur, onions and meat (lamb, beef, goat or camel) that are seen,

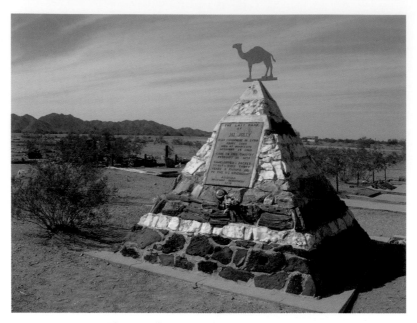

49 The Hi Jolly memorial in Quartzsite, Arizona.

with variations on the name, on plates in Egypt, Iraq, Arabia and Mexico. Lentils and chickpeas, dates and figs, olives and pomegranates all migrated from the oases of the Old World to those of the New. The Arabic for apricot is *al-barquq*, the Spanish *albaricoque*; the Tohono O'odham of the Sonoran Desert call them *wi:ragogi*. Safflower, the substitute for saffron, is one of the oldest crops of arid lands and its original Arabic name is *az-za'farān*. The Spanish is *azafrán* and the O'odham call it *sasafrani*. One of the many O'odham terms for a waterhole is *algibes*, a word that arrived in the Sonoran Desert via the Andalusian Spanish *aljibe* that, in turn, owes its origin to the Arabic *al-jubb*.

The O'odham were far from the only indigenous inhabitants of the Mexican and American arid lands who found their way of life and their culture changed forever by the arrival of the outsiders. Yaqui, Mojave, Pima, Seri, Apache, Hopi, Navajo, Pueblo, Paiute, Zuni – and, disappearing just before the arrival of the westerners, the Hohokam – are peoples who, together with dozens of smaller communities and subgroups, had lived in northern Mexico and the u.s. southwest for at least 12,000 years. All lived, inevitably, with a focus on water supply, either along the desert rivers of the Colorado, the Gila, the Sonora, the Yaqui and the Rio Grande, or, like their cousins in Australia, around reliable waterholes, springs and constructed wells. Like the Aboriginal Australians they would be required to share those waters with the outsiders who contributed disastrously to their destruction. Some of these peoples were nomadic, some agriculturalists, some settled in pueblos, some were hunter-gatherers, but all were societies structured around water.

One of the greatest, and most enlightened, missionary travellers was Father Eusebio Kino, a diminutive Italian Jesuit priest who first came to the New World in 1681 and spent the rest of his life exploring and map-making in the Sonoran Desert and beyond, establishing the land link between California (he was the first to demonstrate that Baja California was not an island) and Mexico City. His journeys in the region he called *Pimería Alta* (after the so-called Pima Indians, more correctly the Akimel O'odham) followed the extensive network of native trails, relying on local guides to navigate and find water. He made multiple expeditions along what would be known as El Camino del Diablo, The Devil's Highway, a 400-kilometre trail from the Sonoran town of Sonoyta to Yuma that crosses some of the most severe landscapes of El Gran Desierto del Altar. In spite of Kino's enthusiasm for conversion of the heathen and their 'reduction' (the gathering of indigenous peoples into settlements and missions), his relationships with the Pima and other Native American groups were good. He described them as industrious and friendly and dispelled many of the myths of the barbaric natives. In his account, *Favores celestiales,* translated into English as *Kino's Historical Memoir of Pimería Alta*, he writes:

> It had been said and reported, but very falsely, that the Pimas of the interior and their neighbors were such cannibals that they roasted and ate people, and that for this reason one could not go to them; but already we have entered and have found them very friendly and entirely free from such barbarities.

He was conversant in the languages of different tribes, was keenly attentive to their health and welfare, introduced domesticated animals, crops, farming techniques and tools, and was fiercely critical of the Spanish enslavement of Native Americans to work in the mines. But the changes that he pioneered also had their downsides. He described himself as 'disconsolate' when one group

> said to me openly that they neither wished to be Christians nor to have a missionary father. On asking them why, they

answered me, first, because they had heard it said that the fathers ordered the people hanged and killed; second, because they required so much labor and sowing for their churches that no opportunity was left the Indians to sow for themselves; third, because they pastured so many cattle that the watering places were drying up.

The introduction of horses, mules, cattle, goats and sheep, never mind people, created a demand for water that the traditional supplies could not fulfil. Furthermore, the value of the herds made them attractive targets for raiding parties of Apaches who had hitherto seen little of interest among the desert tribes, and open warfare broke out. The O'odham were forced to retreat from their traditional lands and to devote much of their energies to military activity.

Father Kino was the last of the enlightened missionaries. Tribal uprisings became an increasingly common threat, and at the same time the colonial focus became economics – the harvesting of food and minerals rather than souls. Furthermore, the outsiders brought disease, just as they did in Australia, and the indigenous peoples suffered the consequences. Some estimates suggest that the number of Native Americans in the Sonoran Desert and the u.s. southwest declined by more than 90 per cent over the next two centuries.

However, such estimates are difficult to make. As with the Aboriginal peoples of Australia, and so many desert societies, there is no written history and we depend on the accounts of the outsiders and limited archaeological evidence, together with oral histories. DNA analysis of the original North Americans, while supporting a major population decline 500 years ago, is far from definitive. Nevertheless, it is a historical fact that, once Columbus had 'discovered' the Americas, centuries of disruption, decline and cultural disintegration followed for the indigenous peoples.

After Mexican independence in 1821 it was only twenty years or so before those peoples faced a new and energetic tide of intrusion and found themselves swept up in the nation-building surge driven by manifest destiny. After the Mexican–American War and the Gadsden Purchase, the United States had a new frontier: the wild and arid West. In the mid-nineteenth century, the perspective from the 'civilized' east coast society was parallel to that of Australia's when viewing the outback frontier: largely unknown and unmapped, wild and occupied by heathen and primitive peoples. But for the u.s. there was a clear destination on the other side, California with its gold and its promise of coastal commerce. The challenge was the 'desert' in between. This was the time when the very word 'desert' was undergoing a fundamental evolution, from uninhabited and uncultivable wilderness regardless of ecology or climate to its modern meaning of arid, and hence an enduring myth of the American frontier was born. Following the Louisiana Purchase of 1803 that expanded the u.s. by more than 2 million square kilometres of the Midwest, President Jefferson wrote of its 'immense and trackless deserts'. In 1806 Zebulon Pike led an expedition to what would later be Colorado and wrote of 'a barren wild of poor land, scarcely to be improved by culture', but 'these vast plains of the western hemisphere may become in time equally celebrated as the sandy deserts of Africa.' The myth was born and would be cemented in the national psyche some sixteen years later when Major Stephen Long of the u.s. Army Corps of Engineers made an official reconnaissance of the border with Mexico east of the Rocky Mountains. He never left the Great Plains, the region that was to become the country's breadbasket, but nevertheless he reported:

> In regard to this extensive section of country, I do not hesitate in giving the opinion, that it is almost wholly unfit for cultivation, and of course uninhabitable by a people depending upon agriculture for their subsistence. Although tracts of fertile land considerably extensive are occasionally to be met with, yet the scarcity of wood and water, almost uniformly prevalent, will prove an insuperable obstacle in the way of settling the country. This objection rests not only against the section immediately under consideration, but applies with equal propriety to a much larger portion of the country . . . This region, however, viewed as a frontier, may prove of infinite importance to the United States, inasmuch as it is calculated to serve as a barrier to prevent too great an extension of our population westward, and secure us against the machinations or incursions of an enemy that might otherwise be disposed to annoy us in that part of our frontier.

On his map, the region to the east and southeast of today's Denver, where today cattle farming and crops contribute around $7 billion to the state's economy each year, is labelled as 'Great Desert'. The map is annotated with the words 'The Great Desert is frequented by roving bands of Indians who have no fixed place of residence but roam from place to place in quest of game.' Both Pike and Long may have had ulterior motives for their designation of desert, Pike to disguise former vice-president Aaron Burr's plan to effect the secession of the new western States (with the help of the British) and Long to support his political views of full development of the eastern U.S. before allowing westward expansion. Regardless, the myth of the 'Great American Desert' would endure and influence the nation's approach to its frontier. Thomas Bradford's 1838 map of the United States continued to categorize much of Colorado as the 'Great Desert' (illus. 50).

As 'manifest destiny' was pursued and settlers travelled west, the myth was dispelled, and once again geology would ultimately come to the rescue. Just as the discovery of the waters of the Great Artesian Basin in Australia transformed the economy, so did the Great Plains Aquifer, first tapped in 1911, in the U.S. But we are still east of the Rocky Mountains – by the time they fell under U.S. control, the true deserts of the southwest were essentially *terra incognita*. Mexican territory on Bradford's map is largely blank, crossed by the Colorado and Gila rivers and notional chains of mountains; Utah and Nevada are labelled as 'Sandy Desert'. There had been few U.S. sources of information on the southwest beyond the Rockies, but one came from an extraordinary man, Jedediah Smith. Mexican control of the region was no barrier to private enterprise, and commercial expeditions by fur-traders and 'mountain men' had long ventured into the west, challenged more by the indigenous inhabitants and the environment than by the authorities (once it was established that they were not spies). In 1826 Smith found himself a partner in a fur company and immediately set off in search of beaver; he had already discovered a route across the Rockies and to the Columbia River, but this time he followed the Colorado River south and then struck off westward, with the help of Native American guides, across the Mojave Desert and through the mountains to California and the mission at San Diego. From there he travelled north and, having collected several hundred kilograms of beaver skins, eventually and after considerable difficulty, found a way back across the Sierras and the deserts of Nevada and Utah to a rendezvous north of the Great Salt Lake. His small party had had to resort to burying themselves in the sand to escape the heat. The following year he repeated his journey to San Diego with a larger party of men and women, but this

50 Bradford's 1838 map of the United States showing the 'Great Desert'.

time returned via a northern route along the Columbia and Yellowstone rivers. Smith's epic itineraries formed the framework for all subsequent exploration of the west and 80 years later the quintessential artist of the frontier, Frederic Remington, would depict his party crossing the Mojave Desert (illus. 51).

With the consolidation of the u.s. by 1853, the doctrine of manifest destiny required urgent pursuit, and the priorities were rail and telegraph links to the west coast where the gold rush had been under way for five years: the Great American Desert was in need of conquest. The emigrant trails to California and the northwest were already being followed by thousands of would-be farmers and settlers; by the late 1850s the California Trail and the Central Overland Route would take pioneers across the desert of Utah and Nevada, following the Humboldt River to the Sierras. That massive range of mountains, the cause of much hardship and suffering, constituted the final obstacle of the many that geology had scattered across the frontier. The western U.S. is geologically young and active, in part torn asunder and in part crushed by the long-lived plate boundary of which the San Andreas fault is but a segment. The Sierra Nevada Mountains are still growing, while to the east, the Basin and Range Province of Nevada and Utah is being stretched, long ranges of mountains separating subsiding desert basins. Journeys westward require repeated crossings of snow-capped ranges and arid valleys. Major Stephen Long may have seen the Great Plains as a barrier to westward expansion, but he had no idea what lay further to the west – constructing a railroad to the coast presented a major engineering challenge. But it was also a major political challenge with regional lobbying for a preferred route made more tense by the looming aspirations of Texas and the South. Two years before he commissioned the import of camels, Jefferson Davis sent out survey parties to report on four possible routes ranging from the far north to the new Mexican border. The Pacific Railroad Surveys included geologists and other scientists, together with artists, to survey, evaluate and document: the reports represent a radical revision to the blanks on Bradford's map, a huge increase in knowledge and the precedent for the scientific surveys that continue today. Understanding the people who actually lived along the possible routes was not a high priority, but, while taking a somewhat positive

51 Frederic Remington (1861–1909), *Jedediah Smith's Party Crossing the Burning Mojave Desert during the 1826 Trek to California.*

view of the official historical treatment of Native Americans to date, the reports represent at least an attempt to document indigenous inhabitants, including references to Spanish descriptions. However, ideas for dealing with them, while occasionally benign, are both condescending and questionable:

> Of all the collateral branches to which our attention was directed by instructions from the department, the one now under consideration seems the most remotely connected with the main object of the exploration. Nevertheless, a knowledge of the inhabitants of the various districts traversed, and their usual mode of subsistence, whether by agriculture, by hunting, by gathering wild fruits and roots, or by plunder of neighboring countries, will tend to elucidate many facts regarding the characteristics and resources of that region, which our hasty reconnaissance could not determine more directly. Besides, a comparison of the various tribes within our borders, showing the effect produced upon each by the policy heretofore adopted by the government, may be useful in determining the course to be pursued towards them in future. In our dealings with this race, it is necessary to understand the peculiarities of their character, and the motives that govern their actions . . . If it should be proved that those tribes, whom we have fostered for years with uniform consideration and substantial benefits, have considerably progressed in civilization, we shall be encouraged, for the sake of humanity, to extend the system which has produced such gratifying results; and, if this can be done at less cost to the national treasury than is required to chastise their aggressions, or to govern them by the fear of a military force, another inducement will urge on the benevolent work of enlightening this remnant of a numerous race. Many thousands of benighted beings now exist under our government without realizing its benefits . . .
>   . . . The aborigines are, upon every side, hemmed in by descendants of a foreign race. Year by year their fertile valleys are appropriated by others, their hunting-grounds invaded, and they themselves driven to narrower and more barren districts. The time is now arrived when we must decide whether they are to be exterminated: if not, the powerful arm of the law must be extended over them, to secure their right to the soil they occupy;

to protect them from aggression; to afford facilities and aid in acquiring the arts of civilization, and the knowledge and humanizing influences of Christianity . . . The labours of missionaries among them have been crowned with success and there appears to be no obstacle in the way to prevent their complete civilization . . . The tribes above mentioned may be divided into three classes: the semi-civilized, the rude, and the barbarous.

The report of the southernmost survey which crossed the desert on either side of the Colorado and the Mojave includes a complete volume that is the first comprehensive description by a geologist, William P. Blake:

Before I reached the surface of the Desert I had been accustomed to regard it as a vast plain of gravel and sand, and supposed that the latter was so deep as to impede the progress of animals and wagons. This, I believe, corresponds with the general impression regarding the Desert. Instead, however, of the whole plain being composed of loose and sandy materials, a great part of it is formed of a compact, blue clay, which has a smooth, floor-like surface, so hard that the passing of mules and wagons scarcely leaves a mark upon it.

He goes on to include an extraordinarily insightful description of desert pavement and desert varnish:

In some places the pebbles are so thickly spread that the surface is entirely formed of them, and no sand or soil is visible. They are also packed together so closely, and lie so even, and are so uniform in size, that the surface is like a floor. Indeed the pebbles look as if they had been pressed into a yielding surface by a heavy roller. These pebbles have a peculiar polished and brilliant surface, looking as if they had been oiled or varnished. The effect produced by the reflection of the sun's rays, from a plain covered with these polished convex pebbles, can scarcely be imagined; each one gives back a ray of light, and the ground seems paved with gems. It is somewhat like the glittering reflection from the ripples of a sheet of water. All this polishing is undoubtedly produced by the constant action of loose sand upon the surface, when driven by the wind. The fact that all the fine sand or dust is removed from between the pebbles near the surface, while it is abundant a few inches below, indicates that the winds have gradually blown it away, leaving the heavy pebbles behind. They thus protect the sand that lies below them. Indeed, the protective power of this surface of pebbles is worthy of remark; for, if they were removed, it could not be long before the thick, underlying strata of sand would be blown away by the impetuous winds of that region . . . The surfaces are not merely polished, but are discolored, a large portion being as black as ebony, and yet having the ordinary gray color of granite or gneiss within. A dark, blackish-brown is a common tint, but it is so deep that it is impossible to decide upon the nature of the rock without first breaking off a fragment. The discoloration is confined to the surface, and does not extend to a perceptible depth.

The surveys showed that constructing a railroad was feasible along any of the four proposed routes but, by the time Congress passed the Pacific Railroad Act in 1862, the Civil War was under way and southern opposition to northern routes was no longer a factor. The act authorized the Central Pacific and Union Pacific Companies to build a transcontinental rail line along the 42nd parallel and in 1869 the construction was completed close to Utah's Great Salt Lake. Twelve years later, the second transcontinental railroad was completed at Deming, in the New Mexico Territory, linking the Atchison, Topeka and Santa Fe Railroad and Southern Pacific Railroad, and following in part Jedediah Smith's route across the desert: the West had been 'conquered' and the frontier was receding, as was the myth of the 'Great American Desert'.

Sixty years before Australia's Edwin Brady published his imaginative description of Australia's lack of deserts and its unbounded potential for development, the U.S. had its equivalent visionary, William Gilpin. A veteran of exploring expeditions and the Mexican–American and American Indian wars, Gilpin was appointed by President Lincoln as the first Governor of Colorado Territory. To describe him as an enthusiast for manifest destiny is a gross understatement. He saw the mission of the U.S. as civilizing, civilizing as progress, and progress as God: the country had a divine purpose. In 1846 Gilpin addressed the U.S. Congress to describe his fanatical vision, the 'Divine Task' and 'Immortal Mission':

The untransacted destiny of the American people is to subdue the continent – to rush over this vast field to the Pacific Ocean – to animate the many hundred millions of its people, and to cheer them upward . . . to agitate these herculean masses – to establish a new order in human affairs . . . to regenerate superannuated nations . . . to stir up the sleep of a hundred centuries – to teach old nations a new civilization – to confirm the destiny of the human race – to carry the career of mankind to its culminating point – to cause a stagnant people to be reborn – to perfect science – to emblazon history with the conquest of peace – to shed a new and resplendent glory upon mankind – to unite the world in one social family – to dissolve the spell of tyranny and exalt charity – to absolve the curse that weighs down humanity, and to shed blessings round the world!

In Gilpin's fantasy, manifest destiny was a global phenomenon, with the U.S. providing the inspirational link between Europe and Asia and extending, as one of his maps clearly shows, to Australia. But there was also much to do at home. In 1860 he published *The Central Gold Region: The Grain, Pastoral, and Gold Regions of North America*, which catalogued, as Brady would do for Australia, the potential development and industrial opportunities. He explicitly denies the concept of the Great American Desert:

There is a radical misapprehension in the popular mind as to the true character of the 'Great Plains of America,' as complete as that which pervaded Europe respecting the Atlantic Ocean during the whole historic period prior to Columbus. These Plains are not deserts, but the opposite, and are the cardinal basis of the future empire of commerce and industry now erecting itself upon the North American Continent. They are calcareous, and form the Pastoral Garden of the world.

The conflicting views of the potential of the American west during the key decades of the nineteenth century were in part driven by political and personal agendas, but they also reflect a period of extreme variations in climate that would have created differing views depending on whether observations were made during periods of drought or rains. Historical descriptions and modern analysis of the climate record

52 John Gast, *American Progress*, 1872.

preserved in tree growth-rings show that the mid-1850s to mid-1860s were years of severe drought. Extreme dry conditions returned in the 1870s, causing the most devastating swarms of locusts ever experienced in the U.S. (although the creatures would become mysteriously extinct by the turn of the century). This was followed by a period of relative wetness on which settlement capitalized at a rate far beyond what we would call today the 'carrying capacity' of arid lands. The subsequent droughts of the 1890s proved catastrophic for man and beast.

But climatic change would be only one contribution to the catastrophe that befell the indigenous men and beasts: manifest destiny was the primary cause. In Gilpin's view, all Native Americans looked alike, all spoke the same language and none had a place in his vision. For decades the rhetoric paralleled that of Australia and was based on the concept of the conflict between civilization and savagery. It was also a rhetoric and 'science' that was underlain by the convenient misapplication of Darwin's work, published at an inflammatory time in the history of relations between white and indigenous Americans. The emerging body of experts in the new science of anthropology would describe how the 'barbarous tribes of America have remained in utter darkness for thousands of years' and, while praising them for rising from the lowest stages of savagery to, at least in some cases, the middle stage of barbarism, positioned them several thousand years behind 'the Aryan family' and 'Civilization'. The tensions between policies of assimilation and eradication dragged on, but once increased settlement and land appropriation led to more Native American uprisings and raids, the latter view tended to hold sway. Earlier treaties and land grants were ignored and the process of deportation into prisoner-of-war camps ('reservations') became common. The stereotype of the 'noble savage' was replaced by one of the violent marauder, and it was even argued that the inferiority of the indigenous tribes was demonstrated by their willingness to 'submit to extermination' – it was all the Native Americans' own fault. Kit Carson, the American folk hero of the Wild West, led the assaults on the Navajo tribes in 1863, under orders to shoot to kill any men who refused to submit to captivity, to capture all women and children and to destroy livestock and crops. The orders came from General James Carleton, head of the army in New Mexico, who cautioned that 'an Indian is a more watchful and a more wary animal than a deer. He must be hunted with skill.' The campaign culminated in the infamous 'Long Walk' of the Navajo hundreds of kilometres eastwards, away from their homelands and into the country of their enemies, the Apaches. Thousands were incarcerated and many died. They were crammed into a 'reservation' of only 100 square kilometres and attempts at enforcing civilization through agriculture proved impossible. By the late 1860s public opinion had turned against Carleton, and the surviving Navajo were returned to a newly defined reservation on their lands in New Mexico and Arizona with token payments and gifts of livestock. Today the Navajo Nation is the largest semi-autonomous territory governed by Native Americans, covering 71,000 square kilometres.

As for the Pima, the 'sand Papagos', correctly the Tohono O'odham or 'Desert People', the Gadsden Purchase created an international border severing their lands where before there had been only a country of lost borders. They were refused dual citizenship, but for many years that mattered little and they crossed the border regardless. Today, however, that southern border of Arizona has become an emotional and expensive political symbol in the latest southwest desert war – against illegal immigration. Perhaps 20,000 Tohono O'odham live on a reservation on the U.S. side of the border, several thousand to the south. All are caught in the middle of conflicts between drug cartels, the agenda

53 Thomas Crawford, *Progress of Civilization*, 1863.

of border security versus the needs of the O'odham and the humane business of saving illegal immigrants from death in the desert – not to mention the question of who pays for what.

Once the Civil War was over and the newly re-united States could focus energetically on manifest destiny, Native Americans would virtually vanish from the primary narrative. They are dramatically illustrated doing so in the strange but iconic painting of *American Progress* (illus. 52).

Commissioned in 1872 by George Crofutt, the publisher of a popular series of western travel guides, John Gast's image captures the national mood. The nation is represented by a diaphanously clad female figure floating mysteriously but inevitably westward, the Star of Empire on her head, the enlightenment of a school book under her arm, and the telegraph wires in her hand. Before her and the advancing civilization flee not only Native Americans but wild animals. As the accompanying text commented, 'This rich and wonderful country – the progress of which at the present time, is the wonder of the old world – was until recently, inhabited exclusively by the lurking savage and wild beasts of prey.' The darkness in the west is being dispelled by the radiance of the east and the civilized world.

Gast was not the first to translate rhetoric into image, and one only has to visit the U.S. Capitol in Washington, DC, to see the evidence. The Senate Wing of the building was designed and built in the 1850s and included massive classical motifs. The pediment of the east-facing wing was commissioned to illustrate the 'history of the struggle between civilized man and the savage, between the cultivated and the wild nature' and, designed by Thomas Crawford, *Progress of Civilization* does this most effectively (illus. 53). Once again, America is an allegorical female

54 Emannuel Leutze, *Westward the Course of Empire Takes its Way*,
1861, mural in the u.s. Capitol.

figure and, to her left, beyond the scene of necessary deforestation, is a
'dying chief contemplating the progress of civilization'.

Enter the House wing of the Capitol, gaze up the west stairway,
and your eyes cannot help but be drawn to the six-by-nine-metre mural
entitled *Westward the Course of Empire Takes its Way* (illus. 54). This
massive and highly popular work by the German painter Emmanuel
Leutze (famed for his earlier national icon of Washington crossing the
Delaware) is manifest destiny encapsulated on a grandiose scale. Leutze
worked on it continuously from July 1861 to November 1862; as Confederate troops approached during the early stages of the Civil War, he
added the American flag to his earlier design.

Leutze also added an African American boy leading a mule, but
among the multitude of figures there is not a single Native American.
The light now shines in the west and enigmatic fires can be seen, perhaps of native villages. But look closely at the dark images included in the
scrolls around the top of the picture and they include, in Leutze's own
description, a Native American 'creeping and flying' from the American
eagle, another 'creeping, discharging an arrow at the hunter' and a third
'covering himself with his robe sneaking away from the light of knowledge'. Such was the role to which the insiders had been relegated in the
narrative of manifest destiny. Today, the situation of the indigenous

North American is little different from that of the Aboriginal Australian and, in *Desert Solitaire*, Edward Abbey commented that

> it's the same the whole world over – one big wretched family sequestered in sullen desperation, pawed over by social workers, kicked around by the cops and prayed over by the missionaries . . . [the] general aim over the long term has been to change Indians into white men, a process called 'assimilation' . . . the usual banal, unimaginative if well-intentioned proposals made everywhere, over and over again, in reply for a demand for a solution to the national and international miseries of mankind. As such they fail to take into account what is unique and valuable in the Navajo's traditional way of life and ignore altogether the possibility that the Navajo may have as much to teach the white man as the white man has to teach the Navajo . . . Navajo poverty can be cured . . . It is doubtful, however, that the Navajo way of life, as distinguished from Navajos, can survive.

Water

The city of Phoenix, Arizona, is one of the driest in the U.S. and has an aridity index that clearly qualifies it as being in the desert, yet it boasts a population of 1.5 million, the tallest fountain in the U.S. and a voracious demand for locally grown salad. The city was founded on the ruins of a complex irrigation system that was typical of the desert engineering skills of the Hohokam people who, by the thirteenth century, had constructed hundreds of kilometres of canal systems to exploit the variable and unpredictable flows of the Gila and Salt Rivers. By the time outsiders first reached the region, the Hohokam (whose name in Pima means 'the ancient ones' or 'the ones who went away') had disappeared. Whether this was for reasons of failing water supply, salt incursion into their agricultural lands, famine or disease is unclear. In 1867 the Hohokam system in Phoenix was reconstructed and the new settlement named in the correct expectation that a great city would arise from the ashes of the old civilization. But today Phoenix struggles for water, its usage far exceeding supplies from local aquifers and rivers, not to mention from the distant and diminishing reservoirs of the Colorado River. The carrying capacity of the region is overwhelmed by demand and unrealistic expectations.

The origins of this problem, in Arizona and across the arid lands of the U.S., can be firmly placed in two disastrous pieces of nineteenth-century legislation. In 1862 the Homestead Act was passed to encourage settlement and development of the west. For $1.25 per acre, purchase of up to 160 acres of public land was allowed, together with a commitment to build and farm. But not only was there a problem with size – 160 acres is little more than half a square kilometre – but the way in which the act was drafted led to it being exploited by speculators, cattlemen, railroad developers and miners. In 1877 the Desert Land Act attempted to rectify some of the issues that had become apparent. Up to 640 acres could be purchased and a commitment to irrigate and 'reclaim' had to be given. But this was still open to corruption and speculation, with large tracts around sources of water being filed on by consortia rather than individuals, a woefully inadequate way to regulate and develop the use of arid lands.

In 1878 a one-armed Civil War veteran and geologist (who went on to become Director of the United States Geological Survey) published arguably the most important and radical document of manifest destiny and resource management. The document was completely ignored and the consequences reverberate today. John Wesley Powell had lost his arm at the Battle of Shiloh, but this did not stop him organizing his extraordinary expedition down the Colorado River in 1869, including the first, and epic, journey down the Grand Canyon. The six survivors brought back with them not only remarkable stories but a wealth of scientific data. Powell combined the results of this and other expeditions into his *Report on the Lands of the Arid Region of the United States*. In the preface he writes that 'The redemption of the Arid Region involves engineering problems requiring for their solution the greatest skill.' He believed that significant tracts of arid land would prove amenable to agriculture, but only with careful planning and legislation:

> To a great extent, the redemption of all these lands will require extensive and comprehensive plans, for the execution of which aggregated capital or cooperative labor will be necessary. Here, individual farmers, being poor men, cannot undertake the task. For its accomplishment a wise prevision, embodied in carefully considered legislation, is necessary.

He analysed water supplies and watersheds, and, in a heroic calculation, stated that pasturage farms in the arid lands that constitute 'more than four-tenths of the area of the entire country . . . to be of any practicable value, must be of at least 2,560 acres, and in many districts they must be much larger'. In other words, the provisions of the Desert Land Act ignored reality and underestimated the minimum area by a factor of four. He also recommended allocating a billion dollars to irrigating a billion acres, and that fundamental revisions to the land laws were required if the west was to be sustainably developed. Land allocation must be on the basis of water supply, and water supply allocated among states and individuals according to realities of geography and geology. He published a remarkable map showing the major drainage districts of the western U.S., the limits of which he argued should form the basis for the definition of state boundaries, with communities developed on the principle of equitable sharing of water resources (illus. 55).

But it was too late and too radical. Resource competition between the states was already a problem and vast areas of critical water supply had already been locked up by speculators, a development that would lead, understandably and inevitably, to considerable anger on the part of the indigenous inhabitants. If Powell's prescient ideas had been listened to, the desert communities of the U.S. would look very different today, and Phoenix would not exist. The settlement of the southwestern U.S. required learning – the hard way – the truth of Powell's warnings and of Peter Wild's definition of desert in *The New Desert Reader*: 'a place where habits learned in humid areas are bound to fail'. Wild goes on to refer to the myths of Europeans, developed in humid places, that were based on 'a divinely sanctioned ticket for exploitation, not with seeking an equilibrium with the land'. His description of the indigenous Americans is true of the inhabitants of arid lands the world over:

> So the Indians were not so much 'lovers of the earth' or 'ecological saints' as some whites mistakenly enjoy stereotyping them. They were practical people who over eons of evolutionary trial and error achieved a fairly stable and benign relationship with the earth. Lacking the technology that has given Europeans a false sense of conquest in the deserts, the native peoples did not always survive: they died from thirst, starvation, and diseases related to malnutrition, as skeletal remains bear out. Those who did manage to fill their bellies despite the harsh demands of the

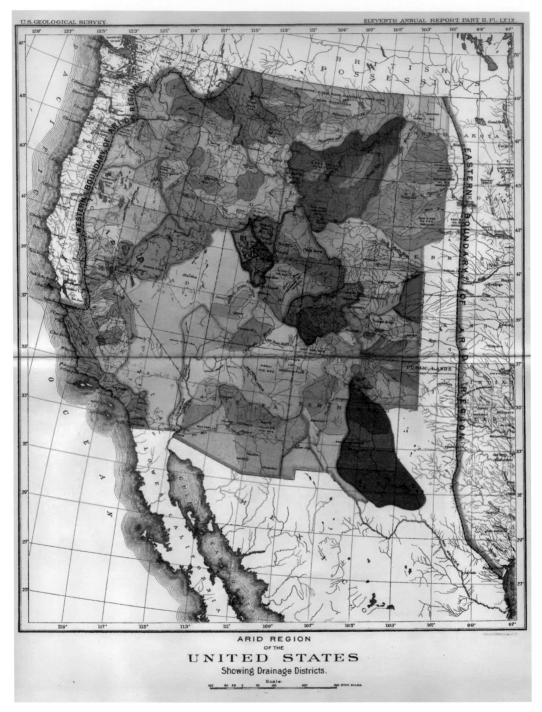

ARID REGION
OF THE
UNITED STATES
Showing Drainage Districts.

Scale:

55 Powell's proposed organization of the western United States.

desert environment did so in small numbers – itself an asset in desert survival – and in ways that did not overburden the fragile resources on which they depended for their livelihoods.

Their 'equilibrium with the land' provided the key knowledge that the insiders of arid lands possessed that the outsiders did not, and the resulting stories and conflicts are the same across the globe. It is no wonder that the spiritual beliefs of the original Australians and the Native Americans hold so many parallels: an intimate relationship with the land and the landscapes, and a focus on water – Hopi and Zuni rain ceremonies feature the same serpent ancestor as do those of the Aboriginal peoples of the red centre. Understanding and managing water resources is the key to desert societies.

In the fourth century AD, the Hohokam were beginning to flourish on the foundations of water management in the deserts of the southwest U.S., while in the Sahara of southern Libya, the great civilization of the Garamantes was in terminal decline through failing irrigation.

The deserts of the Old World have followed a very different historical trajectory from those of the New. Certainly they have long been frontiers to a variety of external interests and been subjected to millennia of attempts at cultural dominance and exploitation, but they have retained a degree of internal social autonomy and continuity that would have been impossible had they been a focus of New World nation-building. As Wilfred Thesiger wrote in *Arabian Sands*:

> As I rode along, I reflected that nowhere in the world was there such continuity as in the Arabian desert. Here Semitic nomads, resembling my companions, must have herded their flocks before the Pyramids were built or the Flood wiped out all trace of man in the Euphrates valley. Successive civilizations rose and fell around the desert's edge: the Minaeans, Sabateans, and Himyarites in southern Arabia; Egypt of the Pharaohs; Sumeria, Babylonia, Assyria; the Hebrews, the Phoenicians; Greeks and Romans; the Persians, the Muslim Empire of the Arabs and finally the Turks. They lasted a few hundred or a thousand years and vanished; new races were evolved and later disappeared; religions rose and fell; men changed, adapting themselves to a changing world; but in the desert, the nomad tribes lived on, the pattern of their lives but little changed over this enormous span of time.

That is not to say that insiders of the Old World deserts have not faced challenges, witnessed and participated in profound change and today face greater struggles than in the past. But, on the whole, they have not suffered the extent of cultural disintegration inflicted on the indigenous peoples of Australia and North America. The very fact that Old World deserts were regarded as frontiers and barriers by those whose 'habits were learned in humid areas' meant that the people who lived in them and knew, in particular, the water supplies, held a commanding position in terms of facilitating commerce. Trade between European societies and sub-Saharan Africa, China and the Middle East was, for much of history, entirely dependent on the inhabitants of the intervening arid lands. Because of this, the Garamantes flourished. From at least 1,000 BC to the seventh century AD, this highly developed society controlled vast swathes of the hyper-arid Sahara in southern Libya and the surrounding region of the Fezzan, but it is only in recent years that they have been truly appreciated. Work led by David Mattingly, of the University of Leicester, has revealed, with the aid of satellite imagery and excavation, the extraordinary extent and sophistication of a people first described by Herodotus. This work has completely dispelled the view of Greek and Roman historians that they were barbarians and savages (not to mention the idea that their cattle's horns were so large that they had to walk backwards). In the 1950s, even the great archaeologist Sir Mortimer Wheeler described them as 'predatory nomads', brigands whose only minor trappings of civilization were borrowed from the Roman Empire. But Mattingly has revealed the first desert civilization that grew independently of a river system, one that had writing, art, sophisticated architecture, textiles, metallurgy, agriculture – and irrigation technology.

While nobody knows exactly where the Garamantes originally came from, it is likely that a significant change in the North African climate was the stimulus for a settled life. After the end of the last Ice Age around 12,000 years ago, the climate was dramatically wetter than today, and the savannah-like conditions, ideal for hunter-gatherer societies, are beautifully illustrated by the abundant rock art across the Sahara that depicts elephants and hippos roaming what is desert today. But around 5,000 years ago the rains diminished and the region began to enter the long period of aridity that continues now. The rock art records this change, with cattle replacing exotic animals, and it is likely that the Garamantes adapted by establishing a more settled way of life. They did so at the strategic crossroads of trans-Saharan trade routes at their capital of Garama, near today's town of Jarmah, in the heart of the desert more than 1,000 kilometres from the coast. Garama is located in the Wadi al-Ajal, a long east–west depression bounded on the north by the dunes of the Ubari sand sea (home of the lakes and the 'worm-eaters' encountered in chapter Two), and to the south by towering rocky cliffs and a barren rock plateau. Tens of thousands of graves have been identified, including small pyramid tombs, together with houses, multi-roomed palaces and baths echoing Roman design. The finer architecture was of dressed stone, the more common of robust mud-brick construction. It is likely that more than a hundred thousand people lived along the wadi, controlling tens of thousands of square kilometres of territory; they tended herds and grew oasis crops of wheat, barley, sorghum, millet, figs, grapes, dates and cotton, all of which was only made possible by the *foggara* that the Garamantes constructed.

Based on original Persian engineering, the foggaras – *qanats* or *falaj* in Arabia and the Middle East, *karez* in the Gobi (from the original Persian) – were the key to desert cultivation the world over for millennia. This ingenious system relies on the fact that, adjacent to mountains or plateaus, the level of the groundwater may be deep, but the water table rises with the topography. The surface of the water table, the top of the underground zone of saturated rocks, mimics the topography and is often closer to the surface in the hills. Tunnel into that water table from lower ground into the hills and water will naturally flow down from the higher levels to be distributed among the cultivated plots of the oasis (illus. 56). It is an elegantly simple idea that requires huge amounts of skill and hard labour. The diagram shows a cross-section of the basic design of a foggara or qanat. The 'mother well' is excavated to a depth below the water table in the hills, often to 30 metres or more, and then a gently sloping but narrow channel is begun from the bottom. The tunnelling and later maintenance is continued and facilitated via a series of shafts every 10 metres or so, which, together with the main tunnel, would be lined with brick or early forms of concrete.

Each of the shafts would become surrounded on the surface by a pile of excavated rock and thus the paths of the foggaras can be still traced today – in Wadi al-Ajal, thousands of kilometres of them. Look on Google Earth along the high ground to the south of the string of cultivated areas of today's Germa and Awbari, and the alluvial fans are apparently covered with multitudes of linear traces linking

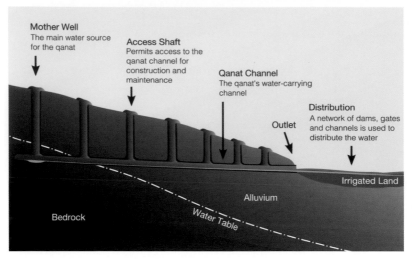

Mother Well
The main water source
for the qanat

Access Shaft
Permits access to the
qanat channel for
construction and
maintenance

Qanat Channel
The qanat's water-carrying
channel

Distribution
A network of dams, gates
and channels is used to
distribute the water

Outlet

Irrigated Land

Alluvium

Bedrock

Water Table

56 The structure of a foggara or qanat.

the high ground with the fields (illus. 57). Look closely, and the tell-tale regular trails of shaft openings and surrounding piles of debris reveal that these are the courses of Garamantean foggaras, some still in use today.

In Iran, the lines of the qanats can be used to trace active earthquake faults, for the line will be suddenly broken and displaced several metres to the side by movement on a fault. The tunnel would, of course, be broken and the consequences for water supply disastrous – there are places where the tunnelling can be seen to have begun all over again following an earthquake. For the Garamantes, it was not earthquakes that proved disastrous, but their voraciously efficient consumption of water. The water table dropped and the foggaras ran dry. By the seventh century AD the civilization was in terminal decline, perhaps suffering also a decrease in trade following the collapse of the Roman Empire. When Islamic invaders swept across the desert there was still a king in Garama, but he ruled over a mere shadow of its former prosperity. The foggaras of Garama may be mostly dry but the technology survives across the Sahara, with new systems still being constructed to water the oases. I have seen working, but ancient, falaj systems in the Oman, still maintained and supplying hundreds of millions of cubic metres of water per day to the fields and towns.

But how did the Garamantes build such an extensive and complex feat of engineering? The answer is another key to the success of their civilization: slaves. The Garamantes were skilled desert route-finders

57 Traces of foggaras in the Sahara. East–west scale 600 metres.

and navigators and controlled trans-Saharan trade, trade that included, as it would until very recent times, slaves from the south as well as gold, salt, glass and gemstones, some of them local. It was slave labour that built and maintained the Garamantean empire, and perhaps slaves who provided the ranks of their military. Herodotus described them as having 'no warlike arms at all' and being incapable of self-defence, but he was wrong. Rock art depicts chariots and warriors, and it was undoubtedly military aggression that procured slaves from their southern neighbours. The outposts of the Roman Empire along the coast were attacked by the Garamantes and the Garamantes were attacked by the Romans, who were repulsed, despite being possibly the first to use camels in the Sahara. Ironically, the Romans not only traded for slaves with the Garamantes, but took them as slaves themselves.

The Romans were the outsiders of the ancient world who viewed everything beyond their civilization as savage and barbaric. In an early version of 'manifest destiny', in the *Aeneid*, the poet Virgil recounts how Aeneas received a message from the underworld that Augustus Caesar (Virgil's patron) would herald a golden age of empire stretching 'beyond the Garamantes', the definition of the ends of the earth.

The script that is found inscribed on Garamantean tombs is related to one still used today, *Tifinagh*, the traditional writing system of the Tuareg, who inherited the role of trade masters of the Sahara and pirates of the desert. 'Tuareg', or the singular 'Targui', is not the name they use for themselves, but rather *Imohag* or the Berber *Amazigh*, 'Free Men', and *Kel Tagelmoust,* the 'People of the Veil'. 'Tuareg' is derived from the Arabic for 'lost souls' or those abandoned by God. The ethnic origins of Saharan insiders are complex and obscure; the centuries of trade and movement created a mix of sub-Saharan, Mediterranean and desert peoples. The Tuareg and the Berbers are more or less the same people, the Tuareg language, Tamasheq or Tamahaq, being a branch of Berber, possibly originating from the Phoenicians, and, in turn, the Garamantes. No one knows where the Tuareg came from, with even modern DNA evidence being ambiguous, but they became the symbol of the Saharan insider.

Romance and reality

The Tuareg were – and are – emblematic of the contradictions inherent in outsiders' views of desert insiders. Theirs is an image of the noble nomad, the lord of the desert, cultured, dignified, aloof. There are strong elements of truth in this image: the Tuareg social structure is sophisticated and, in many ways, enlightened, their artisanship is exquisite, and their mastery of the harsh environment extraordinary – as they themselves say, 'the desert has no secrets from the Tuareg' (illus. 58). But their longevity as a people is also based on their ferocity and their efficiency at running a protection racket based on violence and intimidation. To the Tuareg, everyone else is an outsider and their allegiances are fickle, driven by self-interest and a strong desire for freedom.

For centuries, the 'blue men' (after the dye of the tagelmust) dominated Saharan trade through guile and brutality. The Arab saying that 'the scorpion and the Tuareg are the only enemies you meet in the desert' rang true not only for adventuresome Europeans, who were warned by the Arabs of these 'masters of mutilation and torture', but also for other desert peoples. The Tebu, a tribe of black African origin living in the region of the Tibesti Mountains of the central Sahara, had their capital at Bilma, a major centre of salt mining and the heart of the trade. The Tuareg routinely raided and fought with the Tebu, but avoided killing too many – they were needed for the manual labour that the Tuareg disdained but was vital to the continuity of salt supply for the caravans that were the basis of Tuareg wealth. And the Tuareg prided themselves on being white. Behind the veil (worn only by the men for physical or psychological reasons, or both) their features are more Mediterranean than sub-Saharan, and this may well have provided nineteenth-century Europeans with a degree of ethnic comfort that led them to the early descriptions of nobility. The unveiled women were particularly attractive to outsiders, although their powerful role in the matrilineal (but not matriarchal) structure of Tuareg society may have been challenging to the social norms of early nineteenth-century European thinking.

The blue men had ferociously resisted every attempted incursion into their realms, from the Romans to the Ottomans. They had reached a pragmatic, but by no means peaceful, accommodation with the tide of Islam that swept across North Africa from the seventh century, subscribing nominally to some of its practices, but retaining their traditional beliefs, customs and superstitions – hence the 'lost souls'. Islamic motifs on Tuareg jewellery and leather goods are there to ward off the evil eye and other malevolent spirits rather than to express devotion. They are fiercely independent, freedom being a fundamental value for the Tuareg, reflected in their saying that 'Freedom is the desert's water, and water is the body's freedom.' Their traditional and determined nomadic, borderless, lifestyle emphasized this, and brought them into constant conflict with the settled communities of the oasis towns and any authority that had the temerity to try to impose itself on the desert. The oases had goods that the Tuareg needed, particularly camels, and were important to them for trade, some of which took place conventionally, but often procurement was by force. To the outside world, Timbuktu was long a fabled city, while for the Tuareg (whose eleventh-century summer campsite by the River Niger may well have been its origin), it was a target. And Timbuktu, together with neighbouring towns in the region, has remained a target into modern times. The Tuareg ferocity for independence, exacerbated by outsider erosion of their livelihood, led to the rebellions of the 1960s and 1990s and, most recently, their pragmatic if short-lived alliance with Islamic extremists and the violent occupation of Timbuktu in 2012. These recent events in Mali drew international attention to the city and, in particular, its treasure-trove of knowledge, its libraries. It has been easy from the Eurocentric perspective of history to ignore the great empires of the Sahel and the desert during the Middle Ages, the successors to the Garamantes.

The reason for the Tuareg camp on the Niger was, inevitably, control of trade, particularly salt, slaves and gold. Gold would drive trans-Saharan trade for centuries, but where did it come from? Just as Californian gold provided the stimulus to cross the deserts of the u.s., so did the gold deposits of the Senegal River system fundamentally influence Saharan history. And, just as much of California's gold was panned and sluiced from river sands, so were the riches of what are now the borderlands of Mali and Senegal. These were placer deposits, gold grains and nuggets torn from their mountain veins and transported by the rivers to be concentrated in the sands and gravels as a result of their relative heaviness. One of the main mining districts was Bambouk (as named by the French) or Bambuhu, described in the early nineteenth century in the *Edinburgh Encyclopaedia* (an attempt at competing with *Britannica*):

> Gold is so plentiful, that it is obtained by merely scraping the surface of the earth, which is clayish and sandy. When the mine is rich, it is wrought only to a depth of a few feet. In separating the gold from the earth, the larger pieces only are obtained, as the lesser pieces are washed away with the water . . . The kingdom is traversed by the mountains of Konkodoo, which abound with gold.

Mali remains today Africa's third largest gold producer, much of it being extracted by the same artisanal – and environmentally and

58 Tuareg men and camels.

ethically dubious – methods as more than a thousand years ago. These riches were closely guarded by the rulers of Mali, who in 1235 threw out the Tuareg from their camp and began the building of Timbuktu and the expansion of the Malian Empire to control more of the gold supply chain. The city grew into a centre of trade, religion and learning. Ibn Battuta visited in 1353, disliked the food and found reprehensible the fact that 'the women servants, slave-girls, and young girls go about in front of everyone naked, without a stitch of clothing on them', but he admired its wealth and culture:

> Most of its inhabitants are of the Massufa tribe, wearers of the face-veil. Its governor is called Farba Musa . . . On certain days the sultan holds audiences in the palace yard, where there is a platform under a tree, with three steps; this they call the 'pempi.' It is carpeted with silk and has cushions placed on it. [Over it] is raised the umbrella, which is a sort of pavilion made of silk, surmounted by a bird in gold, about the size of a falcon. The sultan comes out of a door in a corner of the palace, carrying a bow in his hand and a quiver on his back. On his head he has a golden skull-cap, bound with a gold band which has narrow ends shaped like knives, more than a span in length. His usual dress is a velvety red tunic, made of the European fabrics called 'mutanfas.' The sultan is preceded by his musicians, who carry gold and silver guimbris [two-stringed guitars], and behind him come three hundred armed slaves.

The Massufa, 'wearers of the face-veil', had helped Battuta cross the desert and were probably Berber, or Tuareg, peoples, but their society relied on black slaves, 'the most submissive to their king and the most abject in their behaviour before him'. The king was the *Musa*, and the most famous was Mansa Musa, who features prominently on the Catalan Atlas as 'Musse Melly', wearing a golden crown, holding a golden sceptre and contemplating a golden sphere (see illus. 37). In 1324 Mansa Musa made the pilgrimage to Mecca after travelling across the desert to Cairo. His entourage consisted of 60,000 men including a personal retinue of 12,000 slaves and, it is said, 15,000 camels, each one laden with gold. His spending spree in Cairo caused the local gold market to collapse for twelve years; in 2012, *Celebrity Net Worth* named him as the wealthiest man of all time, with a worth of $400 billion in today's terms. He also put his wealth to good use, consolidating Timbuktu's commercial and intellectual role, defending it against desert raiders and building the great Djinguereber Mosque, a classic of mud-brick architecture and now part of the World Heritage Site. But the kings would become weak, the people rebelled and in the early fifteenth century the Tuareg took the city back. Meanwhile, the rival Songhay Empire was growing in power and prosperity, and, using cavalry and canoes, took Timbuktu in 1468. After his visit in the early sixteenth century, the Spanish-born Berber writer, traveller and diplomat who would become known as Leo Africanus left some of the most detailed descriptions available at the time to Europeans, and commented that:

> Here there are many doctors, judges, priests and other learned men, that are well maintained at the king's cost. Various manuscripts and written books are brought here out of Barbarie [the coastal regions] and sold for more money than any other merchandise . . . The people of Timbuktu are of a peaceful nature. They have a custom of almost continuously walking about the city in the evening (except for those that sell gold), between 10 p.m. and 1 a.m., playing musical instruments and dancing. The citizens have at their service many slaves, both men and women.

Ironically, it was the Tuareg who carried many of the books and manuscripts – and, importantly, paper – to Timbuktu as part of their diversified trading activities. The city was one of the major centres of scholarship and knowledge in the world, and its records comprise hundreds of thousands of manuscripts collected in family libraries (some in the Tifinagh script), most of which were heroically saved from destruction in 2012 (illus. 59).

By the end of the sixteenth century, Timbuktu and the Songhay Empire were conquered by the Moroccan army, the scholars were deported and the city and its culture faded from the map. Its reputation and romance remained, however, long after the flow of gold had ceased, with a European mythology of streets paved and roofs covered with gold. But no European had been there and much of North Africa remained not just a vast blank on the maps, but also a blank in western knowledge, informed largely by the accounts of Leo Africanus. Sir Joseph Banks, having explored the world with James Cook, was not alone in regarding this ignorance as an embarrassment. On 9 June 1788 Banks and a number of his titled colleagues met in a private room in the St Alban's Tavern in London and formed the 'Association for Promoting the Discovery of the Interior Parts of Africa', otherwise known as the African Association. At the top of their agenda was determining the actual course of the River Niger and reaching Timbuktu. Thus began the great period of exploration that continued through the nineteenth century. The Niger was an enigma, a river that appeared to flow eastward into the desert. To join the Nile? To disappear in the sands? To flow into a great interior lake? Or to take some other strange course? But it was a route into the interior, and the African Association dispatched a series of explorers, including an American and a German as well as members of the British military, to solve the problem. For years, the mortality rate was 100 per cent, and no real light was shed until Mungo Park (who would himself perish on his second expedition) reached the Niger. But the river's true course would not be confirmed until 1830 when Richard Lemon Lander, together with his brother, traced the river to its mouth in the Gulf of Guinea. Lander had been a servant on earlier ventures sent out by the African Association that consisted of naval officers who, after acrimonious months in the desert, communicated with each other only in writing but at least reached Lake Chad, which they wanted to name 'Lake Waterloo'.

Meanwhile Timbuktu had become the goal of a race, a North African competition between Britain and France that would endure for more than a century. In 1824 in Paris, the Société de Géographie offered 10,000 francs to the first non-Muslim to reach the city and, importantly, return. In 1825 the African Association in London and the British Government instructed Captain Alexander Gordon Laing to leave for Tripoli and organize an expedition southward to Timbuktu and the Niger, a journey compellingly recounted and documented in Frank T. Kryza's book *The Race for Timbuktu*. Taking time first to marry the daughter of the British Consul, Laing departed Tripoli two days later for what would prove to be an expedition of heroic success and failure, plagued by disease and betrayal. Laing relied on the help of both the Sultan, the *Bashaw*, in Tripoli and of Tuareg guides, a reliance built, in both cases, on sand. The warning Laing had received that 'The sacred word of a Targui is like water fallen on the sand, never to be found again' proved all too accurate and applied equally to the Bashaw. A local sheikh, who had supposedly been paid by the Bashaw to support Laing, in fact had received nothing and

59 A leaf of a book from the Timbuktu libraries.

came to an arrangement with the Tuareg to murder Laing and share the camels and other valuables being carried by his caravan.

In early February 1826, somewhere in the dunes of today's southern Algeria, Laing was attacked in the night, suffering more than twenty horrific wounds from sabres and bullets. He wrote to his wife that he had a 'very severe cut on my fore Finger' and asked her to excuse his handwriting. But he informed the Consul in Tripoli that he was 'nearly murdered' and in some detail listed the wounds to his head, neck, arms and legs and that his right hand had been virtually severed. 'I am nevertheless doing well,' he wrote, 'and hope yet to return to England with much important geographical information.' Miraculously, Laing lived and continued south with his surviving – and loyal – companions; they spent a long period recovering and regrouping in the desert camp of a friendly sheikh. On 13 August 1826 after a journey of 399 days rather than, as he had estimated, a few weeks, Laing was the first white man to see Timbuktu in centuries. What he saw was a squalid, decaying, stinking and disease-ridden city, as Kryza comments, 'not even the palest shadow of the city abounding in wealth and architectural wonders that he – and all of Europe – had imagined'. The Tuareg were in control, but the city was in turmoil, threatened by ferociously Muslim Arab powers. After a stay of 35 days, during which he apparently documented the people, the place and its manuscripts, Laing had to leave, probably accompanied only by a freed slave, a young Arab and two camels. He was never heard from again. The slave was later found and recounted how Laing had been murdered by a local sheikh only three days after leaving the city. There was, infuriatingly, no sign of Laing's journals, and there never would be.

Laing had, at the cost of unimaginable suffering and eventually his life, accomplished half the mission. The Société de Géographie prize would later be claimed by René Caillié, who reached Timbuktu from the west, disguised as a Muslim in a slave ship on the river, in April 1828. He returned, destitute and in rags, to the bosom of the French authorities in Morocco, who refused to believe him. The Société de Géographie eventually and reluctantly accepted his story and awarded him the prize. However, some 80 years later, the French, obsessed with the proving that Caillié had in fact been the first to even reach the city, dispatched an army officer based in Algeria, Alexandre Bonnel de Mézières, to investigate. It was through his efforts that relatives of people who had known Laing in Timbuktu confirmed the story and the probable bones of Laing and his Arab companion were found beneath a tree in the desert some 50 kilometres north of the city. It seems likely that the journals had been destroyed by Laing's assassins as Christian magic. Caillié himself had investigated what had happened to Laing and, fortunately, his narrative survives, first published as *Travels through Central Africa to Timbuctoo; and across the Great Desert, to Morocco, Performed in the Years 1824–1828.* His account of what he had heard of Laing's death supported that given by Laing's freed slave and his disillusioned description of the reality of Timbuktu must echo what Laing had felt (illus. 60):

> This mysterious city, which has been an object of curiosity for so many ages, and of whose population, civilization, and trade with the Soudan, such exaggerated notions have prevailed . . . I looked around and found that the sight before me, did not answer my expectations. I had formed a totally different idea of the grandeur and wealth of Timbuctoo. The city presented, at first view, nothing but a mass of ill-looking houses, built of earth. Nothing was to be seen in all directions but immense plains of quicksand of a yellowish white colour . . . though one of the largest cities I have seen in Africa, [it] possesses no other resources but its trade in salt, the soil being totally unfit for

cultivation. The inhabitants procure from Jenne every thing requisite for the supply of their wants, such as millet, rice, vegetable butter, honey, cotton, Soudan cloth, preserved provisions, candles, soap, allspice, onions, dried fish, pistachios, &c.

Although admiring their craftsmanship, Caillié had little good to say about the Tuareg, describing their viciousness and procurement methods:

> The house of my host Sidi was constantly infested with Tooariks and Arabs. These people visit Timbuctoo for the sole purpose of extorting from the inhabitants what they call presents, but what might be more properly called forced contributions . . . When the chief of the Tooariks arrives with his suite at Timbuctoo, it is a general calamity, and yet every one overwhelms him with attention, and sends presents to him and his followers. He sometimes remains there two months, being maintained all that time at the expense of the inhabitants and the king, who sometimes give them really valuable presents, and they return home laden with millet, rice, honey, and preserved articles.

For the rest of the nineteenth century and well into the next, the Sahara would be the stage of colonial conflict. Any original agendas for the pursuit of knowledge and the filling in of blanks in the map (together with, at least by the African Association, a moral purpose to abolish slavery) became secondary to empire building, conquest and commerce. As with the deserts of the New World, after the idea of vast inland bodies of water had been discredited, attention turned to engineering plans for trans-Saharan railroads and, indeed, the *creation* of an inland sea.

In 1827 as Caillié was making his way to Timbuktu, the last Ottoman ruler of Algeria, angered by unpaid French debts, struck the French consul over the head with a fly whisk; the French invaded and the Gallic hegemony over the desert began. In 1884 fourteen countries, none of them African, began a meeting in Berlin that would divide up the entire continent of Africa. Territories were imposed, borders drawn where none had existed – or, geographically or culturally, *should* exist. It was a land grab under the auspices of 'orderly extension of European influence' and 'the development of trade and civilization'. After the fall of Napoleon III, France needed to find a place for 22,000 refugees from Alsace-Lorraine

60 Caillié's view of 'Timbuctoo'.

and vineyard workers made destitute by the ravages of *phylloxera*. North Africa offered the place and, of course, the opportunity to regain lost grandeur and pursue a worthy '*mission civilisatrice*'. Within a few years France controlled almost all of the Sahara, no great concern to the British Prime Minister, Lord Salisbury, who declared that it was 'nothing but light soil in which the Gallic cock can scratch', or, in an alternative version, 'Let the Gallic cock sharpen his spurs on the desert sand.' The governor-general of Algeria, Jules Cambon, responded:

> Very well, we will scratch in this sand. We will lay railway-lines, we will put up telegraph-poles, we will make the artesian water-tables gush to the surface, and in the oases we will hear the Gallic cock crowing his most melodious and happiest fanfare from the rooftops of the Kasbah.

The residents of the Kasbah were not happy with this idea, nor were any of the desert insiders. History has done little to assuage or understand the Tuareg, and, like transnational nomads of arid lands everywhere, they have been largely ignored, except when erosion of their freedom and marginalization has caused them to respond with their traditional ferocity. Tuareg 'uprisings' have occurred regularly for over a hundred years, most recently in Niger and Mali. Since 2008 *National Geographic* staff writer Peter Gwin has travelled among the Tuareg of the region and written memorably on how they 'struggle to survive amid the turmoil of North Africa'. In 2011 he reported from the isolated and spectacular Aïr Massif in central Niger, west of the old salt headquarters of Bilma, where the Tuareg were waging war against government forces. Their school had been destroyed, old men killed and buried, helicopters deployed against them and land mines laid by both sides. Drought had threatened the Tuareg way of life for some time, and Gwin reports how he was told that 'Animals are everything to a Tuareg . . . We drink their milk, we eat their meat, we use their skin, we trade them. When the animals die, the Tuareg dies.'

The government had been issuing uranium mining permits across traditional Tuareg lands, but sharing none of the profits, and the nomads had had enough. The conflict in both Niger and Mali was exacerbated by Colonel Qaddafi, who trained and armed the Tuareg militias while providing millions of dollars to the governments. Qaddafi then recruited Tuareg mercenaries during the 'Arab Spring' of Libya, and Libyan arms in large quantities found their way across the non-existent borders of the desert to the militias. Not all Tuareg supported the rebellions, and thousands of refugees continue to cross and recross the desert. Shortly after Gwin left a new cease-fire was announced, the army overthrew the president and elections were held; the extent to which the new president will address the needs of the Tuareg remains to be seen. The following year events in Mali provided a grim illustration of the complexity of politics in the lawless expanses of the Sahara. Tuareg rebellion and demands for freedom and independence become inextricably caught up in drug- and people-smuggling and Islamic extremism. The chaos in Mali began with the Tuareg National Movement for the Liberation of Azawad (MNLA) declaring independence, deepened with the military *coup d'état* and escalated out of control with the participation of the Islamist group Ansar Dine. The conflict generated deep ethnic divisions both among the Tuareg and between them and communities of Arabs and 'black Africans'. At the time of writing, Mali's new president, Ibrahim Boubacar Keita, is faced with the monumental task of finding a way to satisfy deeply divided and antagonistic peoples of his war-torn country. How the Tuareg abide by their proverb 'kiss the hand you cannot sever' will be a determining factor for the future, but the reality is that the Sahara cannot be controlled without the Tuaregs' participation.

61, 62, 63 Tuareg craftsmanship.

La Pensée sauvage

The Tuareg character can be described – by the Western standards of 'civilization' – as violent, unprincipled, fickle. And yet. Their society is complex and highly structured, women are powerful and respected, their fierce independence is, in many ways, admirable, their knowledge of, and relationship with, their land is intimate, they have dignity and their metal and leather craftsmanship is exquisite and sophisticated (illus. 61–3).

The Tuareg illustrate, together with the Native Americans and the Aboriginal peoples of Australia, the utter impossibility of a Western mind truly understanding their culture. Instead, history and anthropology have resorted to describing them as 'primitive' or 'savage', at the same time yielding to the temptation to qualify such terms with words such as 'noble'. We have thankfully emerged from the period of exploited 'Darwinism' and eugenics, but the conflict between connotations of 'civilized' and 'barbaric' endure. As I cautioned at the beginning of the previous chapter, the field is strewn with cultural and intellectual traps, and any kind of balance is difficult to achieve. As a consequence anthropology and philosophy are constantly enlivened by intellectual conflict between opposing 'outsider' schools of thought. A leading participant in these debates in the twentieth century was Claude Lévi-Strauss (who hated 'travelling and explorers'). Lévi-Strauss had written that, in his youth, he had 'three intellectual mistresses', one of which was geology (the others were Freud and Marx), and so I confess a bias towards his views. The geological muse convinced him of the value of looking carefully beneath the surface of things, in particular so-called 'primitive societies':

> Other societies are perhaps no better than our own; even if we are inclined to believe they are, we have no method at our disposal for proving it. However, by getting to know them better, we are enabled to detach ourselves from our own society. Not that our own society is peculiarly or absolutely bad. But it is the only one from which we have a duty to free ourselves: we are, by definition, free in relation to the others.

Lévi-Strauss believed that a society cannot be denied humanity on the basis that they lack writing and therefore 'history'. When Lévi-Strauss had taken up a chair of 'Religions of Primitive Peoples' in one of France's *grandes écoles*, he immediately changed it to 'Religions of Peoples without Writing Systems'. Few of the desert insider societies have writing systems (even the Tuareg use theirs sparingly and certainly not to write histories or their poetry), and yet they have a strong sense of their identity and their origins and an enquiring and comprehensive vision of the world around them. In what is generally regarded as his greatest work, *La Pensée sauvage* (1962, translated as *The Savage Mind*, though it could also be translated as 'The Wild Pansy'), Lévi-Strauss wrote the following, perhaps words to consider when outsiders contemplate the desert insiders:

> It is forgotten that each of the tens or hundreds of thousands of societies which have existed side by side in the world or succeeded one another since man's first appearance, has claimed that it contains the essence of all the meaning and dignity of which human society is capable and, reduced though it may have been to a small nomad band or a hamlet lost in the depths of the forest, its claim has in its own eyes rested on a moral certainty comparable to that which we can invoke in our own case. But whether in their case or our own, a good deal of ego-centricity and naivety is necessary to believe that man has taken refuge in a single one of the historical or geographical modes of his existence, when the truth about man resides in the system of their differences and common properties.

FIVE

Mind and Matter, Body and Soul

CLAUDE LÉVI-STRAUSS felt that 'Objects are what matter. Only they carry the evidence that throughout the centuries something really happened among human beings.' He was a great collector, and many of his treasures are now in the spectacular Musée du quai Branly, the intellectual inspiration for which came very much from Lévi-Strauss. Opened in 2006, beside the Seine and in the shadow of the Eiffel Tower, the museum consolidates ethnographic collections previously dispersed around Paris and prides itself on being the place 'where cultures converse'. The collections and the displays are a celebration of the idea that it is objects that matter, objects that speak to us, the outsiders, in representing the inspiration of a culture, of a people's response to environment, heritage and beliefs. Being a French museum, the collections from North Africa are comprehensive and stunning in their diversity, both in the physical displays and in the online galleries. In these we begin to see the inspiration of the desert that is the topic of this chapter, together with the tensions and contrasts of the insider–outsider viewpoints.

Two objects from the quai Branly are shown in illus. 64 and 65. On the left is a typically exquisite example of the Tuareg craftsmanship introduced in the previous chapter, a *clé de voile*, a piece of jewellery used to secure a woman's veil. Made from silver, copper and brass, the design incorporates symbolism that speaks powerfully of Tuareg culture and spirituality. The symmetry tells of a cosmos and a world in balance, containing opposites in equilibrium with each other – earth and sky, desert and tent, the four cardinal directions, male and female, the union of all necessary to the life and health of the Tuareg and all Berber people. Many of the motifs echo the letters of the vowel-less *Tifanagh* script of the Garamantes and their descendants, the Berber *Amazigh*, the

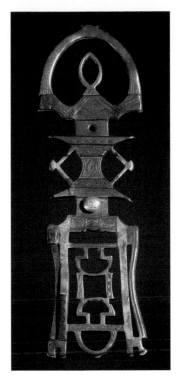

64, 65 Early 20th-century Tuareg veil pin, and Jean-Baptiste-Ange Tissier's
Algerian Woman and her Slave, 1860, both in the Musée du quai Branly.

'free humans'. Here is an object that matters, telling us (to the extent that, as outsiders, we can read them) stories of a society, its world view and its beliefs, quite apart from its artistic skills.

On the right, from 1860, roughly the same time that the veil pin was crafted, is *Algerian Woman and her Slave*, a painting by Jean-Baptiste-Ange Tissier. Tissier was an official artist to the Second Empire of Napoleon III, typically recording in reverent detail scenes such as Napoleon being presented with the new plans for the Louvre. He also occasionally devoted himself to recording aspects of the colonies, of which this painting is an example. It is rare to find European 'objects' in the collections of the quai Branly, but this painting appears on the same Maghreb gallery page of the museum's website as the veil pin, and the contrast is startling. In among the strikingly beautiful examples of jewellery, textiles and ceramics is a languidly sensual odalisque and her slave, stars of Orientalism, the outsider's view of North African culture.

The desert has long been a source of inspiration, a strangely fertile stage for the human imagination. Western culture discovered in the desert a place so different from its temperate homelands that it became a place to explore the exotic, the mysterious, the threatening beauty of the Sublime, a place to escape to, a place that offered insights into the soul and the self. The desert has provided refuge and peace for the most ascetic of spiritual movements and, in contrast, the backdrop for post-apocalyptic and violent writing and film. The landscapes of the desert are, in themselves, characters in literature, cinema and the visual arts. It seems that the desert is possibly only rivalled as an inspirational setting by its apparent opposite, the sea. The desert is seductive, with some strange allure that, once experienced, invites – or even compels – return. In the words of Wilfred Thesiger, 'this cruel land can cast a spell which no temperate clime can match', or Edward Abbey: 'There is something about the desert . . . There is something there which the mountains, no matter how grand and beautiful, lack; which the sea, no matter how shining and vast and old, does not have.' The need to return to the desert is something experienced in common by otherwise utterly different individuals. Isabelle Eberhardt, the angst-ridden, cross-dressing, drug-addicted vagabond writer of wonderful prose, wrote of the triggers of homesickness:

> And so, he whose soul was elect during his far-off and successive exiles, need only an Arab-sounding word, an oriental melody, a perfume, even a simple bell ringing behind the wall of some barracks, to evoke with piercing clarity verging on pain a whole world of memories of the land of Africa, dormant, almost extinct, buried in the silent necropolis of his soul.

From a very different viewpoint, Ralph Bagnold, soldier, engineer, scientist and quintessential Englishman, echoed Eberhardt's sentiment precisely:

> And then comes some trivial sense-impression – the hot-varnish smell of a car standing in the sun, a cloudless sunset, the finding of sand grains in the pocket of an old coat. Out comes the map again; and the eye hovers over some blank space still farther away which nobody has yet reached. Happy calculations follow about petrol and distance – dreams of just one more desert trip.

And Mary Austin: 'A land of lost rivers, with little in it to love; yet a land that once visited must be come back to inevitably. If it were not so there would be little told of it.'

These are, of course, the views of outsiders who see the desert very differently from those for whom it is home. Yet the allure is also strong for the insiders, together with a sense of homesickness regardless of how cruel their home can be. In the early nineteenth century, Alexander Burnes, a Scottish explorer of Central Asia, wrote on seeing the Karakum Desert: 'I cannot imagine a sight more terrible.' But the view of a local nomad was that 'Every time I think about the sunset in the desert, my heart bleeds for those poor people who have never seen that beauty.' Hassanein Bey, Westernized Egyptian though he may have been, felt, at heart, his Bedouin roots when he wrote:

> The desert is terrible and it is merciless, but to the desert all those who have once known it must return . . . The desert calls, but it is not easy to analyse its attraction and charm . . . It is as though a man were deeply in love with a very fascinating but cruel woman. She treats him badly and the world crumples in his hand; at night she smiles on him and the whole world is a paradise. The desert smiles and there is no place on earth worth living in but the desert.

The inspiration of the desert in the human imagination, outsider and insider, has created a vast body of art, literature, poetry, music, photography and film, spiritual and worldly, beautiful and banal. In contemplating this topic, I am reminded more than ever of Edward Abbey's warning: 'you cannot get the desert into a book any more than a fisherman can haul up the sea with his nets.' The task is impossible, and what follows can only be a sampling, in many ways a personal response to the sheer scope and diversity of the topic.

Paint and varnish

A few years ago, travelling through the remote landscapes of Egypt's Western Desert in the tyre tracks and footsteps of Ralph Bagnold, a number of my companions were rock art enthusiasts and my eyes were opened to the compelling mysteries of these extraordinary expressions of human inspiration. Exploiting the graphic potential of removing

66, 67 Carved rock art from Egypt's Western Desert.

the dark veneer of desert varnish to reveal the lighter rock beneath has been an artistic medium for desert people the world over for millennia (illus. 66, 67). Add to that the palette of natural pigments for painting and, on the grand scale of the Nazca Lines, the manipulation of desert pavement, and the desert offers a dramatic variety of artistic media.

The global collection of desert rock art is glorious enough in its own right, but the fact that it inspires in us a deep human resonance and connection with our past, at the same time remaining completely elusive in terms of its meaning and motivation, has stimulated great flights of fantasy and unfounded speculation. The so-called 'Cave of the Swimmers' in one of the wadis running out of the Gilf Kebir plateau in the southwestern corner of Egypt is perhaps the most emblematic example of desert rock art. Discovered in 1933 by the intrepid but enigmatic Hungarian explorer and spy László Almásy, the cave (and Almásy) featured in Michael Ondaatje's book *The English Patient* and the Oscar-winning film. While paintings do indeed include strange human figures in postures that could represent swimming (illus. 68), they have been also variously interpreted as flying figures and mermaids.

Like most examples of desert rock art, the age of the paintings is difficult, if not impossible, to measure, but these paintings were certainly made thousands of years ago in times when the climate of the Sahara, as suggested by the menagerie commonly depicted, was quite different from today. As we shall see in chapter Seven, it was not long ago that the arid wadis of the Gilf Kebir formed part of a great river system – it is quite reasonable that these *are* swimmers. Then again, that is simply our interpretation. The fame of the cave resulted in its becoming a tourist destination, albeit for visitors who are willing and able to make the journey across hundreds of miles of hyper-arid desert. When I visited the cave, the tragic consequences of this were horrifyingly apparent: graffiti and irreparable damage. The motivation of the original artists may be mysterious, but that of visitors to this art gallery who feel compelled to paint their names on it is truly incomprehensible.

The entire region is rich in rock art, many locations, thankfully, less visited than the Cave of the Swimmers. In 2002 Colonel Ahmed Mestakawi, an Egyptian reserve army officer, ex-border patrol officer and then desert guide, explored the area with Massimo Foggini, an Italian multimillionaire (who insisted on champagne each night in the desert). They discovered what became known as the Foggini-Mestakawi cave, although a later falling-out led to the Italian's name being dropped. It is not so much a cave as an open shelter beneath an overhanging cliff, half-filled with drifting sand. Topographically modest and unimposing as

68 The Cave of the Swimmers.

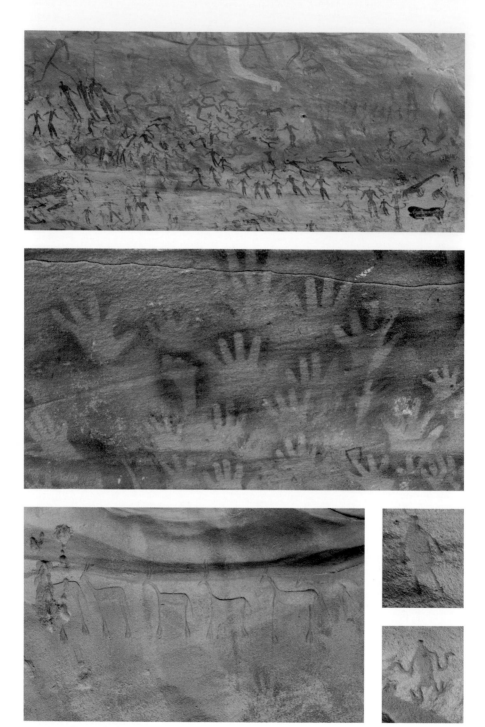

69–73 The Foggini-Metsakawi cave; note generations of over-painted images (top), delicate carvings (bottom), and strange figures (bottom right).

it may be, it vies for the title of the largest single rock art site in Africa. It is a 5,000-year-old Louvre, with hundreds of works, many painted, some carved, overlapping successions of artistic genres. I rarely find myself tempted to use the term 'awe-inspiring', but that was the sensation I felt as I approached the site. It is a place of wonder.

A small catalogue of the diversity of this art gallery is shown here (illus. 69–73). Dynamic human figures who seem to spontaneously animate, the human hands (including a clenched fist) that resonate with the humanity and individuality of each artist, exquisitely carved gazelle, ostriches and bizarrely leaping human figures. And, inevitably, the un-interpretable creatures that consistently, the world over, lead some observers to talk of extraterrestrials. But what was this place, what are many of these figures doing, what motivated the artists? All fertile ground for speculation with little basis. This kind of 'primitive' art has been described as everything from adolescent graffiti to evidence of shamanism or the depiction of aliens; there is an implicit sexist assumption that the artists were men, but also the suggestion, based on the hands, that women played a key role. In its presence, however, whether at the Mestakawi cave, in the Australian red centre, gazing at the great Atacama geoglyphs or Utah's 'Newspaper Rock', the viewer does not really need an explanation. This desert art is both inspired and inspiring, and a large part of our inspiration is the freedom to imagine and connect with very human expression from the deep past.

'In the desert, you see, there is everything and nothing . . . it is God without mankind'

Perhaps because of the strong psychological effect of the desert, in Mary Austin's view the place 'where the borders of conscience break down', it is difficult to believe that there is not a strong element of spirituality of some sort in all desert rock art. Possibly those early artists were responding to the role that the desert has always played for the human imagination, the role of a place for the soul. There are many Tuareg sayings that echo the one quoted in the preface that describes 'lands full of sand for the well-being of the soul': 'water cleanses the body, but the desert cleanses the soul'; 'for the body the desert is a place of exile, whereas for the spirit the desert is paradise.' For thousands of years, mystics, philosophers, pilgrims and shamans have sought an indefinable something in the desert and often found it. From St Anthony and St

Jerome to Albert Camus, Paul Bowles, Isabelle Eberhardt, Edward Abbey and countless others, the desert has provided a place of self-discovery – in a conventional religious way or very emphatically otherwise.

Around 3,000 years ago, it is said, an old man gathered his family, livestock and possessions and left the Mesopotamian city of Ur to travel westward into the desert to the new land that had been promised to his descendants. The difficulties of his journey and his family problems have become legendary, his legacy global. Abraham – Abram, Ibrahim – would become the patriarch of the three religions of the Book, the great monotheistic religions of the desert. Out of the desert came powerful gods and prophets, and back to the desert have gone monks, ascetics, romantics and those (particularly in the Christian tradition) on the margins of human society in search of the divine and themselves.

At the heart of the Abrahamic religions are the Five Books of Moses, known in the Old Testament as Genesis, Exodus, Leviticus, Numbers and Deuteronomy. In the Hebrew of the Torah, using the opening words of each, these appear as *Bereshit* ('In the beginning'), *Shemot* ('Names'), *Vayikra* ('He called'), *Bamidbar* ('In the desert') and *Devarim* ('Words'). In the Qur'an, these books and their prophets are recognized and respected, together with the Gospels, as earlier revelations (Surah 2:136):

> Say (O Muslims): We believe in Allah and that which is revealed unto us and that which was revealed unto Abraham, and Ishmael, and Isaac, and Jacob, and the tribes, and that which Moses and Jesus received, and that which the prophets received from their Lord. We make no distinction between any of them, and unto Him we have surrendered.

From the beginning the symbol of the desert is common and powerful in the Bible. The Garden of Eden was created as an oasis for Adam and Eve, from which, having initiated the concept of original sin, they were thrown out – into the desert. So began the eternal theme of exile to the desert, continued in Genesis with Abraham fleeing drought and famine to Egypt. There he had a son with Hagar, the slave of his wife, Sarah, who had been unable to bear children. The resulting friction led Hagar to flee Sarah's anger and escape to the desert, where she was persuaded to return by an angel and gave birth to a son, Ishmael. By this time Abraham was 86 years old. Despite their advanced age, Sarah then gave birth to Isaac and the ensuing rivalry between the boys caused Hagar and Ishmael to be banished, albeit after being freed. For the second time, Hagar found herself abandoned in the desert, the desert of Paran which, by some interpretations, was in the Arabian Peninsula. The water supplied by Abraham ran out and they were on the verge of death when an angel again appeared and created a well. In the Islamic account, Hagar's search for water in the desert hills took place close to Mecca and a reenactment of this, together with drinking from the well, which is close to the *Kaaba*, remains a key part of the pilgrim's hajj today. The image of the exiled Hagar as the mother of outcasts and an icon of feminism have inspired paintings by countless artists from Rubens (who depicts a finely dressed Hagar seated beneath a tree in the traditional setting of 'wilderness') to Chagall. She appears in literature from Defoe and Shakespeare to Salman Rushdie and Margaret Atwood.

Troubles in Egypt later required Moses to lead the Israelites across the Red Sea and into the Sinai desert, where he had earlier encountered the burning bush, to begin their forty years of wandering (it should be noted that the number 'forty' in the Bible, when referring to days, nights or years, is not to be taken literally, but as representative of a long period of time, generally involving struggle). As always in the desert, the challenge for Moses was providing food and drinkable water for his complaining people, and it was only through divine help that bitter waters were turned sweet and manna rained from heaven. The key event of this period took place at Mount Sinai, where the Ten Commandments and the Torah were revealed to Moses, the Five Books revered by all the Abrahamic religions.

The message from the desert wanderings of Moses and the Israelites was clear for all of these faiths: man could only survive in the desert through the grace of God. The words at the head of this section that describe the desert as the place where God is and man is not are from a strange story by Honoré de Balzac. 'A Passion in the Desert' tells of a Napoleonic soldier separated from his troops, captured by local tribesmen, escaping and being forced to take refuge in a desert cave. There he finds himself in the company of a female 'panther' (most likely a Saharan cheetah, today an animal that, remarkably, continues to survive, albeit endangered). This 'sultana of the desert', bizarrely anthropomorphized, cares for the soldier who, in return, 'grew passionately fond' of her, referring to her as 'Mignonne', his darling. However, the relationship 'ended as all great passions do end – by a misunderstanding'.

After he admires an eagle in flight, Mignonne apparently becomes jealous, bites him and he kills her: 'It was as though I had murdered a real person.' The soldier is rescued and tells his story to the narrator whom he meets at a circus menagerie. Balzac never visited North Africa, but the soldier's view of the desert as God's place accurately reflects the beliefs of the Abrahamic religions. There is an Algerian saying, 'The desert is the Garden of Allah, from which the Lord of the faithful removed all superfluous human and animal life, so that there might be one place where He can walk in peace.' Man can only be sustained 'in a desert land, and in the waste howling wilderness' through God's will: 'the desert shall rejoice, and blossom as the rose' as long as man does not sin. If he does, then the desert is the symbol of God's wrath: 'And thy heaven that is over thy head shall be brass, and the earth that is under thee shall be iron. The Lord shall make the rain of thy land powder and dust: from heaven shall it come down upon thee, until thou be destroyed.' Thus the desert became the place of testing, judgement, punishment, purification, self-denial and sacrifice, a theme dramatically continued through the New Testament in Christianity.

The Old Testament book of Isaiah refers to 'The voice of him that crieth in the wilderness, Prepare ye the way of the Lord, make straight in the desert a highway for our God', words commonly regarded as foretelling the arrival of John the Baptist and Jesus. The desert is the stage for John's praying and fasting, and for the ministry and ultimate testing, the temptation, of Jesus: 'And he was there in the wilderness forty days, tempted of Satan; and was with the wild beasts; and the angels ministered unto him.' In the Greek gospels, the place where John the Baptist appears is *eremos*, desert, from which comes the word 'hermit'. Over the centuries, the desert drew hermits in search of enlightenment and testing, experimenting with the ascetic to attain purity and discover divine truth. The image of the saint confronting temptation in the desert became an enduring one, Saint Jerome being a popular subject in the classical tradition in works by Leonardo and countless other Italian and Flemish artists. In all of them Jerome finds himself in exotic surroundings, but they are most certainly not arid (although one version from the early sixteenth century by Joachim Patinir does feature two camels beside what would seem to be an Alpine lake). The most iconic, diverse and persistent imagery is that of Saint Anthony, Anthony of the Desert, leader of the Desert Fathers. Anthony was born into a wealthy family in Lower Egypt; it is believed that at the age of 35, towards the end of the third century, he disposed of all his possessions and withdrew to an old fort in the Eastern Desert. He remained there alone for perhaps twenty years while a group of disciples established themselves in caves and huts around the fort. They persuaded him to emerge and for a number of years he devoted himself to instruction and organization before once more returning to a solitary life. Inevitably, Anthony was confronted by temptation, reportedly in many forms of monsters and demons, and, in some descriptions, the Queen of Sheba and naked women. The French writer Gustave Flaubert spent much of his life working on a long and blasphemous account of a single night in *The Temptation of St Anthony; or, a Revelation of the Soul*, an attempt to create a French *Faust*. He published the final version – to widespread and vicious disdain – in 1874. Flaubert was inspired by a painting he had seen by the Flemish Renaissance artist Pieter Bruegel the Elder (or a follower). Bruegel was a pioneer of grand landscape painting and this work is a dramatic example, although, once again, hardly resembling the Egyptian desert (illus. 74). The scene is filled with grotesque creatures, the sky crowded with floating demons. St Anthony appears twice, on the ground in his hovel and above being carried away by Satan.

Flaubert's work inspired Freud and Bruegel's painting inspired Cézanne. Indeed, the Temptation of St Anthony has been a frequently recurring theme for artists from Italian frescoes of the tenth century

74 School of Pieter Bruegel, *The Temptation of St Anthony, c.* 1550–75.

75, 76 Details from Hieronymus Bosch,
Triptych of the Temptations of St Anthony, c. 1501.

through to the work of Max Ernst and Salvador Dalí. But undoubtedly the most famous – or infamous – portrayal of the torments of the saint is the extraordinary triptych by Hieronymus Bosch, a work that surely might have inspired Bruegel. Looking at this work in Lisbon's Museu Nacional de Arte Antiga, I found it difficult to believe that it was painted at the very beginning of the sixteenth century and that Bosch was a devout believer rather than an eccentric contemporary of Dalí. The three panels display a dense narrative, packed with grotesque, obscene and nightmarish figures in scenes thought to reference events and descriptions in the Five Books of Moses. Anthony is featured four times, the extent and diversity of his temptations and torment painted in meticulous and disturbing detail (illus. 75, 76).

Hermits, particularly St Jerome, St Anthony and John the Baptist, feature frequently in many of Bosch's works, illustrating the power of the tradition in religious thinking. Anthony became known as the founder of the 'Desert Movement', most importantly the eremitic Desert Fathers from the third to the seventh centuries. However, the tradition has its roots from long before in ascetic Judaism, from which desert communities originated throughout the lands of the Israelites – it was one of these that produced the Dead Sea Scrolls. At the height of the desert movement, thousands of monks lived, tested themselves and sought purification across the arid landscapes of Egypt and Palestine. As did the less celebrated Desert Mothers, thousands of women ascetics; twelve female desert saints are recorded, but since the accounts were entirely written by men, their lives and works are far less well known.

Visions, miracles, revelations and madness are what the desert has to offer the hermit and the mystic. The very nature of the desert has offered the opportunity for removal, solitude, self-examination and the quest for the divine for thousands of years, and continues to do so. For the mystic and atheist Jewish writer Edmond Jabès, born in Egypt and exiled in 1956 as a result of the Suez Crisis, the word 'desert' has become a metaphor for which, to 'give it back its strength', one has to return to the real desert and 'its exemplary emptiness'. Nevertheless, in much of his challenging writing and philosophy, Jabès himself uses the void and the silence of the desert as a metaphor. *The Book of Margins* contains a foreword by Mark C. Taylor, philosopher of religion at Columbia University, in which he quotes Jabès in conversation:

It is very hard to live with silence. The real silence is death and this is terrible. To approach this silence, it is necessary to journey to the desert. You do not go to the desert to find identity, but to lose it, to lose your personality, to be anonymous. You make yourself void. You become silence. You become more silent than the silence around you. And then something extraordinary happens: you hear silence speak.

This is the 'baptism of solitude' of Paul Bowles, the spell of the desert:

Here, in this wholly mineral landscape, lighted by stars like flares, even memory disappears; nothing is left but your own breathing and the sound of your heart beating. A strange, and by no means pleasant, process of reintegration begins inside you . . . For no one who has stayed in the Sahara for a while is quite the same as when he came.

It is the place where, for Mary Austin, 'the borders of conscience break down' and, for the Desert Fathers, where God is and man is not.

Songs of the desert

The desert resonates for all the religions of the book. Josephine Lazarus was an eloquent essayist and the less well-known sister of Emma, the poet whose immortality was guaranteed by the words, 'Give me your tired, your poor, / Your huddled masses yearning to breathe free.' Addressing the challenges faced by the Jewish community in the United States in the early years of the twentieth century, Josephine wrote that 'We still bear in our soul the soul of the desert – the wide, vast spaces, the great silence, the great solitude, the silent watches of the night under the calm, large stars of the East, the flight of the alone into the Alone.' The desert still resonates, but of the three religions it does so with most vigour in Islam.

In 610 the angel Jibra'il (Gabriel) brought to the 40-year-old Prophet Muhammad his first revelations from God on a desert hill not far from Mecca; the revelations continued over more than twenty years and were gathered into the Qur'an. Within 200 years Islam had been spread through conversion and conquest from Arabia to Central Asia, and through North Africa to Spain. The desert was the literal birthplace of Islam, its early adherents were desert peoples and its language was the language of the desert. In the tradition of the time, Muhammad was sent as a child into the desert to live with the Bedouin to learn the eloquence of spoken Arabic and the self-discipline and morality of the desert tribes. The desert has always been at the core of Islam and, just as a desert-dweller rarely refers to the landscapes of his home, the desert features in a different way and far less prominently in the Qur'an than it does in the Bible. The desert is simply one part of God's creation. It is, of course, a place where man can survive and water be provided only by the grace of Allah, who 'quickened a region that was dead'. That in itself is a cause for celebration and this message can be accompanied by educational advice (Surah 39:21):

> Hast thou not seen how Allah hath sent down water from the sky and hath caused it to penetrate the earth as watersprings, and afterward thereby produceth crops of divers hues; and afterward they wither and thou seest them turn yellow; then He maketh them chaff. Lo! herein verily is a reminder for men of understanding.

Water is what defines paradise, an oasis, a garden of flowing streams that is the opposite of the desert. In a modern photograph by George Steinmetz of a roadside restaurant on the edge of the desert of the Empty Quarter, a young man sits in front of a wall-sized mural of what could be the gardens of Versailles; in a street cafe in Marrakech, above a devotional poster of Mecca, is a large and fanciful poster of a lush garden, multi-coloured flowers and a cascading fountain. The descriptions in the Qur'an of the opposite of paradise are not of a desert, but of something far worse: hell is a place of blazing fires and boiling water and on judgement day the 'hills become a heap of running sand'.

While the Qur'an is at the heart of the long tradition of Arabic literature and poetry, it is a tradition that long pre-dates it. The Arabs had a deep love for their language and its form and resonance, a love that expressed itself in an oral culture of poetry composition and recital, often sung. It was, inevitably, oral, since the nomadic lifestyle does not encourage libraries. The poetry narrated epic stories of love, warfare, heroism, tribal history, everyday nomadic life, journeys and rain, and was felt to be inspired by desert spirits, the *djinn*. The earliest preserved examples of written poetry are the so-called 'Hanged Poems' or *Mu'allaqat*, works of seven tribal poets whose works were so respected that, in the sixth century, they were transcribed and 'hung' in the religious building of the *kaaba* at Mecca a century or so before it was transformed by Islam. These poems follow a strict structure and metre, that of the *qasida*, an elegiac ode that begins with a journey to an abandoned desert camp and a recollection of lost love, and continues with a celebration of the poet's horses and camels, together with scenes of tribal events and warfare; allusions to seduction are common. The metre may have had its roots in the pace of a camel. The *qasida* concludes with a section praising the writer and his tribe. These, like all Arab poetry, are works *of* the desert but not directly *about* the desert, for it is a given, the setting and context in which life and events unfold. Muhammad declared the greatest of these poets to be Imru-ul-Quais, whose *Mu'allaqat* ode is considered the oldest example of pre-Islamic poetry. It begins with the classic memory:

> Stop, oh my friends, let us pause to weep over the
> remembrance of my beloved.
> Here was her abode on the edge of the sandy desert between
> Dakhool and Howmal.
> The traces of her encampment are not wholly obliterated
> even now;
> For when the South wind blows the sand over them the
> North wind sweeps it away.

And ends with rain:

> The clouds poured forth their gift on the desert of Ghabeet,
> till it blossomed
> As though a Yemani merchant were spreading out all the rich
> clothes from his trunks,
> As though the little birds of the valley of Jiwaa awakened in
> the morning
> And burst forth in song after a morning draught of old, pure,
> spiced wine.
> As though all the wild beasts had been covered with sand
> and mud, like the onion's root-bulbs.
> They were drowned and lost in the depths of the desert
> at evening.

The tradition of Arab poetry continued through the spread of Islam, which encouraged for the first time its written recording and it continues to thrive today. The desert is always present, but as a stage, an inevitable setting, the symbol of freedom, the place to escape the evils of a settled life. In *Lyrics of the Sands*, the American photographer Gloria Kefayeh pairs stunning desert images with extracts of poems, including the odes of the *Mu'allaqat*. An early Islamic poet whom she quotes is Mutammim bin Nuwayra al-Yarbuee:

> Many a dusty desert, long a wilderness, across which the
>   thirsty camels hasten with stones hot underfoot,
> Have I crossed on a fine strong she-camel, moving swiftly,
> Even when the night is dark, passing from the unknown to
>   the known.

Poetry and song remained fundamental to Bedouin culture into modern times. Wilfred Thesiger:

> When moved, Arabs break easily into poetry. I have heard a lad spontaneously describe in verse some grazing which he had just found: he was giving natural expression to his feelings. But while they are very sensible to the beauty of their language, they are curiously blind to natural beauty. The colour of the sands, a sunset, the moon reflected in the sea: such things leave them unmoved.

And Hassanein Bey records songs sung for camels as a caravan is on the move:

> In companies the sand dunes
> Marched to meet them,
> Pointing the homeward way.
> The sand dunes hide many wells
> That brim with waters unfailing.
> You come to their margins like bracelets
> Wrought of gold and rare gems in far countries.

In the 1970s Clinton Bailey, for his fascinating compilation *Bedouin Poetry From Sinai and the Negev*, recorded the recital of a poem that he translated as 'The Best Things in Life: a Bedouin's Credo'. The poem begins:

> God, grant me the ten things that make life worthwhile,
>   Inscribe them for me as my fate:
>
> First, a tent held by tent-ropes spread wide,
>   Where horsemen will meet when they're out on a ride;
>
> Second, a wife of good training and breed,
>   Who, when guests come, directly will bring what they need;
>
> Third, a mare who'll beat stallions though bound on one side,
>   And a far-shooting rifle to hold while I ride;

He continues to wish for powerful sons, cover (both literal and meta-phorical) to protect his daughters, goats, camels, a hajj, and salvation from hell at judgement day when Gabriel will retell his good deeds.

The survival of Bedouin poetry and song is threatened by the erosion, often forced, of the nomadic way of life. Nevertheless, the image and metaphor of the desert continues to be a foundation of modern Islamic verse. Assad Ali is one of the most highly respected modern Arabic writers, a retired professor from the University of Damascus who explores themes of Islamic mysticism and Sufism. Regrettably, only one of his works is easily available in English, but *Happiness Without Death: Desert Hymns* is, although challenging for a non-Muslim reader, both beautiful and extraordinary. The 30 poems are philosophical and inspirational reflections on the first verses of the Qur'an as they were revealed chrono-logically, and the voice of each is 'the Desert', a voice, as Camille and Kabir Helminski describe in their introduction, both 'from the desert and of the desert'. The second poem, 'Paradises of Your Gifts', begins:

> I, the Desert,
> Love You my God and pray to You.
> I was a weed through which the winds whistled;
>   You sharpened me,
>   so, by Your virtue, I've become
>   a pen with which you teach.
> I was barren and inactive;

You planted life and movement in me,
and made me a destination
to which pilgrims come in search
                    of knowledge and wealth,
and You gave me unimaginable gifts.

Throughout the vast body of Arabic literature, while there have always been women poets, the dominant voice is male; and yet '*sahraa*', 'desert' is feminine. The fifth of Assad Ali's hymns ends with the words 'Accept this prayer from your pleading maidservant, the Desert.'

The male domination of poetry and song in the Arab world continues today, but this is by no means the case in other desert cultures. Among the Tuareg, women play key roles in society and the household, including as the primary educators and the dominant storytellers, song-writers and poets. The tradition of the *griot* and the *griotte* is a long one, originating in the days of the Mali Empire and its founder, Sundiata Keita, and is common to a number of North African cultures. The griots, 'the keepers of memories', occupy the fascinating and diverse role of storytellers, diplomats, negotiators, marriage brokers, historians, genealogists, jesters and praise-singers at weddings and other events. The Tuareg say that when a griot dies, a library has burned to the ground. In the complex Tuareg caste system, the griots are artisans, 'blacksmiths', working in metal, wood and leather, and are regarded as having mystical powers through their association with the spirit world. This, together with their colourful and extrovert nature, means that they are frowned upon by the nobles while being intrinsically necessary to the functioning of their society. The women, the *griottes*, play an equally important role and recently have been singing for peace and reconciliation in Mali. Their music is intensely rhythmic and, like the Bedouin songs, dominated by drumming and traditional stringed instruments, in particular the *kora*, a multi-stringed form of harp.

This music has also been vital in the growing fame of 'Tuareg desert rock', led by the band Tinariwen, who have taken traditional desert music and blended it with Dylan, Chuck Berry and Hendrix into a unique, compelling and ever-expanding repertoire. Complex layers of driving rhythm are overlain by distinctive vocals and innova-tive guitars. The music is regarded as a message to the community and the outside world. The names and sounds of musicians from the Sahara – including, though certainly not limited to, Etran Finatawa, Toumani

Diabaté, Ali Farka Touré, Omara 'Bombino' Moctar, and the glorious female singer Fatoumata Diawara – become more global each year. The Tuareg musician Bombino is featured in the award-winning 2010 documentary film *Agadez: The Music and the Rebellion*, in which we are reminded that the origin of 'Tuareg' is the Arabic for 'lost soul' or 'rebel' but they call themselves *Imohag* or the Berber *Amazigh*, 'free men'. After two of his musicians were executed by the military, Bombino was forced to flee Niger: the discussion in the film is very much about freedom and what it means to be free.

The 'golden voice of Africa', Salif Keita, is extraordinary not only for his singing and his albinism, but because, as a direct descendant of the founder of the Mali Empire, he is a noble and should not be a singer at all. He has performed, along with many of the leading musicians of the desert, at Mali's annual Festival of the Desert. It is tragic that this event, at the time of writing, is no longer as securely accessible as it was.

Indigenous women from Australia's deserts also have a long tradition as educators, storytellers and singers, in addition to being the main calorie providers. Traditional songs and dance are, naturally, intimately linked to stories of the Ancestors and accounts of song lines and the Dreaming. As such, they are ritually divided between men and women. While the red centre has an equivalent modern growth of indigenous music to that of the Sahara, it is almost entirely dominated by men. Aboriginal country, rock and reggae music are immensely popular and provide an important means of cross-cultural understanding, but their themes are, understandably, often bitter stories of struggle and oppression. Women are rare participants. As Åse Ottoson of the Australian National University has written in 'The intercultural crafting of real Aboriginal country and manhood in Central Australia', country music is 'an important means for Aboriginal men in Central Australia to articulate contemporary forms of manhood and indigeneity'. However, while contemporary music of the Aboriginal peoples may be a male domain, art certainly is not; many of today's leading artists are women. As the Australian government website states:

> Painting and other art forms allow the women's stories and knowledge of country to be passed on. This expression also links the women to ceremonies, travelling in and knowledge about their country as well as their family histories.

77 Rose Nanala, *The Gathering*, 1965, acrylic.

It is often forgotten that the contemporary Australian Aboriginal art now admired and highly valued the world over has only been in existence since the early 1970s. Yes, it has its origins deep in traditional Dreamtime motifs of sand drawing and body painting, but the 'acrylic dots' are a modern expression. In 1971 Geoffrey Bardon, a teacher at a remote community in the Western Desert, encouraged children to try painting in the style of the designs of the adults, whom he then involved. The result was a large mural of the Honey Ant Dreaming, the dots used as a disguise for secret elements of the design. In spite of public interest being aroused by the work, it was painted over by the disapproving non-indigenous authorities. This was, however, the beginning of a dramatic and iconic movement in Australian art (see illus. 2). The paintings are intimately rooted in the desert and can perhaps be viewed (at least simplistically through the eyes of an outsider) as depictions of mental maps of place, memory and tradition. The image shown in illus. 77 is an example from the Great Sandy Desert and the Warlayirti artists' community. It is in my own collection and is titled *The Gathering*. Painted by Rose Nanala, both of whose parents were well-known artists, it depicts a scene from her childhood in the desert, some of the country around the Canning Stock Route; the long features are the dunes (the *tali* in Rose's language), the colours referencing different vegetation types and food sources. Around the waterhole the shapes are people gathered (probably women), with bark baskets (*coolamons*) or digging sticks. The desert is vibrant.

Many indigenous Australian artists are now producing dramatic work radically different from the traditional 'dot paintings', subjects of land and mythology remaining the focus. These paintings are a reminder that for Aboriginal peoples, who have no word for 'landscape', the desert is an ordered and harmonious place. In contrast to the Christian story of the fall from paradise, creation stories for Native Australians (and Americans) tell of a rise, from subterranean chaos into the sun and an intimate, ordered, relationship with the environment. Figurative painting (except for animals) is rare – the human body may itself be a canvas for the stories, but not in itself an object of interest.

Orient and Occident

While Native Australian artists may have little interest in depicting the human figure, in Islam it is prohibited. This may have limited the scope of Islamic art, but it encouraged alternative modes of expression in design, and, in particular, calligraphy that flowered into an art form in its own right, gracing manuscripts, textiles and mosque ornamentation. One of the most creative and expressive modern calligraphers is the Iraqi Hassan Massoudy, who often uses quotations from classic and modern writers, Arabic and Western, as inspirations for his works. The work shown here is a typically glorious flowing piece representing the words of the revered thirteenth-century Persian poet and Sufi mystic Rumi: *Woman is a ray of divine light* (illus. 78).

This is indeed the sentiment of much of Arabic poetry, women being cherished and respected (as long as they did not bring shame to their tribe or recite poetry). Yet that light is commonly, like the women themselves, hidden. Perhaps surprisingly, however, there is a strong thread of the sensual and even the explicitly erotic in Bedouin poetry. In Clinton Bailey's compilation, lines are found such as 'By God, what a maiden I've just now beheld' and 'From her firm upturned breasts I tore open the shirt'; a girl is described as having white cheeks and black eyes and breasts the size of a 'bustard's egg' (ostrich eggs are also used as analogies). Resonance with these very human emotions can arguably be seen in one of Wilfred Thesiger's more extraordinary photographs of Bedouin at a well (illus. 79).

It is probably necessary to admit that the response of a Westerner to this woman is coloured by a sense of the exotic, and therein lie the roots of one of the most contradictory narratives of the desert as inspiration and a quintessential division between the insider and the outsider: Orientalism. Nineteenth-century Britain was bookended by scandalous publications: in 1812 Lord Byron published the poem that would make him famous, *Childe Harold's Pilgrimage*, and in 1885 Sir Richard Burton's *The Book of the Thousand Nights and a Night* became available for private subscription. Both spoke of escape to foreign lands and cultures to indulge sexual proclivities unacceptable in the homeland and, as such, represent the century's great fascination with, and indulgence in, the exotic. Byron wrote the lengthy poem in his early twenties, during and after a three-year tour of Europe and the Levant. Childe Harold ('childe' being a medieval term for a young nobleman before knighthood) is the first Byronic hero, Byron himself: 'Few earthly things found favour in his sight/ Save concubines and carnal companie.' Harold is a flawed hero on a journey, struggling (eloquently) against himself and the world, beset by angst. The desert offers, once again, a place of refuge from the world:

Oh! that the Desert were my dwelling-place,
With one fair Spirit for my minister,
That I might all forget the human race,
And, hating no one, love but only her!

Burton was an enigma, described as an imperialist or as a cross-culturally sensitive outsider to his own culture who defended the rights

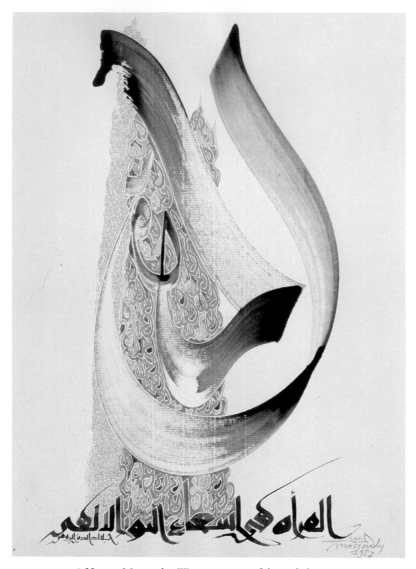

78 Hassan Massoudy, *Woman is a ray of divine light*, 1987.

of indigenous peoples. The true nature of this extraordinary man is undoubtedly at neither extreme, but the arguments persist. He spoke more than
25 languages and dialects and was an explorer, a military man, a diplomat
and, always, a devoted hedonist. He wrote in *Zanzibar*:

> Of the gladdest moments in human life, methinks, is the
> departure upon a distant journey into unknown lands. Shaking
> off with one mighty effort the fetters of Habit, the leaden weight

of Routine, the cloak of many Cares and the slavery of Hope, one feels once more happy. The blood flows with the fast circulation of childhood.

This was the view of the explorer, certainly, but also that of a man who sought opportunities to stimulate his blood circulation. Burton was an Orientalist in the context of both nineteenth-century imperialism and self-indulgence. The term came into wide use following Edward Said's controversial book of the same name, published in 1978. Said described the traditional meaning as that in which

> a very large mass of writers, among whom are poets, novelists, philosophers, political theorists, economists and imperial administrators, have accepted the basic distinction between East and West as the starting point for elaborate theories, epics, novels, social descriptions, and political accounts concerning the Orient, its people, customs, 'mind,' destiny and so on.

79 Wilfred Thesiger: Sa'ar Bedouin watering at a well in Yemen.

As Tissier's work in illus. 65 demonstrates, Said might well have added 'artists'. This Orientalism was intimately linked with the conflicts we have seen in the last two chapters, the 'civilized' versus the 'uncivilized', the outsider versus the insider, and the role of social Darwinism in the justification of colonial repression. As Europe discovered and conquered much of the rest of the world, the Occidental's view of the Oriental as exotic, as 'other' and as threatening 'civilized' society gained currency. The controversy arose as Said continued this view into modern times in which western culture, institutions and governments display 'a manner of regularized (or Orientalized) writing, vision, and study, dominated by imperatives, perspectives, and ideological biases ostensibly suited to the "Orient"'. The 'Orient' covers a vast swathe of diverse cultures from Turkey to China and Japan, but today 'Orientalism' is no different from the nineteenth century in that the focus is primarily on the Arab world. As we shall see, approaches to the issues of managing arid lands today are often tinged with what can only be described as modern Orientalism.

Orientalism in the nineteenth century developed in parallel with the exploration of North Africa and the Middle East, and with the growing dominance and narratives of colonial powers. French Orientalism found its home in North Africa, the British version in Arabia and the lands of the Bible. Byron was only one of countless Europeans (and, eventually, Americans, including Mark Twain) to embark on a Grand Tour in quest of classical sites and, where possible, biblical locations. In addition to having to journey through the lands of the Ottoman Empire dominated by Islam, the truth of the Holy Land was somewhat of a shock – the 'land flowing with milk and honey' was dusty desert and 'the shining city on a hill' a somewhat dilapidated provincial town. The seeds of Orientalism were sown, and, through the eyes of writers and artists, the culture and landscapes came to be romanticized and distorted. In the 1830s the Scottish artist David Roberts travelled extensively through Egypt and the Middle East and produced a vast number of watercolours and sketches which proved immensely popular, but they seem today somehow sanitized, the desert struggling in an attempt to equal the conventional beauty of the traditional European landscape, figures unrealistically posed. In trying to sketch Jerusalem, Roberts wrote that 'I have often laid down my pencil in despair'; later, when the Pre-Raphaelite artist Holman Hunt spent time in the Holy Land in quest of the face of Jesus, his depiction is indeed of a shining city on a hill.

On a secular and salacious level, it was the clichéd fantasy of the harem that captured the imagination of Western male artists – it would only be later when women travellers gained access and wrote accounts that reality competed with fantasy. This fantasy was particularly the vision of French artists, who were apparently not particularly intent on seeking their Christian roots in North Africa and the Middle East. A long succession of painters travelled to the colonies and elsewhere in search of the exotic, both in the landscape and in the odalisque. Gustave Guillaumet, Léon Belly, Jean-Léon Gérôme, Eugène Fromentin and Nasreddine Dinet are the prominent painters of French iconography, but Eugène Delacroix also visited Morocco and Algiers as part of a diplomatic mission in 1832 and produced some luminous watercolour sketchbooks and paintings. Matisse would later visit and comment that 'I have found landscapes in Morocco exactly as they are described in Delacroix's paintings.' Nevertheless, while inspiring Picasso, *The Women of Algiers in their Apartment* by Delacroix is a classic work of Orientalist sexual fantasy. A number of the Orientalist painters spent long periods of time actually travelling and living in the colonies – Dinet, while continuing to paint copious numbers of voluptuous nudes, moved to the Algerian oasis town of Bou-Saada in 1904, converted to Islam and was a vocal critic of colonialism. The desert is rarely a subject in its own right in the works of the Orientalists, but forms a sweeping backdrop to many of the figurative works. Belly's *Pilgrims Going to Mecca* (illus. 80) and Fromentin's *The Land of Thirst* (illus. 81) are fine examples. Fromentin wrote eloquently of his desert journeys, fascinated by 'the colour of emptiness'.

In the same year that Dinet moved to the desert, Isabelle Eberhardt drowned a few hundred kilometres to the southwest (chapter Two). Born in Switzerland in 1877, Eberhardt was the illegitimate daughter of an aristocratic woman of Russian descent and a former Russian Orthodox priest turned anarchist. In most ways the outcast of the family, she was essentially raised as a boy, cropping her hair and dress-ing accordingly. She became addicted to the contemporary writing of Pierre Loti (actually Louis-Marie-Julien Viaud), a diminutive and highly imaginative Frenchman who travelled North Africa and Turkey as, in the tradition of Orientalism, an escape from his own culture and an opportunity for self-indulgence. While Loti's tormented, melan-cholic and highly fanciful writing was at the same time adored and derided in his home country, it was deeply attractive to the young Isabelle.

She saw in him a soulmate and felt 'the *same sad calls* towards the *Unknown*, towards an *Elsewhere*'. Loti may have been sympathetic to Islam and its cultural history, but the young Isabelle eagerly immersed herself in it, learning Arabic by the time she was sixteen, voraciously consuming Sufism and its poetry and ultimately spending most her life dressed as an Arab man. Although she may have been influenced by Loti, and during her sojourns in North Africa vigorously promiscuous, nevertheless at heart she was the antithesis of the typical Orientalist. To describe Isabelle Eberhardt's motivations as mysterious is very much an understatement, but through her writing and influence she contributed importantly to the subversion of colonialism. Eberhardt has been the subject of a forgettable 1991 film (with Peter O'Toole), Timberlake Wertenbaker's first published play, *New Anatomies*, and a modern opera, *Song from the Uproar* by the New York composer Missy Mazzoli. However, she is still best approached through her writing. The desert, its skies 'religious in their vastness', and its people captured her soul and her writing captures the reader: 'Oh Sahara, menacing Sahara, hiding your beautiful, grave soul under your bleak, desolate emptiness. Oh yes, I love this country of sand and stone.' Melancholy was also deeply ingrained in her soul: 'One must never look for happiness: one meets it by the way – but it is always going in the opposite direction.'

Lost borders, little rain and the Sublime

As Isabelle Eberhardt was immersing herself in the melancholy of the Sahara, across the world another woman was writing with equal eloquence of the Mojave Desert. Mary Hunter Austin opened the desert and its people to her readers with the same meticulous detail and, often, the same sense of melancholy. In her classic *The Land of Little Rain*, published the year before Eberhardt's death, she wrote, 'And yet – and yet – is it not perhaps to satisfy expectation that one falls into the tragic key in writing of desertness?' The expectation was that of her eastern audience, who were still struggling to come to grips with the reality of their desert frontier, but the contrast between the beauty of the landscape and the tragedies of its human inhabitants is a thread that runs through all of Austin's work. Ten years earlier she had published a short story, 'Mother of Felipe', in a San Francisco magazine. A moving account of the death of a son, mourning, burial and re-burial, it begins

80 Leon Belly, *Pilgrims Going to Mecca*, 1861.
81 Eugène Fromentin, *The Land of Thirst*, c. 1869.

with a description of the contradiction of the desert as a place of beauty
and threat:

> A country to be avoided by the solitary traveler, with its hard,
> inhospitable soil, and its vast monotony of contour and color.
> A country sublime in its immensity of light, and soft unvarying

tints – fawn, and olive, and pearl, with glistening stretches of white sand, and brown hollows between the hills, out of which the gray and purple shadows creep at night. A country laid visibly under the ban of eternal silence.

It seems in retrospect almost tragic that the deserts of the western u.s. captured the imagination of 'civilized' east coast society not through the words of Mary Austin, but through those of a contemporary writer, John C. Van Dyke, who was, to all intents and purposes, a charlatan. His book *The Desert* was published in 1901, a couple of years before Austin's first major work, *The Land of Little Rain*; it remains routinely described as a classic of desert literature and in a sense it is. What it is not is an intimate personal account of the place. Van Dyke was a prominent art historian and critic at Rutgers University, who took the elitist view that the desert is a canvas that, like all art, represents an aesthetic that could not properly be appreciated by the common man. And as for the ability of the desert insider to appreciate his surroundings, 'Doubtless, a wealth of color and atmospheric effect was wasted upon the aboriginal retina.' The writing style is hyperbolic, littered with exclamation points and passages such as 'That beam of light! Was there ever anything so beautiful!' and

> High in the zenith rides the desert moon. What a flood of light comes from it! What pale, phosphorescent light! . . . And far away against the dark mountains the dunes of the desert shine white as snow-clad hills in December.

Van Dyke did indeed visit the deserts of the southwest, but, as Peter Wild argues convincingly in his introduction to the reprint of the book, rather than setting out bravely and alone into the wilderness, as he claimed, he spent much of his time at his brother's ranch and on a train. Reading his account today brings no sense whatsoever of personal experience, of observations and reactions that are genuinely Van Dyke's. It contains numerous inaccuracies, including patently incorrect descriptions of desert creatures. When Van Dyke describes the coyote, the reader is left to wonder if he had ever actually seen one: 'The prairie wolf or coyote is not at all like the gray wolf. He seldom runs after things, though he does a good deal of running away from them.' When Mary Austin recounts how she had 'trailed a coyote often, going across country', the reader believes her typically idiosyncratic description – it is something she has witnessed:

> The coyote is your true water-witch, one who snuffs and paws, snuffs and paws again at the smallest spot of moisture-scented earth until he has freed the blind water from the soil. Many water-holes are no more than this detected by the lean hobo of the hills in localities where not even an Indian would look for it.

Van Dyke can be viewed as an American Orientalist who happened to travel westward. His early environmentalist enthusiasm for the preservation of the desert is undermined by his close association with Andrew Carnegie, at the same time a philanthropist and one of the great robber barons of east coast society and commerce, to whom Van Dyke dedicated his book. *The Desert* reveals more about how that society came to perceive its far-flung frontier than about the place itself; it was reprinted fourteen times before 1930 and the modern edition still sells a thousand copies a year. Meanwhile, Mary Austin, though recognized and respected today, struggled to make a living. Nevertheless, she had gained wide respect by the time she published *The Land of Journey's End* in 1924, described in the *New York Times* as 'written out of such knowledge of the region, its characteristics and inhabitants as, possibly, is shared by no other general writer, and with an understating, love and sympathy that tip her pen with flame and color'.

Both Austin and Van Dyke were, in their own contrasting styles, influential in shaping the perception of America's arid lands in the eyes of an east coast society to whom those landscapes were entirely alien. Peter Wild's definition of the desert as 'a place where habits learned in humid areas are bound to fail' applies as much to the aesthetic as the practical. As the American historian, writer and conservationist Wallace Stegner commented in his essay 'Thoughts in a Dry Land':

> Scale is the first and easiest of the West's lessons. Colors and forms are harder. Easterners are constantly being surprised and somehow offended that California's summer hills are gold, not green. We are creatures shaped by our experiences; we like what we know, more often than we know what we like . . . Sagebrush is an acquired taste, as are raw earth and alkali flats.

Often called the 'dean of Western writers', Stegner also observed that in order to see the American west as beautiful,

> You have to get over the colour green; you have to quit asso-
> ciating beauty with gardens and lawns; you have to get used to
> an inhuman scale; you have to understand geological time.

Van Dyke was an admirer of John Ruskin and, in his own way, perhaps among the first writers to apply Ruskin's ideas of the Sublime in art and the landscape to the desert. While the idea that a natural scene could evoke in the observer's imagination a sense of overwhelming violence and threat originates with Kant, it was thoroughly explored by Ruskin, and, in the 1920s, by the German theologian Rudolf Otto with his theories of the *numinous*, closely related to the Sublime. For Otto this concept underlay all religion and was made up of three components: the *mysterium* (a sense of the wholly other beyond normal experience), which is *tremendum* (inspiring the feeling of overpowering terror, dread and one's own nothingness) and *fascinans* (in spite of the threat, having an irresistible and mystical allure). Whether the numinous or the Sublime, this surely describes the power of the desert as the place of spirituality – of every kind – that we have considered here, 'a land', in the words of Mary Austin, 'whose beauty takes the breath like pain'. In her fascin-ation with the desert and its relationships with the people in it, she would have enjoyed a conversation with the modern Chinese-American geog-rapher Yi-Fu Tuan. Tuan continues the contemplation of the Sublime with his ideas on human geography, the place as the context for religion, art, philosophy and psychology. He escaped China with his family in 1940, moving eventually to the u.s. via Australia, the Philippines and the uk. It was at the University of California, Berkeley, in the 1950s that he devel-oped his passion for the desert, spending long periods alone in the Mojave and writing his PhD thesis on desert landforms. In the preface to *Topophilia* he wrote how

> The desert, including the barren parts and (I would even say)
> especially those, appeals to me. I see in it purity, timelessness, a
> generosity of mind and spirit. The bleached skull in the desert,
> far from evoking the odor of death, suggests something clean
> and noble that may crumble into dust but is exempt from the
> humiliation of decay.

His interests moved on from conventional geography to the consideration of the relationships between culture and landscape, the perceptions of insiders and outsiders: 'Of course, peoples of the desert (nomads as well as sedentary farmers in oases) love their homeland: without exception humans grow attached to their native places, even if these should seem derelict of quality to outsiders.'

His first major article on his thinking was 'Mountains, Ruins, and the Sentiment of Melancholy' – Isabelle Eberhardt would also perhaps have enjoyed a conversation. Tuan's best-known book, quoted above, is *Topophilia: A Study of Environmental Perception, Attitudes, and Values*, published first in 1974, a complex work in which he explores how we experience a place, a landscape, with senses beyond simply the visual. He describes the occasion as a student when he and a few friends had slept out in Death Valley and how, on waking, he was presented with a scene 'of such unearthly beauty that I felt transported to a supernal realm and yet, paradoxically, also at home, as though I had returned after a long absence'.

Austin and Eberhardt opened the twentieth century to the idea of a desert aesthetic, opened the public's eyes to a more accurate understanding of the place and its people and ushered in a long period of recalibration of our perception of arid lands. Mary Austin was a member of the somewhat eccentric groups that gathered in Santa Fe and Taos, 'artists' colonies' that were the precursors of the utopian communities that would spring up on the margins of the desert and society. In 1921 the *New York Times* described Taos as 'the garden of Allah in the New World; an oasis of twentieth-century culture in a vast desert of primitive nature'. These groups were fluid, but the epicentre was the Taos property of Mabel Dodge Luhan, wealthy patron of the arts, writer and friend of Austin. Among the artists and writers who spent time in spiritual retreat at the Taos oasis were many whose names would become renowned. Ansel Adams was a great admirer of Austin and the two collaborated on *Taos Pueblo*, a limited edition, large-format book of Adams's photographs and Austin's writing; later they would publish an edition of *Land of Little Rain* illustrated by Adams. Laura Gilpin, the photographer whom Adams called 'one of the most important photographers of our time', was also a guest of Luhan and, inspired by the landscapes of Taos and Santa Fe and the people in them, went on to be a dramatically innovative photographer, producing luminous works until her death in 1979. Among the Taos artists embraced by Luhan were George Bellows, Edward Hopper and Georgia O'Keeffe, along with dance choreographer Martha Graham. It was at Taos that Carl Jung had his first conversation with a non-white person, a Hopi elder, an experience that made him appreciate that he was trapped 'in the cultural consciousness of the white man'. With Austin and Luhan as champions of Native Americans and their culture (Luhan had married Tony Luhan, a member of the Pueblo people), the topic was a constant theme of discussion. Writers included Willa Cather, Aldous Huxley, Gertrude Stein, Thornton Wilder and D. H. Lawrence, who wrote that 'New Mexico was the greatest experience from the outside world that I have ever had. It certainly changed me forever', and

> the moment I saw the brilliant, proud morning shine high up over the deserts of Santa Fe, something stood still in my soul, and I started to attend . . . In the magnificent fierce morning of New Mexico one sprang awake, a new part of the soul woke up suddenly and the old world gave way to a new.

Certainly his time in New Mexico was significant for Lawrence and inspired perhaps some of his best writing, although not the great American novel that Luhan had hoped for. He did, however, write some mildly satirical descriptions of those literary women and the occasional inconsistencies in their approach to Native American rights.

The Taos group of Mabel Dodge Luhan was influential in re-framing the desert for the twentieth century. It was not, however, exactly utopian and was certainly not the first to seek the inspiration of the desert for such communities. Some years after his sojourn in Taos, Aldous Huxley, increasingly and controversially disconnected from world events (most importantly the Second World War), withdrew to the Mojave Desert where he found 'an expression of divine joy'. In the hope that the climate would help his failing eyesight, Huxley devoted himself to reflection, mysticism and writing on a ranch 100 kilometres east of Los Angeles. The property was set amid the ruins of the failed socialist utopian colony of Llano del Rio, established in 1914 by Job Harriman, a Marxist lawyer from Los Angeles who had failed twice to be elected mayor of the city. Within a few years, over a thousand people lived there, setting up farming, schools, a sawmill, a theatre and a library. Unfortunately, they strayed from utopian ways, and internal strife, economic incompetence and the wrath of local ranchers over their excessive use of water led to the colony being ended and dispersed in 1918. Huxley, having gazed out at the ruins each day of his retreat in the desert, would later write an essay, 'Ozymandias, the Desert Utopia that Failed', in reference to Shelley's famous poem: 'Round the decay / Of that colossal wreck, boundless and bare / The lone and level sands stretch far away.' The story of Llano del Rio served to reinforce Huxley's view of dystopia rather than utopia. As a hermit himself, Huxley reflected on the early Christian mystics, including St Anthony, in 'The Desert', its 'boundlessness and emptiness', and the fact that 'The desert can drive men mad, but it can also help them to become supremely sane.' He goes on to observe the modern dystopian developments of the desert and that 'The wilderness has entered the armament race, and will be in it to the end. In its multimillion-acred emptiness there is room enough to explode atomic bombs and experiment with guided missiles.' Observing the survival skills of the desert's non-human inhabitants, he speculates on the chances of human survival, after which, if it does occur, is 'transfiguration; beyond and including animal grace is the grace of that other not-self, of which the desert silence and the desert emptiness are the most expressive'.

Llano del Rio was the first in a long tradition of desert communities of the American west established and sought out by modern ascetics, followers of counter-cultural mystics (genuine or not), extraterrestrial mediums, and general misfits and outliers of society. Hari Kunzru swept many of these characters into his complex, compelling and masterfully written novel *Gods Without Men* (2012), a title that echoes Balzac. The story is centred around Pinnacle Rocks, a fictional three-fingered Mojave geological landmark long perceived as mystical. Sub-stories follow a Spanish friar and silver miners, together with the Native American mythology of the place. The Ashtar Galactic Command, a UFO cult, plays a prominent role, as do a fake Iraqi town (and its real Iraqi 'inhabitants') built by the military in the desert for exercises, a disintegrating British rock star facing his demons and the shape-shifting trickster Coyote god. The central story is the disappearance of the four-year-old son of a Sikh non-believer (a creator of Wall Street financial algorithms) and his Jewish wife; they have come on vacation to the desert in search of family healing.

The motivation of nineteenth-century Orientalists and hermits to seek in the desert opportunities for freedom and self-discovery is echoed in the real-life counter-cultures of modern times. In 1991 The San

82 Burning Man festival in the Black Rock Desert.

Francisco Cacophony Society 'in pursuit of experience beyond the pale of mainstream society today' began holding its festivals on a playa lake in the Nevadan desert. The Burning Man festival has become a counter-cultural gathering every year since, 'an opportunity to leave your old self and be reborn through the cleansing fires of the trackless, pure desert'; participants of every stripe number in excess of 50,000 (illus. 81) and the event culminates in the very pagan ritual burning of a wooden effigy. In the words of Mojave Desert artist Diane Best, 'people go to the desert to re-invent themselves' – even temporarily.

Journeys and strangers

The U.S. novelist John Gardner is reported to have remarked that there are only two plots in all of fiction: someone goes on a journey and a stranger comes to town. This is, of course, open to discussion, but these categories describe essentially all desert films. The playa lake-bed where Burning Man is held is in the Black Rock Desert and the classic *Bad Day at Black Rock* falls firmly into the second group. Thanks to a typically fine performance by Spencer Tracy (and a startlingly young Lee Marvin), the story of a remote town (when Tracy arrives, it is the first time that the train has stopped there in four years) with a dark secret and a dystopian male population is transformed into a still very watchable movie. The town is run by the sociopathic Reno Smith, played by Robert Ryan, who at one point comments to Tracy that 'Somebody's always looking for something in this part of the West . . . But to us, this place is our West, and I wish they'd leave us alone.' Filmed in the Black Rock Desert, however, it was not – the Sierras in the background testify to the location as Lone Pine, in the Owens Valley just down the road from Mary Austin's house and a favourite western filming location. The entire and enduring Hollywood genre of the 'western' would not exist without the lingering romance of manifest destiny – and the desert landscape.

The desert movie should perhaps be a genre in its own right. The setting has provided the backdrop, and often a character, for countless movies from the first version of *The Garden of Allah* (1916) through the Oscar-winning *Lawrence of Arabia* and *The English Patient*, to James Bond and *Quantum of Solace* and *No Country for Old Men*, via *Zabriskie Point* and a host of often truly mediocre offerings over the last century. The best of the three versions of *The Garden of Allah* starred Marlene Dietrich and Charles Boyer and was made in 1936 by David O. Selznick. It is in the grand tradition of Orientalist films involving white women, the Sahara and a stranger, most often an exotic Arab but in this case a Trappist Monk. The silent film *The Sheik* (1921) recounts a dramatic and romantic entanglement between Lady Diana Mayo and Sheik Ahmed Ben Hassan, played by Rudolph Valentino, who was launched as a star as a result (in the sequel, and Valentino's last film, *Son of the Sheik*, 1926, he played both roles). Fifty years later, the theme would be reprised, this time based loosely on fact, in *The Wind and the Lion*, in which an American woman (Candice Bergen) falls into the hands of Mulai Ahmed er Raisuli, a Berber brigand played by Sean Connery. The reality was that, in 1904, an American businessman was kidnapped by the very real Raisuli, creating an international incident, but his gender was changed in the film for the sake of romantic require-ments. Completely fabricated military engagements between Berbers, Germans and Americans were added. The film's style owes much to *Lawrence of Arabia*, *The Sheik* and *The Four Feathers*, of which there have been no fewer than seven versions, beginning in 1915. A story of empire, cowardice and redemption set against the epic backdrops of the Egyptian and Sudanese desert in the attempt to relieve General Gordon at Khartoum, the 1939 version is the classic. The Khartoum theme was repeated in the 1966 film of the same name and is memorable only for the spectacular double miscasting of Charlton Heston as Gordon and Sir Lawrence Olivier (with a skin colour as strange as his accent) as the rebel leader, the Mahdi.

The desert lends itself perfectly to the 'someone goes on a journey' story and there are endless examples in film, a few of which are memorable. In *Lawrence of Arabia* the slow, intensely suspenseful, threatening and entirely silent arrival on a camel of Omar Sharif as Sherif Ali, across the wide empty desert, is perhaps one of the most gripping sequences in the cinema of the desert. It was a scene that was effectively echoed in the strange psychological drama *The Passenger* (1975). In this film by Michelangelo Antonioni, the troubled Jack Nicholson uses the chance discovery of a corpse to re-invent himself. In an early scene the reporter, Locke, played by Nicholson, completely unequipped both logistically and psychologically for solo desert travel, becomes stranded, with no water and his Land Rover embedded in the sand through his incompetence. In the distance a man on a camel slowly approaches, the camera following his progress – and he rides by, completely ignoring Locke.

A geologist watching many of these movies suffers from conflicting emotions: a thorough enjoyment of the landscape, attempting through its geology to identify the location, and often complete disdain for and frustration with the incompetence of the protagonists. A friend once suggested that there is really only one story: someone does something stupid. This certainly covers films such as Antonioni's *Zabriskie Point* and finds its ultimate realization in the interminable desert film *Gerry*. In this 2002 work by Gus Van Sant, Matt Damon and Casey Affleck become, for close to 100 minutes and through their own stupidity, terminally lost in magnificent desert landscapes that mysteriously fluctuate between Argentina, Death Valley and Utah.

The 'someone goes on a desert journey' theme is made for Australia and became fundamental to the flowering of that country's cinema as it explored the cultural legacy of the red centre. Capitalizing on the landscapes, the wildlife, a little nudity and the outsider's perception of Aboriginal people's spiritual journeys, *Walkabout* experienced a varied reception when it was released in 1971, called by some critics 'a masterpiece' before essentially disappearing until the director's cut became available in 1996. In its cross-cultural pessimism it is a prescient indictment of the insider-outsider relationships that were discussed in chapter Three and there was much controversy at the time about whether it was a properly 'Australian' film. But it was also in many ways a celebration of the outback environment and people. The year 1971 was ground-breaking for Australian cinema with the release also of *Wake in Fright*, a dark and violent film noir with Donald Pleasence that fits into both the journey and the stranger comes to town categories. *Walkabout* was the first of many films to star David Gulpilil, the wonderful indigenous actor (whose name was misspelled in the original credits). Gulpilil was sixteen in *Walkabout* and went on to become an activist for Aboriginal rights and take roles in, among other films, *Rabbit-Proof Fence* and *The Tracker*, further classics of desert journeys. Gulpilil also appears in what I think is the finest of the Australian outback films, *The Proposition*, released in 2005. The award-winning film (screenplay and haunting score written by Nick Cave) reinvents the tradition of the western, and again celebrates the landscape. With memorable performances by Ray Winston and John Hurt, it is, however, a physically and culturally violent film, with dystopian echoes of the American writer Cormac McCarthy.

It is only in the last few years that films by indigenous Australians have gained international attention. In 1992 Rachel Perkins, an Arrernte woman from the desert east of Alice Springs, set up Blackfella Films, a production company for work by Aboriginal people that has been creating award-winning factual and narrative films, shorts and features, ever since.

Warwick Thornton describes how, as a DJ, he had been hanging around the studios of the Central Australian Aboriginal Media Association radio station in Alice Springs for twenty years waiting to make a feature film. In 2009 he did: *Samson and Delilah* is a brutal, heart-rending and extraordinary story of youth and the challenges for Aboriginal peoples of retaining dignity in today's Australia. It was shown at film festivals worldwide, won an award at Cannes, and Aboriginal cinema was propelled, rightly, on to the global stage.

And what of insider cinema from other arid lands? It is understandable but unfortunate that a nomad is not inclined to carry a camera. Nevertheless, every country has its film-makers and its national industry and their work is sometimes accessible to a Western audience. Nacer Khemir is a Tunisian director whose *Desert Trilogy* has gained international recognition. Khemir describes himself as deeply influenced by the stories of *One Thousand and One Nights* and Sufi mysticism, and both form strong elements in his films, in which, as he also says, the desert is a character in itself. On his love of the desert, he has commented that:

The desert is a literary field and a field of abstraction at the same time. It is one of the rare places where the infinitely small, that is a speck of sand, and the infinitely big, and that is billions of specks of sand, meet. It is also a place where one can have a true sense of the Universe and of its scale. The desert also evokes the Arabic language, which bears the memory of its origins. In every Arabic word, there is a bit of flowing sand. It is also one of the main sources of Arabic love poetry.

The films themselves, *The Wanderers of the Desert*, *The Dove's Lost Necklace*, and *Bab'Aziz, The Prince Who Contemplated His Soul*, made between 1986 and 2005, are fairy tales; they are filled with complex layers of fables and imagery that can be challenging for the Western viewer. But at the same time they are hypnotic and fascinating in their visual richness, with the score, as well as the desert, being an intimate part of the narrative. The first is clearly in the 'stranger comes to town' category, with a teacher arriving at a remote desert village, almost uninhabited except for the strange ghostly procession in the sands that men feel compelled to join. Mythology becomes a mysterious reality when Sinbad's boat, complete with sail, appears in the desert. In *The Dove's Lost Necklace* are layered stories of the quest for lost love and gardens in the desert. *Bab'Aziz* is another journey story, that of a blind old man travelling in a spiritual quest across the desert with his granddaughter to attend a meeting of dervishes and die. In discussing the motives for the film, Khemir states that 'Fundamentalism, as well as radicalism, is a distorting mirror of Islam. This movie is a modest effort to give Islam its real image back.'

Gerardo Olivares, although Spanish, has made two films that tell stories of people in the Sahara. In times when the appalling deaths of desperate migrants attempting to cross the desert make regular news, his film of 2007, *14 kilómetros*, makes for depressingly topical and compelling viewing. Fourteen kilometres separate Africa from Europe, but for a young woman fleeing forced marriage and abuse and a would-be footballer and his brother who leave Niger for a better life, the distance is infinite. A kind of 'docudrama', the film superbly draws the viewer into their personal stories of hope, anguish and tragedy. Football is the entire theme of Olivares' film *La gran final*, an eclectic and utterly delightful story of groups of people in the Sahara, the Gobi of Mongolia and the Amazon rainforest united in their determination to find a means of watching the 2002 World Cup final between Germany and Brazil. The Saharan caravan succeeds in rigging up a TV antenna on the sculpture that replaced the lone tree of Ténéré after it had been demolished by an inebriated truck driver (chapter Six), the Mongolians steal electricity from a transmission line and in the Amazon the Indian Brazil fans, after discovering that their women had taken the cables of their own TV for jewellery, eventually succeed in watching the game from outside the hut of forest workers.

There is a thriving film industry in many countries of the Sahara and the Sahel, the language commonly French, the distribution far from global. Malian director Cheick Oumar Sissoko's *Guimba the Tyrant* is a visually stunning story, set at some undefined time in the past, of lust and a despot's downfall. Part slapstick comedy, part political satire, the film features a griot as its chorus and commentator – 'A griot has no shame, but he has scruples.' *Bamako*, by Abderrahmane Sissako (not to be confused with Sissoko), is most definitely a political commentary, a courtroom drama in a Malian village courtyard. Improbably, the World Bank and the International Monetary Fund are on trial for causing social and environmental degradation, but the viewer's disbelief is creatively suspended. The testimony of an old man, officially denied his say, sung and chanted, and untranslated (the court would not have understood his dialect either), is memorable cinema. Sissako's highly acclaimed *Timbuktu* was selected to open the Palme d'Or competition at the 2014 Cannes Film Festival.

The breadth and variety of ways in which the desert has played a role and provided the critical setting for film-making is spectacular, the moving image in a static landscape. This brief and very personal survey only begins to open the window on to that variety. It is impossible not to at least mention some omissions: *The Story of the Weeping Camel*; Werner Herzog's strange *Fata Morgana* and *Where the Green Ants Dream*; *Nostalgia for the Light*, Patricio Guzmán's luminous reflection on the desert and the legacy of Pinochet; *Rango*, the animated feature on water wars; *Ice Cold in Alex* and the other classics of the North African campaign; all the spaghetti westerns set in Spain; *Ashes of Time* (martial arts in the dunes of the Gobi); *The Gods Must be Crazy*.

The desert as a setting for spiritual and counter-cultural exploration, for real and imagined utopia and dystopia, has been enthusiastically exploited in film. Huxley wrote *Ape and Essence*, his post-war, post-apocalyptic revisit of *Brave New World* in California where the novel is set; much of the work is written as a screenplay, and Huxley worked on a stage version – a precursor to the *Planet of the Apes* films. The *Mad Max* franchise has spawned countless, largely forgettable, films in the same vein.

Cinema has also explored the fact that the desert has long been the last refuge of eccentrics – whether attracted to or created by the character of the place – and the marginalized: *Bagdad Café*, *Bombay Beach*, *Raising Arizona*. In Wim Wenders's *Paris, Texas* an amnesiac stranger walks out of the Devil's Graveyard in the desert of southwest Texas and into a ramshackle bar in which a crude sign declares: 'The dust has come to stay. You may stay or pass on through or whatever.' Ry Cooder's superb slide guitar soundtrack resonates with both the real and the urban desert of the film. The documentary *Amargosa* tells the story of the real-life eccentric Marta Becket, a dancer from New York City who in 1967 removed herself to Death Valley Junction (population fewer than twenty) and spent decades restoring and performing in the Armagosa Opera House. Together with the adjacent hotel, the buildings featured in David Lynch's *Lost Highway*. And the desert offers opportunities for solitude and refuge in the quest for, and manufacture of, illicit pharmaceuticals: *Crystal Fairy*, television's *Breaking Bad*. The list goes on.

Does the desert look back?

In his *Blue Highways: A Journey Into America*, William Least Heat-Moon, a writer of both Native American and European roots, crafted one of the great journey narratives. In it he writes eloquently of one of the fundamental sources of the inspiration of the desert: the place as a voice, as a character: 'The desert does its best talking at night, but on that spring evening it kept God's whopping silence; and that too is a desert voice.' He continues:

> The immensity of sky and desert, their vast absences, reduced me. It was as if I were evaporating . . . I looked out the side window. For an instant, I thought the desert looked back. Against the glass a reflection of an opaque face. I couldn't take my attention from that presence that was mostly an absence.

In West Texas:

The night, taking up the shadows and details, wiped the face of the desert into a simple, uncluttered blackness until there were only three things: land, wind, stars. I was there too, but my presence I felt more than saw. It was as if I had been reduced to mind, to an edge of consciousness. Men, ascetics, in all eras have gone into deserts to lose themselves – Jesus, Saint Anthony, Saint Basil, and numberless medicine men – maybe because such a losing happens almost as a matter of course here if you avail yourself. The Sioux once chanted, 'All over the sky a sacred voice is calling.'

This is the desert of Paul Bowles, of Isabelle Eberhardt, of Mary Austin, of Albert Camus, of Jack Kerouac.

And, as a voice, does the desert have a gender? In the opening scene of the film of *The English Patient* the texture of the dunes is one of feminine sensuality. The desert in Arabic is a feminine noun, and women writers and artists working in the aggressively masculine American desert frontier routinely saw the desert as feminine. But not passively feminine. Mary Austin wrote one long descriptive sentence that begins, 'If the desert were a woman, I know well what like she would be: deep-breasted, broad in the hips, tawny, with tawny hair, great masses of it lying smooth along her perfect curves.' Decades later the Hispanic American writer Pat Mora, in her collection of poems titled *Chants*, includes 'Unrefined':

> The desert is no lady.
> She screams at the spring sky,
> dances with her skirts high,
> kicks sand, flings tumbleweeds,
> digs her nails into all flesh.
> Her unveiled lust fascinates the sun.

The intimate relationship between women writers and the American desert continues. In *Tséyi': Deep in the Rock, Reflections on the Canyon de Chelly*, Navaho poet Laura Tohe includes two stunning poems contrasting 'Male Rain' and 'Female Rain'. And in *a rambling chronicle* Neysa Griffith includes a description, an answer to a riddle, that beautifully captures the essence of the desert:

what empties fullness
and fills emptiness
is the desert

Women's voices have long created powerful views of the desert. To
Mary Austin and the U.S. writers we can add not only Isabelle Eberhardt
but also Mildred Cable and Gertrude Bell (chapter Seven). Simone de
Beauvoir wrote that 'The Sahara was a spectacle as alive as the sea.' A
contemplation of the desert and the sea is sufficient for an entire book
in its own right. Far beyond the simple analogies of 'seas of sand', the
two seemingly contrasting environments have proved fertile ground
for writers and philosophers. W. H. Auden explored the desert and the
sea extensively, not only in his mystical schemes of the real world versus
paradise and hell, but in *The Enchafèd Flood* and in *The Sea and the Mirror*,
his commentary on Shakespeare's *The Tempest*. He has Alonso urging
Ferdinand to find a way of ruling 'Between the watery vagueness and / The
triviality of the sand' and, in some early versions (as discussed by Arthur
Kirsch in his textual notes on the poem), Alonso ruminates at length:

> Both are dreadful in their own way; our fear of the sea
> Is our terror of the unknown; our fear of the desert
> Is our terror of others; being exposed ourselves.

I am painfully reminded, again, of Edward Abbey's comment on
the fishermen hauling up the sea in his nets: my net is inevitably coarse.
I have included no discussion of the Nobel Prize winning work of
J.-M.G. Le Clézio, notably his lyrical novel *Desert*, nor *Quarantine*, Jim
Crace's startling revisionist narrative of Christ in the desert. I have not
introduced T. S. Eliot's view of despair and the desert in 'The Waste
Land'. I have not recounted the modern epic and painful desert journeys
of Geoffrey Moorhouse (*The Fearful Void*) or Robyn Davidson and her
beloved camels (*Tracks*, now also an internationally acclaimed film). I
have not reminded the reader of *The Desert Music*, the strange
collaboration between William Carlos Williams and Steve Reich, or the
equally difficult composition *Déserts* by Edgard Varèse. I should recognize
the often lurid role played by the desert in today's video games. I have
not paid tribute to the glorious sweeping landscapes of the desert
through the paraglider-born photography of George Steinmetz. And,
on the grand scale, I have not begun to explore the way in which art and

83 *Desert Breath,* land art in the Egyptian desert by Danae Stratou
and the D.A.ST. Arteam, 1997.

desert landscape join in the land art, the 'earthworks', of Robert Smithson, Michael Heizer, Richard Long and so many others. Long's circles in the Sahara and the Gobi, Heizer's massive *City* in the Nevada desert, Jim Denevan's ephemeral designs in the Black Rock Desert – all are formed from the land, are part of the land and ultimately return to the land. In 1997 Danae Stratou, Alexandra Stratou and Stella Constantinides completed their 100,000-square-metre earthwork *Desert Breath* in the Sahara close to the Red Sea (illus. 83). It is an intricate and precise design of spirals and cones of sand, protruding and inverted, with, occasionally, a small body of water at its centre. As the creators comment, 'Desert Breath still exists, becoming through its slow disintegration, an instrument to measure the passage of time.'

The passage of time. In 1996 (or 01996) computer scientist Danny Hillis teamed up with Stewart Brand, writer, editor and entrepreneur, to begin work on the Clock of the Long Now project with the intention of constructing a series of clocks that would run, unattended, for 10,000 years. Brand wrote that

Such a clock, if sufficiently impressive and well-engineered, would embody deep time for people. It should be charismatic to visit, interesting to think about, and famous enough to become iconic in the public discourse. Ideally, it would do for thinking about time what the photographs of Earth from space have done for thinking about the environment. Such icons reframe the way people think.

The first clock is under construction in a mountain in the desert of West Texas, the second is planned for the high desert of Nevada, described by Brand as 'a timeless landscape'. Timeless, vast, emptying fullness and filling emptiness: an inspiration.

SIX

Ancient and Modern, Boom and Bust

THE CLOCKS OF THE Long Now contemplate 10,000 years into the future. The science of geology, the clock of the very long then, peers deep into the past, calibrates it to the present and, in turn, applies its conclusions to contemplating the future. Rocks tell stories in their own language, the geologist translates, interprets and retells those stories, linking them together into a narrative that spans a time scale that may be a challenge to comprehend but at least makes sense. However, it is a narrative that can never be continuous for so many stories have been lost.

There is a story from the hills of northwestern South Africa, a story of fast-flowing rivers flushing their cargoes of sand and gravel down from the hills, then drying up, their beds exposed to winds that played with the sand, blowing it into dunes that grew and wandered and smothered the old river landscape. Then some moisture returned and the tops of the dunes were covered in rippled layers of sand grains, their journeys slowed by sticking to the damp surface which developed mud-cracks as it was alternately moistened and dried out. It's a story of climate change, which took place 3.2 billion years ago.

The story comes from the so-called Barberton Greenstone Belt, one of oldest preserved pieces of continent on the planet, and the 3.2-billion-year-old sandstones are the oldest evidence of the work of the wind that we have so far discovered. And sand*stones* they certainly are: the primeval rivers and dune sands have been caught up in the tortured history of the early earth, baked to temperatures of several hundred degrees Celsius, buried and cooked deep in the earth's internal oven, smashed and contorted by the turmoil of early crustal formation and destruction. Yet they have preserved their story and retained evidence of their origin. However, as is so often the case, that story raises more

84 The Navajo Sandstone in Arches National Monument.

questions than it answers: there was a land surface across which dunes grew and migrated, but was it a desert? After all, great stretches of dunes often develop today along temperate coasts and, with the exception of being regularly rained on and more vegetated (as well as being the home of renowned golf courses), they look little different from those of the desert. Conditions were clearly arid enough for the wind to do its work, but there were no plants or animals whose remains as fossils would testify to a desert rather than a coastal environment. The limited preserved extent of the sandstones precludes mapping out a great sand sea as opposed to a coastal dune strip. Nevertheless, these are remarkable rocks, the earliest *aeolian* sandstones (from Aeolus, the mythical Greek keeper of the winds), testifying to early continents, early weathering and erosion under a violently hot atmosphere (with little oxygen) but a weak sun. What they do not do definitively is help answer the apparently simple question: have there always been deserts on our planet? And, anyway, how would we know?

We know the age of these sediments (within a few million years) because they contain older pebbles of igneous, once molten, rocks, and younger molten rock later forced its way upwards through the sediments. Those igneous rocks contain pristine minerals which, as they crystallized from their molten state, incorporated uranium atoms. Those radioactive uranium atoms decay to lead at a constant and well-known rate and, once trapped inside the newly formed crystal, start a geological clock of the very long now ticking. The ages of the pebbles and the younger igneous rocks thus 'bracket' the age of the sandstones. The answers to how we know that the rocks were originally sediments deposited by the wind, and whether there have always been deserts are rather more complex.

Visit the stunning landscapes in the National Parks of the deserts of the American west and you will become convinced that the entire region is made of nothing but sandstones in all their glorious palettes: reds, ochres, hennas, umbers burnt and raw, pale creams and yellows, and you will be faced with vistas such as that shown in illus. 84, in the Arches, inspiration for Edward Abbey.

Look closely and the rocks appear to have been treated to some crazed brushwork, sweeping curved strokes overlain by subsequent swirls in a different direction. What is their meaning? Is there a story here and how do we read it? There is, of course, a geological story, but in order to interpret it, we have to go back to basics, to the cornerstone of the means to understand our planet's past, a simple but powerful idea described by a cumbersome and inelegant word: *uniformitarianism*. The idea was first formulated by the late eighteenth-century scientific visionary (not to mention doctor, farmer, mineralogist, geologist, chemist and philosopher) James Hutton, often referred to fondly as 'the father of modern geology'. Hutton had the then heretical view that rocks record unimaginably immense lengths of time and that in the earth's history he saw 'no vestige of a beginning, no prospect of an end'. He appreciated that he had two choices to interpret that record: to create entirely fictional accounts or to make the apparently simple (but radical) assumption that they were formed by the same geological processes that he could see occurring in the present. That groundbreaking concept was uniformitarianism (although it would not be termed such until the following century). It simply said that rivers, oceans, deserts, glaciers, rain and wind, volcanoes and earthquakes work in the same way today as they have done during the entirety of our planet's history. If we understand the records they are leaving today, then we can interpret the stories of the rocks. Taken to an extreme, it views geological processes as always having worked at the same rate – a counter to the views of the so-called 'catastrophists' of Hutton's time who saw the earth having been sculpted rapidly by a series of devastating and unique events of

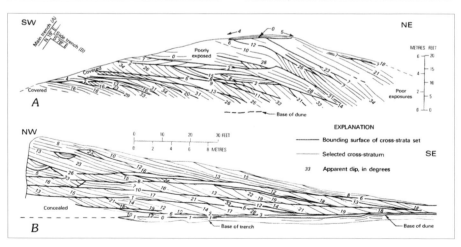

85 U.S. Geological Survey geologists revealing the internal structures of a dune.
86, 87, 88 Photographs and diagram showing the structural complexity.

explicitly biblical proportions such as the Great Flood. We know, of course, that the extreme view of a uniform rate of earth processes is far from true and that with alarming frequency our planet has been subject to massive volcanic eruptions, inundation by ice, impact by meteorites and mass extinctions of life. But, while varying in rate and frequency, those processes have remained the same. The earth works today in essentially the same way it always has – the laws of physics have not changed – and, by understanding processes today, we can read the stories of the past.

By following this logic, the exotic patterns in the sandstones of Arches National Park tell us that we are looking at ancient sand dunes, part of a vast sand sea that covered much of the western U.S. 200 million years ago. The forensic evidence for this conclusion is that if we are bold enough to bulldoze a trench through a modern sand dune we see that the interior structure of the dune shows exactly the same complex patterns displayed in the ancient Navajo Sandstone. Half a century ago, geologists from the U.S. Geological Survey did exactly that: they carved trenches through a dune at White Sands National Monument, New Mexico (illus. 85–8).

Although they used liberal quantities of water to stabilize the sand, this was a risky endeavour and probably one that would be frowned on in terms of health and safety today. But, as the photos and diagrams show, there on all scales are the distinctive patterns of the Navajo Sandstone, diagnostic evidence that much of the western U.S. was desert. The patterns are called cross-bedding, structures that can be formed in sands transported by rivers and ocean currents, but on this large scale they are the work of the wind. More evidence of desert conditions can be assembled. Changing the scale of investigation, the Navajo sandstones of Arches can be traced over large areas of Utah, Colorado, Arizona and Nevada – they form the dramatic landscapes of Zion and the Canyonlands national parks and numerous other destinations, and can be up to 700 metres thick. These are the hallmarks of a great sand sea, an erg, akin to those of the Sahara and Arabia today. Change scale to the microscopic and the sand grains themselves provide further forensic evidence. Sand in the desert is blown enormous distances by the winds and, in the process, the grains crash into one another, chipping off their sharp edges, and they become smooth and rounded.

Dust (as we shall see) is blown away, but even a strong desert wind can only move grains up to a certain size – the range of grain sizes in

89, 90 Desert sand grains: from a modern dune (left) and ancient Navajo Sandstone; each view approx. 2 mm across.

a sand dune is relatively small (it can be described as well-sorted, unlike the mix of pebbles, gravels, sand and silt transported by a river). And often the grains display delicate shades of reds, pinks and oranges, aridity and atmospheric chemistry conspiring to coat them with a thin veneer of iron-rich clay minerals. Compare the microscope views of the sand grains from a modern dune with those from the Navajo Sandstone, and the resemblance is startling: the range of grain sizes is limited, they are rounded and smoothed and they are reddish-orange in colour (illus. 89, 90). The evidence is beginning to come together through the forensic application of the principle of uniformitarianism, but caution is still required. Sandstones can be red for reasons other than being from a desert and, like all good forensic science, different lines of evidence all pointing to the same conclusion are required for a reliable diagnosis.

The Brigadier and how deserts work

The empirical evidence for identifying ancient deserts is compelling, but we need to understand more: if cross-bedding is characteristic of dunes, how does it form? Exactly how does the wind move and deposit sand? Why do dunes come in so many different shapes and sizes? Why does a sand sea form where it does, more or less surrounded by gravel plains? Where does the sand come from?

For centuries, desert travellers, caught in sandstorms, were only too aware of the role of the wind in the desert, yet even the great scientific progress of the nineteenth century contributed little to understanding the details. The fifteenth-century description by the intrepid wandering monk Felix Fabri remained essentially as accurate as anything for the next 400 years. He observed how:

> in the wilderness there are exceeding strong winds and violent whirlwinds, whereby the sand is carried about and caught up with great force from the whole surface of the ground, and so the sand moves about with the wind like running water; wherefore some have named the wilderness 'the sea of sand.' Moreover, high mountains of sand are carried by these whirlwinds from one place to another in a single night, so that, where to-day is a flat plain, to-morrow you will find a lofty mountain piled up. This moving about of mountains takes place daily in windy weather; yet is not the whole mass moved at once, but the top is blown away by the wind, down to its foundation on the ground, and is piled up in another place, and then a new mountain is formed, four or five miles from where the first one stood. Sometimes great valleys are filled with sand, and if the storm lasts, in place of the valley a mountain arises, and so, where three days ago there was a deep valley, to-day there rises a high mountain. So also immovable rocky mountains are covered by the fluid sand, so that, where yesterday one saw rocky mountains, to-day one sees nought but sand.

Among the nineteenth-century North African colonial powers, it was the French who devoted most attention to describing their desert territories, sometimes surmising startlingly bizarre origins for dunes through earthquake vibrations or assuming them to have solid rock at their core. It would take an ingenious British military man, with an enquiring mind, time on his hands and a love of the Egyptian desert, to lay the groundwork for understanding the desert that has lasted for more than 70 years. Essentially every research paper or book published today on the transport of sand by the wind and the formation of dunes makes reference to *The Physics of Blown Sand and Desert Dunes*, published in 1941 by Ralph Alger Bagnold. We met the then Major Bagnold in the first chapter, gazing out over the Great Sand Sea and being seduced by the blank areas on the maps. In the 1920s and early '30s, Bagnold made a series of epic motorized expeditions across the Western Desert of

Egypt, Sudan and Libya, observing, documenting and questioning. He wrote that:

> In 1929 and 1930, during my weeks of travel over the lifeless sand sea in North Africa, I became fascinated by the vast scale of organization of the dunes and how a strong wind could cause the whole dune surface to flow, scouring sand from under one's feet. Here, where there existed no animals, vegetation or rain to interfere with sand movements, the dunes seemed to behave like living things. How was it that they kept their precise shape while marching interminably downwind? How was it they insisted on repairing any damage done to their individual shapes? How, in other regions of the same desert, were they able to breed 'babies', just like themselves that proceeded to run on ahead of their parents? Why did they absorb nourishment and continue to grow instead of allowing the sand to spread out evenly over the desert as finer dust grains do? More basically, what kind of upward physical force must be exerted on the mineral grains to make them rise against the force of gravity, lifting them to such a height that they can strike one's face like little hammers? No satisfactory answers to these questions existed. Indeed, no-one had investigated the physics of blown sand. So here was a new field, I thought, one that could be explored at home in England under laboratory-controlled conditions.

He found stimulus in the observations and measurements that had been made by Model T-driving desert military surveyors and geologists, but he was an engineer looking for quantification and an analysis of the physics. Having grown up in an engineering household where if a piece of equipment was needed it would be designed and made, he combined his desert observations with measurements in a self-constructed wind tunnel back at Imperial College in London (in space simply loaned to him since he was 'only' an amateur scientist). His equipment was unique and exquisitely designed, capable of making detailed and accurate measurements of the sand he was blowing through it. The mathematics was rigorous and the equations he developed still form the foundations for today's research. He described accurately how wind initiates the movement of sand grains, how moving grains create a feedback relationship with the wind, how blowing sand behaves as a fluid, how the amount of

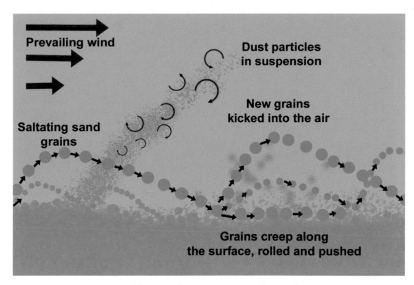

91 How sand grains move in the wind.

sand moved varies with wind velocity and a host of other details. A key observation was the different ways in which sand is moved: fine grains in suspension in the air, capable of being blown around for great lengths of time, larger grains leaping across the surface of a dune, banging into each other and kicking off more grains from the surface (a process termed 'saltation', from the Latin for 'jump') and finally, the largest and heaviest grains being nudged and rolled along the surface, a process called 'creep', or 'reptation' (illus. 91).

In 1938 Bagnold returned to the desert to test out his laboratory results in reality:

> My work necessitated waiting for a sand storm to blow up . . .
> A heavy one blew up within a few days. I was well prepared for
> it except, alas, I had lost my sand goggles. I spent some very
> uncomfortable hours sitting in the open, directly exposed to a
> violent sand blast, trying to keep my eyes open while taking
> readings from an array of gauges and sand traps. The purpose
> of eyelashes was very evident. Fortunately, I managed to get some
> reliable measurements which nicely confirmed my wind-tunnel
> measurements made in London.

His now classic text was published while he was pioneering desert war-fare in the North African campaign, but lay more or less academically dormant until the 1970s, for Bagnold was scientifically far ahead of his time. However, by the time of his death in 1990 at the age of 94, the then retired Brigadier was a hero of desert research, a Fellow of the Royal Society and the winner of awards from a spectrum of illustrious international scientific societies; in his early 80s he had advised NASA on likely conditions on Mars in preparation for surface exploration.

Bagnold's work explained why dunes are not simply overgrown ripples, why dunes appear to be self-accumulating, leaving broad stretches essentially devoid of sand between them (saltating grains bounce energetically off a pebbled surface and keep on going until they become embedded in a dune) and how cross-bedding originates. Dunes, most dramatically the crescent-shaped ones, the barchans, migrate as sand is blown up and off their windward slope and flows down the steep lee slope, the 'slip face'. A strong wind will cause avalanches that successively build layers (beds) of sand resting approximately at the angle of repose of the slope and the dune migrates (illus. 92).

A new avalanche may scour out the previous layers and a change in the wind direction will create new layers at different angles – hence the complex patterns in the excavated White Sands dune and the ancient deserts of the American west, the orientations of which tell us which way the winds were blowing long in the past. However, in detail the avalanching of sand and granular flow and indeed the strange behaviours of granular materials in general present a challenge to the finest research minds today. Why, for example, as observed by Marco Polo, Charles Darwin and Ralph Bagnold, some dunes will 'sing' during avalanching, generating pure musical notes, booming sounds or imitations of a didgeridoo, is a question that has created heated scientific arguments and has yet to be satisfactorily answered. Different theories suggest electrostatic phenomena, reverberation and amplifying effects between different layers within the dune and avalanche synchronization.

Dunes are far from simple and Bagnold remained perplexed by their behaviours and complexities, as, in many respects, does aeolian research today. The extraordinary variety of sand dunes is reflected in the vocabulary of desert insiders. Just as the Inuit are reported to have many words for snow, so does the Arab for dunes: *abam, argoob, fuluq, draa, hadh, hasansuba, 'irg ma 'kuf, khait, nefud, niqa, qa'id, qawz, qarhoud, qatarat, rabbadh, ramlah*; the hollows between the dunes: *huqna, seif, shamtut, zibar*. A sand-driving wind is the *ajaj*, soft sand is *ath-ath, fesh-fesh or beth-beth*. Wilfred Thesiger wrote, in *Arabian Sands*:

These enormous piles of sand, produced by vagaries of the winds which blew there, conform to no known rule of sand formation. The Bedu call them *qaid* . . . These *qaid* are known individually to the Bedu, for each dune has its own shape, which does not change perceptibly with the years; but all of them have certain features in common.

Dunes and dune fields occur over a dramatic range of shapes and sizes, from small individual barchans a couple of metres high but moving along at up to 100 metres a year, to gigantic star dunes and *draas*, 'mega-dunes' that barely move at all but on top of which smaller dunes cluster (illus. 93), to the ergs and sand seas such as the immense Rub' al Khali that covers 650,000 square kilometres of the Arabian Peninsula. Individual longitudinal dunes in Australia's red centre can stretch continuously for nearly 200 kilometres.

The advent of satellite imagery created the opportunity to view the complexity of desert dunes, their shapes, patterns and changes on a large scale. But integrating that scale with the behaviours of the individual sand grains that make up these landscapes remains the holy grail of aeolian research. It is, for example, clear that feedbacks occur on all scales: the saltation of individual sand grains in the wind influences the flow of air over the surface which, in turn, influences the movement of the sand. On a larger scale, the topography of a sand sea interacts with the lowermost layer of the atmosphere, the waves of sand creating atmospheric waves that determine the large-scale development of the dune field, the thickness of the atmospheric boundary layer limiting how big the dunes can grow. In turn, the sand sea, and the desert as a whole, become players in the earth system, participating in the dynamic relationships between oceans, atmosphere, land and life. Add the fourth dimension, time, and the complexity of the system, despite the best efforts of geologists, physicists, fluid dynamicists, engineers and biologists, continues to remain beyond our ability to describe in any kind of integrated, holistic way.

The tallest dunes in the world are in the Gobi Desert's Badain Jaran sand sea, some reaching 500 metres in height; bizarrely, they harbour more than a hundred lakes in the hollows between them (Badain Jaran is Mongolian for 'Mysterious Lakes'). Bizarre, but therein lies the secret of these towering dunes: water. The water table is close to the surface and moisture permeates the sand and stabilizes the dunes. Water is never far

92 Avalanches pour down the slip face of a dune.

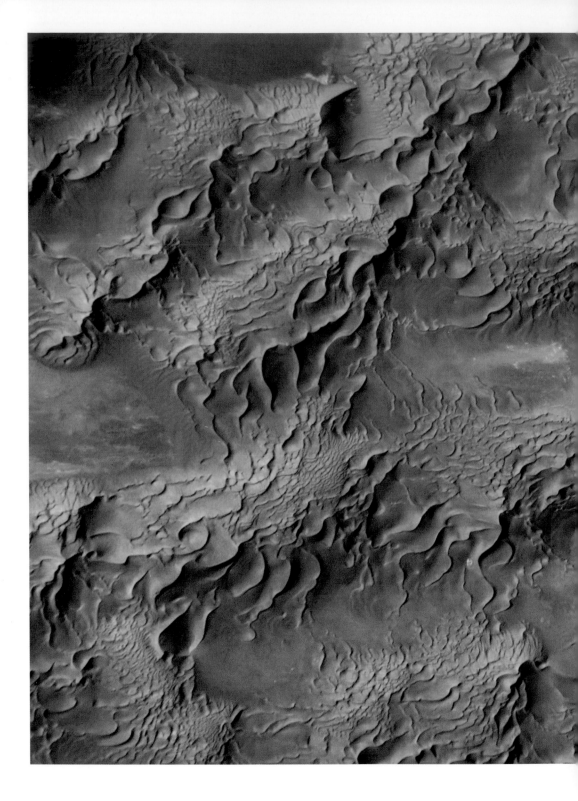

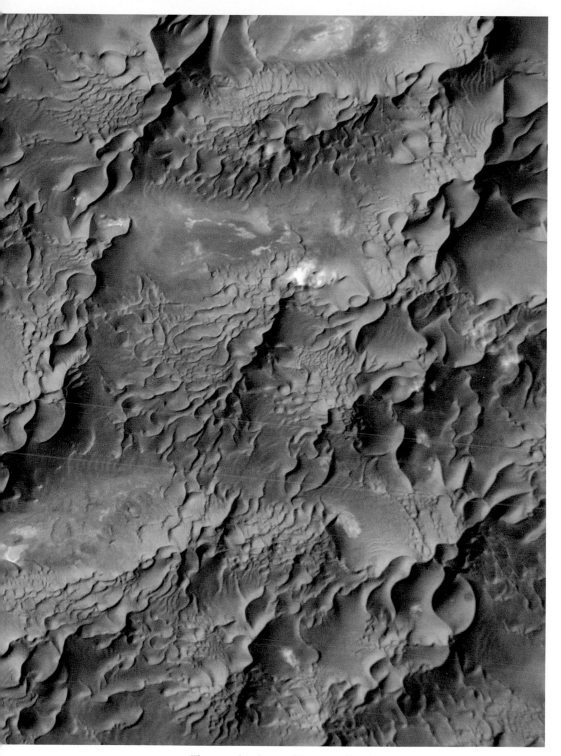

93 The complex dunes of Issouane, Algeria.

away in the desert, but for dehydrated travellers even a few metres below their feet make it fatally inaccessible. However, on a microscopic scale it can, surprisingly, be almost everywhere, even in the heart of a sand dune whose surface is hyper-arid. In a recent and on-going, typically international, research project, workers from Qatar, the u.s., Switzerland, France and Mauritania have been probing the interior of moving sand dunes. In Qatar, instruments capable of recording long-term changes in temperature and humidity were buried in the slip face of a barchan dune, soon to be deeply buried by avalanches of sand. The dune was on the move, migrating at a speed of 26 metres per year, and fifteen months later the instruments emerged from the sand on the windward side. The data they carried with them were a revelation. Periodically during their entombment a few millimetres of rain had fallen, quickly drying in surface temperatures that could exceed 60°c, but the water that had percolated down into the sand was sheltered and preserved for months. So now we begin to understand how a little rain, even in the hyper-arid desert, can temporarily inhibit the movement of dunes and provide grazing for herds of the nomadic Bedouin of the Empty Quarter who, as Thesiger recounts, are very well aware of how this works:

> I asked how much rain was required to produce grazing, and he answered, 'It is no use if it does not go into the sand this far,' and he indicated his elbow. 'How long does it have to rain to do that?' 'A heavy shower is enough. That would produce grazing that was better than nothing, but it would die within the year unless there were more rain. If we get really good rain, a whole day and night of rain, the grazing will remain green for three and even four years.'

The measurements from the heart of the Qatar dune revealed not only the dynamic environment within the sand but also that there can be enough moisture for significant periods of time to support microbial life, signs of which the experiment detected. The closer we look, the less of a desert the desert becomes.

Forensic evidence

Great thicknesses of extensive, large-scale, cross-bedded red sands with rounded and well-sorted grains are all clues that point to a likely desert origin. But more evidence is needed if we are to interpret the ebb and flow of aridity across the planet over the last few billion years. Dunes and even sand seas may be dramatic and ubiquitous in our imaginations, but desert landscapes are made of far more than sand. Illus. 34 in chapter Two summarizes the complexity and diversity of desert features as we see them today, but we have to ask which of these are likely to be preserved in the rock record long after the desert has gone, and what will they look like, how will we recognize them? The key is to analyse all the environments at the heart of the desert, and at those beyond its borders, to identify the influence of the desert and its interactions with climate; only then can a more complete story be told.

Again, water has a vital role to play. Ephemeral though desert rivers may be, they leave behind distinctive testaments to their work, the kinds of valley-filling channel sands and gravels of illus. 27, the gigantic aprons of detritus that make up the alluvial fans of illus. 31 and 33, the deposits left behind when flash floods and mudflows come to rest. The evaporitic salt deposits and cracked mud of the playa lakes, the cemented crusts of silica, gypsum and limestone, desert soils, pebbles coated in desert varnish – if the circumstances are right, all can be turned to rock and preserved over hundreds of millions of years. And, as moving dunes today cover the old river beds, so are alternating layers of windblown and waterborne sediments preserved. The red sandstones on which Nottingham Castle was built, home of Robin Hood's nemesis sheriff, tell exactly this story, sediments flushed by ephemeral desert rivers sandwiched between dramatically cross-bedded dune sands. And all of this was happening at the same time that the great sand sea of the Navajo Sandstone was accumulating: 200 million years ago was an arid time on planet earth.

'After the desert has gone', and 'if the circumstances are right' – easy to say, but what do we mean? The desert conditions that the Navajo Sandstone bears witness to continued, with occasional minor interruptions, across the western U.S. for tens of millions of years; then at the top of the pile the desert sands are scoured and eroded and the next sediments, the ones immediately overlying, are marine sands and muds – the seas had come in and overtaken the desert. Why, then, are the desert sands preserved? Why had the storms, waves and currents of the encroaching sea not washed them away? The great thickness of the Navajo helps, but it is likely that water, once again, had a key role to play. A sand sea on the scale represented by the Navajo can only form if a number of critical conditions are met: there must be a copious source of sand of the right size, there must be strong enough and long-lived winds to transport it, and there must be an atmospheric or topographic effect that slows down the winds and causes them to dump their load. As I can verify, any obstruction in the desert, such as my collapsed tent, will cause even the violence of a sandstorm to slow ever so slightly and build up a small dune in its lee. For a sand sea to develop this effect has to operate on a very large scale. Mountain ranges can slow the wind's velocity and cause dune fields to accumulate: the Great Sand Dunes National Park in Colorado is a dramatic example of this. For an erg to form, the most propitious circumstance is a conspiracy between the winds and a regional-scale topographic depression, ideally one in which the underlying earth's crust continues to subside, constantly creating space for new piles of sand to accumulate on top of older ones. It seems quite likely that most of the sand seas that have survived through geologic time owe their longevity to this kind of process, for, as the pile of sand subsides, it sinks below the water table. Not only will the water stabilize the sand, but minerals dissolved in it will begin to glue, or cement, the grains together, starting the process of turning sand into sandstone, and ultimately armouring the desert deposits against the attacks of the incoming seas which themselves cause the water table to rise.

The preservation is imperfect, the gaps considerable, but enough forensic evidence can be found to catalogue the great deserts of our planet's past. The South African dunes from 3.2 billion years ago may or may not represent a true desert, but there are unlikely to be older ones exposed on the earth's surface. Much of the first 2 billion years of the earth's history were chaotic, violent and hellish, a troubled youth appropriately termed the Hadean eon. Catastrophic extraterrestrial impacts, one possibly blasting the moon into orbit, churned and melted the solidifying crust. We have evidence that small continental fragments must have existed prior to 4 billion years ago, but it is unlikely that there was a sufficient expanse of land on which a desert could develop and the necessary water and atmospheric chemistry to make the sand to supply it. Tortured crustal terrains such as that at Barberton are testimony that certainly by 3 billion years ago, familiar processes were under way: rivers were flowing, winds were blowing, dunes were being formed, and it is possible that there were microbial crusts to help stabilize the sands.

Strong and conflicting opinions continue to be exchanged as to whether or not plate tectonics as we know it was up and running by this time, but major changes were under way. Around 2.5 billion years ago, the great oxidation event changed the atmosphere forever, newly evolved bacteria flooding it with toxic oxygen: earth surface processes evolved, with weathering as we know it providing the material for rivers, the oceans and the winds to play with. Within a relatively short time, there is ample forensic evidence for all kinds of deserts across the growing continents and there were probably many more which did not survive or which we haven't yet found. From then on the record grows and given that the atmospheric, oceanic and topographic conditions causing today's deserts have operated for hundreds of millions of years, there is no reason to think that our planet has ever been entirely desertless. The only possible exception would have been, if the theories are correct, the 'snowball earth' events of around 700 million years ago, but even then, if there were small areas of land remaining above the ice, it can be assumed that they would have been hyper-arid since the atmosphere had so little water available.

For the next couple of hundred million years, deserts were indeed deserts. With the exception of microbes, the land had no life whatsoever, no animals, no plants. Then, around 490 million years ago, in a coastal desert in what is now southeastern Ontario, Canada, creatures came out of the sea and, scuttling tentatively across the dunes, left us our oldest evidence of land invasion. The creatures were probably arthropods, that great group of invertebrate animals that includes insects, spiders and crustaceans, and may have been the primitive shrimp-like creatures whose fossilized remains are found in the sediments of the neighbouring seas. But, not surprisingly, no fossils are found in the dune sands, just the tracks and trails of the first animals to explore the land. In sediments deposited some 60 million years later, there are plant fossils and all the evidence for a complete and recognizable land ecosystem: the stories of landscapes and life would be from then on forever intertwined.

For much of our planet's history, deserts have been a feature, sometimes in greater abundance than others, but there is one period that can be described as the era of the desert, a time when aridity ruled much of the earth. It began around 260 million years ago, in the midst of what is called the Permian period, lasted close to 100 million years, and included the greatest catastrophe that life on earth has ever witnessed. The rocks of Nottingham Castle and the Arches National Monument testify to the later part of this saga of aridity, but it had begun long

94 The supercontinent of Pangaea.

before and for a single, global, reason: the supercontinent of Pangaea had welded itself together (illus. 94).

As continents wander around the globe under the driving forces of plate tectonics, the distribution of land and ocean changes, and the changing geographies influence ocean and atmospheric circulation and therefore climate. Continents and continental bits and pieces have periodically behaved gregariously in the past, most recently clustering together to form Pangaea ('entire earth'). This not only changed oceanic circulation but meant that huge areas of land were far removed from the influence and moisture of the oceans: aridity spread across the great landmass. Life was challenged, but arid-adapted plants did well, as did insects, all establishing niches and expanding into new ones. However, it was ideal, as deserts are today, for reptiles, and in particular the 'mammal-like' reptiles, the *therapsids*, which were the size of a large dog and had vicious teeth. They lived alongside the ancestors of the dinosaurs and were themselves the ancestors of mammals.

The forensic evidence for extensive Permian deserts shows up on essentially every continent except for Antarctica where there was no ice, but temperate forests and coal-forming swamps. In Scotland, the cross-bedding of gigantic dunes appears in the wall of the old Ballochmyle Quarry, now sadly filled in (illus. 95). The rocks that contain the huge natural gas fields of the southern North Sea and elsewhere in Europe were formed in these deserts. The brownstones of New York and the Smithsonian Institution were built from desert sandstones of this period.

An idea of what the world looked like at this time can be gleaned not only from the stories of the rocks, but from modelling the processes of the oceans, the atmosphere and the continents, the earth system. The principles and methods of today's climate modelling (something we shall return to in more detail) can be applied to any period in the earth's past, clearly with a whole series of caveats and considerable uncertainty. But calibrate a model with the testimony of the rocks, interrogate its sensitivities and key factors, and it can be a useful part of the narrative. Exactly this has been done recently by German and Norwegian researchers who generated a series of world maps using the same Köppen-Geiger Climate Classification that we saw in the first chapter (with a different colour scheme). The example in illus. 96 maps Pangaea, the climate

95 The Permian dunes of Scotland.

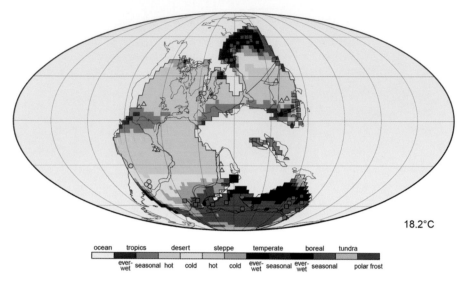

96 A model of late Permian Pangaean climate zones.

zones, and examples of diagnostic 'climate indicative sediments': 60 per cent of the planet's land was arid, desert or steppe.

These were warm times: the assumption for the global average temperature is, in this case, 18°C, compared to perhaps 14°C today (although the concept and measurement of 'global average temperature' is a thorny and controversial issue). But what is particularly interesting about the Permian climate model is that the annual mean temperatures can be changed from 7°C to over 30°C and the extent of the arid lands varies only a little: it was the continental mass of Pangaea that caused the aridity.

Life may have been challenged by the deserts' spread, but it went on – until something truly dreadful happened: 252 million years ago, in the space of a mere 200,000 years, more than 85 per cent of the planet's marine species were wiped out. The loss on land may not have been as great, but the evidence suggests that the majority of animal and plant types perished. This was the Permian mass extinction, the 'great dying', the most catastrophic loss of biodiversity in the last 600 million years – far, far worse than the event that would later end the reign of the dinosaurs. Mass murder on a global scale, but what was the killer? This question has stimulated a vast research literature, numerous hypotheses and considerable scientific controversy. There is a school of thought that advocates an extraterrestrial impact event, greater than the one that later killed off the dinosaurs, but the evidence is scarce. The majority view blames the eruption of monumental volumes of lavas in Siberia. The timing is right and the (geologically) sudden explosion of molten rock covering millions of square kilometres must have had a devastating effect on the atmosphere and the oceans. Along with the lavas, carbon dioxide, sulphur dioxide and dust in huge volumes were injected into the atmosphere, causing acid rain and changes to the chemistry of ocean waters. Along with carbon dioxide, methane (an even more potent 'greenhouse gas') was released through burning peat and the melting of the gas previously frozen in the sediments of the oceans. An already hot global climate became hotter, wildfires broke out across Pangaea, landscape-stabilizing vegetation was destroyed and the bare land laid waste by the erosion of uninhibited flash floods.

This kind of disastrous scenario can be pieced together from what we know of the effects of huge volcanic eruptions and from the frustratingly disrupted record of the rocks. That record, as is always the case, is more continuous in the oceans than on land, particularly when the land is arid to begin with and then subject to the kind of devastation that occurred at the end of the Permian. Deserts are hardly the ideal environment for extensive preservation of geological and biological stories. We can look at the testimonies of marine sediments from the time and chart the changes in the sediments pouring into the oceans, the extinction of species and the wholesale modification, potentially toxic, of water chemistry. But correlating the record from the ocean with the patchwork of evidence from the land is difficult. It's as if you live in a small town where the library archives are very incomplete indeed, with many successive volumes of old newspapers missing. The collections of the main city library are more complete, but those newspapers only contain indirect references to what was going on in your town.

Deciphering the stories of ancient deserts and charting their history is challenging at the best of times, but it is particularly difficult over the period of the great dying. And answering the question of what exactly was the killer has proved impossible. The evidence is circumstantial and incomplete: the Siberian volcanic eruptions themselves did not cause the mass extinction, but their effects probably did. But was it the effect of global temperatures, ocean acidification, reduction in atmospheric and oceanic oxygen, acid rain, wildfires, aridity or any conspiracy of these that was the actual killer? The debate continues to rage in scientific circles. Life took a long time to recover from the great dying, but there were extraordinary cases of survival, especially on land, where desiccation-tolerant varieties of plants and reptiles, particularly the therapsids, struggled through to become the founders of the arid land's new ecosystem and, ultimately, many of the desert life forms today. They would, however, be dethroned by the emergence of the dinosaurs, who first appeared in South America around 230 million years ago but were prevented from migrating to North America for millions of years, quite probably blocked by the great barrier of the desert. Bacteria and other microbes, as usual, had few if any problems surviving the mass extinction and the aridity.

The search for the mass murderer, with acid rain, lack of oxygen and aridity the prime suspects, raises an obvious question: how do we even know that these were suspects 250 million years ago? The fact that we cannot return, even if we were mad enough to want to, to look around the earth as it was then, is the underlying challenge for constructing a geological narrative. Uniformitarianism is a powerful companion, guiding us in reading the visible stories of the rocks, but there are other details, further clues that can contribute to the forensic case. It is some of these that have helped the search for the Permian smoking gun: proxies.

Circumstantial evidence

It is a regrettable fact that we can't measure the rainfall, temperatures, atmospheric composition or biological activity of 250 million years ago; direct measurements of the earth's processes and changes are only available for the last 150 years or so, which is unfortunate, since those processes are of profound importance to us as we try to understand how our planet's climate works. So, not being able to measure these things directly, we have to look for circumstantial evidence, things that we *can* measure that reflect in some way the things we would like to measure but can't. This kind of vicarious evidence is referred to as a 'proxy', a stand-in for the real thing. The library that is the history of our planet is missing many volumes, and many that we have are not the originals; there are works that we know existed but all we have left is the indirect evidence. Many of the works of Aristotle (in many ways the first proponent of the idea of uniformitarianism and role of geological time) are, in all likelihood, not his original writings, but compilations of the lecture notes of his students: they too can be thought of as proxies.

In some respects, *all* geological evidence is a proxy: we can't measure ancient aridity, but large-scale aeolian cross-bedding, specific kinds of sand ripples, evaporites and rounded sand grains are the results of it and, together, suggest the presence of a desert. But there are more subtle and more quantitative kinds of proxy evidence. For the relatively recent past, for example, tree rings provide not only a chronology, but in their width and density an indication of the vigour of growth, the health of the tree and therefore the state of the environment (temperature, rainfall, the availability of nutrients) in terms of whether it was good or bad for the tree. There is still an underlying role for uniformitarianism: we must assume that trees in the past behaved much in the same way that they do today, which, for the last few thousand years, is probably a reasonable assumption. But the character of a tree ring is not, in itself, a direct measurement of environmental factors and we have had, so to speak, to go somewhat out on a limb, or a series of limbs, to deduce climate from tree rings. Furthermore, the tree ring measurements from one tree are far from sufficient to make any conclusions other than about the small area around that particular tree. We need data from demonstrably the same time from many different trees in many different locations, the data from all of which, having received whatever statistical treatment we feel is appropriate, must point to the same general conclusion. And there is therefore the risk of sampling bias – data collected in a way that is at best not representative and, at worst, chosen to support a particular hypothesis. Proxies present thorny issues, but they can provide remarkable insights, even though it is not unknown for different conclusions to be drawn from exactly the same data.

Over the last few decades, a wide variety of proxy measurements have been developed that shed light on past conditions on the earth, the palaeoclimate. A number of these are based on the fact that key elements, particularly oxygen, hydrogen and carbon, come in different isotopic forms. For example, in every few hundred normal carbon atoms there is one that is slightly heavier as a result of having an extra neutron. The heavy isotope is ^{13}C, having thirteen neutrons compared to its common ^{12}C colleagues. The same occurs with oxygen, ^{16}O being the normal atom and the isotope ^{18}O the heavier version. The weight difference between the isotopes may be small, but it is significant. Water contains mostly ^{16}O but also a small proportion of ^{18}O (so-called 'heavy water'). As water evaporates from the surface of the ocean, the lighter is more agile, easier to remove from the surface, and so the ocean becomes relatively enriched in ^{18}O, the atmosphere relatively depleted. But as the surface of the sea becomes increasingly warm, even the heavier water molecules will be caught up in evaporation: the *ratio* of the isotopes in the ocean will have changed. Enter the Foraminifera, forams for short, tiny single-celled marine creatures that thrived throughout the oceans for the last 600 million years. Each foram makes a shell for itself from calcium carbonate extracted from the water in which it lives; calcium carbonate contains oxygen atoms and the proportion of light to heavy oxygen will be the same as that of the water. As the forams die their shells sink to the sea bed to build up thick layers of sediment which will eventually be turned to rock, heaved back to the surface of the earth and exposed as limestone. These rocks contain the oxygen isotope record of the time over which the sediments originally accumulated. Measure the oxygen isotope ratios and the way in which they change is a *proxy* for ocean temperature, which, in turn, reflects atmospheric temperature. It is an elegant and powerful line of evidence, but, of course, not quite as straightforward as we would like. For example, melting ice sheets will not only cool the ocean but add water whose oxygen isotope composition reflects the atmospheric conditions when the snow originally fell. Different species of forams have different lifestyles in different parts of the oceans with different temperatures – we need to think hard about the circumstances under which the oxygen isotope data originated. But at least relative changes in isotope ratios provide an insight into relative changes in temperature. The records from widely different locations from the time of the Permian mass extinction show a significant warming of the oceans, quantifiable in the 6–10°C range, devastating for the majority of life on earth.

The temperature record from proxy data points to a warm earth at the time of the great Pangaean deserts, but it is not in itself evidence for aridity; as we saw in the first chapter, it is difficult enough to define and measure aridity today, never mind hundreds of millions of years ago. There is currently no proxy for drought and aridity in the earth's past, other than the traditional geological evidence from the rock record. The isotopes of carbon can be indicative of ecosystem health, since plants prefer to use the lighter isotope in photosynthesis and therefore the relative concentration of light and heavy carbon in fossil organic material and limestones provides a hint of biosphere health or stress, with aridity one possible cause for the latter. For the relatively short period of time in which large mammals have been grazing the land, their fossilized teeth have been proposed as an aridity proxy: the longer they are (the measure of hypsodonty), the better they are adapted to a tough diet and wear and tear, quite possibly as a result of the fibrous and abrasive plants typical of parched conditions. The oxygen isotopic content of any tooth enamel that remains is an indicator of the temperature (or at least the vigour of evaporation) of the water the animals were drinking. The dentistry of ancient ungulates may reveal climatic secrets. There is also some work that is indicating a possible aridity proxy through organic molecules produced by different kinds of microbes that respond to the alkalinity and therefore the aridity of the soil in which they live. This is promising, but, given the prominence and importance of understanding palaeoclimates, our inability to decipher ancient droughts is frustrating; we must fall back on the evidence of the dunes, yet even that is fraught with uncertainty.

As the narrative of geological time continues and the record becomes younger, the evidence improves in both quality and quantity, and more forensic techniques are available. The deserts of today contain long histories of aridity (probably more than 20 million years in the Atacama, more than 7 million years in the Sahara). Of particular interest is that those histories are not ones of sustained levels of aridity, but rather a history of fluctuation, of ebb and flow between semi- and hyper-arid as the climate changed. The movement of active dunes was prevented as vegetation grew, the winds died down or precipitation increased, even slightly. When the climate dried out, the dunes resumed their march and these episodes of activity and stabilization are recorded in the sands.

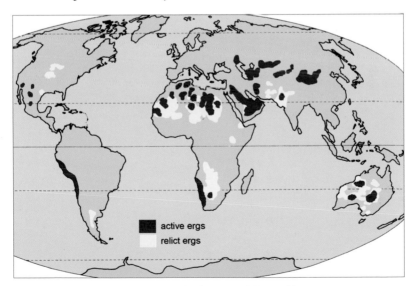

97 Active and relict ergs of the world.

These kinds of changes can even be seen in historical times: the largest dune field in the western hemisphere can be found in the prairies of Nebraska, appropriately, part of the 'Great American Desert'. These dunes are vegetated and immobile today, but a thousand years ago they were on the move and they were periodically resuscitated by the droughts before and during the pursuit of manifest destiny, causing problems for the settlers' wagon trains. Navajo oral histories provide first-hand evidence of changing vegetation and fluctuations in dune activity. Dunes cover around 5 per cent of the global land surface today, but most are stable. The map in illus. 97 shows the current distribution of active and 'relict', immobile, ergs, a snapshot in time. The map would have looked very different a few thousand years ago and will change significantly in the future.

In order to decipher the history of phases of erg activity, a means of determining the age of a particular layer of sand is required. For a long time this was simply not possible: the desert is far from an ideal environment in which to preserve the mineral and fossil materials that provide the geological clocks, and, even should carbonaceous remains be available, carbon dating only works for ages younger than 60,000 years. However, over the last couple of decades two remarkable clocks have been developed that have revolutionized our ability to decipher the stories of the deserts and transformed our understanding of how they work. Once again, isotopes are the key. Once a sand grain, typically quartz, is buried, it is bombarded from its surroundings by natural radiation from isotopes of potassium, thorium and uranium. The radiation strips away electrons from the mineral atoms but those electrons remain trapped in the crystal structure of the sand grain, a store of energy that can be released simply by shining light onto the grain. In doing so, the energy of the trapped electrons is released as light and the grain glows, it luminesces. The longer the grain has remained buried, away from sunlight, the more electrons are trapped and the more energy will be released. Since isotopes are predictable, we know the rate at which electrons are produced and so we have a clock. 'Optically stimulated luminescence dating' (OSL) gives us a measure of how long our sand grain has been in the dark, for when it re-emerges into the sunlight the clock is reset.

However, once the grain is back at the surface, it is bombarded by extraterrestrial cosmic rays which themselves reorganize some atoms into new isotopes, and the longer the grain remains at the surface, the more isotopes accumulate: now we have a clock that measures how long a grain has been exposed on the surface. As with all such measurements, data from one sand grain is far from sufficient, and huge numbers of analyses are required to come to a statistically acceptable conclusion. And nature creates all kinds of complications in the story of an individual sand grain that can cause ambiguities and complications in interpreting the data, but these methods have given us a means of quantifying episodes of desert activity and have provided extraordinary insights into the dynamics of arid lands.

For example, detailed studies of dunes from the Kalahari and the Namib deserts have produced chronologies of periods of movement and stability over the last 80,000 years or so. There are some significant correlations of events between different types of dunes from widely different locations, in general correlating with the global history of pulses of glaciation. However, the data from different areas can show significant conflicts, and correlation of the timings of dune movements with proxies for temperature, wind and oceanic upwelling from the continuous archives of neighbouring ocean sediments raises some interesting and challenging questions. It seems that different parts of the same sand sea can be active at different times, and that dune movement is more a measure of changing wind strength than a reliable indicator of aridity: the same burial ages coming from large numbers of sand grains must reflect accumulation and therefore a reduction in the strength of the winds.

It's a complex environment, the desert, but while we are only beginning to understand it, other forms of life have known it well for close to 500 million years.

Xerocoles and xerophytes

The work of Roy Chapman Andrews, palaeontologist and Gobi explorer, was introduced in chapter Two. In a series of pioneering expeditions, he and his colleagues discovered a desert treasure of superbly preserved vertebrate fossils, including the now famous dinosaurs, the old Chinese 'dragon bones' – and their eggs. Some of the greatest treasures were unearthed at Bayn Dzak, the Flaming Cliffs, towers of red sandstones illustrated in one of the reports of the expedition geologists (illus. 98). These rocks bear all the hallmarks of a desert from 75 million years ago, the late Cretaceous Period, a desert in the desert.

98 *The Flaming Cliffs of Bayn Dzak*, painted by C. Lester Morgan after a field
sketch by Frederick K. Morris of the Chapman Andrews expedition.

In *The New Conquest of Central Asia*, the somewhat oddly titled
report of the expeditions, Chapman Andrews wrote:

> On July 13, George Olsen reported at tiffin that he had found
> some fossil eggs. Inasmuch as the deposit was obviously Cretaceous
> and too early for large birds, we did not take his story very seri-
> ously. We felt quite certain that his so-called eggs would prove to
> be sandstone concretions or some other geological phenomena.
> Nevertheless, we were all curious enough to go with him to
> inspect his find. We saw a small sandstone ledge, beside which
> were lying three eggs partly broken. The brown striated shell was
> so egglike that there could be no mistake. Granger finally said, 'No
> dinosaur eggs ever have been found, but the reptiles probably
> did lay eggs. These must be dinosaur eggs. They can't be any-
> thing else.' The prospect was thrilling, but we would not let
> ourselves think of it too seriously, and continued to criticize the
> supposition from every possible standpoint. But finally we had to
> admit that 'eggs are eggs,' and that we could make them out to
> be nothing else. It was evident that dinosaurs did lay eggs and that
> we had discovered the first specimens known to science.

The rocks in which the dinosaur bones and eggs (illus. 99), together
with a large variety of mammals, are found are variable in character.

There were clearly migrating dunes, but there are also sediments that indicate periods of greater precipitation and flash floods – all in all, a typical desert story of fluctuating aridity. But the preservation of the eggs, quite possibly broken and consumed by a hungry predator, is extraordinary and there are beautiful examples from other sites within a couple of hundred kilometres of the Flaming Cliffs. So extraordinary that workers from the American Museum of Natural History, the original sponsor of the expeditions, together with colleagues from the University of Rochester, have recently tried for the first time the proxy methods of oxygen and carbon isotope analysis on the shells. The shells of today's descendants of the dinosaurs, the birds, contain an isotopic signature of the environment in which the mother laid them. The results from eggshells (and tooth enamel) 75 million years old, while not entirely definitive, contain all the signals of a climate varying from extremely arid to more moist. This supports the story of how the dinosaurs died: their remains are typically found in massive sandstones with no internal structure, no cross-bedding indicative of being buried in an arid dune – besides which, it hardly seems likely that a dinosaur would be slow enough to be caught by avalanching sand. Rather, it would seem that they were trapped by the catastrophic and large-scale collapse of a dune saturated with water, a diagnosis supported by the fact that the skeletons are preserved in postures suggestive of a sudden and violent death. The

THE FIRST NEST OF DINOSAUR EGGS, DISCOVERED BY GEORGE OLSEN AT SHABARAKH USU IN 1923. Two eggs and part of another are shown lying on the surface. The small sandstone ledge in the background was removed intact and sent to the Museum. In the center of the block of stone thirteen other eggs were discovered, 1923.

99 The original Mongolian dinosaur egg discovery.

Gobi dinosaurs have become famous and valuable. Could these remains have been the origin of the multicultural dragon legends that travelled along the Silk Road? They are certainly today a commodity of commercial trade, often illegal.

It would not be long, geologically speaking, before the Mongolian dinosaurs would, together with all their relatives, be wiped out by the mass extinction at the end of the Cretaceous. But many members of the remarkable menagerie of other creatures whose remains are found with them, including 30 species of lizards and a diversity of mammals, would make it through and thrive as the ancestors of today's communities in arid lands. Unfortunately, that evolutionary path is far from easy to trace, for the desert does not care much for the conservation of biological archives. We know that, while the climatic conditions that followed the mass extinction were hotter and more humid than today, arid environments must have had a role to play, albeit a lesser and more discontinuous one than at present. Our planet has become, on average, more arid over the last few tens of millions of years, but the extent of drylands has varied significantly and their fossil legacy is patchy at best. The detailed lineage of today's desert ecosystems remains incomplete and controversial. As aridity took over lands that had been previously semi-arid or temperate, did species of plants and animals adapted to drylands migrate with the desert or did the existing inhabitants adapt to the new conditions? The answer is far from clear and the lost borders of arid ecosystems have long stimulated heated debate in the corridors of biological science.

Chuckwalla Land: The Riddle of California's Desert is David Rains Wallace's fascinating description of his quest to decipher the biological ancestry of the deserts of the American southwest (the Chuckwalla is a rather stocky lizard, an iguana, *Sauromalus obesus*). His quest fails, simply because the scientific story has not yet been put together. This failure is in large part a result of the lack of data which, in itself, reflects not only the imperfect archives but also the fact that the desert has hardly been a focus of evolutionary biology. As Wallace points out, Charles Darwin essentially ignored deserts, regarding them as an 'evolutionary backwater', the great man and his successors preferring the lure of the teeming rainforests and the clement environments of temperate lands. Darwin records from his travels in Chile that 'While travelling through these deserts one feels like a prisoner shut up in a gloomy court, who longs to see something green and to smell a moist atmosphere.' After all, the ideas about evolution developed by Darwin and, from the jungles of Southeast Asia, Alfred Russel Wallace, were about competition, and the perceived lifelessness of the desert seemed hardly conducive to evolutionary excitement. This situation remained unchanged for decades, and it is only now that we are beginning to appreciate the extraordinary diversity of desert life, from microbial to mammalian, and how these systems fit into the games of evolution.

Xerophytes and xerocoles, plants and animals that like dryness. The image of the struggle for survival in the desert is somewhat anthropocentric and exaggerated. Yes, the environments are harsh and death in the desert is never far away, but for the xeric communities, the arid lands are their home and they are cleverly adapted to their harshness. There may not be dense populations of them, but their diversity can be astonishing: the Sonoran Desert described in *Chuckwalla Land* is home to 3,000 plant species, countless thousands of invertebrates and more than 500 different vertebrates. A typical hectare of Australia's desert is home to more lizards (around 400) than any other hectare on earth. Like every other desert, no one has accurately counted the number of kinds of insects, but there are more than 1,000 species of ants (food for 230 species of birds in the outback). There are crocodiles in the Sahara, elephants in the Namib, fish in Death Valley, frogs in the Atacama, tulips in the Negev and truffles in Arabia. No one knows the true scope of the desert's microbial jungle. The deserts of the world offer such a rich variety of micro- and macro-environments that their levels of biodiversity should hardly be surprising, and ecosystems vary widely from one environment and one desert to the next. The best way to sleep in the hyper-arid desert is outside, in a sleeping bag or a swag on the ground, gazing at the image of infinity that the sky presents. Wake up in the morning and any idea of 'lifelessness' vanishes with the myriad tracks and trails of nocturnal activity in the sand. Wake up in the Australian outback and it may well be to a riot of colour of flowers and birds, as well as to countless tracks and trails. Across the borderlands of any desert, the species richness escalates at an astonishing rate. Travel a few hundred kilometres south from the hyper-arid Sahara into the drylands of the Sahel and you will encounter ten times as many mammals; the plant diversity will have increased a hundredfold.

The adaptations developed by desert life are, first and foremost, to deal with the problems of desiccation and they are impressively diverse. The lack of water can be dealt with in three ways: behaviour, physiology and morphology. By far the most common behavioural adaptation is

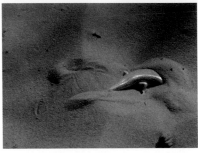

100, 101, 102
The disappear-
ing sand fish.

simply to live underground and only come out in the cool of the night, hence the tracks and trails in the morning. Insects, mammals, marsupials, lizards and amphibians all burrow, dig and tunnel, and have often developed morphological specializations to become expert excavators, sometimes to the point where they seem to be swimming, rather than burrowing, through the sand. From the west coast of North Africa through to the deserts of Arabia can be found a variety of 'sand skinks', otherwise known as 'sand fish' (illus. 100–102). These little lizards have an ultra-smooth skin whose nano-scale structure reduces friction with the sand, a chisel-shaped snout and very strong limbs. Put a sand fish down on the sand and it will simply disappear in a fraction of a second, the unique motion of its limbs and body enabling it to 'swim' beneath the surface, a talent that has been the subject of robotics research and development.

It's a clever means of avoiding predators, but not strictly *burrowing* since the sand collapses behind it, as it does behind the marsupial moles of Australian deserts, which are indeed marsupials but not moles. They are known as the *itjaritjari* by Aboriginal peoples who describe them disappearing into the sand 'like a man diving into water', exactly like the sand fish. But unlike the skinks, they spend essentially their entire lives moving underground and are blind, with no external ears. Their head is ideally shaped for tunnelling and their front feet are shovel-like, the rear ones specialized in moving sand out of the way. Being marsupials, they have a pouch, but it faces backwards so as not to collect sand. Shy and elusive creatures, there are many mysteries about the marsupial moles, but the reason that they are called 'moles' is because they look and behave very much like them, a fine example of a common evolutionary phenomenon in desert ecosystems: convergence.

There are often basic solutions to thriving in a particular environment and, in the course of evolution and under the pressures of natural selection, widely different creatures will come up with the same approach: birds, insects and bats are the classic examples of the convergent evolution demonstrated by flight. Having shovel-like feet is a solution for effective excavation of loose sand and this is a convergent evolutionary tool developed by marsupial moles, common moles and a wide variety of lizards. There are a number of geckos that live in the sands of the Namib Desert, all of them descended from their brethren that were adapted for climbing trees and rocks. Among them is the wonderful rainbow-coloured, translucent palmatogecko (illus. 103). Their climbing relatives are adept at doing so because of microscopic dry adhesion forces generated by millions of tiny hairs on the pads of their feet. These, however, are of no use digging in the sand, and indeed are a problem because the sand clogs up the hairs, and so, as aridity took over, the geckos evolved to discard the hair and grow webbed feet with spiny scales. Several different lineages of geckos responded to life in the new desert by doing exactly the same thing on several different occasions in the last 5 million years or so as the climate fluctuated.

Another behavioural example of convergent evolution in arid lands is the strange habit of hopping. This is a highly energy-efficient means of moving rapidly across the open landscapes of the desert and is not only the obvious skill of the kangaroo, but is adopted by the jerboas of North Africa and Asia, the appropriately named kangaroo rats of the u.s. (which can cover 2.5 metres in a single hop) and the wide variety of hopping mice in Australia. Kangaroo rats demonstrate yet another example of convergent evolution that is common among desert creatures, physiological adaptation via a metabolism that is incredibly good at conserving water. Most desert rats, including the kangaroo rats, never drink water: they obtain essentially everything they need from the seeds and insects collected during their nocturnal excursions from their burrows. They obtain their water supply from these metabolic processes, they have no sweat glands, their metabolic rate is extremely low and the workings of their remarkable kidneys produce highly concentrated urine. Having no

103 The palmatogecko.

need to drink and little to urinate clearly offers a significant advantage in desert life. And, strangely enough, rat urine offers us a very valuable way of reconstructing geologically recent desert history. Rats collect vegetation, seeds and nuts and construct a pile of it, a midden, in their burrows or caves, which they typically urinate on. The concentrated urine dries and crystallizes, gluing the midden material together so that it can be preserved for tens of thousands of years, thus providing a record, whose age can be determined by carbon-14 (radiocarbon) dating, of the changing vegetation – and therefore climate – of the desert.

The mammals and marsupials of the desert are warm-blooded creatures, endotherms: regulating their body temperature through their internal metabolism, they avoid the heat of the desert day. The geckos and other lizards have a different problem: they are ectothermic, having no internal mechanism for body temperature regulation (the only mammal that is ectothermic is the bizarre naked mole rat of the deserts of East Africa). Lizards need the warmth of the sun to stimulate their metabolism, but at the same time, while being tolerant of a wide range of temperatures, they cannot allow themselves to heat up too much. The staggering variety of lizards in the desert is testimony to how efficiently they manage their way of life. They bask in the sun, but their skin is adapted to filtering ultra-violet radiation to avoid damage to internal organs; they scamper at high speed across rock and sand, they cool off in the shade and retire underground when things get rough. Ectothermy gives lizards a huge advantage in the desert, for it requires little energy to operate: a day's food supply for a small bird will keep a lizard of comparable size going for a month and, should the food supply disappear, they can simply lower their metabolic rate to virtually nothing and practise another common form of desert adaptation: they can estivate, remain dormant, for long periods of time.

The ability to estivate (or acstivate) is again a powerful competitive skill in arid lands; like hibernation, it conserves energy but, most importantly, it conserves water and can be employed whenever home dries up. It is a strategy used by a variety of animals and even birds. Varieties of nightjars found in the drylands of the u.s. and Africa have been found huddled in cracks in the rocks with no signs of pulse or breathing and an alarmingly low body temperature (the Native Americans of the Hopi tribe call them 'the sleeping ones'). The birds are responding to a lack of their normal insect diet *and* to lower temperatures, and so this is also a form of hibernation. However, it is the desert amphibians who are the professional estivators. Amphibians are seriously challenged by arid conditions since their skins are porous and their need for water substantial. There are relatively few desert frogs, toads or salamanders, but the ones who are there have developed some astonishing adaptations. Amphibians cannot survive in the harshest parts of the desert, but as long as the possibility of some sources of water exists, in the oases or the borderlands, they can flourish. In drought conditions, the Australian 'water-holding' frog *Litoria platycephala* retires to the relative cool of its burrow, secretes a multilayered mucus 'cocoon' around itself and waits for rain – for years. Aboriginal peoples find these frogs, squeeze them to release the water they have stored up in their bladders and skin pockets, and replace them. When the rain does come there is a frenzy of activity in the desert. Life cycle modifications are yet another common form of adaptation to aridity and amphibians excel at this. Life in the desert has been described as 'boom and bust' or 'pulse and reserve', long periods of dormancy and torpor, punctuated by periods of hyper-activity in procreation and growth. Michael Mares, the veteran investigator of desert adaptation and evolution, has described how amphibians 'breed explosively' after a drought. Huge numbers of eggs are laid frenetically,

104, 105 Thorny and horned.

to hatch typically within a day. Larval development sets speed records and some forms of larvae are carnivorous and cannibalistic. An evaporating pond on a desert playa is the dramatic scene of nature red in tooth and claw – one of the keys to life in the desert is speeding some things up and slowing other things down. Reptile eggs can lie dormant for long periods of time, buried in the sand until the vital level of moisture is reached.

The strategies for living in the desert, whether adopted by animals (including humans), insects or plants, are of clever innovations to make the most of what little there is. In chapter One, we encountered the Namibian beetle that collects the meagre condensation from the atmosphere, but this kind of technology is not only employed by beetles. Consider the two portraits here: on the left is the wondrous Australian thorny devil (rather cruelly named *Moloch horridus*, after the ancient sacrifice-loving god and angel of Satan), on the right, *Phrynosoma cornutum*, the horned lizard of Arizona, also the official State Reptile of Texas (illus. 104, 105). Despite the similarities in their bizarre appearance, they belong to two very different lizard lineages that have evolved for 150 million years on two totally separated continents: the similarities are a dramatic example of convergent evolution and the technology of drinking. The complex shapes and micro-structures of their scales are cleverly designed and use capillary action to draw any condensation out of the air and channel it to their mouths. Hygroscopic (water-retaining) mucus around their mouths adds to the efficiency of the process and their tongue and jaw create a pumping action that ensures the continuous flow of collected water.

The similarities between the thorny devil and the horned lizard extend to their camouflage and, remarkably, to their diet: they both live almost exclusively on ants and their jaws and tongues are specialized for myrmecophagy. They have no need for big teeth and strong jaws to chew on large prey, simply swallowing the ants directly, standing almost motionless beside an unsuspecting column of ants that delivers a constant supply of food. There is little risk of a food shortage, given the ant population of the Australian desert and, for the lizards of the U.S. southwest, 100,000 or so species of insects. The arthropods, in terms of variety, adaptation and sheer numbers, rule the desert. In large areas of Australia there are probably several hundred tonnes of termites in every square kilometre, and in Africa a single swarm of locusts may weigh thousands of tonnes. Termites, ants, beetles, spiders, flies, bees, wasps, centipedes, scorpions and locusts use almost every arid adaptation trick in the book: ectothermia, burrowing, nocturnalism, metabolic water management, insulation, radiation shielding, modified life cycles, estivation. Scorpions have demonstrated the lowest metabolic rates ever measured in a living organism, will eat almost any insect and can detect the vibrations of food's presence metres away. When food is not available they don't need to eat for a year and can resuscitate after being frozen – scorpions are tough. As are desert ants. In the Sahara, *Cataglyphis bombycina*, the silver ant (illus. 106), and its cousin *Cataglyphis*

106 Silver ants and their nest.

fortis are the most heat-tolerant creatures known (except, of course, for some types of microbes).

To forage on the carcasses of the less strong, these ants wait in their nests, preparing heat shock proteins, until the heat of the day becomes intolerable for their predators, and then boldly go about their business with body temperatures up to 50°c and ground temperatures in the 60s. The proteins help protect them, as does their reflective silver colouring, and they move at an amazing speed (the human equivalent of over 400 kilometres per hour) on unusually long legs for an ant, keeping themselves off the searing ground surface. Their extraordinary navigational abilities guide them back to the nest by the shortest route. Even so, the silver ants can only spend twenty minutes outside before they succumb and become food for their colleagues.

Insects form the framework of any desert ecosystem – and termites are invariably the 'keystone species', the 'ecosystem engineers'. The most ubiquitous (and irritating) vegetation in the Australian outback is spinifex, strictly *Triodia*. This coarse, tough grass grows in landscape-smothering tussocks (illus. 109), and its spiky leaf tips contain small shards of silica that have a habit of embedding themselves in the skin of passing animals, including humans.

Spinifex performs an important function in terms of dune stabilization and is a key participant in the fire ecology of the desert, but it is essentially inedible for animals and would smother the land and clog the ecosystem if left unchecked. In other climates, plant debris is cleared by wood-decaying fungi, but the desert is too dry for them. However, crucially, termites eat spinifex and there are a lot of them. Spinifex may be an archetypal feature of the landscapes of the outback, but so are termite mounds. They come in a bewildering array of shapes and sizes, each one extending far below the surface for water supply and providing a complex climate-controlled home to a community of hundreds of thousands of individuals (illus. 107, 108). The termites consume the spinifex (along with a vast variety of other organic matter) and keep it under control, but they cannot digest it. For that, through a remarkable example of symbiosis, they require the specialized microbes in their gut that convert the cellulose to acetate, a kind of vinegar that then feeds the termites. Termite mounds provide safe havens for a variety of other creatures (some lizards lay their eggs in them) and the process of their construction moderates the desert soils, influencing water infiltration and evaporation, changing the structure and permeability.

107, 108 Termite mounds in the Australian outback.

This, in turn, promotes plant growth and diversity, the entire vertebrate and invertebrate burrowing ecology and the food chain as a whole. Termite mounds in the Sahara and the Sahel are referred to as 'houses of the devil', but without this 'keystone species' arid lands would be very different – it has been estimated that most or all of the biomass produced in the Chihuahuan Desert is consumed by termites.

Termites may be seen as destructive and threatening as they go about consuming your house, but in the desert they are a vital and constructive part of the natural system. However, insects do exist that

109 Spinifex country.

110 A tree before the locust plague of 1915.

truly are threatening and destructive in arid lands, a scourge and a plague, insects that feature prominently in the Bible:

> For they covered the face of the whole earth, so that the land was darkened; and they did eat every herb of the land, and all the fruit of the trees which the hail had left: and there remained not any green thing in the trees, or in the herbs of the field, through all the land of Egypt.

Locusts. In their non-swarming mode, desert locusts are relatively harmless solitary grasshoppers, but when circumstances change them to their gregarious form, a 'phase change' that includes body shape and metabolism as well as behaviour, their swarming is catastrophic. In a bad year of outbreaks, locusts can populate 20 per cent of the earth's land surface, affecting more than 60 countries and one in every ten people on the planet; swarms can travel more than 100 kilometres in a day, each individual consuming its own weight in food. The young locusts abandon their solitary lifestyle and begin to band together in ever-larger groups, and then they march. With their final moult, they

111 The same tree after the plague.

become adults, spread their wings and take off in their tens of millions. Tens of millions of insects in need of protein and salt which they find in vegetation, seeds, carrion, dung and themselves: locusts are cannibals. Is it fleeing to avoid being eaten by their relatives behind them that stimulates the swarm? Surveying for the early signs of locust swarming sent both Ralph Bagnold and Wilfred Thesiger on desert expeditions, but unfortunately our ability to predict and control has not made many significant advances since. The more we investigate their habits and what drives them to congregate, the more mysterious locust behaviour becomes. It seems that protein and salt deficiency is a primary cause and that rains after a drought stimulate congregation. Strangely they prefer low nitrogen plants from areas of degraded soil, so could nitrogen fertilizers discourage them? And are we making the problem worse by overgrazing and the resulting soil degradation as well as by increasing the areas of grassland for animal fodder and biofuels? Are there specific biochemicals associated with the swarming phase change that could be (safely) targeted? We have no answers and so the biblical plagues continue to destroy crops and natural vegetation over vast areas year after year.

The great locust plague of 1915 stripped essentially every piece of vegetation from a vast swathe of the lands of southern Syria and Palestine, devastating the food chain. The Library of Congress holds a remarkable photographic record, including the 'before and after' images of a tree, shown in illus. 110 and 111.

The xerophytes, the plants of the drylands, have evolved an astonishing variety of adaptations to combat desiccation, fire and consumption by animals and insects. The tree may have no means of preventing its defoliation by locusts, but it probably survived. Defence against predators is important for a desert plant, but, once again, the priority is water management. In her luminous accounts of the flora of the Mojave, Mary Austin wrote:

> If you have any doubt about it, know that the desert begins with the creosote. This immortal shrub spreads down into Death Valley and up to the lower timber-line, odorous and medicinal as you might guess from the name, wandlike, with shining fretted foliage.

The creosote bush, *Larrea tridentata* or greasewood, demonstrates the ultimate drought tolerant skills of the xerophytes: it has root systems that both spread laterally and penetrate to depth, taking advantage of surface and subsurface moisture. Its tiny leaves minimize water loss and can orient themselves to reduce the direct heat of the sun; the plant cells themselves can withstand extreme desiccation. And from an original central plant that dies off after several decades, the creosote can clone itself into a ring of genetically identical growth. The so-called 'King Clone' of the Mojave has been dated as 11,700 years old, one of the oldest living organisms on earth (illus. 112).

The dominance of the creosote gives way northward to the rule of the sagebrush, again aromatic and medicinal, the extra in so many westerns. These plants may dominate but they are players in an astonishingly diverse flora of the arid lands. Edward Abbey observed from his trailer in the Arches National Monument:

> the princess plume with its tall golden racemes; the green ephedra or Mormon tea, from which Indians and pioneers extracted a medicinal drink (contains ephedrine); the obnoxious Russian thistle, better known as tumbleweed, an exotic;

pepperweed, bladderweed, snakeweed, matchweed, skeleton-weed – last-named so delicately formed as to be almost invisible; the scrubby little wavy-leaf oak, stabilizer of sand dunes . . .

For plants, water management is all about photosynthesis and transpiration, water movement and evaporation through leaf pores, the stomata. Photosynthesis can, of course, only take place in daylight hours, using the energy of sunlight and some complex biochemistry to manufacture the plant's nutrients from carbon dioxide and water. But as temperatures rise, the most common photosynthetic process, referred to as C3, reflecting the way carbon atoms are clustered during processing, becomes less and less efficient. A small minority of plants, specially adapted to hot and arid lands, use a different carbon dioxide delivery process and biochemical pathways that avoid this inefficiency. These are the C4 plants, and their close relatives, the so-called CAM photosynthesizers. C4 plants only evolved around 25 million years ago, but they did so multiple times and in different places, another example of convergent evolution. They treat carbon isotopes differently from C3 plants, and so they can provide proxies in palaeoclimate analyses. Only a small percentage of plant species use C4 or CAM photosynthesis, but they are extremely important – they include around half of all grasses and many crops, for example millet and maize. Both C4 and CAM plants operate more of a closed system, can efficiently divide daytime and night-time processes and, vitally, can close their stomata during the day, substantially reducing water loss. However, they are not the only plants to modify stomata opening hours. Cacti, agaves and aloes close their stomata during the day and store carbon dioxide overnight for photosynthetic processing the next day – they are nocturnal plants.

Just as the palm tree is the image of the North African desert and spinifex is the floral icon of the Australian outback, the saguaro cactus appears in just about every American desert cartoon. And for good reason: *Carnegiea gigantea* is endemic to the Sonoran Desert and, growing up to 13 metres tall and weighing more than 8,000 kilograms, can dominate the landscape. The saguaro typifies the water management skills of cacti – more than 90 per cent of it is water (illus. 113). The shady ribs of the saguaro can expand to collect water when it is available and contract to conserve it when it is not. The spines, really modified leaves, customize air circulation around the plant, collecting condensation, and the skin is thick and waxy to reduce evapotranspiration.

112 The King Clone creosote of the Mojave.

113 The mighty saguaro cactus.

114 A lone acacia in the Moroccan Sahara.

115–20 Outback flora.

121 Resurrection plants waiting for rain in the Egyptian Sahara.

There are more than 1,500 species of cactus, all of them native to the Americas, but their adaptive skills are shared by many desert plants around the world. Among the thousands of species of *Euphorbia*, many are xerophytes, having independently exploited the same solutions to aridity, including spines, fleshiness and root systems; the evolutionary lineages, both divergent and convergent, are complex and, so far, largely undecipherable.

Many of the huge variety of acacia trees and shrubs, the thorn trees or wattles, are xerophytes, found in deserts from Africa to Australia (although the Australian varieties are rarely thorny). The sight of a lone acacia, apparently flourishing in the middle of an arid gravel plain, is startling (illus. 114), and raises immediate questions. Desert plants are typically widely spaced but this is surely taking an ecological principle to an extreme. How did it get there and how did it grow? Is it the sole remnant of a grove of acacias from better times? How could a single seed germinate and continue to find adequate water in order to grow its roots to a sustainable depth?

But it's a common sight, the most famous acacia being the Tree of Ténéré in the heart of the Sahara of northern Niger. No one knows how long this tree lived in its splendid isolation, protected and revered, some 400 kilometres from any other, a landmark for caravans. Its death is infamous, knocked down in an extraordinary feat of navigation by a probably inebriated truck driver in 1973. The original tree is now in the national museum, in its place a simple metal sculpture that featured in the delightful film *La gran final* (2006, *The Great Match*; see chapter Five). In the 1930s, a well was dug close to the tree and its roots were revealed probing the water table 36 metres below the surface; therein lies one of the adaptive skills of the acacias. Not having much ability to store water or manage photosynthesis, their roots are deep and they shed their leaves in times of drought. Indeed, acacias essentially enter a state of estivation during hard times, appearing desiccated and withered, only to revive with leaves and flowers when the rains come. The Australian wattles, nearly a thousand species of which are native to that continent, are dramatically different from the lone trees of the Sahara and they dominate the exuberant diversity of the flora of the outback (illus. 115–20) that is largely uninhibited by grazing mammals (with the exception today of the feral camels).

The ability of some xerophytes to practise the floral equivalent of estivation, essentially shutting down completely and waiting for rain, is demonstrated in the extreme by a variety of appropriately named 'resurrection plants'. There are a number of species that have this skill, all of them employing a mysterious combination of genetic, metabolic, biochemical and morphological tricks to survive extreme desiccation. Several of them are popularly known as the 'Rose of Jericho', brought back to Europe in amazement by Christian pilgrims to the Holy Land (illus. 121). These shrivelled clumps of utterly desiccated twigs can remain this way for decades and then, with the first rain, unfurl, drop seeds that germinate within hours and, in their own way, briefly flourish. A life cycle modification that mimics the boom and bust of other desert life forms: long periods of boredom punctuated by flashes of frenzied activity.

Lone acacias and scattered resurrection plants are more or less self-contained, but the desert ecosystem as a whole is a complex network of interdependencies. There are endless positive interactions among and between plants and animals, mutual dependencies of seed dispersal and pollination, shade, microclimates and safe havens – lizards in termite mounds, owls nesting in saguaro cacti. Species adapted and evolved together, divergently and convergently, migrating and exploiting specialized life skills as climates changed. Around 200,000 years ago a new species, not particularly well adapted to aridity but intelligent and innovative, faced the deserts of North Africa, found ways to cross it, and changed the planet forever: *Homo sapiens*.

122 Below, the first shuttle radar image showing river valleys
invisible beneath the sands in a conventional image, top.
The radar 'strip' is 50 km across.

SEVEN

Barriers and Corridors, Imports and Exports

I draw attention to the presence of the crocodile in the lakes of Mîherô and also at the head of Ouâdi-Tedjoûdjelt, in a place called Tadjcradjeré, on the south edge of Tasîli du Nord. The major floods that took place at the time of my journey to Tikhàmmalt prevented me from going myself to verify the similarity of this amphibious animal to those of the Nile or of the Niger, but the information that was given to me by individuals who had seen the crocodile in Egypt and within the Sudan was precise and definite. The dread that it inspires in serfs living by the water, the tithe it takes from the herds that go to drink from the lakes, the injuries from which some Touaregs bear scars leave me no doubt in this respect. According to the Touaregs, this reptile remains hidden within underwater caves during the winter and emerges in the spring on the shore. In the mating season, they say, the females emit cries similar to those of camels in rut. Nevertheless, the existence of so large an animal within small lakes of merely a few hectares in a country where rains are rare seems at first improbable. The history and the recent observation of the existence of the crocodile in similar regions, however, allows me to place this saurian within the faunal nomenclature of the country of the Touareg of the North.

HENRI DUVEYRIER was a French geographer and Saharan explorer with, for his time, remarkably enlightened views of the Tuareg. The paragraph above (translated by the author) is from his account of his journeys, *Les Touareg du nord*, published in 1858. It seems at first glance fanciful: he is, after all, talking of the mountains of the Tassili n'Anjer, deep in the heart of the Sahara of southeastern Algeria, and he is describing crocodiles, alive and well in the gueltas, the permanent or semi-permanent rock pools and small lakes. But this is not fantasy, Duveyrier was not deranged by the desert – a crocodile skeleton resides in an Algiers museum, probably the last of the Tassili n'Anjer population, shot by a French army sergeant in 1908. Crocodiles are known to be living today in the gueltas of the Tibesti Mountains and the Ennedi Plateau of northern Chad, a few hundred kilometres southeast of where Duveyrier heard of them. Significant populations of the hardy amphibians have been identified from more than 60 localities in the mountains and ephemeral river beds of southern Mauritania, often practising estivation to make it through the frequent periods of desiccation. It is highly likely that there are more crocodiles eking out a living in remote and isolated homes across the desert, but they simply have not yet had the privilege of a visit by western observers.

These crocodiles, together with other totally water-dependent fauna, including fish, are indeed isolated: they have no way out. But their presence raises the obvious question of how they got there in the first place. We clearly need to examine any assumptions on the timing and duration of Saharan aridity and its effectiveness as a barrier to animal (including human) migration. One obvious clue lies in the fact that the Tassili n' Anjer is a UNESCO World Heritage Site, not for the crocodiles, but for its 10,000-year record of human occupation, testified to in stunning rock art. The power of the landscape is echoed in the power of the art, one of the most important collections in the world: engraved and carved into rock and desert varnish, and exquisitely painted on the walls and roofs of caves, are thousands of depictions of humans and a menagerie of animals. But these are animals that are hardly indigenous to today's hyper-arid Sahara: elephant, giraffe, gazelle, rhinoceros, hippopotamus, lion – and crocodile – all testaments to a rather different Sahara. A few years after Duveyrier's travels, the great French geographer, anarchist, naturist and vegetarian Élisée Reclus wrote how 'The tribes of the Algerian Sahara say that at the time of the Romans the Ouad-Souf was a great river, but someone threw a spell on it and it disappeared.' This was, ironically, the same valley that bewitched Isabelle Eberhardt, who wrote of its dunes as 'a strange ocean frozen mid-tempest, solidified – only its surface, partner to the winds, flowed ceaselessly in the silence of the unchanging centuries.' Eberhardt may have been seduced by the idea of the unchanging desert, but her view was wrong. The desert is about nothing but change. Nevertheless, the scale of change is difficult

to comprehend: yes, the art of our desert ancestors depicts less arid
times, a more forgiving environment than today – but rivers?

Out of – and possibly into – Africa a few times

In November 1981 the ultimately ill-fated Space Shuttle *Columbia* was
launched on its, and the programme's, second mission. Much of the
mission's focus was on testing and demonstrating the safety and performance of the craft, but among the instrumentation it carried was
a device called the Shuttle Imaging Radar-A, a technological shot in
the dark cobbled together from spare parts of an earlier radar satellite.
It was an idea, a suspicion, that radar, through its ability to penetrate
clouds, vegetation and, possibly, soil, could reveal something different from conventional remote-sensing instruments. And reveal something
different it most certainly did. As the shuttle took one fly-past over the
Selima sand sheet of the southern Egyptian desert (scene of many of
Ralph Bagnold's exploits), the radar instrument peered down at the
almost featureless sand. When the data were processed, NASA staff were
shocked. The image here shows, at the top, the conventional satellite view
of the desert, together with the path of the radar imaging and, below,
the radar view (illus. 122). The instrument, like an X-ray, ignored the sand
and looked a few metres below the surface to the solid rock beneath.
There, in clear and extraordinary detail, were river valleys.

It was, as the principal investigator would later describe it, 'just a
fluke', but a fluke that would kickstart the intensive development of
radar technology and revolutionize our understanding not only of the
desert's past but of our own.

Charles Darwin had always felt that Africa was the cradle of humanity, the home of all our ancestral lineages, but until the 1920s the
conventional wisdom was that we originated in Asia where the oldest
scraps of human-like remains so far had been found. Then, in 1924, a
three-year-old child's skull was discovered in South Africa, dated from
around 2.8 million years ago. Inevitably, academic controversy raged
for years until the findings were accepted and the first of many revisions
to the tree of human evolution was made: *Australopithecus africanus*
officially took its place as a low branch on that tree. The branch would
expand, notably with the addition of *A. afarensis*, better known as Lucy,
and her relatives. But exactly where they came from remains unclear, as
do the origins of another older, isolated group, the *Ardipithecus* family

that includes *Sahelanthropus tchadensis*, a distinctly ape-like character who walked upright on the shores of a crocodile-infested lake in what is now the Djurab Desert of northern Chad more than 6 million years ago. This is the place in the narrative of our origins where geology meets anthropology and archaeology, and, just as piecing together a complete geological story is made impossible by the discontinuity of the archives, so is our own story. The cemeteries of our predecessors are in locations vulnerable to natural turbulence and predators, and what remains is a meagre and fragmented record. The graves have no inscriptions. We cannot link the *Sahelanthropus* and *Australopithecus* groups and we cannot definitively link either of them to ourselves. Indeed, there may well never have been a link and our quest to find one is perhaps more a reflection of a modern human need for a genealogical tree than the reality of our ancestry. But all of these hominins (itself, as opposed to hominids, a relatively new term resulting from revisions to the evolutionary story) were most definitely African and most definitely living in climatically challenging times.

Our planet's climate has always changed, shifting in part in response to cyclic changes of the earth's orientation and passage around the sun, and in part as a result of migrating continents influencing oceanic and atmospheric circulation, all this, as we have seen, mixed in with occasional catastrophic volcanic eruptions and complex feedbacks. Around 4 million years ago, geological records from both ocean and land show the beginning of a long-term, but fluctuating, cooling trend and the onset of regular ice ages. Along with the cooling trend came increasing aridity. Carbon isotope analyses of the tooth enamel of our possible australopithecine ancestors show a significant change in diet around 3.5 million years ago from fruits and herbs to C4 grasses. This, together with separate evidence of the move towards carnivorous habits, is indicative of a change to drier savannah conditions. Aridity became pronounced around 1.8 million years ago, the same time that our undeniable ancestor, big-brained and long-legged *Homo erectus*, strode on to the scene. But exactly where that scene was is now the subject of considerable and vociferous academic debate. Archaeological work at the Dmanisi site in the Georgian Caucasus had already shown *erectus*-like remains from 1.77 million years ago, but in 2011 further excavations revealed that the site was already occupied 1.85 million years ago, stirring huge controversy with the possibility that *Homo erectus* originated in Eurasia and migrated into Africa. Further flames are added to the academic fire by the possibility that the diminutive and difficult Indonesian 'hobbit', *Homo floriensis*, first discovered in 2003, was a descendant of primitive australopithecines whose short legs, conventional wisdom had it, never enabled their going anywhere beyond Africa.

So it seems that however compelling and romantic a concept 'Out of Africa' may be, it requires a radical rethink. Clearly, although in the popular imagination the 'Out of Africa' idea applies to anatomically and behaviourally modern humans, *Homo sapiens*, there had been migrations of our probable ancestors long before that. A further problem with the idea is that it is intimately linked with the attractive concept of the 'family tree', a simple series of branches, all but one of which failed, the successful branch crowned by ourselves as a result of our brave conquest of the Sahara Desert and the world. Perhaps the views of the great palaeontologist and evolutionary theorist Stephen J. Gould are closer to the unpleasantly complex truth:

> Humans are not the end result of predictable evolutionary progress, but rather a fortuitous cosmic afterthought, a tiny little twig on the enormously arborescent bush of life, which if replanted from seed, would almost surely not grow this twig again.

It may be that, in our determination to define the tree of life, we are missing the bush, looking in the wrong places with the wrong ideas. And, in our instinctive view of the desert as a barrier, we are missing the corridors – after all, the crocodiles did not cross the desert in the sense of making their way across the dunes, they simply took advantage of opportunities that opened up to them. The conventional view that *Homo sapiens* appeared around 200,000 years ago and then waited patiently for 140,000 years for the Nile to stabilize as a potential itinerary is now firmly superseded, both by archaeological data and by the revelations of the Space Shuttle *Columbia*.

Archaeological sites demonstrate that hominins have, at least periodically, resided in, and to the north of, the Sahara for more than 2 million years, and stunning results from improved satellite radar imaging capacity, combined with the confirmation of their geological implications, have shown how. It is now dramatically clear that the old river valley underlying the Selima sand sheet is but a glimpse of major river systems crossing the entire Sahara, river systems that, whenever aridity ameliorates and the rains come, can be rapidly reactivated, greening the desert and opening it up to man and beast alike.

In chapter Two, in considering the key role of water in sculpting desert landscapes, we saw how a large valley descending from the great plateau of the Gilf Kebir in extreme southwestern Egypt looks exactly as we would expect a major mountain river system to look, except for its total desiccation (illus. 27). We now know, thanks to the work of Egyptian, American, French and British geologists, that when rains have fallen on the plateau in greener times, this valley has carried a river that is simply a tributary of a huge regional river system likely draining north and west into the Mediterranean. Named after a remote Libyan oasis under which it lies, the Kufrah River can be traced from far to the south, where it quite possibly drained 'mega-lake' Chad, northward through a vast inland delta beyond which it disappears under the sands (illus. 123). For deciphering the story of the desert and our own history, this is buried treasure indeed.

Not only does a vast system of Saharan rivers, lying dormant beneath the desert, estivating beneath the sands until the next period of a green Sahara, provide the corridors, periodically, for our ancestors (and crocodiles) to migrate, but it also supplies the plentiful source of sand for building the sand seas when aridity returns. These rivers may also give us clues to today's distribution of underground water courses across the desert – the Kufrah River may be responsible for the Kufrah oasis. But how often have these corridors been activated? The answer lies in the roughly twenty cycles of glaciations and intervening warm periods that have been the hallmark of the last few million years of our planet's history. A glacial episode in high latitudes causes deepening of aridity in the tropical regions, the retreat of the ice subsequently leading to more humid conditions.

When *Homo erectus* was on the move, these cycles were relatively short and benign, but around a million years ago glacial periods became more severe and longer-lasting, typically operating on 100,000-year cycles. When *Homo sapiens* first appeared, the timing was bad – in the midst of what was the coldest, the most severe, glacial episode of them all. From around 125,000 years ago the ice retreated and ushered in 50,000 years of relatively benign conditions, only to be followed by the return of the ice sheets and the last major glacial episode. This reached its peak around 20,000 years ago, the 'Last Glacial Maximum', or LGM, when deserts were in general at their greatest extent. 'In general' simply

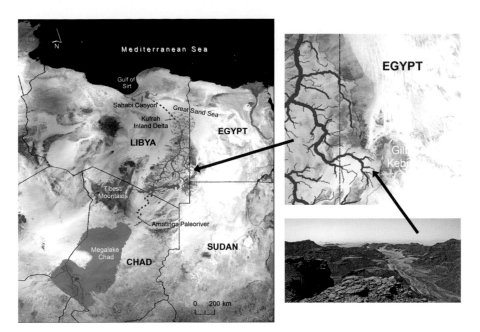

123 The Kufrah River system of the eastern Sahara and the tributary valley of the Gilf Kebir.

because regional changes to atmospheric circulation, the jet stream and the monsoons meant that aridity was not global: the deserts of the American southwest, for example, experienced increased rain and the development of huge lakes. But North Africa and the Middle East were most definitely arid, the dry climate showing no improvement until around 12,000 years ago. Our migrating ancestors were faced with profound changes to their habitats and the available corridors along which populations could move. Even in times when North Africa was habitable, moving beyond that region was still a challenge. There were three possible ways out: across the Strait of Gibraltar, across the northern Sinai to the Levant, and into the Arabian Peninsula across the narrow Bab el Mandeb, the 'Strait of Grief' between what are today Djibouti and Yemen.

Since the spectacular stalactites and stalagmites of limestone caverns only grow when there is water available, their history provides yet another proxy for alternating periods of aridity and humidity. Such deposits ('speleothems') from caves in Israel's Negev Desert reveal a relatively wet period from around 140,000 to 110,000 years ago, coinciding with the first known appearance of *Homo sapiens* in the Levant. We had clearly made it out of Africa, but by what route? Oddly, the evidence for migrations along the Nile is meagre, and it is likely that groups already established along the North African coast simply set out eastward as the desert conditions ameliorated. This excursion is regarded as 'abortive', there being no evidence of onward move-ment or long-term residence – but then again, the available evidence is hardly abundant. The straits between Africa and Europe and Arabia would seem difficult for our ancestors to traverse; the periods of dra-matically lower sea levels that would have reduced, but not eliminated, the distance to be crossed were also periods of extreme glaciation and aridity. There is little evidence, human or animal, of a significant Gibraltar connection, but a different story seems to be unfolding in the Arabian Peninsula. The archaeological archives have only begun to be deciphered in recent years, but they are rich. Evidence of human occupation dating from more than 125,000 years ago is being revealed in the coasts, deserts and mountains, ancient river systems and lakes have been mapped beneath the desert sands, and proxies show periods of abundant water supplies. Rock art was long unrecognized in Saudi Arabia, but today, thanks to Bedouin reports, more than 2,000 sites have been identified. It seems quite likely that the 'out of Africa' story may well need to be overlaid with an 'out of Arabia' saga.

Our enterprising ancestors had found their way around the world long before the LGM, surviving and adapting (rather like the crocodiles) in environmental refuges when times were bad, moving on when conditions improved. We survived not only ice and aridity, but vol-canism: 74,000 years ago the Sumatran volcano of Mount Toba staged a 'mega-eruption', darkening the planet's skies and plunging it into a 'nuclear winter' in the midst of an ice age. The world population of *Homo sapiens* may well have been reduced to fewer than 10,000 people. But we are survivors. By the time the ice sheets staged their final retreat, we were a global phenomenon, poised to move on into civilizations and societies.

Cradles, civilizations and climate

The history of mankind is intimately interwoven, pragmatically and spiritually, with the desert, but in particular the desert margins, the 'lost borders'. The end of the last great glacial episode was not the end of climate change: the rock art of the Sahara is but one example of human records of fluctuating aridity and 'greening' of the deserts of the world. The archaeological and geological archives tell of the onset of semi-humid conditions in the southern Sahara around 10,500 years ago, after which the desert margin shifted perhaps 800 kilometres northward over just a few centuries. Extreme aridity returned perhaps 5,000 years later, causing humans and animals to flee the desert. There is even a 'model' referred to as the 'Saharan pump' that sees the human history of the region being driven by suction into a greening desert followed by expulsion as a result of aridity. The timing and nature of changes in the Gobi Desert or the Australian red centre may differ in detail from those of the Sahara, but the cyclic nature of aridity is a global phenomenon and plays a crucial role in the human story.

To the outsider, the desert is always a barrier, routinely associated with the qualifying adjective 'impassable'. The barrier may be regarded as the ultimate defence, whether fictionally by the states of Narnia or Oz, or historically by the Turkish garrison at Aqaba whose guns were pointed towards the sea rather than the 'impassable' Nefud Desert out of which T. E. Lawrence charged with his Arab forces. The Italian forces in Libya during the Second World War suffered for their delusion that the surrounding desert was 'impassable' to the likes of Ralph Bagnold and his Long Range Desert Group, indulging in 'piracy on the high desert'. The desert may be seen as a barrier to progress, as was the case with Australia or the manifest destiny of the United States. As John Steinbeck wrote in *Travels with Charley*, 'The Mojave is a big desert and a frightening one. It's as though nature tested a man for endurance and constancy to prove whether he was good enough to get to California.'

But the insider knows that the desert is never a total barrier. As Antoine de Saint-Exupéry (as close to an insider as an outsider can get) commented, 'What makes the desert beautiful is that somewhere it hides a well.' Know the water and you know the desert and the corridors that render it no longer impassable. This is something that, as just one example, the Tubu women of the Ténéré Desert are experts at on their trading journeys. Extraordinary navigators, they use sand-ridge orientations, dune-counting and the stars to travel for days to find a well a mere metre across, hidden in the sand sea – a shopping expedition with a difference across landscapes of death. A well allows a desert crossing, water close to the surface on a larger scale permits an oasis, perhaps with hundreds of thousands of date palms, but a river provides the resources for a society, for a 'civilization'. Rivers facilitated and channelled the migrations of our ancestors and the great desert rivers of today – the Nile, Tigris, Euphrates, Niger, Amu Darya (Oxus), Jordan and Colorado – set the scene for human social development that led, for better or for worse, to where we are today.

'The Fertile Crescent' resonates in our human roots, and for good reason. The fertility represents the lands linking the Mesopotamian rivers with the Nile, crescentic in shape as it follows the contours of rainfall and skirts the borders of the Syrian and Arabian deserts, the landscapes where the desert meets the sown. Hunter-gatherer societies took advantage of climatic improvements and by 10,000 BC had begun to domesticate sheep, goats and cattle, and to cultivate wild grasses from the drylands: wheat, millet, barley, all with seeds that are easily stored and transported. These initiatives undoubtedly took place independently in different places at different times, and the sequence is a contentious topic. As is the thorny question of whether agriculture preceded settlement or vice versa. But the implications are clear for the development of two different lifestyles. Domestication of animals allowed the flourishing of pastoral nomadism, increasing the security of mobility in environments that changed on annual and longer-term scales. Agriculture underpinned the rationale for settlement, the security of fortifications, the continuity of resources and a communal approach to economics. This separation has, as we shall see, always been blurred, but the myths of nomadic lifestyles and their incompatibility with settlement have long underwritten a distorted narrative of inevitable conflict.

The story of human settlement is one that continues to be re-drafted as new data conflict with the prevailing narrative, the conventional wisdom. In the dryland foothills of Turkey's Zagros Mountains, where rivers rise to join the Euphrates, excavations continue at a site that has fundamentally challenged that conventional wisdom. Göbekli Tepe is the world's oldest monumental construction identified to date, successive circles of huge stones weighing more than sixteen tonnes, carefully wrought and decorated with endless sophisticated carvings of animals, from bulls to ants and lions to scorpions. The oldest date from 11,600 years ago, millennia before the pyramids and 6,000 years before the embarrassingly rustic Stonehenge. What it was, we don't know. There are no signs so far of agriculture or habitation, but workers must have been housed and fed, even if the construction was purely for religious purposes. Further discoveries in the area of possible settlement from the same time continue to upset traditional views.

Göbekli Tepe enjoys a hot steppe climate, according to the Koppen-Geiger classification – annual rainfall today averages over 400 millimetres, but it all comes in the winters with typically no precipitation during the summer months. Follow that precipitation contour westwards along the Fertile Crescent, and it passes through the Jordan Valley and the Dead Sea, near which lies Jericho, one of the oldest established human settlements. By around 9,000 years ago, dryland agriculture was well established, together with the compelling human logic of settlement. With a couple of thousand inhabitants, mud-brick houses, a protective ditch (and, later, a wall), the location of Jericho was determined not only by the nearby River Jordan, but by the abundant springs that allowed the oasis town to grow.

That word 'determined' raises the need for caution. As we consider the complex and enduring relationships between human societies and aridity, we tread the contentious grounds of geographic (or environmental) determinism. The idea that the physical environment not only influences but causes social change, cultural development and human evolution is an old one, possibly originating with Aristotle. But it flourished in the late nineteenth and early twentieth centuries in the wake of Darwin's work, and provided convenient support for its misapplication by colonial powers eager to justify their actions in the abhorrent terms of civilization versus barbarism. After all, if one can confidently state that a tropical climate causes indolence and an inferior intellect, and that those characteristics define an absence of civilization, then essentially all of sub-Saharan Africa is *terra nullius* for the imperial brand of barbarism. As discussed in chapter Two, Darwin's own views did little to counter this ideology.

By the middle of the twentieth century the ideology of environmental determinism had fallen into disrepute, only to be revived, albeit somewhat moderated, in more recent years as we have come to understand the rapidity with which regional climates can fluctuate and to recognize those changes as an unavoidable backdrop against which human history is played out. It remains, however, the subject of heated debate – the popularity of Jared Diamond's *Guns, Germs, and Steel*, published in 1997, continues to stimulate academic argument and publication today. The problem would seem to be that this is an ideology, an attempt to compress, in a rather unscientific way, the complexities and non-linearity of both the earth system and human culture into a favoured paradigm. The requirements for proving causation become lost in the smoke and dust. Groups of humans have always found themselves in a specific environmental setting at any specific time. If that setting provides what they need at that time, then they stay; if it doesn't, or if it changes, with the seasons or over the longer term, then they seek to adapt or move elsewhere. If the lands they find themselves in are suitable for goats, then they raise goats, not pigs. If written records are useful for agriculture and commerce, or the allocation of water resources, then they develop writing. And so on, and so on. Humans are part of any geography, responding and adapting to achieve what they perceive as necessary and beneficial; there is always a network of causation small and large operating in the background, but strict geographical determinism it is not. Unfortunately, as we shall see in the final chapter, the views of outsiders and, importantly, policy-makers are still tinged with the misconceptions of colonial environmental determinism.

Along the Fertile Crescent, along the flood plains of the Tigris and Euphrates, settlements developed, then towns and, eventually, cities and empires. With increasingly sophisticated agriculture and animal domestication, it made sense for communities to pool their resources, to construct grain and other food storage, to develop and administer common water supplies, and to share skills. Along with these motivations came rulers, laws, administrations, bureaucracies, politics and conflicts. But exactly how the process of congregation took place remains the subject of debate, as do the early economies. The city of Eridu, now in the Iraqi desert tens of kilometres from the current course of the Euphrates, was the earliest and southernmost of the Sumerian cities of Mesopotamia and the home of the gods. Founded around 7,500 years ago, Eridu, and its nearby sister city of Ur, were not desert cities but ports at the head of the Persian Gulf, on the delta of the Tigris and the Euphrates whose cargoes of mud and sand would conspire with falling sea levels to slowly fill the Gulf and extend the shoreline 200 kilometres southwest to its position today. The earliest cities had their backs firmly to the desert and developed in an environment analogous to that of Basra today and, in particular, the tragically drained marshes (now partially restored). This model, supported by the collaborating disciplines of geology and archaeology, runs contrary to the long prevailing views of aridity and the necessary underpinning of extensive canal systems: these early cities were delta towns, the New Orleans of Mesopotamia.

In the foothills of the Zagros east of Göbekli Tepe, there is evidence at Tel Brak for substantial urban growth around the same time as Eridu and Ur, but based on a dryland pastoral and agricultural economy. However, while this and neighbouring urban centres of northern Mesopotamia had a challenging history punctuated by drought, the southern cities flourished. For 2,000 years, the Sumerian city of Uruk, now located on a dry and abandoned channel of the Euphrates, was a centre of Mesopotamian civilization. Like Eridu, for a long time it was also situated close to the waters of the delta, and it was further watered by a canal system from the river, supplying the gardens that made up a third of its huge area of more than 5 square kilometres. Uruk grew into an early city-state, home of King Gilgamesh whose epic story became the oldest piece of great literature that we have. Rival city-states dependent on the ever-shifting channels of the Tigris and Euphrates grew and declined, but a significant consolidation into the Akkadian Empire took place around 4,300 years ago, stretching from Ur in the south northward to Nineveh and the cities of the Zagros and Taurus mountain steppes along the northern fringe of the desert. Nevertheless, the Akkadian Empire, for all its glory, was remarkably short-lived: it had essentially collapsed within little more than 100 years. Why?

Theories abound – invasion, political strife and disintegration have been regarded as the primary causes, all human in origin. However, excavation of one of the key Akkadian sites and primary supplier of grain to the empire, Tel Leilan in northeastern Syria, suggests a different story. The ruins marking the collapse are covered first by a thin layer of volcanic ash, and then by a metre or more of windblown sand and silt, strongly suggesting that environmental factors, a sudden onset of aridity, an encroachment of the desert, were at work. Today, the region is very much dependent on seasonal winter rains and at the mercy of summer drought. During dry seasons and periods, large volumes of dust are blown out of the desert and steppes, southeastward to the Persian Gulf, and it is in those marine sediment records that the archives of aridity are stored. These archives have been accessed by taking cores of the sediments below the sea floor and analysing the telltale contributions of dust particles as a proxy for changes in regional aridity. A dramatic increase in incoming dust shows up at around 4,100 years ago, along with volcanic ash. Forensic chemistry ties the ash and dust to the layers at Tel Leilan and provides the smoking gun for the collapse of the empire: a major period of drought, lasting perhaps 300 years and probably resulting from atmospheric shifts in the inter-tropical convergence zone and El Niño cycles, destroyed the breadbasket and the economy of the Akkadian Empire. Environmental determinism if you wish, but geology and archaeology collaborate to tell the story.

And the evidence continues to build that this was not just a regional disaster of drought and famine, but a global period of aridity that challenged societies from Tibet to Europe. In Egypt, the flowering of civilization attained one of its peaks during the period of the Old Kingdom, four dynasties of dynamic culture, development and pyramid building from around 4,700 years ago. But after 500 years of prosperity, royal squabbling, civil wars, social fragmentation and economic turmoil heralded the end of an era and, 4,200 years ago, the Old Kingdom collapsed. The Egyptian sage Ipuwer gave a graphic description of an environmental and social catastrophe: 'The desert claims the land. Towns are ravaged, Upper Egypt became a wasteland . . . Food is lacking . . . Men stir up strife unopposed. Groaning is throughout the land, mingled with laments.' The Nile is both bountiful and fickle, and it seems that it had essentially dried up, its annual floods no longer providing the resources on which the Old Kingdom had flourished. The story is revealed in the sediments of the lakes of the Nile Delta, where 7,000 years of climate archives are preserved. In those archives are the records of pollen, blown by the winds and carried by the river; the types of pollen from 4,200 years ago show a sudden and dramatic change from humid to arid plants. Furthermore, layers of charcoal testify to dryness and fire. The end of the Old Kingdom was marked by social turmoil, but social turmoil induced by drought, famine and the failure of the Nile, brought on by the same climatic changes that destroyed the Akkadian Empire.

This was only the latest in a series of fluctuations between humid and arid conditions. The muds of the delta lakes show an earlier drying that brought to an end the long period of the 'green Sahara' and, according to some, triggered the very start of pharaonic civilization. For years, the prevailing view of the rise of the Egyptian kingdoms echoed that of Herodotus: they were a gift of the Nile, a welcoming corridor through the desert. However, during the long wet period following the end of the ice ages, the Nile most likely stabilized into a river system that was simply too bounteous, with huge annual floods leaving behind nothing but marshlands unwelcoming to settlement and agriculture. At the same time, to the west, the savannahs of the Sahara supported large numbers of people and animals, settled and pastoral nomads. Cattle were first domesticated in the eastern Sahara 7,000 years ago and used for milk as well as meat – researchers from the University of Bristol have recently shown that fatty acids from unglazed pottery at sites in the Libyan Desert are dairy fats. But when the desiccation cycle of the 'Saharan pump' began 5,300 years ago, there was massive retreat from spreading desert conditions, including eastward migration into the increasingly hospitable Nile valley. The early pre-dynastic Nile settlements appear to have started around 5,600 years ago and the first kingdom of the ancient Egyptians was established. In other words, the first peoples of the great pharaonic civilization came from the desert. There is a growing body of archaeological evidence to support this: we find, for example, that sophisticated technologies were developed in the desert earlier than in the Nile valley. There continues to be a great deal of controversy around this idea (including very personal animosities between its extreme proponents and its more pragmatic supporters), but the evidence of ongoing trade and trade routes between the pharaonic Egyptians and their desert brethren on whom they relied is clear.

It is worth noting that even the precise history of Saharan aridity is troubled by conflicting evidence. While dust records from the sediments of the Atlantic support the view of a sudden onset of aridity around 5,300 years ago, a recent project by Canadian, German and Belgian researchers tells a somewhat more subtle story. Lake Yoa in northern Chad is a saline lake whose sediments miraculously preserve, in extraordinary detail, 6,100 years of environmental archives. The lake's longevity, and the preservation of sediments that would normally be blown away in the wind during dry periods, is the result of its lying close to the underground water table – it has remained a lake, or at least damp, for all that time. Every year a little less than 2 millimetres of sediment have typically accumulated in the lake, each layer showing alternating winter and summer conditions. Each layer preserves the remains of micro-organisms and pollen in addition to windblown sand and dust, and from these proxies a detailed story can be reconstructed. That story tells of tropical savannahs until 5,600 years ago when the first signs of aridity appear – but not rapidly or drastically. The lake became saline around 3,900 years ago, but today's hyper-arid conditions were not established until 700 BC. As is so often the case, the proxies do not necessarily agree with each other and decipherment of the complexities continues.

However, the history of mutual relationships between the communities along the Nile and the desert pastoral nomads is a typical one. Settlement may highlight the contrasts between sedentary and nomadic lifestyles, and increasing aridity may induce changes from agriculture to pastoralism, but the distinctions have often been exaggerated and the true relationships between the desert and the sown ignored to suit a given ideology. Nomadism has always been, and remains, more complex and sophisticated than it has often been given credit for.

On the move, collaboration and conflict

In the preface to the fascinating collection of viewpoints and case studies *Desert Peoples: Archaeological Perspectives*, Mike Smith and his colleagues write:

> For centuries, deserts have captured the public imagination as places of extremes. These are landscapes that might be perceived as impenetrable barriers to human occupation or instead as the domain entered into by individuals pursuing revelatory experience. They are of course also the same terrain through which the Tigris and Euphrates Rivers passed and which, when hydraulically 'tamed,' became the agricultural powerhouses of the Near East. Desert societies have also been central to the anthropological imagination.

The book's focus is on hunter-gatherer societies, but the imaginative role applies equally well to pastoral nomads. As I noted when attempting, in chapter Three, to review objectively the interactions between insiders and outsiders, there is a potential trap of romanticism and that same trap is no less present in our views of nomadism, and particularly the interactions between nomads and settled communities. While archaeologists, anthropologists, ethnographers and sociologists are well aware of this trap and scrupulously try to avoid it, their work often translates into over-simplification, in the minds not only of a typical outsider but of governments and policy-makers with preconceived agendas. In *Nomads, Tribes, and the State in the Ancient Near East: Cross-disciplinary Perspectives*, archaeologist Jeffrey Szuchman succinctly sums up these challenges:

The term nomad, or more precisely pastoral, or sheep- and goat-herding nomad, is itself a complex concept, and scholars have long struggled to identify and overcome the multiple biases that affect the interpretation of Near Eastern nomadism. Although the word 'nomad' no longer conjures up the image of mythic and inscrutable creatures, fiercely independent and existing outside the purview of the civilized world, this romantic notion was not easily vanquished, and one can trace a long tradition of Western travelers and scholars who perpetuated the myth of the stateless nomad, along with a false binary state-nomad opposition. A second myth that has been put to rest is that of the barbaric nomad, sweeping in from the desert to occasionally overwhelm bucolic villages and their defenseless inhabitants.

In place of the mythical noble nomad and the barbaric nomad, scholars have focused not on the nomad per se, but on the nature of pastoral nomadism as an economic adaptation. This focus on pastoral economics has brought to light the fact that there are indeed many different types of pastoral nomadism in the Near East, depending in part on the natural environment.

The book raises the question of whether the integration of pastoral nomads with sedentary populations is so complete as to undermine the entire traditional concept of nomadism and fundamentally question the idea that tribes and states are incompatible. But the narrative of myths of nomadism is an ancient one and arguably the divisions originally evolving from early settlement led to the familiar ideas of conflict between 'civilized' and 'barbaric', views of evolutionary superiority derived from Darwinism and the entire 'outsider–insider' conflict. Once city-states were established, it would not take long for these social divisions to manifest themselves. Baghdad became a flourishing city and international centre of learning where the Abbasid Caliphate was established in the ninth century. The long-lasting Abbasid rule was famous not only for its scientists and scholars, but also for its poets, among whom was Omar Khayyám, author of the *The Rubáiyát* and himself an astronomer and mathematician. Among his predecessors was Bashshár ibn Burd, of Persian origin, an influential writer and a man intensely proud of Persian civilization and his own lineage. In a poem addressing all the Arabs, after extolling the wealth of his family, he describes, with astonishing hubris, his father:

> He was not given to drink the thin milk of goatskins,
>   or to sup it in leather vessels;
> Never did my father sing a camel-song, trailing along
>   behind a scabby camel . . .
> Nor did I dig for and eat the lizard of the stony ground,
> Nor did my father warm himself standing astraddle a flame;
> No, nor did my father use to ride the twin supports of
>   a camel-saddle.
> We are kings who have always been so through the
>   long ages past.

Bashshár hated and despised the Bedouin as primitive and 'outside the purview of the civilized world', a view perpetuated since Cain, the farmer, slew his brother, the herder. For the Western outsider, the cultural barrier between his way of life and that of a pastoral nomad is, as the desert is perceived to be, impassable. Even Wilfred Thesiger, who became as close to the Bedouin as any outsider, relying as he did on their friendship and knowledge to survive the Rub' al Khali, recognized the ambiguities and conflicts. In his view:

> All that is best in the Arabs has come to them from the desert: their deep religious instinct which has found expression in Islam; their sense of fellowship which binds them as members of one faith; their generosity and sense of hospitality; their dignity and the regard which they have for the dignity of others as fellow human beings; their humour, their courage and patience, the language which they speak and their passionate love of poetry.

Yet when he describes the Arab conquest of North Africa:

> These desert Arabs were avaricious, rapacious, and predatory, born freebooters, contemptuous of all outsiders, and intolerant of restraint . . . Only in the desert, they declared, could a man find freedom. It must have been this same craving for freedom which induced tribes that entered Egypt at the time of the

Arab conquest to pass on through the Nile valley into the interminable desert beyond, leaving behind them the green fields, the palm groves, the shade and running water, and all the luxury which they found in the towns they had conquered.

The cultural and social histories of arid lands from Morocco to Mongolia and Tucson to Santiago are narratives of the relationships between the desert and the sown. The Arabic language has its roots in the dialects of nomadic desert tribes, and, as Thesiger remarks, 'It was the customs and standards of the desert which had been accepted by the towns-men and villagers alike, and which were spread by the Arab conquest across North Africa and the Middle East.' While T. E. Lawrence comments accurately that 'Bedouin ways were hard even for those brought up to them and for strangers terrible: a death in life', ancestral ties to desert roots remain powerfully resonant for many city-dwelling Arabs. Hassanein Bey, graduate of Oxford, son of a university professor, grandson of the last admiral of the Egyptian fleet, Olympic athlete, MBE, adviser to Kings Fuad and Farouk and a diplomat of influence until his death in 1946, nevertheless wrote, as he began one of his great desert crossings, 'I was no longer an Egyptian of today, but a Beduin, going back to the desert where his father's fathers had pitched their tents.'

There is little romance, at least to Western eyes, and even to villagers with nomadic roots, in nomadic life today (illus. 124, 125). Poverty and lack of access to health care and education are almost inevitable consequences of mobility, isolation from 'mainstream' society and a lowly position on the social ladder in the eyes of governments and policy-makers. As will be considered in more detail in the last chapter, this is one of the major issues in understanding and managing the social and environmental challenges of arid lands today. To view pastoral nomads as 'outside the purview of the civilized world' and to misrepresent their role in society as a whole is a serious error. Not only are nomadic tribes the people who truly know the desert, but they are, and have always been, also an integral part of the social structure of oases, villages and towns of the lost borders. A nomadic group does not possess everything it needs, nor do the town-dwellers. Nomads need agricultural products and tools and farmers need meat, milk, hides, salt and woven goods. Seasonal changes mean that nomads will settle in towns and oases during hard times, and most Bedouin families, for example, have

124, 125 Berber nomads in the Moroccan Sahara.

agricultural interests and members who specialize in managing them. Trade between the desert and the sown is vital for both, but conflicts over land use, water and status are inevitable.

The first genocide of the twentieth century, featured in Thomas Pynchon's novels *V* and *Gravity's Rainbow*, was committed against the pastoral nomads of the Kalahari and Namibian deserts. Between 1904 and 1908, 65,000 Hereros were slaughtered by the German colonial authorities and settlers. Women, who hold an influential role in Herero society but were described in the German press as 'black amazons swinging clubs and castrating their foes', were specifically targeted. Many were thrown into concentration camps or driven into the desert to die of thirst – their wells were poisoned. Twenty years later, Stalin would set in motion another genocidal event, the catastrophic 'collectivization' and 'sedentarization' of Kazakh nomadic populations under his First Five-Year Plan of 'revolution from above'. Nomads slaughtered their livestock rather than hand them over. In 1929 there were an estimated 36 million livestock in Kazakhstan – horses, goats, sheep, cattle and camels. In 1934 the number was only a little more than 4 million. The resultant famine of the early 1930s killed close to 1.5 million Kazakhs, 38 per cent of the country's population. The nomadic societies of Kazakhstan had been critical components of the fabric of the country, descendants of the Mongol Empire that retained the social structure of the three hordes, the Great, the Middle and the Lesser. That structure was essentially destroyed but remains embedded in the collective memory of Kazakhs today. In the distinctly twenty-first-century metropolis of Almaty, everyone knows to which horde, or *juz*, they and their friends and business associates belong, and to which tribes within them. The Great Juz are still the herdsmen, the Middle the intellectuals and lawyers, and the Lesser the warriors in the informal relationships of cosmopolitan Kazakhs today.

The Kazakh hordes were territorial, and therein lies another myth of pastoral nomadism: tribes wandering entirely at random, with no organization to their management of resources or territory. Nothing could be further from reality. Just as the nomads know the water in the desert, they know its seasons, the cycles and locations of pasturage for their herds and food for themselves, and its routes. Many nomadic groups maintain seasonal encampments with permanent structures. T. E. Lawrence, in noting that every Bedouin knows the stone that marks the limit of the district of his tribe, observed that:

Men may have looked upon the desert as a barren land, the free holding of whoever chooses but in fact each hill and valley in it had a man who was its acknowledged owner and would quickly assert the right of his family or clan to it . . . The desert was held in a crazed communism by which Nature and the elements were for the free use of every known friendly person for his purpose and no more.

The desert is most emphatically not *terra nullius*, and to assume so has led to disastrous policies. Today's Middle East bears turbulent testimony to this.

The desert queen

To describe Gertrude Margaret Lowthian Bell as a remarkable woman is a significant understatement. If, in the early years of the twentieth century, anyone understood how the tribal societies of the desert worked and was in a position to facilitate knowledgeably and intelligently the politics and borders of the Middle East in the aftermath of the First World War and the demise of the Ottoman Empire, it was she. Born to a wealthy industrialist family in the northeast of England in 1868, this 'child of spirit and initiative' (according to her stepmother) was, at the age of nineteen, the first woman to earn a first-class degree in Modern History from Oxford, taking a mere two years to do so. Her uncle was a diplomat posted to Teheran and, after graduating, Gertrude set off to visit him, a trip that began her lifetime addiction to Persia and Arabia, to Arabian culture and peoples and to the desert: 'Oh the desert around Teheran! . . . I never knew what the desert was until I came here; it is a very wonderful thing to see.'

She learned Persian and Arabic and, among her many other activities, set about translating the mystical Sufi poetry of Hafiz. Her travel addiction extended to becoming one of the finest women Alpine climbers of her day, often shocking her companions by removing her skirt for ease of movement. But it was her love of the Middle East that was her primary motivation. She developed a keen interest in archaeology and participated in excavations of sites in northern Mesopotamia and the southern reaches of the Tigris and Euphrates. In 1909 she revealed and mapped the great Abbasid palace-fortress of Ukhaider in what would later become – under her despairing eyes – Iraq. She travelled to Jerusalem, Damascus,

Beirut, Palmyra, and ventured to the Syrian territories of the eclectic religious sect of the Druze during a period of uprisings and violence between neighbouring communities and with the Ottoman Turks. These journeys were daring for any Westerner, and for a woman extraordinary. Gertrude manipulated Turkish bureaucracy in order to travel at all (often without proper permissions), utilized local guides and, where unavoidable, Turkish military escorts, and would ride her horse using a male saddle and a split riding skirt of her own design – she began effectively not disguising herself as a man but adopting male habits. It was her remarkable language skills and ability to recite classic Arabic poetry, often more fluently and more broadly than her hosts, that gained her not only access, but welcome in remote, male-dominated, tribal encampments. Her attitude was simply that 'Opportunities of enlarging the circle of your acquaintance should always be grasped, especially in foreign parts.'

Her love of the desert and her desire to experience remote communities and immerse herself in their culture led her to set out, in 1913, on her most ambitious and dangerous journey: a 2,500-kilometre round-trip by camel from Damascus across the Nefud Desert to the northern Arabian oasis of Hail. The challenges of the terrain were the least of her concerns: Hail was the capital of the Rashid tribe, who were in a constant state of war not only with the Turks but with the forces of King Abdul Aziz ibn Saud, who was determined to bring all of Arabia under his control. Other Westerners had visited Hail, but not easily – the eccentric Charles Montagu Doughty had been nearly murdered there some two decades before Gertrude set off. And whenever Gertrude set off, she did so in style. Her caravan was not large by the standards of the day, but she had her travelling wherewithals well organized and did not believe in deprivation. Her baggage contained hats, veils, parasols, evening dresses, fur coats (the desert is cold in its winter nights), a Wedgwood dinner service, silver candlesticks, a folding canvas bed and bath, and theodolites; a case of rifles, telescopes, binoculars and silver cigarette cases were gifts for the sheikhs who would be her hosts along the way.

Gertrude Bell reached Hail and, finding herself thrown into the midst of ongoing family feuds ('In Hayil, murder is like the spilling of milk'), was immediately placed under house arrest, in the hands of slave girls, eunuchs and the harem (illus. 126–8).

She not only had her unique and informed perspective on Arab society, but she was also a woman, which gave her access to parts of that society rarely seen or described by Westerners. The harem at Hail was

126, 127, 128 Gertrude Bell's view of a Hail welcome (top left);
Turkiyyeh, a Circassian woman slave who befriended Bell (top right);
Bell's camp with nomads (bottom).

classic: 'straight from the Arabian Nights . . . There they were, these
women, wrapped in Indian brocades, hung with jewels, served by slaves.'
Elsewhere in the desert, however, she encountered less romantic versions:

> The harem was shockingly untidy. Except when the women folk
> expect your visit and prepared for it, nothing is more forlornly
> unkempt than their appearance . . . Sheikh Hassan's wife was
> a young and pretty woman, though her hair dropped in wisps
> about her face and neck, and a dirty dressing gown clothed a
> figure which had, alas! already fallen into ruin.

Bell returned safely to Baghdad shortly before the First World War broke out. She sought to support the war effort in the Middle East with her knowledge of the desert and its tribes and kings and, after initially being turned down (she volunteered with the Red Cross in France), 'Major Miss Bell' was dispatched to Cairo to address the chaos that was British policy in the region. As the first woman officer in the history of British intelligence, it was an uphill battle. Not only was profound ignorance of, and a general lack of interest in, Arab affairs widespread among the diplomats, advisers and policy-makers, but they were also all male and largely misogynists. One of the most influential individuals in the process, who would eventually be responsible for the Sykes-Picot Agreement of 1916 that parcelled up the Middle East, was Sir Mark Sykes. Sykes, perhaps irritated by his conviction that Gertrude had employed trickery to reach the Druze territories before he could, was not one of her great admirers. He wrote to his wife, 'Confound the silly chattering windbag of conceited, gushing, flat-chested, man-woman, globe-trotting, rump-wagging, blethering ass!' But Gertrude was a stubborn woman, and determined. She strongly disliked Sykes and his description of the Arabs as 'animals' and 'diseased'. She was a devoted supporter of Arab self-determination, in similar ways to T. E. Lawrence, with whom she periodically worked, and was on personal terms with many of the Arab leaders (illus. 129). 'I see visions and dream dreams,' she declared, but in the end they were dashed.

Amid the disintegration of the now enemy Ottoman Empire, the competing interests of the French, the Russians and the British, and the ungovernable rival tribal societies of the Arab deserts, borders were imposed where none belonged, promises given that could not be kept and countries defined, most notably Iraq. Gertrude Bell was painfully aware that 'Political union is a concept unfamiliar to a society which is still highly coloured by its tribal origins . . . The conditions of nomad life have no analogy with those of the cultivated areas.' In the wake of the Paris Peace Conference of 1919, in which the final, unworkable, map of the Middle East was drawn, A. T. Wilson, the leading British representative in Baghdad with whom Gertrude had had a fractious relationship, wrote:

The very existence of a Shi'ah majority in Iraq was blandly denied as a figment of my imagination by one 'expert' with an international reputation, and Miss Bell and I found it

129 Abdul Aziz Ibn Saud, British administrator Sir Percy Cox
and Gertrude Bell, Basra, 1916.

impossible to convince either the Military or the Foreign
Office Delegations that Kurds in the Mosul vilayet [province]
were numerous and likely to be troublesome, [or] that Ibn Saud
was a power seriously to be reckoned with.

In 1922 Gertrude Bell returned to her love of archaeology and took
up the post of Director of Antiquities in Baghdad where she completely rebuilt the museum and its collections. She died in Baghdad in
1926 and, while the name of T. E. Lawrence is today unknown there, the
name of 'Miss Bell' is still fondly remembered, at least in some quarters.
The bust of Gertrude Bell that had been prominently on display in the
museum was looted, along with many of the treasures, in 2003.

Empires and ungulates

The early empires of Mesopotamia were simply the first of a series that
would rise and fall throughout Eurasia and North Africa, culminating in
the disintegration of Ottoman and European hegemony in the first half
of the twentieth century – which Gertrude Bell was witness to and a
participant in. Empires arose to some extent from ideologies and religions, but were dominantly cultural and survived through trade and
military power. Successful pursuit of both trade and warfare on an
imperial scale is very much dependent on transport efficiency, to which
the horse and the camel provided the key advantage. The history of

animal domestication is a blurred one, key events probably taking place in different locations at different times, but it seems likely that the horse was first domesticated in the drylands of Kazakhstan around 5,600 years ago and, around 600 years later, the dromedary in Arabia and the bactrian camel in the margins of the Gobi Desert or Iran. The horse provided speed and the camel enormous carrying capacity and desert endurance, the ingredients of empire.

Theories and paradigms of imperial rise and fall abound in the annals of historians and social scientists, but Peter Turchin, of the University of Connecticut, is one of the few to seek quantification and science in the analysis of history. Working, in his own words, 'at the interface between biological, mathematical, and social sciences', Turchin seeks to identify the mechanisms underlying the dynamics of social and cultural history, and, in particular, the most likely reasons for the rise and fall of empires among the many hypotheses. Hoping at the same time to enable history to become a predictive science (in a way not dissimilar to our geological application of uniformitarianism), Turchin has proposed 'an entirely new discipline: theoretical historical social science. We could call this "cliodynamics", from Clio, the muse of history, and dynamics, the study of temporally varying processes and the search for causal mechanisms.' It is hardly surprising that this is dynamically controversial in academic circles, but it is also fascinating and provocative. Introducing his article 'A Theory for Formation of Large Empires' (2009), Turchin writes:

> Between 3000 BCE and 1800 CE there were more than sixty 'mega-empires' that, at the peak, controlled an area of at least one million square kilometres. What were the forces that kept together such huge pre-industrial states? I propose a model for one route to mega-empire, motivated by imperial dynamics in eastern Asia, the world region with the highest concentration of mega-empires. This 'mirror-empires' model proposes that antagonistic interactions between nomadic pastoralists and settled agriculturalists result in an autocatalytic process, which pressures both nomadic and farming polities to scale up polity size, and thus military power. The model suggests that location near a steppe frontier should correlate with the frequency of imperiogenesis. A worldwide survey supports this prediction: over 90 per cent of mega-empires arose within or next to the

Old World's arid belt, running from the Sahara desert to the Gobi desert.

Turchin charts empires, environment and transport, plus dominant weaponry (in particular the small, compact bow that could be used from horseback) to correlate imperial power with animal transport and the confrontation between the desert and the sown. He cites the well-documented views of the agrarian empires that see the nomads as non-human, and those of the nomad empires (most dramatically, the Mongols) that regard city-dwellers as targets for extermination. He lists 42 'mega-empires' of Eurasia and North Africa that flourished in the arid zone and its margins, all of which depended on the horse, and many, additionally, on the camel. He develops quantitative mathematical models to examine how societies increased in scale and hierarchical complexity not simply through increasing numbers but through more complex and non-linear processes of selective pressure and competition implied by any evolutionary succession. Controversial? Yes. Environmental determinism? Possibly. But a compelling story certainly, and the echoes of conflict across the borders of arid lands continue to reverberate today.

The horse may have been fleet, but its desert endurance, as explorers found to their cost, is very limited. It was the camel that not only carried the burden of empires but pioneered the corridors across the desert. It may seem odd, given the camel's lack of success in modern America, but it was there that it originated, as the genus *Protylopus*, around 45 million years ago. It was small, around the size of a large cat, but would be succeeded by giants. *Titanotylopus* and *Gigantocamelus* roamed North America until around 300,000 years ago, typically 3.5 metres tall, and they raise the question of whether their humps evolved for fat storage in cold climates. Ancestors of today's camelids made their way across the Isthmus of Panama to beget the llama, the guanaco, the alpaca and the vicuña, while others ventured across the Bering Straits to evolve into the bactrian and, probably later, the dromedary. The camels' ancestors that remained in North America were likely slaughtered by our own Neolithic forebears.

Exactly why bactrians have two humps and dromedaries only one remains unclear, but dromedary embryos go through a two-humped stage, suggesting descent from the bactrian. They are very different creatures in many ways, the bactrian being more massive and hirsute, prepared for the cold of the Gobi, and capable of carrying even greater loads than the impressive capacity of the dromedary. Neither can be described as being fully adapted to the desert, in the sense of the creatures we saw in the last chapter. In spite of their powers of endurance, in general, being domesticated animals, they need man's help with food and water. However, the only remaining truly wild population of camels, a group of perhaps 600 bactrians on the margins of China's Taklamakan Desert, survive despite man's best efforts. The feral camels of Australia do well enough, in part (and to the anger of the ranchers) thanks to agriculture. The relationship between man and camel is a long one, but its origins are poorly documented. Camels appear in Saharan rock art, but the first written accounts are from the seventh century BC when an Assyrian king used camels in his war with Egypt, and from 46 BC when Caesar defeated one of the Berber kingdoms of North Africa and took 22 dromedaries captive. It is generally thought that it was the enterprising Nabateans, who settled around Petra 2,000 years ago and developed a sophisticated and complex irrigation system to support their terrace agriculture, who first routinely employed camels in their extensive trade across the region. The camel caravan was born.

The last wild dromedaries probably disappeared 5,000 years ago, but their domesticated relatives proved to be a great success story, underpinning desert societies and trade for millennia. Their evolution had equipped them in any number of extraordinary ways to do the job required of them. Their feet, eyes, ears, lips, mouths, teeth and stomachs, not to mention their fat-storing humps, all contribute to their remarkable capacity to plod through blowing sand and dust for days on end, and subsist on the most desiccated and unappetizing vegetation, while providing milk and meat for their owners. Even their blood cells are uniquely different and helpful, with an ability to swell and store water. Camels only sweat at extremely high temperatures and normally lose no water from their blood. There are many bizarre aspects of a camel's physiology and metabolism that contribute to its character – male dromedaries (but strangely not bactrians) carry in their throats a repulsive and malodorous inflatable sac, the dulla, that they extrude from their mouths during their rutting phase. They are the only ungulates to mate in a sitting position and one of the few animals to pace, proceeding by moving both legs on the same side at the same time, producing a distinctly strange sensation that can lead to seasickness when riding the ship of the desert.

But the camel's pace is to be treasured in its steadiness, a fact noted and scrupulously measured by early Western explorers. Captain Sir Alexander Burnes, who travelled across central Asia and the deserts of the Kyzylkum and Karakum included in his account, *Travels into Bokhara* (1834), comprehensive calculations and concluded that a string of 52 camels 676 feet long moves over its own length in 218 seconds, giving an average speed of 3,700 yards per hour 'in soft ground'. He compares this favourably with other estimates, but his camels were perhaps a little slow or the ground particularly soft since the more generally accepted average velocity is 3 miles per hour and, when necessary, higher.

The average speed of the camel may be an elusive and unimportant statistic today, but it assisted Eratosthenes in making his remarkably accurate estimate of the circumference of the earth in the third century BC. In his now classic calculation, he knew from the sun's rays at Alexandria versus the famous well at Aswan the angular difference between the two places and all he needed was the physical distance between them. He had survey results but confirmed them by establishing the typical time it took for a camel caravan to travel the route and the average speed of the caravan, and came up with 700 stadia per degree of latitude, and a circumference of 252,000 stadia. Depending on which of the various definitions of a stadion he was using, the translation of this varies, but if it was, as seems likely, the Egyptian stadion, his result was within 1.6 per cent of the correct value. Had Columbus used this figure, rather than Ptolemy's, in planning his voyage, he might never have had the courage to set out.

Soon, caravans of tens of thousands of camels would be transporting goods and pilgrims across the deserts of North Africa, Arabia and the Middle East. Mansa Musa's hajj and shopping trip to Cairo (chapter Four) was supported by 15,000 camels and at the height of the pilgrimages across the desert to Mecca, a caravan would consist of 25,000 of the beasts (together with thousands of merchants, soldiers and officials as well as pilgrims). In their vicious Saharan campaigns of 1900 and 1901, the French military requisitioned 35,000 camels, of which 25,000 died of thirst or inexpert handling. Many of the original owners, deprived of their livelihood, died of starvation.

Gertrude Bell described her camel as 'the most charming of animals', an unusual view by an unusual woman. For the way in which a camel is regarded illustrates well the divisions between the desert and the sown, between insiders and outsiders (remember the poem of Bashshar ibn Burd). Rudyard Kipling's initially humpless camel 'lived in the middle of a Howling Desert because he did not want to work' and was 'most 'scruciating idle', refusing to say anything more than 'Humph!' The horse, the dog and the ox were incensed at the camel's refusal to help them with their work for man and complained to the Djinn of All Deserts, who, having located the camel admiring himself in a pool of water (refusing to say anything more than 'Humph!'), gave him his hump so that he could make up the work he had missed through idleness without having to eat.

Felix Fabri, while acknowledging that 'Were it not that nature has so taught camels, that they can go over pathless ground without making any mistake, men never could pass through the wilderness', nevertheless declared them to be deformed and that 'Among us the camels are considered monsters.' William Palgrave, travelling in disguise through Arabia in the 1860s, wrote:

> I have, while in England, heard and read of the 'docile camel.' If 'docile' means stupid, well and good: in such a case the camel is the very model of docility . . . In a word, he is from first to last an undomesticated and savage animal, rendered serviceable by stupidity alone, without much skill on his master's part or any co-operation on his own, save that of extreme passiveness. One passion alone he possesses, namely revenge, of which he furnishes many a hideous example . . .

The litany of Western disdain goes on, but Wilfred Thesiger described the Bedouin's view of the camel's worth (illus. 130, 131):

> 'Ata Allah', or 'God's gift', they call her, and it is her patience that wins over the Arab's heart. I have never seen a Bedu strike or ill-treat a camel. Always the camel's needs come first . . . To Arabs, camels are beautiful, and they derive as great a pleasure from looking at a good camel as some Englishmen get from looking at a good horse.

Thesiger's companions told him:

> Their patience is very wonderful. What other creature is as patient as a camel? That is the quality which above all else endears them to us Arabs . . . It is not hunger nor is it thirst that frightens the Bedu . . . It is the possible collapse of their camels that haunts them. If this happens, death is certain.

Hassanein Bey thought the camel was 'as clever as a horse, if not more clever, and in some ways is more human. Affectionate, devoted, gregarious . . .'. Arabic contains even more words devoted to camels than it does to sand and dunes, specific names for types, colours, breeds, age, sex, skills, condition and character. Pre-Islamic lyric poetry includes the classic form of the qasida, whose introduction is normally a nostalgic account of lost love and praise for the writer's camel that carries him safely across the desert. A not uncommon scene is an encounter with a group of virgins and the slaughtering of a fine camel in order to please and seduce them. For the Bedouin or the Tuareg, life is not life without their camels – and they are experts at camel forensics. All desert-dwellers, from the Tuareg to the Aboriginal peoples of Australia, are, by nature and necessity, expert trackers, but the Bedouin excel. As Thesiger witnessed:

> Here every man knew the individual tracks of his own camels, and some of them could remember the tracks of nearly every camel they had seen. They could tell at a glance from the depth of the footprints whether a camel was ridden or free, and whether it was in calf. By studying strange tracks they could tell the area from which the camel came. Camels from the Sands, for instance, had soft soles to their feet, marked with tattered strips of loose skin, whereas if they came from the gravel plains their feet are polished smooth. Bedu could tell the tribe to which a camel belonged, for the different tribes have different breeds of camel, all of which can be distinguished by their

130, 131 Members of Wilfred Thesiger's party, including his longstanding and faithful young Rashid Bedouin companion, Salim bin Kabina, at far left and with his camel (right).

tracks. From looking at their droppings they could often deduce where a camel had been grazing, and they could certainly tell when it had last been watered, and from their knowledge of the country they could probably tell where.

The Arab forces with T. E. Lawrence carried camel dung with them so that they could scatter it and give the impression of being more numerous than they were. The Murrah tribe of the Arabian peninsula were, and are, the most renowned of the skilled trackers, seeing foot-prints in the sand as family portraits. The Saudi Ministry of the Interior continues to employ around a hundred professional trackers, most of them Murrah, and stories abound of their prowess. The classic is of the Bedouin tracker who, after four days of pursuing a fugitive and his camel, arrived at a settlement and demanded, 'Bring out the man with the eye ailment who rode in one night ago on a white camel with no tail that's also blind in one eye.' His diagnosis was entirely correct.

Gold, salt, silk, paper and slaves

'The history of a great desert like that of a great ocean is the history of its edges, and the efforts of mankind to trade across its corners.' So observed Ralph Bagnold in describing the Libyan Desert in 1936, but it applies globally. As nomads settled, as towns, cities and empires grew, trade became the foundation of societies, new social classes of merchants developed, new systems and ethics of commerce were inaugurated and new currencies were created. Transport was the key, and, for North Africa and Arabia, the dromedary was king, while in Central and Eastern Asia, the horse, the mule, the donkey and, to a lesser extent, the bactrian hauled the precious cargoes. As the simplified map in illus. 132 makes clear, for millennia the major overland trade routes wove their way across the arid lands of Africa and Eurasia, directed by geology, topography and water, and connecting cultures and empires.

The routes across the Sahara served not only to deliver sub-Saharan goods to Europe and vice versa, but also to supply the desert oases and towns. Northward flowed gold, ivory, ebony, spices, cloth and kola nuts (the only stimulant allowed by Islam and therefore a significant component of commerce). Northward also, in endless, suffering numbers, went slaves. Even though they relied on it, nomadic tribes of the oases and towns disdained agricultural labour, and slaves were

132 A simplified map of trade routes of the arid lands.

required to maintain the fields and palm groves. The Arabic name for the Niger River is Neel el Abeed, the river of slaves. Ibn Battuta, who himself at one point travelled with a caravan of 600 black female slaves, describes the King of Mali as being preceded by musicians and 300 armed slaves and salt being mined by black slaves subsisting on dates, camel meat and imported millet. For centuries, from Roman times onward, great caravans of misery followed the route of the Darb al-Arbain, the 'forty-day nightmare', northward from Darfur to the Egyptian oasis of Kharga and on to Assiut. Tens of thousands of slaves would typically start, but only a quarter survive, their bones, together with those of countless camels, littering the route. The colonial period may have seen the official abolition of slavery on multiple occasions, but its history endures in the caste systems of desert societies and, in all likelihood, slavery itself continues today. Inspired by the journeys of Mungo Park, the writer Kira Salak travelled by kayak almost a thousand kilometres along the Niger River to Timbuktu in 2002, describing her destination as 'the world's greatest anti-climax'. In her account for *National Geographic*, she describes her horror at finding modern slavery; she purchased two female slaves and freed them. The Haratin, supposedly freed slaves, constitute a significant but marginalized part of the Saharan population today, but by some estimates up to half of the Haratin population of Mauritania and elsewhere continue to live as de facto slaves.

Southward across the Sahara came dates, horses, brass, copper and other metal goods, glassware, beads, leather, textiles and paper. Paper, as we have noted, to supply the scholars of Timbuktu – the great trade routes carried not only commodities, but ideas, scholarship, medicine, science and literature. But where did this paper come from? By the thirteenth century, probably Italy, where the craft of producing good quality but cheap paper had been perfected. However, paper, that wondrous new product that would change learning forever, had only arrived in Europe in the tenth century, via Spain, from North Africa, Baghdad and the Silk Road. The Silk Road, the icon of the history of globalization, was, for centuries, the greatest network of overland trade and cultural exchange ever known. In its popular interpretation, the term has come to mean much more than originally intended when it was first introduced in the 1870s by the pioneering German geologist, Ferdinand von Richtofen (uncle of the 'Red Baron'). It was never a single road and silk was only one of its more exotic commodities. Von Richtofen applied the term only to the days of the Han Empire from 200 BC to AD 200 when silk moved westward and knowledge of far-flung parts moved east. However, human interactions and trade along this great corridor were under way at least 5,000 years ago. Later in the history of this network of highways linking China with the rest of the world – and vice versa – silk became a currency rather than a commodity. Jonathan Bloom, of Boston College, has provocatively suggested that 'Perhaps the most important product carried along this trade network, however, was paper, a now-ubiquitous material which has had a far greater impact on the course of human civilization than silk, jade or glass ever had.'

Originally developed in China as a wrapping material, its value as a writing medium was appreciated around 2,000 years ago and written culture began to flourish. The technology needed modification to be suitable for the arid climates of Central Asia where the use of already-processed plant fibre materials in linen and cotton was likely developed. Paper then became the medium by which, in particular, religious ideas and documents were exchanged along the Silk Road. Instrumental in this process were two Buddhist pilgrims who travelled to India from China to collect sacred texts and images. Fa-Hsien (the transliterated spelling varies significantly) journeyed across the Taklamakan Desert and the Pamir Mountains in the fifth century, followed by Hsuan-Tsang, who also crossed the Central Asian deserts to Samarkand, in the seventh. These monks provide not only the earliest descriptive accounts of the region, but relied on paper for their precious documents. Hsuan-Tsang described the Taklamakan as

> a desert of drifting sand without water or vegetation, burning
> hot and the home of poisonous fiends and imps. There is no

road, and travellers in coming and going have only to look for
the deserted bones of man and beast as their guide.

At the easterly extent of the Taklamakan is the great dry lake of Lop
Nor and the Kumtag Desert, home of the singing dunes described by
Marco Polo. On the edge of the dunes lies the oasis town of Dunhuang,
a key strategic crossroads on the Silk Road as the routes divided to the
west to skirt the Taklamakan to the north and south. In 1907 the
great explorer and scholar of Central Asia, Aurel Stein, was travelling
in the area when he tracked down a Taoist monk who was the guardian
of treasures, preserved, like the libraries of Timbuktu, by the aridity of
the desert: the paintings and libraries of the caves of Mogao and the
Thousand Buddhas. The caves were centres of worship and meditation
first dug in the fourth century, and it was in these caves that Fa-Hsien
and Hsuan-Tsang and their successors deposited their precious documents. Tens of thousands of manuscripts, textiles and countless exquisite
frescoes and paintings were collected or installed at Mogao and nearby
cave complexes. Stein persuaded the guardian to let him take documents
and paintings (for a fee) and the treasures were routinely removed by
later collectors. The major collections are now to be seen in London, Paris,
Berlin and Beijing, but today the International Dunhuang Project is
devoted to cataloguing, conserving and digitizing the treasures. Not only
were countless early paper manuscripts preserved in the caves, but so
was the first known printed book, the Diamond Sutra, made in AD 868
and now in the British Library.

The desert preserves and this is dramatically true in the Taklamakan.
Husan-Tang had written of lost cities, buried beneath the shifting sands,
and Aurel Stein, following in the footsteps of the Swedish explorer (and
student of von Richtofen) Sven Hedin, revealed ancient burials and settlements. Hedin and Stein also reported finding desiccated bodies, that
'but for the parched skin, looked and seemed like that of men asleep'.
Little light was shed on these until 1988 when Victor Mair, professor
of Chinese language and literature at the University of Pennsylvania,
was leading a Smithsonian tour that stopped in Ürümchi, the capital
of the Xinjiang region where a new museum had recently opened. He
found a small room labelled 'Mummy Exhibition' and its contents were
staggering. Relegated to backrooms for years by the Chinese, because of
the doubts they shed on the conventional history of Chinese civilization,
were half a dozen extraordinary mummies, astonishingly well preserved,

distinctly not Chinese in appearance and dressed in everyday clothes. Thus began a co-operative project between Mair and Chinese and Western colleagues that continues today. Numerous further cemeteries have been excavated and hundreds of mummies revealed, together with sophisticated technologies of metal-working, leatherwork, weaving, foodstuffs, musical instruments and cannabis. Their facial features and clothing caused a great eurocentric stir in the West – they were European in appearance and their clothing included tartans that must speak of emigration from Scotland close to 4,000 years ago. The truth, teased from DNA evidence, demonstrates not wandering Scottish clans but long-lived regional interactions among far-flung groups. The Tarim Basin, crossroads of the Silk Road, has been the stage for a great admixing of peoples, cultures and technologies from Siberia, Eurasia and China for thousands of years.

Horses and camels, exotic animals, woollen goods, carpets and tapestries, military equipment, gold and silver, glass, porcelain, bronze, medicines and perfumes, spices, grapes and wine, tea and rice as well as people, cultures, art, literature and armies moved back and forth along the routes of the Silk Road, linking Europe and Asia but also supplying local needs. The routes connected the oases, some now buried in the sand. In the oases grew an abundance of crops, including famous grapes and melons, many watered by the clever technology of the *karez*, the Asian equivalent of the *qanat* of Persia, the *foggara* of the Garamantes, and *falaj* of Oman. Along the northern route lay a string of fertile and prosperous oases at the foot of gigantic alluvial fans (illus. 33), on the edge of the sands of the Turpan, or Turfan, depression, at 154 metres below sea level the lowest point in Asia. For centuries these oases were the focus of wars between the Chinese and the Uyghurs, the Mongols and the Moghuls (among others). This was never a stable frontier and could hardly be so described today.

Gossiping the Gospel

The mere names of Gobi oases are enough to kindle the imagination. One Cup Spring, Bitter Well Halt, Gates of Sand, Sandy Well Oasis, Inexhaustible Spring Halt, and Mudpit Hollow ('Some people say it is the muddiest oasis in the desert,' my hostess observed with pride).

The writer was a woman who travelled in less style than Gertrude Bell, but for whom the word 'extraordinary' seems equally inadequate. Alice Mildred Cable, together with Eva French and her sister Francesca, set out in 1923 westward through the gate in the Great Wall known as the Traveller's Gate, the Gate of Demons or the Gate of Sighs. Beyond lay the desert, a place of banishment and terror. However, 'We found the desert to be unlike anything we had pictured. It had its terrors, but it also had its compensating pleasures; it subjected us to many and prolonged hardships, but it also showed us some unique treasures.' So wrote Mildred Cable in what is arguably one of the greatest travel accounts ever written, *The Gobi Desert*, published in 1942 with Francesca French. It does not follow a rigorous chronology of their thirteen years along the highways and byways of the Silk Road, but presents a closely observed and informative, and at the same time highly entertaining, account of the people, the towns, the oases, the plants, the animals, the routes, the commerce and the desert itself. There can be few more eloquent descriptions of desert pavement than this:

> By reason of their vivid and varied colourings these stones are one of the Gobi's features of beauty, and sometimes the narrow, faint path passes through a litter of small multi-coloured pebbles, which are rose-pink, pistachio-green, tender peach, lilac, white, sealing-wax red and black burnished by sand, sun and wind as though black-leaded, the whole mixed with a quantity of orange-tinted cornelian, forming a matchless mosaic.

The three women were missionaries who set out to 'gossip the gospel' from place to place, always supplied with religious tracts in multiple languages loaded on their mule carts. They were devoted to their cause but not zealots, and their religious activities only feature in the book in the context of arranging meetings in villages to distribute bibles and pamphlets or, occasionally, being stoned. Like Gertrude Bell, Mildred Cable knew the local languages well – in her case, seven of them, with some challenges: 'The number of intelligent forms which a single Turki primary transitive verb-root is capable of yielding is not less than 28,000 ... Then despair seized us.' And, like Bell, Cable's linguistic ability and gender gave her access to places in the desert societies that had never been described:

Thus we learnt to live in these various homes and among women of many nationalities and to develop, in our nomadic life, the art of being 'at home' in a crowded serai, a Mongol yurt, a Siberian isba, a Chinese courtyard, a mud shack, a camel-driver's tent, or the palace of a Khan . . . Princesses and beggar-maids were alike in the circle of our friendship.

'The Trio' visited the caves at Dunhuang, the lakes amid the dunes, the singing sands, and the great Silk Road commercial centres and oases such as Turpan: 'In the centre of those uncompromising surroundings Turfan lies like a green island in a sandy wilderness, its shores lapped by grit and gravel instead of ocean water, for the division between arid desert and fertile land is as definite as that between the shore and the ocean.' Cable described how residents retreated underground in the heat of the summer and the difficulties of surviving the bitterly cold desert winters. She compares the qualities and prices of different melons, grapes, raisins and sultanas from the different oases, plants such as the Asian relatives of the ephedra that Edward Abbey described from the American deserts, that the local Gobi residents processed with tobacco and 'chew with most evident enjoyment'. They spent sufficient time in the Gobi to be able to observe profound changes, that 'aridity is not stationary but increases steadily, and in the course of even a few years, the decrease in water supply is perceptible.'

'The desert was gracious to us and lavished liberty upon us in the far-flowing vastness of its solitude.' Mildred Cable and her companions loved the desert and its peoples, but all good things have to come to an end. After being caught up in rebellions, being taken captive and coming close to being killed, they made one of their infrequent trips to England under the threat of a Japanese invasion and communist uprisings. In 1938 war broke out between the local warlords and the Chinese and all foreigners were banned. They never returned, but Mildred (and Francesca) left us with an extraordinary legacy of books and journals that documented the previously undocumented and still resonate today.

The desert's greatest export

Travellers call them dust-spouts from their likeness to an ocean water-spout, but the desert-dweller, certain that these waterless places are peopled by *kwei*, calls them dust-demons. The pillar

of sand gives the impression of an invisible being daintily folding
a garment of dust round its unseen form . . . 'This one is the male
and that one the female *kwei*,' said the men; 'you can distinguish
them by the way they fold the dust cloak around them, right
to left or left to right; see how they come in pairs.'

So wrote Mildred Cable as she watched 'sand and stones lifted high
from the ground' with a force that 'nearly swept me off my feet'. Dust-
demons and dust-devils sweep the world's deserts and are commonly
believed to hide a malevolent spirit, a *kwei* or a *djinn*. But, compared
to the wrath of a sandstorm, dust-devils are benign. 'A distant roar, and
a cloud like rolling smoke with a livid edge advances and invades the
sky, blotting out the sun and daylight . . . No progress is possible, and
human beings shelter behind a barrage of kneeling camels from the
flying stones and choking sand.' Anyone, like Mildred, who spends any
time in the desert will probably experience the frightening power of a
sandstorm, and, close to the ground, it is indeed a sandstorm. However,
there is a limit as to how high even the fiercest wind can carry the heavy
sand grains as evidenced by the limited sand-blast height of the rock
formations in illus. 19 and 20. Ralph Bagnold commented that 'The
bulk of the grains flowed as a dense fog, rising no higher than five feet
from the ground. Over it we could see each other quite clearly, head and
shoulders only, as in a swimming-bath.' What the howling desert wind
can carry to enormous altitudes and in enormous volumes is dust. An
estimated two billion tons of dust are blasted out of the earth's deserts
every year (illus. 133). On an average winter day, the deposits left from
the drying of the mega-lake Chad in the Sahara's Bodélé depression
export 700,000 tonnes of dust. The dust will circle the planet within days
and remain in the atmosphere for years, raining gently down on oceans
and land.

In 1845 Charles Darwin reported to the Geological Society in London
on a survey he had made of vessels encountering dust while crossing
the Atlantic. He noted the size and composition of the particles which,
intriguingly, were not simply inorganic mineral grains, but consisted 'in
considerable part of Infusoria and Phytolitharia' – microorganisms and
plant material. The components of the dust swirling around in our
atmosphere are so diverse that Darwin would hardly be surprised by
the revelation that the health of the Amazon rainforest depends on
nutrients blasted out of the Bodélé depression. Dust is one of the jokers

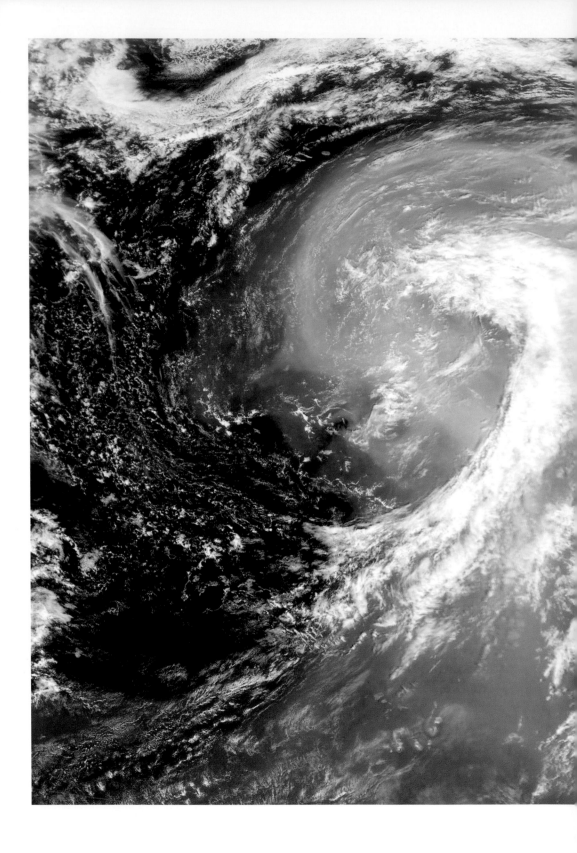

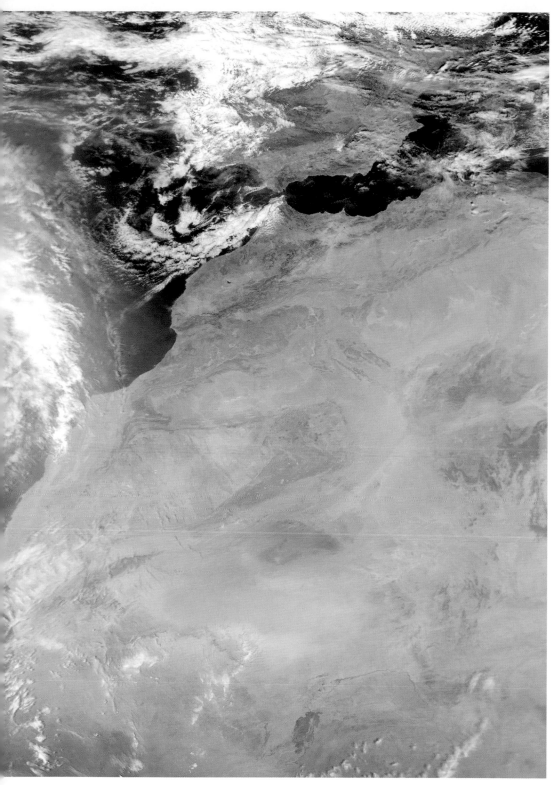

133 A Saharan dust storm heads out into the Atlantic.

in the pack of climate modelling; the processes, impacts and feedbacks within the workings of the earth system are complex to the point of being beyond our ability to decipher and quantify.

We do know that one of the key, but unquantifiable, components of the equations is us. The evidence suggests that the amount of dust circulating in the atmosphere roughly doubled over the course of the last century. We know that dust became a problem in the 'Great American Desert' only after the arrival of the cowboys and their herds, and we predict that another dustbowl may be the future of those lands. Dust tells us much about the past, but the question of what it can tell us about the future of our planet's drylands and their residents and livelihoods is but one of the many challenges we face when we contemplate how best to 'manage' these complex and critical environments.

EIGHT

Feast or Famine, Knowns and Unknowns

ANY NOTION THAT our planet's drylands are somehow inert and sterile, bystanders in the dynamics and workings of our planet, will be dispelled by the extraordinary image in illus. 134. Thanks to the supercomputing abilities of NASA and the data derived from different highly sophisticated satellites, this image is a snapshot of the frenzied activity of aerosols in our atmosphere. These tiny particles, ranging in size from less than that of a virus to approximately the diameter of a human hair, fall into four main categories: salt (blue) is blown from the sea surface, sulphates (white) from volcanoes and fossil fuel emissions, smoke (green) from fires, and, in the great swirling vortices and plumes of red and orange, dust.

Despite our long history of encountering sand and dust storms, Darwin's observations in the Atlantic, and the social and economic catastrophe of America's Dust Bowl in the 1930s, these were regarded as local events. It is only in the last few decades, with the advent of increasingly detailed satellite data, that we have been able to see and measure the true global extent of the role of dust and to begin to understand the part it plays in the workings of our earth system and our societies. Europeans experience periodic downpours of 'blood rain', events regarded as bad omens at least since, in Homer's *Iliad*, Zeus 'shed a rain of blood upon the earth' as his son was killed at Troy. We now know, of course, that the red colour comes not from blood but from Saharan dust. NASA's stunning image dramatically illustrates the fact that, rather than being isolated and inert, arid lands are actively interconnected with the rest of the planet, their influence surging far beyond their lost borders. And those interconnections, those linkages, are not just through the work of dust: there are great rivers, fed by mountain rains, that cross arid lands, bringing with them the erosional debris of mud and sand and the chemical residues of man's agricultural activities. Or

134 NASA's portrait of global aerosols, 2013, extract from visualizations 2006–7.

they don't cross, dying out in the desert either naturally or as a result of dams that deprive the peoples of the drylands of precious water. Roads, railways and pipelines carry products into, out of and across the deserts. Birds and insects move back and forth across the borders of arid lands. People migrate, voluntarily or otherwise, and drugs, arms, desperate refugees and slaves are transported across the deserts on a daily basis.

And yet the mindset remains in much of the outsider world, the conventional wisdom that deserts are deserted, empty, sterile, wilderness spaces to be either largely ignored or used for purposes unacceptable in temperate lands. Where did the UK choose to test its rocketry and nuclear weapons? The Australian desert. The United States exploded the first atomic bomb, nicknamed 'The Gadget', in the New Mexico desert and proceeded to conduct over 800 tests in Nevada. France conducted 17 nuclear tests in the Sahara, the Russians 116 above-ground tests in the Kazakhstan steppe and the Chinese detonated their 45th and final nuclear test in 1996 at the 100,000-square-kilometre site at Lop Nor, a vast dry lake on the eastern end of the Taklamakan Desert. The Lop Nor testing, research and training area is near the archaeological sites of the Tarim mummies and includes a nature reserve dedicated as a refuge for the last of the wild bactrian camels. The reserve is burdened with threats from illegal mining and hunting as well as the legacy of nuclear testing. The bright blue evaporation ponds of the largest potash-producing facility in the world cover an area close to 2,000 square kilometres, readily and incongruously visible in the desert on the satellite images of Google Earth. Military training and weapons testing sites, gigantic mines, spaceports, sprawling 'aircraft graveyards' and prisons for both criminals and indigenous peoples litter the desert from the Mojave to the Gobi via the Australian outback. This is not to say that such facilities and activities are not, at least to some extent, necessary, but the fact remains that the desert is convenient as 'someone else's backyard'. Nor am I arguing for an extremist environmental conservation agenda, but it cannot be denied that in the minds of outsiders, of government and commercial interests, the desert is still too often treated as *terra nullius*, despite being the home of what the United Nations Development Programme refers to as 'the forgotten billion'. Differing agendas and conventional wisdom, together with a reluctance to abandon or even recognize mythologies, create issues and conflicts in the world's drylands that urgently require addressing.

The scientific frontier

Many hundreds of scientific articles around the world report on dust research every year and yet the results highlight what we don't know as much as they add to what we do. Our knowledge of the earth's arid lands grows substantially with each passing year, but these environments remain a scientific frontier just as they were for so long physical frontiers. Regarded – still, in many quarters – as economically marginal, biologically and socially impoverished, and having little impact on the civilized world, the desert attracted little attention compared to, for outsiders, more familiar, more accessible and more politically high-profile environments. In spite of our rapidly growing knowledge, dryland research still lacks the quantity, quality and longevity of high-resolution integrated data that is available from temperate lands, and dust presents a startling example.

Estimates of the annual load of dust in the atmosphere vary from one to more than four billion tonnes; we know that dust particles are critical contributors to cloud formation, but the physical and chemical mechanisms by which this happens and the results in terms of climatic effects are poorly understood. We have only recently discovered the forensic evidence that dust from Africa, the Middle East and Asia reaches California throughout the year and plays a key role in stimulating winter rains and snowfall, and African dust determines the strength of the Indian monsoon. All this dust is composed not simply of inert mineral particles but includes a significant biological, bacterial component.

While many biological particles do not survive the radiation of their trip through the upper realms of the atmosphere, some do, and we have only recently begun to come to grips with the importance of this. In order to be able to understand the behaviour of dust in the earth system, we must be able to track it and analyse it on its journey from origins to destination, from source to sink. Mapping the details, however, the compositions and the annual variations, remains a challenge.

It has been established that by far the largest source of dust in the Sahara (and, indeed, the world) is the Bodélé depression, the site of the old, now dried-out, Lake Mega-Chad, an area of almost 12,000 square kilometres. Unlike other sources, the Bodélé kicks up huge amounts of dust all year, but with month-to-month and year-to-year variations. These variations reflect the strength of a low-level atmospheric jet, a northeast wind that blows most strongly over the winter months, but it is only over the last few years that we have understood some of the details of this. There is now a growing body of integrated ground and satellite data that allows measurement of dust pulses and where they are coming from. As the old lake dried out, it left behind thick layers made up of the siliceous shells of tiny algae, diatoms, and it is the wind erosion of these deposits that is responsible for much of the dust. Many of the details have yet to be understood, particularly for constructing a story that integrates the process from the scale of the surface character and 'erodibility' of the diatomite with local, regional and seasonal wind regimes. Local conditions are key: it has been shown that turbulence created as the wind blows around a sand dune creates a pulse of dust – the dunes have been described as 'dust-mills'.

Tracking the dust's journey is largely a job for satellite observations, satellites such as the Cloud-Aerosol Lidar and Infrared Pathfinder Satellite Observation (CALIPSO), a joint mission by NASA and the French space agency that uses laser reflections to measure cloud cover and aerosols. CALIPSO flies in formation with Aqua, an international satellite mission that carries six different instruments for monitoring surface and atmospheric water, and CloudSat that, as its name implies, watches and analyses clouds. Five instruments aboard NASA's Terra satellite observe the earth's atmosphere, ocean, land, snow and ice, and energy budget; they record optical thickness, a measure of how opaque or transparent the atmosphere is as a result of the density of aerosols. What we find, as is clear from NASA's portrait, is an extremely complex system that changes from hour to hour and year to year. The Sahara may be the planet's greatest source of dust, but it is certainly not the only one. As China knows well, great plumes blow out of the Gobi and every piece of arid land in the world is a dust source. Most of it is entirely natural: estimates differ, of course, but a general figure is around 75 per cent. However, this varies enormously from region to region. North Africa accounts for 55 per cent of global dust emissions, but probably only 8 per cent is anthropogenic. In Australia the anthropogenic contribution is closer to 75 per cent. And the composition of the dust reflects the local ingredients – diatomite from the Bodélé depression, but from elsewhere in the Sahara much of the dust derives from the iron oxide coatings of sand grains being abraded in the wind (hence the blood rains). Where the dust originates from cultivated land, it carries with it the fertilizers and pesticides used there, and dust from mining operations can carry motes of toxic metals. The biological components are a subject of intense investigation since we are looking at a global circulation of microbes, fungi, pollen and the like: potential pathogens. The implications for soils, vegetation, ocean life and human health are significant – so-called Valley Fever, caused by dust-borne fungi, has become the second most commonly reported infectious disease in Arizona.

Dust has profound effects from source to sink and en route between. Where dust originates from sandy soils, those soils become sandier through the winnowing of the fine-grained component, their water-retaining capacity is reduced, and they must await flooding for renewal; flooding has the effect of both reducing, temporarily, the emission of dust and supplying new material for erosion. On its journey through the atmosphere, dust joins other aerosols in influencing cloud formation and precipitation – just one way, as we shall see, in which it moderates climate. Much of it ultimately falls in the oceans, but where it falls on land it forms soils and delivers both nutrients and toxins to living matter. The soils of the Bahamas and the Florida keys are composed almost entirely of African dust. The renewal of soils that support the biodiversity and health of the Amazon rainforest is probably driven by the constant supply of dust from the Sahara. There are, however, two sides to this coin: dust settling on leaves can interfere with photosynthesis and there are suspicions that toxins from pesticides and microbes are damaging Caribbean corals. This two-sided coin presents a challenge, for, while we have made considerable progress in understanding the potential roles of the global dust system, good and bad, its sheer complexity makes it almost impossible to quantify. If we could, however unlikely it may seem, devise a means of reducing sources of dust, should we? If we could, somehow or another, reduce the supply of dust from the Bodélé depression, it would be a massive and highly risky global geo-engineering experiment, not simply a local scheme. The ways in which dust participates in modulating the earth's climate are profound, often opposing, and certainly not well understood.

Dust, together with other aerosols, both absorbs the sun's radiation and reflects it, resulting in warming or cooling. Which of these opposing behaviours a dust particle will exhibit depends on its size and its composition, together with the wavelength of the light: incoming short-wave radiation tends to be reflected and scattered, a cooling effect, but outgoing long-wave (infrared) radiation reflected from the earth's surface tends to be absorbed and retained, warming the atmosphere. Dust clouds over dark areas such as the oceans have a cooling effect, preventing sunlight from warming the waters, but over light-coloured areas, such as sand and snow, the way in which those surfaces would normally strongly reflect incoming radiation (their albedo) is reduced, resulting in warming. Local and regional temperature variations drive the winds and the weather, and, on a global scale, the climate. Data to assess the overall net effect of dust is incomplete and often conflicting; while views, understandably, vary, it seems likely that the net effect is cooling, importantly countering, but by no means coming close to offsetting, other planetary warming processes. This is but one of the reasons that dust is a joker in the pack when it comes to climate modelling. It also plays a critical role as the nuclei for the water droplets that form clouds and clouds are as nebulous in climate models as they are in reality.

If we are to have any hope of rationally addressing the complex issues of our planet's arid lands, we must contemplate evidence from the past and the present and weave this into a thoughtful view of the future. We have no crystal balls – all we have are 'models'. The science of climate modelling is extraordinarily sophisticated and powerful, and becomes more so each day, but it is this very sophistication and power, together with the compelling and often alarming outputs of luridly coloured global maps of the future, that can be misleading in the all-too-human quest for certainty. In 1997 Per Bak, the internationally respected Danish theoretical physicist who worked at, among other institutions, the Brookhaven National Laboratory and the Santa Fe Institute in the u.s. and the Niels Bohr Institute and Imperial College in Europe, published a fascinating book heroically titled *How Nature*

Works. Bak, who died, too young, in 2002, developed our understanding of the role of 'self-organized criticality' in natural processes, behaviours that are non-linear and inherently non-predictable. He used the most simple and elegant of physical models to illustrate this: a pile of sand and the nature of the avalanches down its sides. The book begins with a quotation from Victor Hugo's *Les Misérables*, questions that resonate with our contemplation of the role of dust in the way our planet works: 'Who could ever calculate the path of a molecule? How do we know that the creations of worlds are not determined by falling grains of sand?' In evaluating the challenges of data interpretation, prediction and modelling (both physical and mathematical), a section enticingly titled 'The Philosophy of Using Simple Models: On Spherical Cows', Bak comments that

> Sometimes we feel that our modelling of the world is so good that we are seduced into believing that our computer contains a copy of the real world, so that real experiments or observations are unnecessary . . . We are always dealing with a model of the system, although some scientists would like us to believe that they are doing calculations on the real system when they ask us to believe their results, whether it be on global warming or the world economy.

Per Bak was certainly no 'climate change denier' (nor am I). He was simply emphasizing the importance of awareness of what we don't know as well as what we do and the uncertainties implicit in any model, uncertainties that reflect what we can and cannot measure, and the impenetrable complexities of natural relationships and feedbacks between even the things that we can measure. As Albert Einstein remarked: 'Not everything that counts can be counted. And not everything that can be counted, counts.' What we do not know about dust and clouds far outweighs what we do, and the same can be said of the causes and processes of aridity.

In order to appreciate the great complexity of feedbacks in the global climate system, consider the following: arid lands create dust – dust modulates the climate causing both warming and cooling – warming and cooling change the nature and distribution of precipitation and temperature, increasing or decreasing regional aridity – varying aridity determines the dust input into the climate system. This is a grand loop, within which there are further important details. Iron-rich dust falling directly onto the oceans or through aerosol-containing raindrops is a major source of nutrition for the oceanic ecosystem. Iron acts as a fertilizer for plankton growth which, in turn, removes carbon dioxide from the atmosphere and sequesters it in the sediments of the ocean depths after the plankton (and their predators) die and sink. The importance of this process to the global carbon and energy budgets cannot be overstated – it is likely, for example, the culprit in exacerbating the last ice ages. In a 2011 review, 'Dust cycle: An Emerging Core Theme in Earth System Science', Yaping Shao of the University of Cologne and his colleagues from Australia, Japan, China and South Korea stated: 'The deep ocean contains nearly 85 per cent of mobile carbon on the Earth and ocean phytoplankton is responsible for nearly half the annual CO_2 exchange and a majority of all carbon sequestered over geologic time.' In their conclusions they observe that 'Despite the remarkable progress made in dust research over the past three decades or so, many challenges remain' and summarize the main areas around which more data and analysis are critically needed: quantification of the dust cycle, dust feedbacks, the details of iron fertilization and the specific roles of wind and water erosion in the preservation (or otherwise) of organic carbon in the soil. The authors include a compelling graphic of the scale and scope of the dust cycle in the way our planet works (illus. 135).

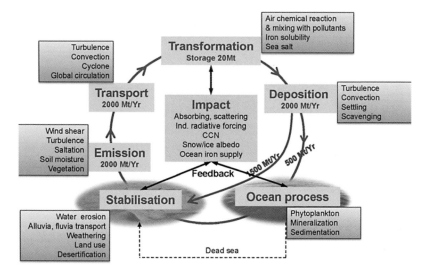

135 The dust cycle and dust's role in the earth system.

Warm and dry, with a chance of dust

Among the terms used in the dust cycle graphic there are two that particularly merit further discussion as we attempt to peer into the future: 'radiative forcing' and the highly provocative 'desertification'. A thorough analysis of the methodologies, the details and the long-term forecasts of climate science is not required to address the pressing issues of today's arid lands and is certainly beyond the scope of this chapter. However, the questions of what drives fluctuating aridity and what the future may hold are important ones if we are to come to grips with those issues.

Understanding climate is about understanding the dynamics of the earth's energy balance. The literature of the science is overwhelming both in its volume and its complexity, but the best place to start is the reports and analyses of the IPCC, the Intergovernmental Panel on Climate Change. Controversial though they may be in some ways, they at least represent a scientific evidence-based consensus. At the time of writing, the Fifth Assessment Report is being prepared for publication, but much of the contributing work and the documentation is available and, for simplicity and consistency, will form the basis of this discussion. The earth system is driven by energy flows. Incoming energy from the sun is harnessed and constantly redistributed by the atmosphere, the oceans, the land surface and plant and animal life, including ourselves. Energy from the earth's interior is contributed to the system through volcanic eruptions and the planet's internal heat. A radiative or climate 'forcing' is any process that causes a perturbation of the energy balance. By definition, since the focus is on warming, a positive forcing causes warming and a negative one cooling. An increase in the sun's brightness and therefore incoming radiation is a positive forcing; the clouds of aerosols from a volcanic eruption that reflect energy back into space are a negative forcing. The 1991 eruption of Mount Pinatubo in the Philippines had a global cooling effect for several years, and the 1815 catastrophe of Indonesia's Mount Tambora conspired with a prolonged period of low solar output to cause 'The Year Without Summer', a year of worldwide agricultural disasters and famine.

Dust, as we have seen, is a powerful agent of radiative forcing, both positive and negative, through a variety of mechanisms, including the 'CCN' of illus. 135, the formation of 'Cloud Condensation Nuclei'. Human activity contributes to the dust load in the atmosphere, both local and global, and we are agents of climate forcing out of proportion to our biomass. Aerosol and gas emissions from fossil fuel burning and widespread changes in land use and vegetation cover are climate forcings. The fundamental question for arid lands is how do the interactions of climate forcings, natural and anthropogenic, collude to cause aridity, how do the time variations, annual and multi-annual, work, and are things likely to get better or worse? Unfortunately, we cannot answer these questions with anything like the certainty that we crave, in part because we simply do not have the data and in part because the complexity of the system, the flapping of immeasurable numbers of butterflies' wings, is beyond our modelling capacity. We can, however, frame some views, albeit with widely varying levels of confidence.

'Desertification' is a highly emotional term and, in the view of many scientists, one that obscures the facts. It has, however, embedded itself in the popular imagination, creating images of the planet Arrakis in Frank Herbert's *Dune* or the post-apocalyptic dystopia of *Mad Max*. The term was first coined in the 1920s by the French naturalist Louis Lavauden while working in Africa, who described it as 'purely artificial' and 'uniquely the phenomenon of man'. This unique blame was unfortunate, but it has, along with the word, endured. The documentation that emerged from the 1992 Rio Earth Summit included a rather more rational definition and summary:

> Desertification is land degradation in arid, semi-arid and dry sub-humid areas resulting from various factors, including climatic variations and human activities. Desertification affects about one sixth of the world's population, 70 per cent of all drylands, amounting to 3.6 billion hectares, and one quarter of the total land area of the world. The most obvious impact of desertification, in addition to widespread poverty, is the degradation of 3.3 billion hectares of the total area of rangeland, constituting 73 per cent of the rangeland with a low potential for human and animal carrying capacity; decline in soil fertility and soil structure on about 47 per cent of the dryland areas constituting marginal rainfed cropland; and the degradation of irrigated cropland, amounting to 30 per cent of the dryland areas with a high population density and agricultural potential.

We talk these days of the issues of rising sea levels, not 'oceanification', but 'desertification' as a term seems unavoidable, together with the impression that the phenomenon is inevitable. But is it? As we have seen, the desert does not represent the final stage of 'desertification' but is rather simply one member of our planet's range of environments and one that has evolved naturally under conditions of water scarcity. Nor does the process of desertification apply to the hyper-arid heart of the desert: it is a phenomenon of the desert's lost borders, precisely as stated in the Rio summary. It is in those lost borders that the 'lost billion' live, not threatened by marauding sand dunes but by land degradation brought on by some combination of climate variations and damaging land use practices.

The most pressing issues of land degradation are clearly in desert borderlands such as the Sahel, the 'shore of the Sahara', but they are by no means unique to the developing world. The residents of Phoenix, Arizona, have adopted the Arabic word for a major dust storm, and headlines such as 'Howling haboob smothers Phoenix' occur with increasing regularity. Individual Arizona dust storms can be more than 150 kilometres across and reach an altitude of 2 kilometres. Blowing dust year-round in the western United States is a major hazard: the largest multiple vehicle pile-up in the country's history took place in California in November 1991, when suddenly reduced visibility caused more than

136 A dust storm approaches Stratford, Texas, in 1935.

160 vehicles to collide, killing seventeen people and injuring hundreds. Arizona highways today carry dust warning systems. The twentieth-century history of the U.S. is marked by the iconic images of the Dust Bowl, underscored by the still evocative words of John Steinbeck and Woody Guthrie (illus. 136). The Dust Bowl was an epic disaster that lasted ten years and was made even worse by the Depression. This passage from *The Grapes of Wrath* applies to those suffering the results of land degradation the world over: 'How can you frighten a man whose hunger is not only in his own cramped stomach but in the wretched bellies of his children? You can't scare him – he has known a fear beyond every other.'

The Dust Bowl was not, however, the first sign of the land degradation that followed the wanton pursuit of manifest destiny. Natural fluctuations in aridity in the American west were part of its history, but they were exacerbated, with dire consequences, by the invasion of millions of livestock that the great naturalist John Muir referred to as 'hoofed locusts'. The natural hardy grasses of the Great American Desert that had been nourished by the gigantic herds of bison were stripped, the soil churned up and eroded and the land degraded. Bison and grasslands had evolved synergistically, but these well-adapted ruminants were displaced by destructive sheep and cattle and decimated by hunters. In the San Juan Mountains of Colorado, a mountain lake has lain downwind of the arid lands for thousands of years, and its sediments have recorded the changing input of dust. Jason Neff, a geochemist from the University of Colorado, has sampled and analysed those sediments and demonstrated that, in spite of the extremely dry conditions that lasted from around AD 900 to 1300, the global 'Medieval Warm Period', little dust was blown into the lake. Until the mid-nineteenth century, that is. 'Then', as Neff describes his results, 'it was like flipping a switch. From about 1860 to 1900, dust deposition rates shot up.' Dust levels rose fivefold, dropping slightly only in the middle of the last century: the hoofed locusts at work. The Dust Bowl was simply the climax of this 'desertification'. *The Wind* (1928) was one of the last silent films and tells the tragic story of a young woman, played by the extraordinary Lillian Gish, driven to madness and murder by the wind and dust of West Texas. A precursor to the Dust Bowl, the film was made in southern California and the Mojave Desert, and was described by Gish, at the age of 90, as 'definitely my most uncomfortable experience in pictures'.

As Texas, together with much of the central and western U.S., China, Australia, parts of the Middle East and, disastrously, the Sahel, faces severe problems of aridity and land degradation today, what can we say about the future? What, if anything, can be done? Like the revelations from the Colorado lake, ocean sediments and cores from the polar ice caps provide us with a record of atmospheric dust in the past and we can reasonably, although not with complete certainty, take dust levels as a proxy for varying aridity. Ice core data can take us back around 800,000 years and show that high dust concentrations coincide with cold periods and the major glacial episodes. An initial cooling and drying of the climate as a result of the regular changes in our planet's orbit and rotation (Milankovitch cycles) is enhanced by more fertilizing dust falling in the oceans, a major draw-down of carbon dioxide and global cooling. Atmospheric dust levels were several times higher during glacial periods than they are today. The ocean sediment record can take us back 4 million years and confirms this relationship. However, as is so often the case with the earth system, the cold and dusty, warm and less dusty relationship is not that simple. Daniel Muhs, a U.S. Geological Survey scientist, comments: 'We're still trying to figure out the chicken and the egg of that. Did glacial periods lead to more dust or more dust to glacial periods? There are a variety of feedbacks. It gets very complicated very quickly.' And, while twenty years of records showed a good correlation between dust levels in Florida and drought in North Africa, that correlation disappeared in the 1990s and Joseph M. Prospero of the University of Miami ('the grandfather of dust studies in the U.S.') worries that 'Now there is no correlation at all, and we don't know what's going on.' Again, the data let us down. We know that shifts in the major climate patterns – the El Niño events, the Pacific Decadal Oscillation, the Atlantic Multi-decadal Oscillation and the structure and location of the jet stream – all influence regional changes in aridity with which they participate in further grand feedbacks. Our ability to quantify and model these climatic mega-games is limited, but we can do our best as long as we make the unknowns and the uncertainties clear.

Drought. First of all, how do we define it? As we have seen, defining aridity is itself something of a challenge and certainly characterizing its duration adds a further complication. Within the vast literature of climate modelling and prediction, the IPCC Special Report *Changes in Climate Extremes and their Impacts on the Natural Physical Environment* is a useful, comprehensive and accessible starting point. In the discussion of drought, that document reviews the problems with definition:

> Though a commonly used term, drought is defined in various ways, and these definitional issues make the analysis of changes in drought characteristics difficult. This explains why assessments of (past or projected) changes in drought can substantially differ between published studies or chosen indices . . . The [IPCC] Glossary defines drought as follows: 'A period of abnormally dry weather long enough to cause a serious hydrological imbalance'. Drought is a relative term, therefore any discussion in terms of precipitation deficit must refer to the particular precipitation-related activity that is under discussion. For example, shortage of precipitation during the growing season impinges on crop production or ecosystem function in general (due to soil moisture drought, also termed agricultural drought), and during the runoff and percolation season primarily affects water supplies (hydrological drought). Storage changes in soil moisture and groundwater are also affected by increases in actual evapotranspiration in addition to reductions in precipitation. A period with an abnormal precipitation deficit is defined as a meteorological drought. A megadrought is a very lengthy and pervasive drought, lasting much longer than normal, usually a decade or more . . . As highlighted in the above definition, drought can be defined from different perspectives, depending on the stakeholders involved.

Furthermore, in any given region, the definition of drought is relative, a comparison with climatic conditions regarded as 'normal' or 'average'. An application of the term to the hyper-arid desert is meaningless and drought does not destabilize the desert. And then there are the 'chosen indices', the varying ways in which drought is quantified. Again, in the same way that we use different ways of measuring aridity, so drought indices can use temperature, precipitation or precipitation versus evapotranspiration, soil moisture and other measures. As the IPCC Report concludes:

> In summary, drought indices often integrate precipitation, temperature, and other variables, but may emphasize different

aspects of drought and should be carefully selected with respect to the drought characteristic in mind. In particular, some indices have specific shortcomings, especially in the context of climate change. For this reason, assessments of changes in drought characteristics with climate change should consider several indices including a specific evaluation of their relevance to the addressed question to support robust conclusions. In this assessment we focus on the following indices: consecutive dry days (CDD) and simulated soil moisture anomalies (SMA), although evidence based on other indices (e.g., PDSI [Palmer Drought Severity Index] for present climate) is also considered.

Any individual climate model (and there are many) will have its own means of approximating and simulating the earth system of atmospheric circulation and atmosphere-ocean interactions and feedbacks, the changing energy balance and radiative forcings, and generating forecasts of temperatures, precipitation and other climate variables over varying lengths of time. Each forecast set depends on assumptions and inputs of atmospheric composition changes (greenhouse gases in particular). The IPCC makes a thorough evaluation of the outputs of selected climate models and compiles them into a consensus view, illustrated by hundreds of maps. Illus. 137 is the summary example from the IPCC Special Report, showing projected annual and seasonal changes in dryness assessed from two indices, CDD and soil moisture anomalies over two different time periods. It is consolidated from seventeen different climate models and is coloured only where two-thirds of the models agree on the sign of the change, in other words whether the area will become drier (reds and yellows) or wetter (greens). The changes are the differences between the average values over the displayed time periods (2046–2065 in the top row, 2081–2100 for the remainder) and the average values over the period 1980 to 1999. The maps show predictions of annual changes (ANN), those for December, January and February (DJF) and June, July and August (JJA). Only one emissions scenario is reflected in these outputs – the possible permutations and combinations are endless and the uncertainties profound. Those uncertainties, the 'confidence levels', are explicitly addressed by the IPCC but not consistently recognized by the readers of the reports.

The outlook is generally for increasing dryness, but by no means globally; warmer temperatures can bring more precipitation. Review the

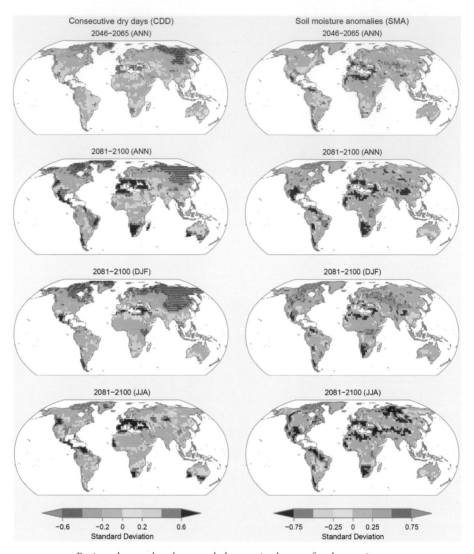

137 Projected annual and seasonal changes in dryness for the coming century.

literature of dryness forecasting for any given region over any given time period and forecasts of increasing drought, 'little change' or increased precipitation can be found. In its summary tables, the IPCC reports the same inconclusive situation at the end of this century for essentially all of the world's major arid lands: '*Low confidence*: Inconsistent signal in CDD and SMA changes.' This is the case for western North America, Australia, the Sahara, Central Asia and the west coast of South America. Only for southern Africa do they report '*Medium confidence*: Increase in dryness (CDD, SMA), except eastern part . . . Consistent increase in area of drought.' In these descriptions, 'Low confidence' reflects 'Medium agreement, Limited evidence' or vice versa.

These results and predictions are of considerable interest, and of importance to the global debate, but modelling scenarios of future climates, quantifying the anthropogenic component and developing long-term counter-measures are arguably entirely separate from addressing the urgent problems of today. They are of no help to a Texas rancher or a resident of the Sahel 'whose hunger is not only in his own cramped stomach'.

Myths and reality

It is perhaps ironic that the challenges of constructively addressing the issues of arid lands and 'desertification' often seem to be those of sorting out the wood from the trees. These are issues of concern to global organizations such as the United Nations and the World Bank, to national and local governments, NGOs, scientists from a multitude of disciplines, environmental groups, commercial interests and, finally, to local communities and individuals. The agendas are correspondingly diverse and, not uncommonly, conflicting.

These are issues of global importance because, as we have seen, the deserts of our planet are not remote and isolated but play an active and involved role in the earth system. Their ecosystems are unique and their societies very much linked to the rest of the world. Climate change inevitably is always in the background, but the question has to be asked as to whether improving long-term predictions and models is really a critical part of the solution to problems that are very much of today. Climate has, after all, always changed, and the societies of arid lands only survive today as a result of their knowledge of, and constant ability to adapt to, changing conditions. Yes, understanding the magnitude and rates of likely near-term changes is important, but there is not a great deal we can actually do about them – the approach must surely not depend on top-down geo-engineering but on bottom-up exploitation of knowledge and adaptation. The health and welfare of desert peoples should not, and cannot, be solely dependent on the reduction of global emissions or grand engineering experiments with the climate. And therein lies the tension beneath the 'debate' over 'managing' the future of drylands and their societies, the familiar contrasts between the views of insiders and outsiders, development versus conservation, the developed and the developing world. The challenge is often maintaining an awareness of what is reality and what is myth, what is conventional wisdom versus appropriate knowledge and how best to apply that knowledge and the science. Substantial numbers of coordinated international programmes and determined individuals are working on these issues, but although there are real success stories, the scale and urgency of the problem requires much more.

Start a review of the available international reports and scientific literature and the volume quickly becomes overwhelming, together with the acronyms. The UNCCD, UNEP, UNDP, GDI, IISD, IIED and IFPRI are but examples of main players who, separately or in collaboration, provide comprehensive, valuable and provocative reports on dryland issues (the documents that I have found most useful and informative are listed in the 'Sources and Further Reading' for this chapter). Two of these, from the United Nations Environment Programme 'Global Drylands: A UN System-wide Response and Global Deserts Outlook', are particularly useful overviews and summarize well the common issues and questions. Under the title 'The Paradigms of Responses to Land Degradation in Deserts', a consensus is described that provides 'a common set of guiding tools for the actions that need to be undertaken'; however, the following comment that 'Since the 1970s, the debate on how to approach the responses to the severe problems of environmental deterioration has remained open' is something of an understatement. The consensus may have been achieved in theory, but translating it into successful practical applications on the ground remains an elusive goal. The summary highlights the need for a multidisciplinary approach to the environmental problems of land degradation:

> The use of natural resources responds to a complex articulation of social, political and economic relationships, and land degradation processes must be analysed in the light of the historical development of local population groups, with particular emphasis on power and social conflicts.

Furthermore, 'The degree to which social participation is essential for land degradation abatement strategies has until recently been underappreciated' and 'responses are imperative'. Arguably, however, the most telling statement is this:

Degradation of natural resources is often associated with poverty around the world. But in many cases, degradation can be triggered by the actions of ambitious international enterprises on a major scale, like mining, oil extraction or the expansion of agricultural frontiers, which often do not generate income [for] or improve the living conditions of local populations.

'Desertification' is a natural process *and* a consequence of human activities, but not primarily those of indigenous societies who, if given a choice, would likely behave and manage their environment very differently. A major component of the problem is that the arid lands of the world disproportionately lie in developing countries where poverty and poor living standards form part of a pernicious feedback loop in the conflict between development, the environment and social welfare. The most disturbing examples of this are in the countries of the Sahel. Each year, the UN Development Programme publishes its assessment and country rankings of Human Development, applying its indices of inequality, gender equality and 'multi-dimensional poverty'. In the 2013 rankings, Niger comes last out of 186 countries, Chad is 184 and Mali is 182. The World Bank reports the percentages of the population who earn less than $2 per day: Niger, 75 per cent; Chad, 83; Mali, 79. Percentages of the relevant age group enrolled in secondary education: Niger, 14; Chad, 25; Mali, 39. Mortality rate of under-fives per thousand live births: Niger, 145; Chad, 150; Mali, 128 (for the UK, the figure is 5). Percentage of the population with access to improved water: Niger, 50; Chad, 50; Mali, 65. Life expectancy in Niger and Mali is 54, in Chad, 49. At the same time, their population growth rates are among the highest in the world regardless of the uncertainty around such statistics and their extrapolation (as has been compellingly evaluated by Swedish doctor and statistician Hans Rosling). Niger will have perhaps 28 million people by 2025, compared to 17 million today, for Chad the numbers are 18 versus 12, and for Mali, 22 versus 15. Enough numbers: they speak, tragically, for themselves. It is in this context of human deprivation – and drought and famine since the 1960s – that some of our planet's most pressing environmental problems need to be addressed. Meanwhile, we should not ignore the fact that this is a situation not entirely limited to the developing world. As we saw in chapter Three, in Australia today Aboriginal people can expect to die twenty years earlier than non-indigenous citizens, are fifteen times more likely to be in jail, and ten times more likely to be murdered. A country that celebrates its indigenous culture as a tourist attraction effectively hides the harsh reality from visitors.

It is not difficult to see how an outsider might well develop a view of land degradation in drylands as an issue that, by its very association with poverty, is inevitable and irreversible but at the same time a problem of only local dimensions. This is a view that needs to be vigorously challenged, and many of the international reports, together with scientists and other individuals working on the ground, are doing so. The case is made nowhere more compellingly than in the publication of the International Union for Conservation of Nature and Natural Resources, *Dryland Opportunities: A New Paradigm for People, Ecosystems and Development* (2009). The authors describe this as a 'Challenge Paper', a 'reappraisal of dryland futures', and write that

> Knowledge is a key component of the human system, and of the interactions between human and ecological systems that lie at the heart of dryland management. But understanding the challenges of sustainable development has been impeded by a number of major misconceptions. It is the aim of this Challenge Paper to show that such perceptions, if applied indiscriminately, function more as myths than science.

The authors define and examine eight key perceptions that 'function more as myths than science', and it is worth quoting them in full here, each myth stated and then refuted:

> 1. *Dryland biomes – compared with other major biomes – are poor, remote and degraded, and apart from having tourist potential, do not really matter globally.*
>
> On the contrary, dryland issues are rapidly increasing in their global significance and call for international economic and institutional response . . .
>
> 2. *Drylands are on the edges of deserts and the deserts are expanding ('desertification') owing to human misuse of the environment (overgrazing, deforestation and overcultivation).*
>
> In place of this view of remorseless degradation, we propose a more balanced view of environmental management based on the concept of resilience.

3. Dryland peoples are helpless (their knowledge and adaptive capacity are weak) in the face of climate variability and change.

In place of despair, we situate drylands objectively within the climate change scenarios and argue that existing adaptive capacity, assisted by sound policy and research, can offer pathways to development.

4. Because of their low biological productivity (when compared to other major biomes), drylands have little economic value except to provide subsistence to those who live there.

We show instead, the real (or total) value of dryland ecosystem services both to local peoples' livelihoods and to national economies.

5. Drylands cannot yield a satisfactory return on investment owing to high risks resulting from low and variable rainfall.

We show that investment in drylands can and does yield a satisfactory and sustainable return, and that poor peoples' private investments are real and significant.

6. Drylands are weakly integrated into markets and because of their remoteness, poverty and low biological productivity, will remain so.

It can be shown that dryland communities have long used markets to drive development, that this economic strategy is expanding rapidly in importance, and that markets can function even under conditions of uncertainty.

7. Dryland communities are conservative and resistant to modernization and institutional change. Governance, rights and institutions are of only local importance and can safely be ignored in favour of new technologies.

We show that equitable rights (in particular, rights to the use of natural resources) and institutional change are necessary and achievable conditions for dryland development.

8. Risk and vulnerability resulting from uncertainty and environmental change can be adequately countered by standard development policy.

Instead, new approaches to risk management are emerging, which build on local and customary practice and directly confront variability.

The analysis is compelling and concludes that:

The Millennium Development Goals cannot be met, nor sustainable ecosystem management achieved, unless drylands are brought back into the mainstream of global development. This Challenge Paper shows the opportunities that exist for achieving these aims, thereby benefiting 41.3 per cent of the earth's land surface and 35.5 per cent of its population. Commonly held presumptions about poverty-environment links require review, and a new set of global drivers of change needs to be identified. A new dryland paradigm should be built on the resources and capacities of dryland peoples, on new and emergent economic opportunities, on inward investment, and on the best support that dryland science can offer.

Powerful and enduring myths and conventional wisdom inhibit the effective application of science and the development of 'a new dryland paradigm', but where did they originate? The answer, inevitably but fascinatingly, lies in the history of colonialism and empires, in the perspectives of Orientalism and in the religiously driven conviction of the superiority of the 'civilized' outsiders. In 1841 David Livingstone arrived as a missionary in the South African outpost of Kuruman on the edge of the Kalahari Desert. His motives were good, in that he believed strongly in the potential to end the slave trade, but unfortunately his chosen means was through 'civilizing' the natives and civilizing meant conversion to Christianity. Kuruman is famous for its desert springs, abundant supplies of fresh water that continue to flow today. But in 1843 they began to dry up and Livingstone seized on this as evidence that the country was being turned into a 'sterile waste'. During his subsequent travels he became convinced that the entire continent was desiccating. Over the following years, the Royal Geographical Society took up the cause and held meetings to discuss global desiccation. Livingstone's mentor, the head of the mission at Kuruman, Robert Moffat, was the leading voice of the Christian view, quoting Milton's *Paradise Lost* and arguing that this 'destitute and miserable land of droughts' was the result of the spiritual failings of the natives and evidence of God's punishment. Livingstone and others placed the blame on deforestation by the natives, and the issue became the foundation for the Europeans to demonstrate their credentials as 'redeemers' and irrigate the Kalahari through damming and diverting tributaries of the Zambezi. Fortunately, this grand geo-engineering project of 'Thirstland Redemption' was never achieved (largely thanks to the reality checks of geologists and surveyors and the return of the rains), but the myth of pan-African desiccation was set in stone.

The narrative of 'blame the natives' underpinned key aspects of colonial policies across the world and, in some quarters, lingers today. *Environmental Imaginaries of the Middle East and North Africa* is an intriguing collection of essays that not only challenge this narrative but document the damage that it has caused in environmental and social management, particularly 'desertification'. As Diana K. Davis and her co-authors describe, one of the greatest 'imaginaries' was that vast areas of today's arid lands had been verdant, forested and agriculturally productive until degraded by indigenous misuse. The French, for example, explicitly declared themselves to be the representatives, the rightful descendants, of the Roman Empire, for which a verdant North Africa had been its granary. 'Restoration' policies were developed and pursued, guided by this entirely imaginary and erroneous belief. Key to these policies was the management of trees and pastureland. Great plantation projects were undertaken, all trees became state property, and pasturelands were divided up and fenced off. The nomads, pastoralists and farmers who, out of necessity, had successfully managed an ever-changing ecosystem for millennia lost control over their lands and their livelihoods. Land degradation and poverty were inevitable. Nomadism was primitive and unacceptable under this system and policies of 'sedentarization' were enforced. It would be reassuring to believe that this misguided approach culminated in the catastrophe of Kazakhstan in the 1930s, but it is one that continues today. Bedouin in the Negev Desert, pastoralists in Mongolia, Khoisan in the Kalahari, all are people whose culture and livelihoods are being lost as a result of policies based entirely on myths and political interests rather than evidence. Nomads inconveniently cross country boundaries and therefore post-colonial national governments commonly regard them as loyal to family and tribe rather than nation, and consign them to the lost borders of political priorities. As Diana Davis writes:

> Critically interrogating the environmental imaginaries of the Middle East and North Africa . . . holds promise for future research that may be able to inform more environmentally sustainable and socially equitable development in the region.

This *is* happening. In 2014, Marcos Easdale and Stephanie Domptail, researchers from agricultural institutes in Argentina and Germany respectively, published a provocative paper titled 'Fate Can Be Changed! Arid Rangelands in a Globalizing World: A Complementary Co-evolutionary Perspective on the Current "Desert Syndrome"'. Extracts from their summary, 'Opportunities to end the marginalization-desertification spiral', are as follows:

> Under an economic system which views ecological aspects of agricultural production as mere side-effects, and under the assumption that consumer values and preferences have co-evolved to favour industrial products, the global socio-economic context is *de facto* marginalizing rangelands, even though they used to be the main source of key agricultural products . . . awareness of the usefulness and appropriateness of traditional knowledge in the design of robust and resilient pastoral systems is rising in the scientific arena . . . Research on alternative systems must become more creative, more participatory and look towards adaptive management . . . far from being an inevitable fate due to the ecological characteristics the marginalization of arid rangelands is the result of political and economic governance choices.

Agricultural, political and social pressures, together with profoundly fluctuating aridity, have created the dire situation in today's Sahel. Pressures on land use have exacerbated conflict between farmers and pastoralists, productivity pressures have resulted in the introduction of cattle breeds not adapted to regional conditions, traditional practices of leaving the land fallow have been abandoned, and European methods of growing crops in cleared and opened fields, utterly inappropriate for the Sahel, have been imposed. Crops need trees and there are trees in the Sahel – not forests by a European definition, but in good times a significant vegetation cover – but, no longer protected as traditions required, they are destroyed for firewood and construction. There *are* success stories in the Sahel and they are underpinned by the collaboration of science and local knowledge. Listening to and involving the people who have successfully survived, albeit not always easily, for hundreds of generations may not seem like a radical approach, but it is. In 1992 the UK organization SOS Sahel published a unique book. *At the Desert's*

Edge: Oral Histories from the Sahel is a compilation, with informed commentary, of interviews with dozens of residents, male and female, young and old, across the borderlands of the Sahara from Sudan and Ethiopia to Mauritania and Senegal. These are the voices of insiders. Obo Koné was 77 years old when he talked with the project team members (sadly he died in 1991). He had spent all his life in the Malian Sahel, and his words capture, as no others could, the complexities and dimensions of the challenges:

> When I was young, the rains were good and the vegetation was thick and green. Plants, men and animals lived together in harmony. The soils were fertile and productive. Then the rain gradually petered out. We began to cut the trees down and lose respect for our old customs. Today we don't really understand what happened: suddenly the rain lost respect for its old cycle – it no longer lasted as long and the hot and cold seasons have been disrupted. Today the environment is sick, the soils are poor and hard, and the trees are dead, having been scorched by the sun. To make up for poor harvests, larger areas of land have been given over to cultivation. We can only afford to leave land fallow for one or two years, compared to four or five years in the past. To make up for this we try to apply more fertiliser . . . If there is no vegetation cover, the wind raises the dust and the top layer of the soil is blown away, leaving the ground bare. On soil which has been stripped of vegetation the water runs off quickly, digging ditches in the ground as it flows . . . I believe these changes can be attributed to the fact that we have lost respect for our customs. We have violated old prohibitions to allow room for modernisation and in so doing we have disregarded God's laws . . . The government today has eased many of our problems and brought us peace. However, in addition to the benefits there have also been negative effects, such as the high taxes we have to pay. As for development projects, I think they are an absolute mess. To begin with, everyone is keen on them. Then after some time certain people, who think they are clever, begin to distrust the project and avoid the work it does. Others, who realise the benefit that they personally can reap, attach themselves to it like leeches and suffocate it. Having said this, it is true that people still believe that development

138 Alkhayna Walet Ibrahim.

projects can strengthen us, and improve the desperate situation in which we find ourselves.

The stories are of change, often for the worse but also for the better – improvements in education and the roles of women are significant examples. Alkhayna Walet Ibrahim, a nomadic Malian woman (illus. 138), comments that: 'Our work has changed. Before women only looked after children and did housework, but now we gather produce that we can sell, trade in tea, and make cushions out of wool and leather to bring in some money.'

However, it is never simple. Education of the younger generation can bring loss of knowledge and reduced respect for culture and tradition, and the creative knowledge and skills of women remain very much under-utilized. There are many disheartening stories of the continuing locust plagues, an effective remedy for which has yet to be developed. The management of water resources is divided and under pressure. Firewood sellers travel increasing distances from outside a particular community to raid what trees remain. However, as stated in the introduction to the book, 'No-one can be left in any doubt that

Sahelians have a thorough understanding of their own predicament, and of the causes of desertification.' Harness this understanding and the results can be astonishing.

A success story

'Desertification' prompts images of an expanding and advancing desert, inevitably and inexorably taking over verdant lands. Stories are written about how many kilometres the Sahara has 'moved' over time. But it is not so. Thanks to the revolutionary technologies of satellite data, the changing conditions across the desert borderlands can be tracked over time. In particular, the constant changes in vegetation cover over the year can be accurately monitored, as we saw in chapter One, by the Normalized Difference Vegetation Index (NDVI) data. Over the years, this powerful tool has demonstrated emphatically that the image of the advancing desert is yet another myth. The 'greenness' of the Sahel fluctuates naturally, but far more importantly, the efforts of a handful of determined people and thousands of resident farmers and pastoralists have resulted in positive changes clearly visible on the satellite imagery. Tens of thousands of square kilometres are now demonstrably greener than they were twenty years ago.

Australian agronomist Tony Rinaudo was serving in Niger with an international missionary organization in the 1970s and '80s when his life's mission became apparent: working to help impoverished communities of the Sahel through agricultural innovation and reforestation. Sometimes referred to as 'the tree-whisperer', Rinaudo developed an approach that was innovative in many respects, but nevertheless relied on local knowledge, traditional methods and the belief and hard work of local farmers. He is the originator of what is now a global, rapid and sustainable methodology of land restoration, Farmer Managed Natural Regeneration, or FMNR. Rinaudo realized that an 'underground forest' remained beneath vast tracts of cleared and degraded land, still-living tree roots and stumps and natural seeds that, if given a chance and protected for a few months, would grow. During the droughts of the 1980s, Rinaudo provided food to farmers and their families in return for continuing protection of the growing trees; when the rains returned, participation dropped, but when the benefits to those who continued became apparent, the movement spread. Tree management was restored to the people who worked the land, the benefits of which were eventually recognized by the government. Farmers began to again use traditional methods of water management for the new trees and for new crops. Digging a planting pit through the hardened surface and adding organic matter created not only a water-conserving environment for plant growth, but attracted termites that processed the organic material for use by the plants and aerated the soil through their tunnelling. Other traditional water conservation methods such as small reservoirs to contain runoff from whatever rain did fall were also brought back into use, aided by cheap and simple technology for their construction. Vitally, the flourishing trees provided shade for a diversity of other crops to be grown beneath them – the temperature beneath them can be more than 20 degrees Celsius cooler than the surrounding open ground – and reduce the impact of the wind, facilitate water infiltration and fix nitrogen into the soil. One tree in particular, the *gao*, a native of the Sahel, is a very effective nitrogen-fixer, but had all but disappeared when the FMNR initiatives began. It has now taken its place again as an essential part of the ecosystem.

Chris Reij is a Dutch agronomist and Sustainable Land Management specialist at the Centre for International Cooperation in Amsterdam and a Senior Fellow of the World Resources Institute in Washington. He also began working in the Sahel in the late 1970s and joined Tony Rinaudo as another driving force in the re-greening of the Sahel. However, such projects do not succeed overnight. It was not until a *New York Times* article titled 'In Niger, Trees and Crops Turn Back the Desert' appeared in 2007 that the world really began to take notice. In it, Reij describes how the scale of vegetation growth surprised even him, and Mahamane Larwanou, a forestry expert at Niger's University of Niamey, relates how the regrowth of trees had transformed rural life:

> The benefits are so many it is really astonishing. The farmers can sell the branches for money. They can feed the pods as fodder to their animals. They can sell or eat the leaves. They can sell and eat the fruits. Trees are so valuable to farmers, so they protect them.

Satellite monitoring, overseen by Gray Tappan, a remote sensing specialist at the U.S. Geological Survey's EROS Data Center, led, in 2009, to the estimation that the area revegetated by farmers in densely populated parts of Niger was close to 50,000 square kilometres and that those farmers had protected and managed at least 200 million 'new' trees over the previous two decades. 'New', because most were regenerated by the FMNR methods. In the 2009 report *Millions Fed* by the International Food Policy Research Institute, Reij, Tappan and Melinda Smale of Michigan State University state:

> Farmers in the Central Plateau of Burkina Faso have rehabili-
> tated at least 200,000 hectares of land . . . If cereal production
> increased by an average of 400 kilograms per hectare – a con-
> servative estimate – farmers have increased their annual harvest
> there by 80,000 tons, or enough to feed about 500,000 people.
> With these increases, farm households that suffered from food
> deficits of six months or more during the early 1980s have been
> able to reduce their deficit periods from six months to two or
> three months, or to zero in some cases.

These techniques are now being applied in more than fourteen countries and are clearly 'resilient' and 'sustainable'. As Reij and his colleagues conclude, 'the process by which these innovations emerged – through experimentation, exploration, and exchanges by and among farmers themselves – is possibly the most vital lesson learned from the Sahel.' In 2013 Chris Reij and Yacouba Savadogo, a farmer from Burkina Faso who has championed traditional water harvesting techniques and FMNR, were very appropriately given Global Drylands Champions awards by the UN Convention to Combat Desertification. Yacouba is profiled in the documentary film *The Man Who Stopped the Desert* and Chris Reij has commented that 'Yacouba single-handedly has had more impact on soil and water conservation in the Sahel than all the national and inter-national researchers combined.' It is a shame that Obo Koné is not still alive to witness these achievements.

What is perhaps most astonishing about this success story is that, in the words of Tony Rinaudo:

> A social, rather than a technical breakthrough, has been achieved.
> The greatest barriers to reforestation were neither the absence
> of an exotic super tree nor ignorance of best practice nursery
> and tree husbandry techniques. The greatest barriers were the
> collective mindset which saw trees on farmland as 'weeds' need-
> ing to be cleared and inappropriate laws which put responsibility

for and ownership of trees in the hands of the government and not in the hands of the people.

This is not high technology, it is not geo-engineering in the normal sense, it is not the result of top-down planning or cutting-edge research. It is very much a success of the bottom-up approach, innovation by local people: it is refreshingly 'barefoot science'.

Water

That 'the desert shall rejoice, and blossom as the rose. It shall blossom abundantly' was a biblical prophecy that, unfortunately, seems to have been taken literally by colonial planners in their mission to bring civilization to the barbaric wilderness. In 1847 Brigham Young arrived on the edge of the Utah desert with his Mormon followers and making it blossom became not only their mission but the mantra of the conquest of arid lands as the manifest destiny of the U.S.

As Tony Rinaudo, Chris Reij, Yacouba Savadogo and countless farmers have shown, the desert can blossom, but only in its own way (illus. 139). The narrative of past abundance and fertility in a European sense that required 'restoration' is an environmental imaginary whose legacy continues. All of the world's arid lands have experienced profound changes in aridity over time, but they and their inhabitants and eco-systems have responded in unique ways. The Sahara may have been savannah a few thousand years ago, but it bore no resemblance to the Forest of Fontainebleau. Along with this narrative came a disastrous attitude: the profligate disregard for the depletion of our planet's primary life-sustaining resource, water.

As we catch up on our knowledge and understanding of drylands as global environments and ecosystems, there are many surprises, challenges to conventional wisdom, lessons to be learned, both positive and negative. As the FMNR projects in the Sahel have so emphatically demonstrated, the most urgent lesson to be learned is from our mistakes over water management. In the same way that a simple hole in the ground is an effective traditional way of harvesting water, we should perhaps ask what the foggaras, the qanats, the karez, the puquios irrigation system of Chile and the Hohokam canals have to tell us about water sustainability – and otherwise. The Hohokam people unaccountably disappeared in spite of – or perhaps because of – their sophisticated water supply

139 The desert blooms in Saudi Arabia.

system, but the one thing we can be sure of is that their per capita water use was substantially less than that of today's Arizona residents. There are compellingly simple but highly innovative ideas being developed for water harvesting. As just one example, the University of Engineering and Technology in Peru's arid capital, Lima, has constructed a single roadside billboard that uses basic water condensation technology to supplement water supply for hundreds of families every month.

Measurements of water use versus available supplies on a global or regional level can never be made without significant uncertainty. The rate at which water moves underground and recharges the great ground-water aquifers of the world is difficult to measure with accuracy, but nevertheless we know enough to draw some clear and irrefutable conclusions. First, regardless of the specific numbers, the data demonstrate unequivocally that large areas of the world are using water at a dramatically unsustainable rate of depletion. As Tom Gleeson of McGill University and his colleagues from the University of Utrecht have recently set out, the water balance of an aquifer can be described by the measure of a 'groundwater footprint'. This is the area of a given aquifer 'required to sustain groundwater use and groundwater-dependent ecosystem services', in other words all the inflows and outflows, both natural and as a consequence of man's activities. In simple terms, if that area is greater than the actual extent of the aquifer, the ratio is greater than one and water usage is not sustainable. Globally, they calculate that figure to be around 3.5. But at the same time, 80 per cent of the world's main aquifers have a footprint less than their area, which means that the 'global value is driven by a few heavily over-exploited aquifers'. And where are many of these? Not surprisingly in the drylands. The footprint for the aquifers of Saudi Arabia is more than 40; for western Mexico, 27; for the High Plains/Ogallala aquifer of the western u.s., 9; and for California's Central Valley, 6. This is a problem particularly in the developed world; the water withdrawal per capita is vastly lower in, for example, the countries of the Sahel than it is in the u.s., the uk or Saudi Arabia. There are substantial and detailed, yet often conflicting, statistics on water use and depletion available from a number of different sources, but the un Food and Agricultural Organization is one comprehensive source, even though the data must still be treated with caution. Their *Aquastat* data reveal that total annual per capita water withdrawal amounts to 1,600 cubic metres for every citizen of the u.s. and 70 for an inhabitant of Niger.

Each year Saudi Arabia withdraws more than 900 cubic metres for every person, a total that is hundreds of times the amount of freshwater that is resupplied to aquifers and surface resources: the country has already used up a substantial proportion of its underground water resources. Eighty per cent of Saudi Arabia's water consumption is devoted to agriculture and vast volumes of its water resources have been expended on the attempt, since the 1970s, to become self-sufficient in wheat production, with at one point 20 per cent of its oil revenues devoted to supplying the necessary water. It is now abandoning this goal, but the country's water use tripled between 1980 and 2006, aquifer levels dropped dramatically and groundwater became brackish in many areas. The application of centre-pivot irrigation systems provided a means of efficient irrigation but prompted massive and questionable projects to make the desert bloom. NASA has dramatically captured these changes in the area of Wadi As-Sirhan, in the northern part of the country (illus. 140, 141). The availability of water in these irrigated areas has resulted in birds changing their migration routes (and increasing their vulnerability to birds of prey and to the pesticides and fertilizers used).

At the southern end of the Arabian Peninsula, Sanaa may be the world's first capital city to run out of water and cities in the southwest U.S. may not be far behind. If John Wesley Powell's sensible proposals for borders and land and water allocation in the Great American Desert (chapter Four) had been adopted, Phoenix and Las Vegas would almost certainly not exist. Nor would the hundreds of square kilometres in Arizona's Yuma County, where average rainfall is less than 100 millimetres per year, be devoted to growing lettuce. Las Vegas, whose name means 'The Meadows', may be a modern oasis of sorts, but as a city – with its more than 60 golf courses – it is irrational and may run out of drinking water in twenty years. A 500-kilometre pipeline has been suggested to bring 300 billion litres of water a year to the city from further north, a grand scheme that, it has been estimated, would lower the water table in some areas by 60 metres and dry up natural springs. The history of wholesale redistribution of water and the damming of major rivers across the western U.S. has created environmental havoc and a situation that is unsustainable. The diversion of water from the Owens River in 1924 to supply the California Aqueduct system resulted in the desiccation of Owens Lake, now the single greatest dust source in the U.S. The Colorado River no longer reaches its delta and marshes in the Gulf of California and legally has no water left to allocate. The Glen Canyon Dam traps 95 per cent of the sediment that would normally find its way down the river and through the Grand Canyon. The equivalent of 30,000 dump-truck loads of sand and mud

140, 141 Wadi As-Sirhan, 1986 and 2013.

are deposited in the reservoir every day, and the future of the dam and Lake Powell is highly controversial. Experiencing today the worst drought in two generations and facing the real possibility of continuing and increasing dryness, the agriculture of Texas and the 'breadbasket' of the western u.s. is unsustainable. Water pricing is not 'reality-based', the groundwater in the Ogallala/Great Plains aquifer is dropping in some areas at a rate of close to a metre a year, and 'water wars' and 'a looming dust bowl' have become headline topics. Yet more than a third of the residential water use in drought-stricken Texas is still devoted to maintaining verdant lawns.

It has to be asked when we will learn that lawns and lettuce, rice, cotton and alfalfa are not the crops of arid lands. The catastrophic destruction of the Aral Sea was the result of the Soviet Union's determination to make the deserts of Central Asia blossom with cotton. In 1932 the Office du Niger was created to instigate grand irrigation projects along the Niger River, particularly in the region of its ephemeral but critical Inner Delta in the Sahel. A massive dam and canals were constructed (by forced labour) to irrigate land for cotton and other thirsty crops to supply the French market. The scheme was a failure, particularly after the abolition of forced labour meant that farmers no longer could be compelled to work. The land was turned over to rice and sugar cane. The Office du Niger still exists as a legacy of colonial policy and is granting rights to large-scale foreign agro-business investors to cultivate vast areas of sugar and rice, together with, yes, cotton. Further dams are planned, including one upstream for hydroelectric power in Guinea. Over the decades, and continuing today, an entire ecosystem has been sabotaged and the livelihoods of several million farmers, fishermen and pastoralists wrecked through loss of land and water rights. West of Egypt's Aswan Dam, in the heart of the desert, are signs welcoming visitors to 'New Toshka City' – which doesn't exist. Regarded by many as a monumental folly, the New Valley development scheme was initiated in the 1990s by pumping water from Lake Nasser into newly constructed canals feeding into a vast desert depression. Lakes formed, roads were built, and the plan was for several thousand square kilometres of agriculture (irrigated by centre-pivot systems) to grow cereals, vegetables and fruit (including strawberries). Twenty per cent of Egypt's population would move to Toshka and other new cities, and the country's chronic food and population pressures would be alleviated. But the lakes, which were expected to replenish declining and salinized aquifers, are drying up, and political turmoil has essentially suspended the project. A Saudi Arabian agricultural business is producing grapes, melons, alfalfa and other crops and is conducting significant research. Not surprisingly, they have declined to grow wheat (although there is talk of devoting large areas to the crop). The project has its proponents and opponents, but more than a billion dollars have been spent, and its sustainability is highly questionable.

There are aridity- and salt-tolerant crops that can be grown in the desert, and irrigation systems that are frugal with water use. Drip irrigation in the Negev is many times more efficient than conventional methods, and the oases in Egypt and elsewhere demonstrate the variety of fruit and vegetables that can possibly be sustainably cultivated. But the problem is always doing so on a scale that realistically addresses the needs of populations such as those of the Jordan Valley and Egypt yet does not deplete and degrade the quantity and quality of available water. Despite its agricultural efficiency and innovation (and its abandonment of wheat as a crop), Israel's depletion of aquifers and water-allocation in a context of political turmoil is a controversial topic. Is the Red Sea–Dead Sea pipeline really the solution?

An ever-improving understanding of aquifer behaviour is providing some answers to water management on a large scale. Satellites measuring delicate changes in the gravitational pull of the mass of a body of underground water are demonstrating, for example, that the ancient waters of the vital Nubian aquifer beneath the Sahara, threatened by

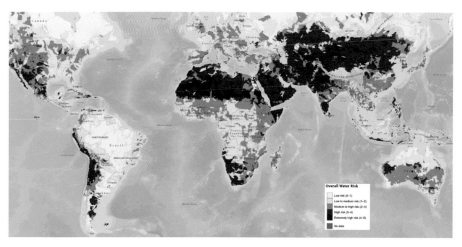

142 Aqueduct world water risk assessment.

Qaddafi's 'Great Man-Made River' project, is, in fact, being recharged faster than we thought – although still not at the rate that it is being used. If there is sufficient political will and cross-border collaboration, then a sustainable usage allocation plan is not impossible. There are glimmers of hope for the Nubian, but, as in most regions of water stress, solutions remain elusive. The World Resources Institute maintains a database and mapping systems of global water issues through its *Aqueduct* programme, readily and interactively available online. 'Water risk' maps display a variety of components of stress on surface and groundwater systems that include seasonal and annual variation, floods and drought, storage, recharge and access. Each component can be examined individually, but the overall risk map is shown in illus. 142. It makes sobering viewing: 56 per cent of irrigated agriculture across the world is facing high water stress.

What can we learn from the desert?

Massive, and often questionable, engineering projects are under way or being seriously contemplated across the world's drylands. A 'Great Green Wall' is being planted across China and another will traverse Africa. Since the late 1970s the Chinese have been planting millions of trees in a project that will stretch 4,500 kilometres across the country in an effort to stop 'desertification'. However, since most of the trees planted are non-native and large numbers die every year, there are real concerns about the ultimate effectiveness and the impact on biodiversity. The African project is somewhat more subtle, having evolved into an integrated plan that includes sustainable farming and water management initiatives, but it requires the collaboration of more than a dozen countries. It was first proposed in the 1980s, a vision emerging from the megalomania of then-president Abdoulaye Wade of Senegal, who described the desert as 'a spreading cancer' that required a 'titanic battle' against it. Now, with the support of international organizations and serious input from environmental science and agronomy, a 'harmonized strategy' was agreed in late 2012. How this controversial 'flagship programme' will emerge into reality remains to be seen.

'Biodiversity' is a term more readily associated with teeming rainforests and European woodlands than arid lands. This reflects the historic myths, the environmental imaginaries and the relegation of drylands to the category of the biologically, economically and socially marginal. Yet, as we have seen, the desert is the home of extraordinary ecosystems, specially and often uniquely adapted to the challenging environment. In 2012 the International Union for Conservation of Nature and Natural Resources, together with partner organizations, published what amounts to a manifesto supporting the UN's Millennium Development Goals on 'Conserving Dryland Biodiversity'. This states:

> The drylands perhaps more than any other biome offer opportunities for achieving both conservation and development objectives simultaneously and in many cases have been shown to do so . . . Some semi-arid and dry sub-humid areas are among the most biodiverse in the world . . . Dryland biodiversity is also central to sustainable development and to the livelihoods of many of the world's poor: the importance of biodiversity to poverty reduction and economic development in the drylands may be greater than in many other biomes . . . Dryland biodiversity also has global economic importance, providing a number of high-value products that fill important niche markets (such as gums and some medicinal plants). Furthermore, at least 30 per cent of the world's cultivated plants and many livestock breeds originate in drylands, providing an important genetic reservoir that is becoming increasingly valuable for climate change adaptation.

Rather than focus on grand-scale engineering projects, it would arguably be more fruitful to consider what can be learned from desert ecosystems and their inhabitants on the small scale. Revelations of the diversity and activities of the microbial-scale component occur on almost a daily basis. Previously unknown bacteria living in the hypersaline pools of Bolivia's Salar de Uyuni ('the Saudi Arabia of lithium') have now been shown to produce biological forms of plastic that could have medical and other commercial applications. Of course, a great deal of work has to be done to develop any commercial-scale use of these biochemicals, and it may not work, but this is typical of the world of 'extremophiles', widespread members of the biosphere whose unique adaptations and chemical products we as yet know little about. We have also come to appreciate that many plants of arid environments, while utilizing novel variations on photosynthesis and other adaptations, still cannot survive on their own, but rely on collaboration with a miniature zoo of fungi, bacteria and viruses in their root systems. This 'microbiome' provides nutrition, nitrogen uptake and protection that allow the plant to survive. Almost all plants live with these endophytes to some extent, but it is aridity-tolerant ones that are of particular interest – yet they are only now becoming the subject of comprehensive study. The exact mechanisms of how these symbiotic communities work remain unclear, but experiments have shown, for example, that spores from grass growing in Yellowstone hot springs, when sprayed on wheat seeds, create almost a doubling of temperature tolerance and a 50 per cent reduction in water requirement. Other work has demonstrated that endophytes from desert plants, when applied to crops such as tomatoes, chillies and feedstock grass, cause a significant increase in yields and drought resistance. The genes of the ancient wild relatives of today's cereals that bestow salt-tolerance have been successfully introduced into durum ('macaroni') wheat and show promise with other strains. These would seem to be approaches to cultivating salinity- and temperature-tolerant crops that are far simpler than genetic engineering.

The microbiotic crusts of the desert are not only being 'cultivated' in China to stabilize shifting sand dunes but are now understood to play a far greater role in the planet's carbon cycle than had been previously assumed. Analysis of satellite imagery of vegetation changes over time has shown that the 'fertilization effect' of increasing atmospheric carbon dioxide levels is particularly visible in arid lands, in part because the efficiency of the vegetation in terms of the amount of carbon used per molecule of water is enhanced when there is more carbon available. The conventional wisdom of biodiversity that long food chains require high 'primary productivity', in other words vigorous plant activity, at their base has been overturned by our understanding of how they work in arid lands. In the desert there are few herbivores and instead plant litter is consumed by the diversity of arthropods, of which termites are the outstanding example. The arthropods are, in turn, consumed by arachnids and reptiles, who are preyed on by birds and mammals, creating a long food chain with tiny creatures as the primary consumers.

The traditional uses of the biodiversity of the desert by indigenous peoples as a supermarket and a pharmacy are only now being seriously evaluated and the results are already, unsurprisingly if belatedly, impressive. Exploring the wonders of the Australian outback, I was overwhelmed by the variety of plant life, almost all of which was entirely exotic to an outsider, and I worked my way through Les

Hiddins's book *Bush Tucker Field Guide.* Of the 175 species he describes, almost all have apparently familiar names: there are yams, tomatoes, bananas, raisins, plums and apples, but none of them have any relation to the originals and only a few bear even a vague resemblance to them – they are white fellah names. The bloodwood apple (or bush coconut) is a gall of the bloodwood tree, a member of the eucalyptus family, and the inner lining of the gall is edible. The blossoms of the tree yield a sweet nectar and from the sap tiny insects produce a crystallized scale, the 'lerp', on the leaves which is sweet and can be dissolved in water and drunk – an equivalent to lerp on desert tamarisk trees may have been the 'manna' of the Bible. The sap of the bloodwood tree is dark red, can be applied in small quantities as an antiseptic and is used in tanning animal skins. The bush tomato comes in a variety of types which are, for the outsider, difficult to distinguish, but while some are extremely poisonous, others constitute a major food source for Aboriginal peoples.

The list of valuable desert plants goes on, and it is the same for the American west. The ubiquitous and uninspiring sagebrush and creosote are used as antibacterials and pain-relievers. Every type of cactus has value as a source of water, food or medicine. The claim by some 'ethnobotanists' that the Sonoran Desert contains more wild edible plants than anywhere else on the planet may be something of an exaggeration, but not much of one. Gary Nabhan, research scientist and 'internationally-celebrated nature writer, food and farming activist', is an enthusiastic advocate for exploiting the links between biodiversity and cultural diversity. In his book *Growing Food in a Hotter, Drier Land: Lessons from Desert Farmers on Adapting to Climate Uncertainty*, he provides comprehensive descriptions of plant varieties and cultivation methods that emulate, rather than imitate, what traditional desert peoples from around the world have learned, arguing passionately and knowledgeably for strategies to replace the thirsty practices of today's agriculture:

> Over the course of four decades, u.s. farmers have failed to hit the water conservation targets that Israeli and other Middle Eastern farmers have achieved in far less time . . . Fortunately, there are a great number of alternative irrigation systems – traditional and innovative – suited to hotter, drier climates, and already being successfully used by farmers around the world.

Take, for example, the use of inexpensive clay pots, known in the Arizona desert as *ollas*. These were described from China more than 2,000 years ago and are increasingly used around the world today, buried in the ground adjacent to a seedling and filled with water so that a continuous, minuscule but adequate, supply of water filters out through the permeable clay. Some of the micro-irrigation techniques Nabhan documents are practicable only on a small scale, but many are also capable of commercial-scale application.

Frankincense and myrrh were valuable commodities of international trade not least because of their pharmaceutical qualities. The list of the traditional medicinal uses of myrrh is a long one, from alleviating blisters, sores and inflammation as an antiseptic, to wart removal and the relief of stomach pains. It would seem interesting to ask why, and 'bio-prospecting', for so long apparently focused on the rainforests, is now rapidly appreciating that desert plants, in their adaptation to severe conditions, manufacture some extraordinary and unique chemicals. We now understand that many desert plants have developed antioxidation defence systems and associated biochemistries that hold substantial promise as alternative cancer treatments. Other plants are being evaluated for their antibacterial properties, influence on blood pressure and numerous other potential applications.

Everywhere we begin to look, there are potential lessons to be learned from the desert. Think, for example, about architecture. As we seek to manage domestic energy consumption in a warming world, we should learn from the designs of passive ventilation, the uses of courtyards, gardens, pools, domes, air vents, vaults and wind towers, the traditional Iranian wind-catching *badgirs* that are characteristic of desert architecture the world over. We should contemplate why desert architecture is often, to the outsider, 'inverted', with the sacrosanct garden, the oasis, on the inside. How shade is routinely provided by upper floors overhanging those below, multiple small openings used versus a small number of large ones, the understanding of thermal mass and maximizing surface areas that radiate the heat at night, the enjoyment of the cool environment below ground level. The use of adobe and mud-brick from the pueblos of the u.s. southwest to the great mosques and urban architecture of Djenné in Mali and the UNESCO World Heritage site of Wadi M'Zab in Algeria: 'Simple, functional and perfectly adapted to the environment, the architecture of M'Zab was designed for community living, while respecting the structure of the family. It is a source of inspiration for today's urban planners.' Increasingly, designers and planners such as the pioneering Iranian-American architect Nader Khalili are indeed using such inspiration. Khalili, who died in 2008, was also inspired by the Sufi poet Rumi, whose poems he translated, and pursued 'a Sustainable Solution to Human Shelter, based on Timeless Materials (earth, water, air and fire) and Timeless Principles (arches, vaults and domes)'. The materials of his dome and vault structures were ceramics and 'superadobe', a combination of sand bags and barbed wire.

And then there are the truly futuristic visions. Prompted by the natural sculptures of tafoni and the strange ability of some bacteria to cement sand grains together into solid rock, Magnus Larsson proposed *Dune: Anti-Desertification Architecture* in response to the Green-Wall Sahara initiative, and Andrew Kudless has been inspired by Frank Herbert's *Dune* to envision *Sietch Nevada* (illus. 143, 144). Fantastic indeed, but also inspiring.

I would suggest, however, that the most important thing to learn from the desert is that it is not deserted. That people have adapted to thrive in arid lands over countless generations and for that they should be respected. The desert is not a dumping ground for human rights and human dignity any more than it is for physical refuse. The desert is not a military laboratory, nor should its landscapes be covered indiscriminately with solar power facilities. Mining and other projects on a scale and with an environmental impact that would not be countenanced in any other environment should, necessary though they may be, be more carefully planned and managed than they often are. Mongolia's economic future is dependent on its natural mineral resources, but this cannot be achieved at the cost of human suffering and environmental degradation. Nomadism and pastoralism are viable ways of life that not only capitalize on a deep understanding of the way arid environments work but are capable of high levels of productivity and commercial value. The wholesale displacement of nomadic tribes in Mongolia or Bedouin in the Negev and North Africa is not only a violation of human rights but is politically and economically myopic. And the world's deserts should not be the graveyards of thousands of desperate refugees every year.

There are choices to be made by those who have the luxury of being able to make them, choices in pursuing an intelligent balance between development and preservation, of sustainability and resilience

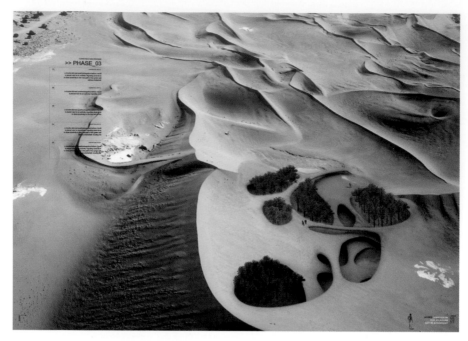

143 Future vision: *Dune*.

144 Future vision: *Sietch Nevada*.

versus degradation and depletion. We need to celebrate the beauty and value of our planet's arid lands and their peoples, and recognize that, imperfect though our knowledge of the desert may be, we have the means to make those choices on all scales, if we have the vision and the will.

145 Desert *dépannage*.

A Personal Epilogue

AS I WAS WORKING on this book, it struck me that, in the interests of personal credibility, I should have spent more time on a camel.

In order to address this immediately, I had little choice other than the tourist route and took off to the Moroccan town of Merzouga and the dunes of the Erg Chebbi. There, with the excellent help of Hassan Mouhou, I met my guide, Ibrahim, and a dromedary named Bob Marley. At the time, I thought this highly entertaining, and conjured up names for the others – Jimi Hendrix, Bob Dylan, Jethro Tull, Jerry Garcia. It was only later that I discovered that most of the camels were called Bob Marley, for the amusement of the tourists, and that in reality they had no names, only numbers inelegantly stapled through their ears (Bob was number 2,222).

My itinerary would be for three days, but we set off in the company of a touring American dance group and the inevitable, but charming, Japanese. They would all only spend one night, after which Ibrahim, Bob and I would set off on our own. But camels are gregarious creatures and the following morning the departure of his friends back to town displeased Bob mightily. We lurched off unhappily, Bob foaming vigorously and malodorously at the mouth, before grinding to a halt within a couple of hundred metres. Since my steed clearly resented my presence and staying on board an irritated camel can be something of a challenge, I dismounted and watched Ibrahim as he attempted to use his camel-knowledge to induce commitment to further progress. This was to no avail whatsoever – Bob had no intention of proceeding (illus. 145).

It was then that I noticed that Ibrahim seemed to be making a call on his mobile phone. I asked him (in French, fortunately our common

language) what the plan was: he grinned broadly and explained that this was a case of *dépannage*, a breakdown, and therefore help had to be summoned. Within an hour, over the dunes, came a young boy leading our replacement vehicle. He took Bob, now clearly delighted and co-operative, back to town for servicing and I mounted my replacement dromedary, whose name, if he had one, I never discovered and so I christened him Alphonse. The next couple of days alone with Ibrahim and the desert were an enormous pleasure and Alphonse tolerated me. However, the delight was, inevitably, moderated by the wear and tear on the nether regions and the sciatic nerve brought on by the bizarre motion of a camel.

146 A desert moment.

Ibrahim knew his desert and its life in detail. A fennec fox in the wild as opposed to those tethered in the arms of children by the roadside for tourist photographs, a 'sand swimmer' lizard revealed in Ibrahim's closed hand and then put through its paces. The nights in the desert held their usual wonder. The couscous and Ibrahim's omelettes and mint tea ('Berber whisky') were all the better for the environment in which they were consumed. For a few days away from London, it was a tonic. And all the more so for the unique moment captured in this photograph: dunes, gravel plains, tamarisk trees, camels and a desert mirage (illus. 146). What more could I want?

Sources and Further Reading

The literature on the deserts of the world, scientific, historic and cultural, is vast. In this compilation of sources, the main sources for the topics in each chapter are listed, together with suggestions for further reading. To facilitate the journey of the curious reader, they are listed under the appropriate subsections of each chapter. Some articles are from scientific journals which may not be easily accessible, but the author can supply copies of some for personal use on request.

Publications that provide global overviews of the desert

Martin Buckley, *Grains of Sand* (London, 2000)
> Buckley's inspiration in the bath to travel the world's deserts resulted in this compelling, entertaining and informative book of his journeys.

Fondation Cartier pour l'Art Contemporain, *The Desert* (New York, 2001)
> In large, coffee-table format, this is an eclectic journey through art, photography, film and history and includes an interview with Wilfred Thesiger accompanied by many of his extraordinary photographs.

Rosslyn D. Haynes, *Desert: Nature and Culture* (London, 2013)

Gregory McNamee, ed., *The Sierra Club Desert Reader: A Literary Companion* (San Francisco, 1995)
> A cross-cultural sampling of desert writing and history, this is a unique and fascinating resource.

Michael A. Mares, *Encyclopedia of Deserts* (Norman, OK, 1999)
> Mares is a biologist and the life of arid lands is the focus of this comprehensive and valuable resource on these ecosystems. Other topics, such as religion and pastoralism, are included.

Nick Middleton, *Deserts: A Very Short Introduction* (Oxford, 2009)

Lisa Mol and Troy Sternberg, *Changing Deserts: Integrating People and their Environment* (Cambridge, 2012)
> This is a highly topical collection of essays that interweave the social and geological issues of the desert.

Jake Page, *Arid Lands* (Chicago, 1984)
> Although a 'classic', this is one of the Time-Life 'Planet Earth' series, and as such retains its value and the quality typical of those publications.

David S. G. Thomas, ed., *Arid Zone Geomorphology: Process, Form and Change in Drylands*, 3rd edn (Chichester, 2011)
> For the earth science, this has been 'the bible' for this book. It is not alone as a text on desert processes and landscapes, but it is comprehensive, up-to-date and accessible.

United Nations Environment Programme, 'Global Deserts Outlook' (2006), www.unep.org

—, 'Global Drylands: A un System-wide Response' (2011), www.unep-wcmc.org
> Two United Nations reports, readily available online, that provide excellent summaries of arid lands, their peoples, the issues and the approaches to solutions.

Michael Welland, *Sand: A Journey Through Science and the Imagination* (Oxford, 2009)
> Sand may be a desert icon, but more broadly it is an uncelebrated hero of our planet and our lives. My book attempts to redress this.

Preface

Edward Abbey, *Desert Solitaire: A Season in the Wilderness* (New York, 1968)

Mary Austin, *Stories from the Country of Lost Borders*, ed. Marjorie Pryse (New Brunswick, NJ, 1987)

Paul Bowles, *Travels: Collected Writings, 1950–93* (London, 2010)

1 Wet and Dry, Hot and Cold

Ralph A. Bagnold, *Libyan Sands: Travel in a Dead World* [1935] (London, 1993)

Felix Fabri, *The Book of the Wanderings of Brother Felix Fabri*, trans. Aubrey Stewart (London, 1896)

form ('creativity and artistic practice in Western Australia'), *Ngurra Kuju Walyja: One Country One People – The Canning Stock Route Project* (2011), www.canningstockrouteproject.com

Robert Frost, 'Desert Places', in *A Further Range* (New York, 1936)

Thomas Medwin, *The Angler in Wales* (London, 1834)

Defining the desert

Mary Austin, *Stories from the Country of Lost Borders*, ed. Marjorie Pryse (New Brunswick, NJ, 1987)

European Space Agency, 'The European Space Agency GlobCover Portal', http://due.esrin.esa.int/globcover

P.C.D. Milly et al., 'Stationarity is Dead: Whither Water Management?', *Science*, 319/5863 (2008)

National Oceanic and Atmospheric Administration, 'Normalized Difference Vegetation Index', www.ospo.noaa.gov/products/land/gvi/NDVI.html

M. C. Peel, B. L. Finlayson and T. A. McMahon, 'Updated World Map of the Köppen-Geiger Climate Classification', *Hydrology and Earth System Sciences*, 11/5 (2007), www.hydrol-earth-syst-sci.net

H. L. Penman, 'Natural Evaporation from Open Water, Bare Soil and Grass', *Proceedings of the Royal Society of London A*, 193/1032 (1948)

D. L. Serventy, 'Biology of Desert Birds', in *Avian Biology*, ed. D. S. Farner and J. R. King (New York, 1971)

C. W. Thornthwaite, 'An Approach toward a Rational Classification of Climate', *Geographical Review*, 38/1 (1948)

United Nations Environment Programme, 'Global Deserts Outlook' (2006), www.unep.org/gdoutlook

—, 'Global Drylands: A un System-wide Response' (2011), www.unep-wcmc. org/resources-and-data

2 Big and Small, Fast and Slow

Edward Abbey, *Desert Solitaire: A Season in the Wilderness* (New York, 1985)

David Quammen, 'Desert Sanitaire', in *Natural Acts: A Sidelong View of Science and Nature*, revd edn (New York, 2008)

Desert landscapes and processes

Ralph A. Bagnold, *The Physics of Blown Sand and Desert Dunes* [1941] (Mineola, NY, 2005)

Charles Doughty, *Travels in Arabia Deserta* (Cambridge, 1888)

James Hutton, 'Theory of the Earth', *Transactions of the Royal Society of Edinburgh*, 1/2 (1788)

David S. G. Thomas, ed., *Arid Zone Geomorphology: Process, Form and Change in Drylands*, 3rd edn (Chichester, 2011)

M. J. Walker, ed., *Hot Deserts: Engineering, Geology and Geomorphology: Engineering Group Working Party Report*, Geological Society of London Engineering Geology Special Publications (London, 2012)

Johannes Walther, *The Law of Desert Formation, Present and Past*, trans. Gabriela Meyer, in *Geological Milestones*, ed. Eberhard Gischler and Kenneth W. Glennie (Miami, 1997)

Peter Wild, ed., *The New Desert Reader* (Salt Lake City, UT, 2006)

Desert pavements and varnish

Ahmed Hassanein Bey, *The Lost Oases* [1925] (Cairo, 2006)

Roy Chapman Andrews, 'The Lure of Mongolia as Described by Roy Chapman Andrews in Interview', *Scarsdale Inquirer* (1 March 1924)

Ronald I. Dorn, David H. Krinsley and Jeffrey Ditto, 'Revisiting Alexander von Humboldt's Initiation of Rock Coating Research', *Journal of Geology*, 120/1 (2012)

Andrew Goudie, *Wheels Across the Desert: Exploration of the Libyan Desert by Motorcar, 1916–1942* (London, 2008)

Anton von Humboldt, *Personal Narrative of Travels to the Equinoctial Regions of America During the Years 1799–1804 by Alexander von Humboldt and Aimé Bonpland*, trans. and ed. Thomasina Ross (London, 1907)

T. E. Lawrence, *Seven Pillars of Wisdom* [1922] (Ware, 1997)

Alfred Lucas, *The Blackened Rocks of the Nile Cataracts and of the Egyptian Deserts* (Cairo, 1905)

Douglas V. Prose and Howard G. Wilshire, 'The Lasting Effects of Tank Maneuvers on Desert Soils and Intershrub Flora', U.S. Geological Survey Open-File Report of 00-512 (2000), www.usgs.gov

Antoine de Saint-Exupéry, *Wind, Sand and Stars* [1939], trans. William Rees (London, 2000)

Michael N. Spilde et al., 'Anthropogenic Lead as a Tracer of Rock Varnish Growth: Implications for Rates of Formation', *Geology*, 41/2 (2013)

Wilfred Thesiger, *Arabian Sands* [1959] (London, 2008)

Michel Vieuchange, *Smara, the Forbidden City: Being the Journal of Michel Vieuchange While Travelling Among the Independent Tribes of South Morocco and Rio De Oro* [1932] (New York, 1987)

Soils and nitrates

Ariel Dorfman, *Desert Memories: Journeys through the Chilean North* (Washington, DC, 2004)

Stephanie A. Ewing et al., 'A Threshold in Soil Formation at Earth's Arid–Hyperarid Transition', *Geochimica et Cosmochimica Acta*, 70/21 (2006)

Arwyn Jones et al., *Soil Atlas of Africa*, European Commission Joint Research Centre (2013), http://eusoils.jrc.ec.europa.eu

Greg Michalski et al., 'Long Term Atmospheric Deposition as the Source of Nitrate and Other Salts in the Atacama Desert, Chile: New Evidence from Mass-Independent Oxygen Isotopic Compositions', *Geochimica et Cosmochimica Acta*, 68/20 (2004)

Ji-Hye Seo, 'Solving the Mystery of the Atacama Nitrate Deposits: The Use of Stable Oxygen Isotope Analysis and Geochemistry', *Journal of Purdue Undergraduate Research*, 1 (2011), http://docs.lib.purdue.edu

Floods

Paul R. Bierman et al., 'Using Cosmogenic Nuclides to Contrast Rates of Erosion and Sediment Yield in a Semi-Arid, Arroyo-Dominated Landscape, Rio Puerco Basin, New Mexico', *Earth Surface Processes and Landforms*, 308 (2005)

Isabelle Eberhardt, *The Oblivion Seekers*, trans. Paul Bowles, new edn (London, 2009)

Fernand Joly, 'Several Flow Events on the Margin of the Algerian-Moroccan Sahara and their Morphological Consequences', trans. Julie Woodward, Arizona Geological Survey Contributed Report 93-C (Tucson, AZ, 1993)

Annette Kobak, *Isabelle: The Life of Isabelle Eberhardt* (London, 1988)

United States Geological Survey, 'Water-Data Report 2009: Rio Puerco near Bernardo, NM' (Denver, CO, 2009), http://wdr.water.usgs.gov

Lakes

N. I. Alfa et al., 'Assessment of Changes in Aerial Extent of Lake Chad using Satellite Remote Sensing Data', *Journal of Applied Sciences and Environmental Management*, 12/1 (2008)

Isabelle Eberhardt, *Prisoner of Dunes*, trans. Sharon Bangert (London, 1995)

Microbes

Carol E. Cleland and Shelley D. Copley, 'The Possibility of Alternative Microbial Life on Earth', *International Journal of Astrobiology*, 4/3–4 (2005)

D. C. Fernández-Remolar et al., 'Molecular Preservation in Halite and Perchlorate Rich Hypersaline Subsurface Deposits in the Salar Grande Basin (Atacama Desert, Chile): Implications for the Search for Molecular Biomarkers on Mars', *Journal of Geophysical Research: Biogeosciences*, 118/2 (2013)

Tim K. Lowenstein et al., 'Microbial Communities in Fluid Inclusions and Long-term Survival in Halite', GSA T*oday*, 21/1 (2011)

Boojala Vijay B. Reddy et al., 'Natural Product Biosynthetic Gene Diversity in Geographically Distinct Soil Microbiomes', *Applied and Environmental Microbiology*, 78/10 (2012)

Cindy L. Satterfield et al., 'New Evidence for 250 Ma Age of Halotolerant Bacterium from a Permian Salt Crystal', *Geology*, 33/4 (2005)

Scale

Paul Bowles, *Travels: Collected Writings, 1950–93* (London, 2010)

Willa Cather, *Death Comes for the Archbishop* [1927] (London, 2006)

C. G. Jung, *Memories, Dreams, Reflections*, trans. Richard and Clara Winston, ed. Aniela Jaffé, revd edn (New York, 1989)

3 Insiders and Outsiders, Civilization and Savagery

Josephine Flood, *The Original Australians: Story of the Aboriginal People* (Crows Nest, NSW, 2006)

form ('creativity and artistic practice in Western Australia'), *Ngurra Kuju Walyja: One Country One People – The Canning Stock Route Project* (2011), www.canningstockrouteproject.com

Sven Lindquist, *Terra Nullius: A Journey Through No One's Land*, trans. Sarah Death (London, 2007)

Maps and travels

Muhammad al-Idrisi, *Géographie d'Édrisi*, trans. Pierre Amédée Jaubert (Paris, 1840)

Ibn Battuta, *Travels in Asia and Africa, 1325–1354*, trans. and ed. H.A.R. Gibb (London, 1929)

Douglas Bullis, 'The Longest Hajj: The Journeys of Ibn Battuta', *Saudi Aramco World*, 51/4 (2000)

Frances Carney Gies, 'Al-Idrisi and Roger's Book', *Saudi Aramco World*, 28/4
 (1977)
J. B. Harley and David Woodward, eds, *The History of Cartography* (Chicago, IL,
 1987–98)
Herodotus, *The History of Herodotus*, trans. George Rawlinson (London, 1875)
Rudyard Kipling, 'The Explorer', in *Collected Verse of Rudyard Kipling*
 (New York, 1915)
Marco Polo, *The Travels of Marco Polo, the Venetian*, trans. William Marsden
 (London and New York, 1908)
F. E. Romer, *Pomponius Mela's Description of the* World (Ann Arbor, MI, 1998)
James S. Romm, *The Edges of the Earth in Ancient Thought: Geography,
 Exploration and Fiction* (Princeton, NJ, 1992)

Australia

'The Australian Landscape: A Cultural History', ABC National Radio,
 www.abc.net.au, 2007
Len Beadell, *Outback Highways: The Gunbarrel Highway Story and Many More*,
 new edn (Chatswood, NSW, 2001)
Edwin J. Brady, *Australia Unlimited* (Melbourne, 1918)
Charles Darwin, *The Descent of Man, and Selection in Relation to Sex* (London, 1871)
Sue Davenport, Peter Johnson and Yuwali, *Cleared Out: First Contact in the
 Western Desert* (Canberra, 2005)
Ernest Giles, *Australia Twice Traversed: The Romance of Exploration* (London, 1889)
Matthew Graves and Elizabeth Rechniewski, 'Mapping Utopia: Cartography and
 Social Reform in 19th Century Australia', PORTAL *Journal of Multidisciplinary
 International Studies*, 9/2 (2012), http://epress.lib.uts.edu.au
Roslynn D. Haynes, *Seeking the Centre: The Australian Desert in Literature, Art
 and Film* (Cambridge, 1999)
Harold Koch and Luise Hercus, eds, *Aboriginal Placenames: Naming and
 Re-naming the Australian Landscape* (Canberra, 2009)
Pat Lowe with Jimmy Pike, *You Call It Desert: We Used to Live There* (Broome,
 Western Australia, 2009)
Thomas J. Maslen, *The Friend of Australia; or, a Plan for Exploring the Interior and
 for Carrying On a Survey of the Whole Continent of Australia* (London, 1836)
Deborah Bird Rose and Richard Davies, eds, *Dislocating the Frontier: Essaying the
 Mystique of the Outback* (Canberra, 2005)
W. B. Spencer and F. J. Gillen, *The Native Tribes of Central Australia*
 (London, 1899)
Charles Sturt, *Narrative of an Expedition into Central Australia: Performed Under
 the Authority of Her Majesty's Government, During the Years 1844, 5, and 6:
 Together with a Notice of the Province of South Australia, in 1847* (London, 1848)
Alfred Russel Wallace, *The Malay Archipelago: The Land of the Orang-utan and
 the Bird of Paradise, A Narrative of Travel with Studies of Man and Nature*
 (London, 1869)
Patrick White, *Voss* (London, 2008)

4 Outsiders and Insiders, New World and Old

Camels

Lynn M. Alperin, *Custodians of the Coast: History of the United States Army Engineers at Galveston* (Galveston, TX, 1977)

Jack Bryson, 'America's Cameleers', *Desert Magazine*, XXVII/8 (1964)

Robert Irwin, *Camel* (London, 2010)

Philip Jones, 'Australia's Muslim Cameleer Heritage', *reCollections: Journal of the National Museum of Australia*, 2/2 (2007)

The American West and manifest destiny

Edward Abbey, *Desert Solitaire: A Season in the Wilderness* (New York, 1968)

William Gilpin, *The Central Gold Region: The Grain, Pastoral, and Gold Regions of North America* (Philadelphia, PA, 1860)

—, *Mission of the North American People: Geographical, Social, and Political* (Philadelphia, PA, 1873)

Vivien Green Fryd, *Art and Empire: The Politics of Ethnicity in the United States Capitol, 1815–1860* (Athens, OH, 2001)

Jerry B. Howard, 'Hohokam Legacy: Desert Canals', *Pueblo Grande Museum Profiles*, 12 (1992), www.waterhistory.org/histories/hohokam2

Eusebio Kino, *Kino's Historical Memoir of Pimería Alta; A Contemporary Account of the Beginnings of California, Sonora, and Arizona*, trans. H. E. Bolton (Cleveland, OH, 1919)

Stephen H. Long et al., *Account of an Expedition from Pittsburgh to the Rocky Mountains, Performed in the Years 1819 and '20* (Philadelphia, PA, 1823)

Gary Paul Nabhan, *Arab/American: Landscape, Culture, and Cuisine in Two Great Deserts* (Tucson, AZ, 2008)

Brendan D. O'Fallona and Lars Fehren-Schmitz, 'Native Americans Experienced a Strong Population Bottleneck Coincident with European Contact', *Proceedings of the National Academy of Sciences of the United States of America*, 108/51 (2011)

John O'Sullivan, 'Annexation', *United States Democratic Review*, XVII/85 (1845)

—, 'The Great Nation of Futurity', *United States Democratic Review*, VI/23 (1839)

United States National Park Service, *Exploring the American West, 1803–1879*, Handbook 116 (Washington, DC, 1982)

United States War Department, *Reports of Explorations and Surveys, to Ascertain the Most Practicable and Economical Route for a Railroad from the Mississippi River to the Pacific Ocean, Made Under the Direction of the Secretary of War, in 1853–4* (Washington, DC, 1855–61), vols I–XII, available at Library of Congress: The Nineteenth Century in Print, www.memory.loc.gov/ammem/ndlpcoop/moahtml/mnchome.html

Davis Parker, 'Icons within an Icon: Representing American Indians in the Artwork of the United States Capitol, 1814–1890', BA thesis, Williams College (Williamstown, MA, 2005)

Richard Seager and Celine Herweijer, 'Causes and Consequences of Nineteenth Century Droughts in North America', Lamont-Doherty Earth Observatory

of Columbia University (2011), www.ldeo.columbia.edu/res/div/ocp/
  drought/nineteenth.shtml
John Wesley Powell, *Report on the Lands of the Arid Region of the United States
  with a more Detailed Account of the Land of Utah with Maps*, USGS
  Unnumbered Series Monograph (1879), available at www.pubs.er.usgs.gov
Peter Wild, ed., *The New Desert Reader* (Salt Lake City, UT, 2006)

The Old World

Leo Africanus, 'Description of Timbuktu' [1526], in *Reading About the World*,
  ed. Paul Brians et al., 3rd edn (Pullman, WA, 1999), vol. II
Ibn Battuta, *Travels in Asia and Africa, 1325–1354,* trans. and ed. H.A.R. Gibb
  (London, 1929)
Réné Caillié, *Travels through Central Africa to Timbuctoo, and Across the Great
  Desert, to Morocco, Performed in the Years 1824–1828* (London, 1830)
Eamonn Gearon, *The Sahara: A Cultural History* (Oxford, 2011)
Peter Gwin, 'Lost Lords of the Sahara', *National Geographic*, CCXX/3 (2011)
—, 'Saharan Insecurity', Pulitzer Center on Crisis Reporting, www.pulitzercenter.
  org/projects/africa/saharan-insecurity-perfect-storm-brewing-desert, 12
  November 2010
Frank T. Kryza, *The Race for Timbuktu: In Search of Africa's City of Gold*
  (New York, 2007)
Claude Lévi-Strauss, *The Savage Mind*, trans. anon (Chicago, IL, and London, 1966)
David Mattingly, 'Garama: An Ancient Civilisation in the Central Sahara',
  World Archaeology, 9 (2005)
James Owen, '"Lost" Fortresses of Sahara Revealed by Satellites', *National
  Geographic News*, www.nationalgeographic.com, 11 November 2011
Douglas Porch, *The Conquest of the Sahara* (New York, 2005)
Wilfred Thesiger, *Arabian Sands* [1959] (London, 2008)
Louis Werner, 'Libya's Forgotten Desert Kingdom', *Saudi Aramco World*, 55/3
  (May–June 2004)

5 Mind and Matter, Body and Soul

Edward Abbey, *Desert Solitaire: A Season in the Wilderness* (New York, 1968)
Mary Austin, *Stories from the Country of Lost Borders*, ed. Marjorie Pryse (New
  Brunswick, NJ, 1987)
Ralph A. Bagnold, *Libyan Sands: Travel in a Dead World* [1935] (London, 1993)
Ahmed Hassanein Bey, *The Lost Oases* [1925] (Cairo, 2006)
Isabelle Eberhardt, *Prisoner of Dunes*, trans. Sharon Bangert (London, 1995)
Gregory McNamee, ed., *The Sierra Club Desert Reader: A Literary Companion*
  (San Francisco, CA, 1995)
Michael Ondaatje, *The English Patient* (London, 2004)
Wilfred Thesiger, *Arabian Sands* [1959] (London, 2008)

Religion

Honoré de Balzac, *A Passion in the Desert* [1830], trans. Ernest Dowson (Seaside, OR, 2010)
Paul Bowles, *Travels: Collected Writings, 1950–93* (London, 2010)
Edmond Jabès, *The Book of Margins*, trans. Rosemarie Waldrop (Chicago, IL, and London, 1993)
David Jasper, *The Sacred Desert: Religion, Literature, Art, and Culture* (Oxford, 2004)

Songs, Arabic

Assad Ali, *Happiness Without Death: Desert Hymns* (Putney, VT, 1991)
A. J. Arberry, *Arabic Poetry: A Primer for Students* (Cambridge, 1965)
Clinton Bailey, *Bedouin Poetry: From Sinai and the Negev* (London, 2002)
Christine Jo Dykgraaf, 'Metaphorical and Literal Depictions of the Desert in the Qur'an', *Arid Lands Newsletter*, 50 (November–December 2001), www.ag.arizona.rdu/OALS/ALN/ALNHome.html
Maysa Abou-Youssef Hayward, 'Communities at the Margins: Arab Poetry of the Desert', *Arid Lands Newsletter*, 50 (November–December 2001), www.ag.arizona.rdu/OALS/ALN/ALNHome.html
Imru-ul-Quais, '*Mu'allaqat* Ode', in *The Hanged Poems*, trans. F. E. Johnson, ed. Charles F. Horne, from *The Sacred Books and Early Literature of the East* (New York and London, 1917), vol. V
Gloria Kifayeh, *Lyrics of the Sands* (London, 2005)
Josephine Lazarus, 'Zionism and Americanism', *Menorah: A Monthly Magazine for the Jewish Home* (May 1905), quoted in Ranen Omer-Sherman, *Israel in Exile: Jewish Writing and the Desert* (Urbana and Chicago, IL, 2006)

Australia

FORM ('creativity and artistic practice in Western Australia'), *Ngurra Kuju Walyja: One Country One People – The Canning Stock Route Project* (2011), www.canningstockrouteproject.com
Roslynn D. Haynes, *Seeking the Centre: The Australian Desert in Literature, Art and Film* (Cambridge, 1999)
Åse Ottosson, 'Aboriginal Music and Passion: Interculturality and Difference in Australian Desert Towns', *Ethnos*, LXXV/3 (2010)
—, 'The Intercultural Crafting of Real Aboriginal Country and Manhood in Central Australia', *Australian Journal of Anthropology*, XXIII (2012)

Orient and Occident

Richard Burton, *Zanzibar: City, Island, and Coast* (London, 1872)
Isabelle Eberhardt, *The Oblivion Seekers*, trans. Paul Bowles, new edn (London, 2009)
Annette Kobak, *Isabelle: The Life of Isabelle Eberhardt* (London, 1988)
Edward W. Said, *Orientalism* [1978] (London, 2003)

The United States

Mary Austin, *Mother of Felipe and Other Early Stories* (San Francisco, CA, 1950)
—, *Stories from the Country of Lost Borders*, ed. Marjorie Pryse (New Brunswick, NJ, 1987)
Susan Goodman and Carl Dawson, *Mary Austin and the American West* (Berkeley, CA, 2008)
Aldous Huxley, *The Complete Essays* (Lanham, md, 2002), vol. V
Kerwin Klein, 'Westward, Utopia: Robert V. Hine, Aldous Huxley, and the Future of California History', *Pacific Historical Review*, LXX/3 (2001)
Hari Kunzru, *Gods Without Men* (London, 2012)
D. H. Lawrence, 'New Mexico' [1928], reprinted in *New Mexico Magazine* (February 1936)
Vera Norwood and Janice Monk, eds, *The Desert is No Lady: Southwestern Landscapes in Women's Writing and Art* (New Haven, CT, 1987)
Wallace Stegner, 'Thoughts in a Dry Land', in *Where the Bluebird Sings to the Lemonade Springs: Living and Writing in the West* (New York, 2002)
David W. Teague, *The Southwest in American Literature and Art: The Rise of a Desert Aesthetic* (Tucson, AZ, 1997)
John C. Van Dyke, *The Desert: Further Studies in Natural Appearances* [1901], facsimile edn, intro. by Peter Wild (Baltimore, MD, and London, 1999)
Yi-Fu Tuan, *Topophilia: A Study of Environmental Perceptions, Attitudes, and Values* (New York, 1974)

Does the desert look back?

W. H. Auden, *The Sea and the Mirror*, ed. Arthur Kirsch (Princeton, NJ, and Oxford, 2003)
Simone de Beauvoir, *Force of Circumstance*, trans. Richard Howard (London, 1965)
Jim Crace, *Quarantine* (London, 1998)
Robyn Davidson, *Tracks* (New York, 1980)
Neysa Griffith, 'A Rambling Chronicle', in *Desert Stories*, ed. Cheryl Montelle (self-published, 2010)
J.-M.G. Le Clézio, *Desert*, trans. C. Dickson (London, 2009)
William Least Heat-Moon, *Blue Highways: A Journey into America* (New York, 1982)
Geoffrey Moorhouse, *The Fearful Void* (New York, 1974)
The Long Now Foundation, www.longnow.org
Pat Mora, *Chants* (Houston, TX, 1984)
George Steinmetz, *Desert Air* (New York, 2012)
—, *Empty Quarter: A Photographic Journey into the Heart of the Arabian Desert* (New York, 2009)
Laura Tohe, *Tséyi': Deep in the Rock, Reflections on the Canyon du Chelly*, photographs by Stephen E. Strom (Tucson, AZ, 2005)

6 Ancient and Modern, Boom and Bust

General

Peter G. Fookes and E. Mark Lee, 'Desert Environments: Landscapes and Stratigraphy', *Geology Today*, 25/5 (2009)

David S. G. Thomas, ed., *Arid Zone Geomorphology: Process, Form and Change in Drylands*, 3rd edn (Chichester, 2011)

Dunes and how deserts work

Anon., 'Why "Singing" Sand Dunes Hum Certain Notes', *Phys.org*, www.phys.org, 25 October 2012

Ralph A. Bagnold, *The Physics of Blown Sand and Desert Dunes* [1941] (Mineola, NY, 2005)

—, *Sand, Wind, and War* (Tucson, AZ, 1990)

Felix Fabri, *The Book of the Wanderings of Brother Felix Fabri*, trans. Aubrey Stewart (London, 1896)

Timothy M. Goodall and Juma D. Al-Belushi, 'A Glossary of Arab Desert Terminology Used in Southeastern Arabia', in *Quaternary Deserts and Climatic Change*, ed. A. S. Alsharhan et al. (Rotterdam, 1998)

Melany L. Hunt and Nathalie M. Vriend, 'Booming Sand Dunes', *Annual Review of Earth and Planetary Sciences*, 38 (2010)

M. Y. Louge et al., 'Temperature and Humidity within a Mobile Barchan Sand Dune', *Journal of Geophysical Research: Earth Surface*, 118/4 (December 2013)

Edwin McKee, ed., A *Study of Global Sand Seas*, usgs Professional Paper 1052 (Washington, dc, 1979)

Edward L. Simpson, Kenneth A. Eriksson and Wulf U. Mueller, '3.2 Ga Eolian Deposits from the Moodies Group, Barberton Greenstone Belt, South Africa: Implications for the Origin of First-Cycle Quartz Sandstones', *Precambrian Research*, 214–215 (September 2012)

Ancient deserts and palaeoclimates

Michael J. Benton and Andrew J. Newell, 'Impacts of Global Warming on Permo-Triassic Terrestrial Ecosystems', *Gondwana Research*, 25/4 (May 2014), summary, www.sciencedirect.com

Charles P. Berkey and Frederick K. Morris, *Geology of Mongolia: A Reconnaissance Report Based on the Investigations of the Years 1922–1923* (New York, 1927)

C. S. Bristow, G.A.T. Duller and N. Lancaster, 'Age and Dynamics of Linear Dunes in the Namib Desert', *Geology*, 35/6 (2007)

Roy Chapman Andrews et al., *The New Conquest of Central Asia: A Narrative of the Explorations of the Central Asiatic Expeditions in Mongolia and China, 1921–1930* (New York, 1932)

Brian Chase, 'Evaluating the Use of Dune Sediments as a Proxy for Palaeo-Aridity: A Southern African Case Study', *Earth-Science Reviews*, 93/1–2 (March 2009)

Brian M. Chase and David S. G. Thomas, 'Late Quaternary Dune Accumulation
    along the Western Margin of South Africa: Distinguishing Forcing
    Mechanisms through the Analysis of Migratory Dune Forms', *Earth and
    Planetary Science Letters*, 251/3–4 (2006)
David B. Loope et al., 'Life and Death in a Late Cretaceous Dune Field, Nemegt
    Basin, Mongolia', *Geology*, 26/1 (1998)
Robert B. MacNaughton et al., 'First Steps on Land: Arthropod Trackways in
    Cambrian-Ordovician Eolian Sandstone, Southeastern Ontario, Canada',
    Geology, 30/5 (2002)
Shaena Montanari, Pennilyn Higgins and Mark A. Norell, 'Dinosaur Eggshell
    and Tooth Enamel Geochemistry as an Indicator of Mongolian Late
    Cretaceous Paleoenvironments', *Palaeogeography, Palaeoclimatology,
    Palaeoecology*, 370 (2013)
Ted Nield, *Supercontinent: Ten Billion Years in the Life of Our Planet*
    (Cambridge, MA, 2009)
Marco Roscher, Frode Stordal and Henrik Svensen, 'The Effect of Global
    Warming and Global Cooling on the Distribution of the Latest Permian
    Climate Zones', *Palaeogeography, Palaeoclimatology, Palaeoecology*, 309/3–4
    (2011)
Ashok K. Singhvi and Naomi Porat, 'Impact of Luminescence Dating
    on Geomorphological and Palaeoclimate Research in Drylands',
    Boreas, 37/4 (2008)

Life

Edward Abbey, *Desert Solitaire: A Season in the Wilderness* (New York, 1968)
Mary Austin, *Stories from the Country of Lost Borders*, ed. Marjorie Pryse (New
    Brunswick, NJ, 1987)
Trip Lamb and Aaron M. Bauer, 'Footprints in the Sand: Independent
    Reduction of Subdigital Lamellae in the Namib–Kalahari Burrowing
    Geckos', *Proceedings of the Royal Society B*, 273/1588 (2006)
Michael A. Mares, *A Desert Calling* (Cambridge, MA, 2002)
—, *Encyclopedia of Deserts* (Norman, OK, 1999)
Philippa Nikulinsky and Stephen D. Hopper, *Soul of the Desert* (Freemantle,
    Western Australia, 2011)
Sara Oldfield, *Deserts: The Living Drylands* (London, 2004)
T. J. Walker, ed., *University of Florida Book of Insect Records* (Gainesville, FL, 2001)
David Rains Wallace, *Chuckwalla Land: The Riddle of California's Desert*
    (Berkeley, CA, 2011)

7 Barriers and Corridors, Imports and Exports

José C. Brito et al., 'Crocodiles in the Sahara Desert: An Update of Distribution,
    Habitats and Population Status for Conservation Planning in Mauritania',
    PLOS ONE, 6/2 (2011), www.plosone.org
Henri Duveyrier, *Les Tuareg du nord: Exploration du Sahara* (Paris, 1864)
Isabelle Eberhardt, *Prisoner of Dunes*, trans. Sharon Bangert (London, 1995)

Out of Africa and ancient rivers

Colin Barras, 'Out of Asia: Our Surprising Origins', *New Scientist*, 2916 (2013)

Tom J. Coulthard et al., 'Were Rivers Flowing across the Sahara During the Last Interglacial? Implications for Human Migration through Africa', PLOS ONE, 8/9 (2013) www.plosone.org

Peter B. deMenocal, 'African Climate Change and Faunal Evolution During the Pliocene-Pleistocene', *Earth and Planetary Science Letters*, 220/1–2 (2004)

Nick A. Drake et al., 'Ancient Watercourses and Biogeography of the Sahara Explain the Peopling of the Desert', *Proceedings of the National Academy of Sciences of the United States of America,* 108/2 (2011)

Stephen J. Gould, *Dinosaur in a Haystack: Reflections in Natural History* (New York, 1996)

Jussi T. Eronen et al., 'Neogene Aridification of the Northern Hemisphere', *Geology*, 40/9 (2012)

Eman Ghoneim, Michael Benedetti and Farouk El-Baz, 'An Integrated Remote Sensing and GIS Analysis of the Kufrah Paleoriver, Eastern Sahara', *Geomorphology*, 139–140 (2012)

Marta Mirazón Lahr, 'Saharan Corridors and their Role in the Evolutionary Geography of 'Out of Africa I', in *Out of Africa I: The First Hominin Colonization of Eurasia, Vertebrate Paleobiology and Paleoanthropology*, ed. J. G. Fleagle et al. (New York, 2010)

Philippe Paillou, Stephen Tooth and Sylvia Lopez, 'The Kufrah Paleodrainage System in Libya: A Past Connection to the Mediterranean Sea?', *Comptes Rendus Géoscience*, 344/8 (2012)

Michael D. Petraglia, Huw Groucutt and James Blinkhorn, 'Hominin Evolutionary History in the Arabian Desert and the Thar Desert', in *Changing Deserts: Integrating People and their Environment*, ed. Lisa Mol and Troy Sternberg (Cambridge, 2012)

Matt Sponheimer et al., 'Isotopic Evidence of Early Hominin Diets', *Proceedings of the National Academy of Sciences of the United States of America*, 110/26 (2013)

A. Vaks et al., 'Paleoclimate and Location of the Border Between Mediterranean Climate Region and the Saharo-Arabian Desert as Revealed by Speleothems from the Northern Negev Desert, Israel', *Earth and Planetary Science Letters*, 249/3–4 (2006)

Cradles

Christopher E. Bernhardt, Benjamin P. Horton and Jean-Daniel Stanley, 'Nile Delta Vegetation Response to Holocene Climate Variability', *Geology*, 40/7 (2012)

Richard Conniff, 'When Civilizations Collapse', Yale School of Forestry and Environmental Studies (2012), www.environment.yale.edu/envy/stories

H. M. Cullen et al., 'Climate Change and the Collapse of the Akkadian Empire: Evidence From the Deep Sea', *Geology*, 28/4 (2000)

Andrew Curry, 'Gobekli Tepe: The World's First Temple?', *Smithsonian* (November 2008)

Julie Dunne et al., 'First Dairying in Green Saharan Africa in the Fifth
     Millennium BC', *Nature*, 486 (2012)
Pierre Francus et al., 'Varved Sediments of Lake Yoa (Ounianga Kebir, Chad)
     Reveal Progressive Drying of the Sahara During the Last 6,100 Years',
     Sedimentology, 60/4 (2013)
Fekri Hassan, 'The Fall of the Egyptian Old Kingdom', BBC History,
     www.bbc.co.uk/history/ancient/egyptians, 17 February 2011
David Kaniewski, Elise van Campo and Harvey Weiss, 'Drought is a Recurring
     Challenge in the Middle East', *Proceedings of the National Academy of
     Sciences of the United States of America*, 109/10 (2012)
Rudolph Kuper and Stefan Kröpelin, 'Climate-controlled Holocene Occupation
     in the Sahara: Motor of Africa's Evolution', *Science*, 308/5788 (2006)
David Robson, 'Civilisation's True Dawn', *New Scientist*, 2937 (2013)
Michael Staubwasser and Harvey Weiss, 'Holocene Climate and Cultural
     Evolution in Late Prehistoric–Early Historic West Asia', *Quaternary
     Research*, 66/3 (2006)
John Steinbeck, *Travels with Charley: In Search of America* (London, 2001)
Harvey Weiss, 'Quantifying Collapse: The Late Third Millennium BC', in *Seven
     Generations Since the Fall of Akkad*, ed. Harvey Weiss (Wiesbaden, 2012)
Emma Young, 'Pharaohs From the Stone Age', *New Scientist*, 2586 (2007)

On the move

Gertrude Bell, *The Desert and the Sown: Travels in Palestine and Syria*, reprint
     (Mineola, NY, 2008)
Gertrude Bell Archive, Newcastle University Library,
     www.gerty.ncl.ac.uk/index.php
Ahmed Hassanein Bey, *The Lost Oases* [1925] (Cairo, 2006)
Lesley Blanch, *The Wilder Shores of Love* [1954] (London, 2010)
Bashshār ibn Burd, untitled poem, trans. A.F.L. Beeston, in *Abbasid Belles
     Lettres*, ed. Julia Ashtiany et al. (Cambridge, 2008)
Niccolò Pianciola, 'Famine in the Steppe: The Collectivization of Agriculture and
     the Kazak Herdsmen, 1928–1934', *Cahiers du Monde Russe*, XLV/1–2 (2004)
Jeffrey Szuchman, ed., *Nomads, Tribes, and the State in the Ancient Near East:
     Cross-disciplinary Perspectives* (Chicago, IL, 2009)
Wilfred Thesiger, *Arabian Sands* [1959] (London, 2008)
Peter Veth, Mike Smith and Peter Hiscock, eds, *Desert Peoples: Archaeological
     Perspectives* (Oxford, 2004)
Janet Wallach, *Desert Queen: The Extraordinary Life of Gertrude Bell, Adventurer,
     Adviser to Kings, Ally of Lawrence of Arabia* (Phoenix, AZ, 2005)

Empires and ungulates

Alexander Burnes, *Travels into Bokhara: Being the Account of a Journey from India
     to Cabool, Tartary and Persia* (London, 1834)
Felix Fabri, *The Book of the Wanderings of Brother Felix Fabri*, trans. Aubrey
     Stewart (London, 1896)
Peter Harrigan, 'Reading the Sands', *Saudi Aramco World*, 55/2 (2004)

Robert Irwin, *Camel* (London, 2010)

Rudyard Kipling, 'How the Camel Got His Hump', in *Just So Stories* (Oxford, 2009)

William Gifford Palgrave, *Narrative of a Year's Journey through Central and Eastern Arabia* [1862–3] (London, 1868)

Peter Turchin, 'A Theory for Formation of Large Empires', *Journal of Global History*, IV/2 (2009)

—, Cliodynamica, www.cliodynamics.info

—, 'Arise "Cliodynamics"', *Nature*, 454 (2008)

—, 'Warfare and the Evolution of Social Complexity: A Multilevel-Selection Approach', *Structure and Dynamics*, 4/3 (2011)

Trade

Jeffrey Bartholet, 'Swept from Africa to the Amazon: What the Journey of a Handful of Dust Tells us About our Fragile Planet', *Scientific American*, 306/2 (2012)

Linda K. Benson, *Across China's Gobi: The Lives of Evangeline French, Mildred Cable, and Francesca French of the China Inland Mission* (Norwalk, CT, 2008)

Jonathan M. Bloom, 'Silk Road or Paper Road?', *Silk Road Foundation Newsletter*, III/2 (2005), www.silk-road.com/newsletter/vol3num2/5_bloom.php

Mildred Cable and Francesca French, *The Gobi Desert: The Adventures of Three Women Travelling Across the Gobi Desert in the 1920s* [1942] (Coventry, 2008)

Eamonn Gearon, *The Sahara: A Cultural History* (Oxford, 2011)

James A. Millward, *The Silk Road: A Very Short Introduction* (Oxford, 2013)

Kira Salak, *Cruelest Journey: Six Hundred Miles to Timbuktu* (Des Moines, IA, 2004)

8 Feast or Famine, Knowns and Unknowns

Dust

Per Bak, *How Nature Works: The Science of Self-organized Criticality* (Oxford, 1997)

Jeffrey Bartholet, 'Swept from Africa to the Amazon: What the Journey of a Handful of Dust Tells us About our Fragile Planet', *Scientific American*, 306/2 (2012)

V. H. Garrison et al., 'Saharan Dust – A Carrier of Persistent Organic Pollutants, Metals and Microbes to the Caribbean?', *Revista de Biología Tropical*, 54/3 (2006)

Paul Ginoux et al., 'Global-scale Attribution of Anthropogenic and Natural Dust Sources and their Emission Rates Based on MODIS Deep Blue Aerosol Products', *Reviews of Geophysics*, 50/3 (2012)

N. M. Mahowald et al., 'Atmospheric Global Dust Cycle and Iron Inputs to the Ocean', *Global Biogeochemical Cycles*, 19/4 (2005)

—, et al., 'Climate Response and Radiative Forcing from Mineral Aerosols During the Last Glacial Maximum, Pre-Industrial, Current and Doubled-Carbon Dioxide Climates', *Geophysical Research Letters*, 33/20 (2006)

Robert Monroe, 'Intercontinental Rainmakers: uc San Diego Researchers Find
that Aerosols from One Side of the World Influence Rainfall in Another',
uc San Diego News Center, www.ucsdnews.ucsd.edu, 28 February 2013
William Putnam, 'Portrait of Global Aerosols 2012', nasa Earth Observatory,
www.nasa.gov/multimedia/imagegallery/image_feature_2393.html
United Nations Development Programme, 'The Forgotten Billion: mdg
Achievement in the Drylands', www.undp.org, 4 October 2011
United States Geological Survey, 'The Effects of African Dust on Coral Reefs and
Human Health', http://coastal.er.usgs.gov
Adam Voiland, 'Aerosols: Tiny Particles, Big Impact', nasa Earth Observatory,
http://earthobservatory.nasa.gov, 2 November 2010
Andrew Warren et al., 'Dust-Raising in the Dustiest Place on Earth',
Geomorphology, 92/1–2 (2007)
Richard Washington and Martin C. Todd, 'Atmospheric Controls on Mineral
Dust Emission from the Bodélé Depression, Chad: The Role of the Low
Level Jet', *Geophysical Research Letters*, 32/17 (2005)
Yaping Shao et al., 'Dust Cycle: An Emerging Core Theme in Earth System
Science', *Aeolian Research*, 2/4 (2011)

Climate projections, 'desertification' and drought

Jason P. Field et al., 'The Ecology of Dust', *Frontiers in Ecology and the
Environment*, 8/8 (October 2010)
Alfredo Martínez-Garcia et al., 'Southern Ocean Dust–Climate Coupling Over
the Past Four Million Years', *Nature*, 476 (2011)
J. C. Neff et al., 'Increasing Eolian Dust Deposition in the Western United
States Linked to Human Activity', *Nature Geoscience*, 1 (2008)
Fred Pearce, 'Head 'em Up, Move 'em Out: Dust is as Much a Part of the Wild
West as Guns, Whiskey and Cowboys', *New Scientist*, 2650 (2008)
S. I. Seneviratne et al., 'Changes in Climate Extremes and their Impacts on the
Natural Physical Environment', in *Managing the Risks of Extreme Events and
Disasters to Advance Climate Change Adaptation*, ed. C. B. Field et al.,
Special Report of Working Groups i and ii of the Intergovernmental Panel
on Climate Change (Cambridge and New York, 2012)
United Nations Sustainable Development, 'Agenda 21', United Nations
Conference on Environment and Development (Rio de Janeiro, 1992),
www.sustainabledevelopment.un.org

Managing land degradation

Nigel Cross and Rhiannon Barker, eds, *At the Desert's Edge: Oral Histories from
the Sahel* (London, 1992)
Jonathan Davies et al., *Conserving Dryland Biodiversity*, International Union for
Conservation of Nature (2012)
Diana K. Davis and Edmund Burke iii, eds, *Environmental Imaginaries of the
Middle East and North Africa* (Athens, oh, 2011)
M. H. Easdale and S. E. Domptail, 'Fate Can Be Changed! Arid Rangelands
in a Globalizing World: A Complementary Co-Evolutionary Perspective

on the Current "Desert Syndrome"', *Journal of Arid Environments*, 100–101 (2014)

Josephine Flood, *The Original Australians: Story of the Aboriginal People* (Crows Nest, NSW, 2006)

Lisa Mol and Troy Sternberg, eds, *Changing Deserts: Integrating People and their Environment* (Cambridge, 2012)

Michael Mortimore, with contributions from S. Anderson et al., 'Dryland Opportunities: A New Paradigm for People, Ecosystems and Development', United Nations Development Programme, www.undp.org (2009)

Fred Pearce, 'Dr Doom-monger I Presume', *New Scientist*, 2351 (2002)

Lydia Polgreen, 'In Niger, Trees and Crops Turn Back the Desert', *New York Times*, 11 February 2007

Chris Reij et al., 'Agroenvironmental Transformation in the Sahel: Another Kind of "Green Revolution"', IFPRI Discussion Paper 00914 (2009)

Tony Rinaudo, 'Farmer Managed Natural Regeneration: Exceptional Impact of a Novel Approach to Reforestation in Sub-Saharan Africa', ECHO Community Global Agriculture Network, Technical Note 65 (2012)

David J. Spielman and Rajul Pandya-Lorch, *Millions Fed: Proven Successes in Agricultural Development,* International Food Policy Research Institute (Washington, DC, 2009)

United Nations Convention to Combat Desertification, www.unccd.int

United Nations Development Programme, 'Human Development Report' (2013), www.hdr.undp.org/en

—, 'The Forgotten Billion: MDG Achievement in the Drylands', www.undp.org, 4 October 2011

United Nations Environment Programme, 'Global Deserts Outlook' (2006), www.unep.org

—, 'Global Drylands: A UN System-wide Response' (2011), www.unep-wcmc.org

Water

Aqueduct: Measuring and Mapping Water Risk, World Resources Institute, www.wri.org/our-work/project/aqueduct

Tom Gleeson et al., 'Water Balance of Global Aquifers Revealed by Groundwater Footprint', *Nature*, 588 (2012)

Leonard F. Konikow, *Groundwater Depletion in the United States, 1900–2008*, USGS Scientific Investigations Report 2013–5079 (2013), http://pubs.usgs.gov/sir/2013/5079

United Nations Food and Agriculture Organization, *Aquastat: Global Water Information System*, www.fao.org/nr/aquastat

Lessons

Burkhard Bilger, 'The Great Oasis: Can a Wall of Trees Stop the Sahara from Spreading?', *New Yorker* (19 December 2011)

Cal-Earth: The California Institute of Earth Art and Architecture, 'About Nader Khalili, Architect and Author', www.calearth.org/about

Les Hiddins, *Bush Tucker Field Guide* (Melbourne, 2002)

Gary Paul Nabhan, *Arab/American: Landscape, Culture, and Cuisine in Two Great Deserts* (Tucson, AZ, 2008)

—, *The Desert Smells Like Rain: A Naturalist in Papago Indian Country* (San Francisco, CA, 1982)

—, *Growing Food in a Hotter, Drier Land: Lessons from Desert Farmers on Adapting to Climate Uncertainty* (White River Junction, VT, 2013)

Sara Reardon, 'Fungus-Powered Superplants May Beat the Heat', *New Scientist*, 2875 (2012)

Julia Rosen, 'Bolivian Bacteria Prove Promising Source of Bioplastic', *Earth Magazine*, 58/11 (2013)

—, 'Desert Plants Feast on Anthropogenic Carbon Dioxide', *Earth Magazine*, 58/10 (2013)

Wallace Stegner, 'Thoughts in a Dry Land', in *Where the Bluebird Sings to the Lemonade Springs: Living and Writing in the West* (New York, 2002)

Acknowledgements

There have been numerous occasions during the writing of this book on which the subject material threatened to explode and doom my ability to keep even a tenuous grip on what I already knew was quite possibly a Sisyphean endeavour. I have many people to thank for bringing me back to my senses on such occasions, most notably my wife, who, had she studied the Book of Proverbs, would undoubtedly have changed the gender of 21:19 to read, 'It is better to live in a desert land than with a quarrelsome and fretful man.'

I have spent periods of my life more or less on my own attempting to decipher the geology of various arid lands, but this book would have been impossible to write without the guidance, help and inspiration of my companions on some unforgettable desert journeys. In the Western Desert, Rob Twigger, Chris Coleman, Isham and his team, and the enduring legacy of Ralph Bagnold. For opening up to me the glories of the Australian outback, Andrew Dwyer and Brendan Eblen of the Diamantina Touring Company. In Morocco, Hassan Mouhou, Ibrahim Ben Salem (of Morocco Excursions) and Alphonse. And, for leading me many years ago to a hidden cave in the Karoo to show me the tiny hand paintings, DeVille Wickens.

I am, as always, grateful for the helpful staff and the extraordinary resources of the libraries of the Geological Society and the Royal Geographical Society in London. For beacons of public domain scientific data, the U.S. government departments of the U.S. Geological Survey, NASA, the National Oceanic and Atmospheric Administration and others are unequalled and deserve global, as well as personal, gratitude.

I am particularly appreciative of the rapid and helpful responses of Mohsen Al-Dajani, Åse Ottoson, Diane Best and Neysa Griffith to my requests for resources and permissions. For ever-reliable support and proofreading: Louise de Bruin, Mark Dalrymple, Walter Vogelsberg and Bea Fausold. For tips and regular encouragement: Pete Newman, Hans-Jörg Begrich, Henry Weisheit and Kate Welland. And, of course, this book would not have existed without the initiation and collaboration of my editor, Ben Hayes, and the stalwart work on my behalf by my agent, Lavinia Trevor.

Photo Acknowledgements and Text Permissions

The author and publishers wish to express their thanks to the following sources of illustrative material and/or permission to reproduce it. Some locations uncredited in the captions for reasons of brevity are also given below.

123RF, Derrick Neill: 105; Mohsen Al-Dajani, *Riyadh, Heart of Arabia* (Riyadh, 2011), by kind permission of Mohsen Al-Dajani: 139; Al-Idrisi, *Tabula Rogeriana* (1154): 36; Australian Government Bureau of Meteorology: 5; courtesy of The Bancroft Library, University of California, Berkeley: 25, 26; Herbert Basedow, 'Group of people, Mount Currie, Northern Territory', National Museum of Australia: 42; Bibliothèque Nationale de France: 35, 37; C14/02, reproduced by permission of the British Geological Survey. All rights reserved: 95; Cresques Abraham, 'Marco Polo's Caravan Travelling to India', Catalan Atlas (1375): 38; *Desert Magazine*, August 1964, illustration by Frank Vohsing: 48; courtesy of Jim Elder, Ottawa, Canada: 90; European Commission Joint Research Centre, Soil Atlas of Africa: 21; European Space Agency: 8, 10; Fairfax Media Limited: 44; courtesy of Peter Fookes, modified by the author: 34; by permission of The Gertrude Bell Archive, Newcastle University Images Y_048, 312, 313, W_056: 126, 127, 128, 129; by kind permission of Eman Ghoneim: 123; Google Earth: 31, 33, 57; © Hans Hillewaert: 3; Image Science and Analysis Laboratory, NASA-Johnson Space Center: 93; IPCC, 'Changes in Climate Extremes and their Impacts on the Natural Physical Environment', Special Report of Working Groups 1 and 2 (2012), figs 3–10: 137; iStock, Alan Tobey, Hulton Archive: 60; photo Klokeid: 112; Magnus Larsson and the Holcim Foundation: 143; courtesy Mark Lee and Peter Fookes: 13 (modified by the author), 97; Library of Congress, Washington, DC: 52 (Prints and Photographs Division), 110, 111 (Prints and Photographs Division, American Colony in Jerusalem collection); collection of the Maison Tiskiwin, Marrakech: 61, 62; *Martumili Ngurra*, 2009, Kumpaya Girgiba, Jakayu Biljabu, Ngamara Bidu, Thelma Judson, Nola Taylor and Jane Girgiba, Martamuli Artists, Shire of East Pilbara: 2; by kind permission of Hassan Massoudy: 78; MATSYS Designs and University of Toronto, Andrew Kudless (design), Nenad Katic (visualization), Tan Nguyen, Pia-Jacqlyn Malinis, Jafe Meltesen-Lee, Benjamin Barragan (model): 144; Musée d'Orsay, Paris: 80, 81; Musée du quai Branly, Paris / Scala, Florence © photo SCALA, Florence: 64 (clé de voile, photo Patrick Gries / Valérie Torre), 65 (Ange Tissier [1814–1876], *L'Odalisque*, 1860, photo Thierry Ollivier /

Text Permissions

Index